STEVE MARRIOTT

ALL TOO BEAUTIFUL

First Edition
Published in 2004 by Helter Skelter Publishing
South Bank House, Black Prince Road, London SE1 7SJ
www.helterskelterpublishing.com

A CIP record for this book is available from the British Library.

Cover design by Simon Halfon.
Contents design and layout by Caroline Walker.
Printed in Great Britain by CPI, Bath.

ISBN 1-900924-44-7

Cover photos:
front cover photograph SKR photos
back cover photograph Julia Noble
authors photograph Rupert Trollope

STEVE MARRIOTT

ALL TOO BEAUTIFUL

BY PAOLO HEWITT AND JOHN HELLIER

Helter
Skelter
Publishing

This book is dedicated to The Marriott family worldwide, the staff of the Helter Skelter shop, past and present plus all the newly arrived Tin Soldiers – Jesamine, Joseph, Anaia, Stirling, Nova, Hope, Natalie and Hayley-Louise.

It is also dedicated to the newest members of the Hellier clan, Dayna and Cameron.

Steve's publicity photo from the Italia Conti school, 1961

'I'm hyperactive, yeah. I've always been like that and I always will be like that. I can't live to other people's rules. I'm sorry. I don't expect them to live to mine. That's just what I do. And I certainly can't live by theirs. If that makes them feel I am out of order then I'm really sorry.'

Steve Marriott talking to John Hellier, 1984.

Contents

Prologue

When they walked into their first ever council flat, the Marriott family couldn't believe their luck. Compared to the accommodation they were used to, 9 Daines Close, Manor Park was stunning. Located on the third floor of a four-storey building, the flat had three bedrooms and a front room that measured twelve by twelve. On the wall was a serving hatch, behind it the small kitchen, and then, to the left – and they couldn't get over this – their very own bathroom. Thirteen years after the end of the Second World War and life for the Marriotts was better than any of them had ever expected.

There were four members in the family, Bill and Kay, the father and mother, Steve and Kay, the son and daughter.

Mother and son were the dominant characters. Between them existed a tight bond that they would both tug on all their lives, forever seeking to impose their iron will upon the other. Even fighting simply drew them closer and closer together.

The son was talented; extremely so. At thirteen years of age he had already left formal education and was now paying his way through the prestigious Italia Conti drama school in Brixton.

The whole family was behind him. They knew he had talent, knew he was destined to be somebody. It was a given in the Marriott family.

As they settled into life at Daines Close the signs of this talent became clearer. Take that night, that cold night in October 1963, when the young Marriott came out of his bedroom and walked into the sitting room to find his mother and father watching the nationally popular variety show *Sunday Night At The London Palladium* on their small black and white television. Round his way – round most people's ways at the time – everyone stayed in to watch this show. It meant they could go in to work the next day and have something to talk about.

Not Steve Marriott. He has little time for light British entertainment. His kicks come from the American R&B records he has been collecting these past few years. That's why he is dressed up to the nines tonight. He is off to a club to listen and dance to the records and sounds of black America.

Music falls out of the television. Instantly, Marriott turns, studies the screen intensely. Four young men from Liverpool are playing their latest disc and in the process busy changing lives across the country. After a minute, Marriott's face relaxes and he screws his nose up.

'Load of rubbish,' he sneers in his fresh, Cockney voice. His father looks round at him. He doesn't confront his son a lot, that's his mum's job. But, he is not standing for this slice of insolence. Son or not, this young man needs taking down a peg or two.

'Steve,' he says, 'when you can sell out the London Palladium like The Beatles have done tonight you can make such judgements, but until then, you'll do well to keep your opinions to yourself.'

'Yeah,' Steve Marriott retorts, buttoning up his coat.

'Well, one day I'll sell out the London Palladium and then you'll see.'

Most families would have laughed at such a declaration from one of their members. The Marriotts knew better. So did their son. Nearly ten years later, in March of 1973, Steve Marriott sold out the London Palladium. Just like he said he would.

Author's Introduction

I had intended to begin this book describing Steve Marriott's last day on earth. My idea for the opening scene was the flight taking him and his third wife, Toni, home from America on Friday, 19th April, 1991, an extremely turbulent journey; the couple argued continually until landing in the UK at around midday.

At that point we would meet their friend, Phil Anthony. He collects the couple from Heathrow airport and drives them back to their 16th century rented house in Arkesden, North Essex. Phil would leave and we would then watch the arrival of Ray Newcomb, another friend who invites the couple out for a meal at the Straw Hat pub in Sawbridgeworth.

We would sit at their table and discover what Marriott ate for his last meal (roast lamb and mint sauce) see his clothes that day (suitably, given his place in Mod history, a silver grey Mohair suit) and then view the actions that led up to him returning home alone at about 1.30am.

There I would have stopped, hopefully with the reader now eager to know more about this unique man.

I had to jettison my plans. In all honesty, you wouldn't have wanted to be around Steve Marriott on his last day on earth. He was vicious, argumentative and tiresome. He had spent the last two weeks of his stay in Los Angeles terrorising Toni. No shrinking violet she but, even her feisty nature and her combative stance could not cope with Marriott's onslaught. The man was simply uncontrollable.

Worse, it wasn't the man she married who was carrying on in this manner – it was Melvin, a bald headed wrestler.

Melvin was Steve Marriott's alter ego, the other side of his dual personality. Melvin first surfaced round about the mid '70s when Marriott was into his second marriage with Pam Stephens. As all his women soon discovered, when Melvin appeared, big trouble followed.

It was Melvin who began the fights – kicked off the arguments. It was scary stuff to be around. When Pam would plead with Steve to stop, he would shout, 'I'm not Steve, I'm Melvin the bald headed wrestler,' and then tear into her some more.

In the morning, Marriott genuinely seemed to have no recollection of his actions. His day would be spent wracked by guilt and remorse.

This is challenging and uncomfortable material and to open the book in such a manner would run the very real risk of putting the reader off Marriott completely.

I couldn't allow this to happen. Melvin was one facet of Steve, a dark facet but not the whole man by a long way. There was so much more to Steve Marriott. Over the last two years, as I have discovered more and more about the man, I could not help but admire his unique spirit, warm to the way Marriott refused to go down, how he allowed nothing in life – the Mafia, the Inland Revenue, the law, the music business – to beat him. Faced with my own day-to-day problems, his life lessons proved to be extremely valuable.

Steve Marriott was a warm, funny man, blessed with incredible talent, energy and charisma. He sang tremendously, he wrote beautifully and he devoted himself to his craft for the whole of his life. He was a true artist. All his life he only did that which his muse demanded, not that which might enrich him.

Music consumed him. He worshipped that beautiful, inspirational force to his dying day. Two, maybe three weeks before his untimely death, he was in a Los Angeles club when he met two fans. He invited them back to his house to play them Charles and Inez Foxx records, explaining how great and vital and important this music was. At age forty-four, he was still spreading the word, still acting as standard bearer for the R&B music he adored so much. He was not alone in his love of this music.

In the '60s, most British artists that mattered – Georgie Fame, Van Morrison, Brian Auger, Rod Stewart, Eric Burdon, Chris Farlowe, Peter Green, The Beatles, The Stones and many others – felt the same way. They displayed an urgency to promote black American music; to reveal to their audiences its wondrous nature.

Rhythm and Blues, or R&B, was the source, the springboard these acts used to forge their own unique music. Today, much to our detriment, that tradition is becoming lost. Back in the day, every young white hipster wanted to sing like Otis or Ray or Bobby. Forty years later, the majority of young hopefuls want to sing like 'Rock' singers, a breed who always lean more to the histrionic than the historic and for whom the expression, stay in tune, might as well been written in Russian.

Not Stevie Marriott. He may well have been the best white soul singer this country ever produced. He's certainly in the top three. Ask Oasis's Liam Gallagher, one of the very few singers today worth listening to. When *Mojo* magazine placed Liam above Marriott in one of those Best Singers lists that all publications love, the young buck, who read the piece while sitting in a Primrose Hill pub, screwed up the mag and threw it on the summer pavement outside in anger.

He knew the truth – knew what an instinctive vocalist Marriott was, how he knew when to go soft, when to race ahead, when to unleash the power, when to hold back; knew in fact how best to use all his musical talents, especially in his Small Faces days.

In that period, 1965–1969, Steve Marriott wrote songs that still transport me to this day. 'Afterglow Of Your Love,' 'Tin Soldier,' 'The Autumn Stone,' 'That Man,' 'I Can't Dance With You,' 'Understanding,' 'All or Nothing,' 'If You Think You're Groovy,' 'The Universal,' 'Donkey Rides A Penny A Glass' – my fingers will tire before the list is complete. His songs were filled with melody, passion, energy, beauty and drive. He was a great arranger as well, imbuing many of his records with a unique musical character. Such was his talent, he could incorporate elements as disparate as East End music hall and screaming rock guitar solos into one satisfying whole.

His writing changed when he joined Humble Pie, did so again in his solo years and there is a case that his muse thoroughly deserted him during this latter period. I tend to disagree. There is still enough great music from this period to fill a lengthy CD. Steve Marriott wrote until the day he died, couldn't stop himself. He loved the job. But he loved performing even more.

That's why in his latter years he was able to play the pubs and the clubs for a grand a night and not feel too bitter about his fate. Onstage, wherever he was, he became whole, became one. He did feel resentment at other lesser talents who had left him behind to become much bigger stars – the Rod Stewarts of this world – but he did so not out of jealousy but a sense of injustice. Marriott had been raised to believe that talent was the only benchmark. The more the talent, the better the rewards. When he discovered that success in the music business owes as much to other factors – a willingness to schmooze, to play the game, to stay meek, keep quiet, not upset people – he reared up in anger. Pound for pound, he was as good as any of his contemporaries, yet in the end they got the mansions and stadium shows while he got the pub circuit.

That wasn't right, it ran contrary to his sense of fairness.

His complex personality didn't help him. On the one hand a sensitive artist who could write subtle and evocative lines such as 'All I need are your whispered hellos,' on the other a man of dirty, ribald humour who displayed no tact whatsoever. His unstoppable penchant for winding up or annoying people in high places inevitably interfered with his career. His first hit combo, The Small Faces were the first to be banned from the prime music show, *Top Of The Pops*. The reason? Marriott believed the show's producer was retiring and confronted him with the words: 'I'm glad you're leaving; I always thought you were a major cunt.'

The producer thanked Steve for the gesture but told the singer he wasn't actually leaving, it was someone else who was. The next day, a short-lived ban was enforced.

Not that Marriott cared too much. 'Fuck 'em' was a phrase he often used throughout his life just as in the same manner he used humour to deflate the pompous and the boring.

Many of his actions were hilarious, sometimes surreal. Pouring mint sauce over a neighbour's plastic lambs or taking to the stage in a bathrobe are acts worthy of Spike Milligan himself. (No surprise then that as a kid, Marriott loved The Goons. So did his Aunt Sheila. The pair would sit at the kitchen table listening to the radio show whilst his father Bill Marriott sat nearby, angrily rustling his newspaper, telling them to keep their laughter quiet. In the downstairs toilet at his last home in Essex was a bookshelf full of Spike Milligan books.)

The base of his humour was earthy and forged from his East End sensibility. The same went for his appeal to the opposite sex. From an early age, Marriott was a rogue and a charmer. Ask the women.

They loved his cheek, his openness, his shoes and his girl-like features. In the '60s, especially when clothes were his passion, Marriott displayed both male and female qualities, a duality that fascinates and attracts women. On stage or in the studio, he looked like a doll but he sang like a man. He was all too beautiful.

Marriott's four main relationships were loving and turbulent but none of his long-term partners will have a word said against him. Those who do criticise him, found his energy too overpowering, his actions too wild. His non-stop chatter, his outlandish behaviour, his filthy mouth, it was all too much. Most others, though, warmed to him. For them he had a heart that was big and warm and exceptional.

In reading this book, I hope you can see through his faults and be drawn to Steve Marriott in the way I was. I hope the words inside lead you to his music, that his work gives you the thrill it gives me every time I hear it. I know my co-author, John Hellier, feels the same way and on that particular subject I have to say this. I could not have been gifted a better man for this job. Not only was his research absolutely exemplary but John's ability to calmly fulfil everything I asked of him, whether it be at seven in the morning or twelve at night, was amazing.

He has been like that all the way through this journey and that means one thing – any success that this book attracts is as much to do with him as it is anybody else.

Paolo Hewitt, London, Autumn 2003

Those Who Have Served Us

Many people knew Steve throughout his life and without them, their time, their patience and generosity, especially in giving us material never before made public, this project would never have been completed. Myself and John are truly indebted. We thank you all.

Specific thanks from Paolo go to; Tiny Arif, Sarah-Jane, *Il Maestro*, Marco and Danny, Mark and Lou Baxter, Johnny and Inki, George and Jenny, Pete and Chris G., Chris and Vicki, Mr Lewisohn, and Mr Wells, the boys at FAB records, Kevin Johansen, Stevie Cradock, Tolga, Mark and Jo, G.C., Sir Chalfont, Des Hurrion, Signor Manzi and all the Howards of Conchar, past and present.

Specific thanks from John for contributions to this book go to the following.
BIG, BIG THANKS TO IAIN McGONIGAL AND STEVE LETFORD FOR THE DEFINITIVE MARRIOTT DISCOGRAPHY.

Also

Gill Hellier
Julian and Melanie Hellier
Lynne Rossi
Lynda Crockett
Brian Finlay
Terry Bramley
Laurie O'Leary
Pam Marriott
Kay and Kay Marriott
Toby Marriott
Manon Brown
Ken Hawes
Jim Leverton
Hugh Janes
Dave Clark
Detlef Mittmann
Klaus Witt
Toni Marriott
Keith Altham
Chris Welch
Jerry Shirley
The late Greg Ridley
Dave Clempson
Dean Powell

Uli Twelker
Roland Schmitt
Steve Ellis
Mick Eve
Paul Gorman
Rick Wills
Kenney Jones
Ian McLagan
Simon Hickling
Ann Moody
Glen Matlock
Billy Nicholls
Jimmy Winston
The late Stanley Unwin
Allen Ellett
John Perry
Dave Fowell
Marilyn Einsor
Paul Einsor
Rupert Trollope
Brian Chalmers
Deborah Hicks
Chris and Vicky

PART ONE

FROM ABSOLUTE BEGINNINGS

302 Strone Road (John Hellier)

Chapter One

Things Are Going To Get Better

The Marriott family – mother and father Kay and Bill and their children, Steve and Kay (slightly confusingly for this narrative, daughter and mother share the same name) – step out onto today's printed pages from a world now vanished. London's East End was the area where the Marriotts would make their home for many, many years: the area whose traditions and unique culture would serve to shape all of their characters.

Those forces have now disappeared into the ether of London's rich and mysterious past and were beginning to do so when Stephen Peter Marriott arrived upon this earth on January 30th, 1947.

For it was at this time, just after the Second World War, that the twin forces of technology and new housing policies combined to move major centres of work out of London taking the workers with them.

Nearly halfway through the 20th century, the children of families who had lived in London's East End for generations, no longer woke up in Brick Lane or Bow but in Essex, or the newly built satellite towns, such as Basildon or Stevenage. With them went their culture. Within twenty years of their departure, Kentucky Fried Chicken would be more popular in the East End than the pie and mash served in Cooke's famous shops.

Yet despite this migration, Steve Marriott's East End has never lost its status as one of London's most mythologized areas.

In books such as Jane Cox's *East End Life and Traditions* or Gilda O'Neil's recent best seller, *My East End*, the same ideals and principles are repeated again and again. East End people are the salt of the earth. They are tough but loving people bound together by geography, living side by side in an area where unconditional help was always on hand.

'You'd rally round if someone needed you,' says a woman in O'Neill's book. 'If someone was unwell, you'd mind her kids, make sure she had a bit of grub.'

'When I think of the East End,' says another, 'I think of all the warmth. Within a radius of two or three streets you had your own little community. Like a village, it was.'

In Jane Cox's book, we encounter a Mrs Morris, mother of seven, who breaks her leg and is hospitalised. She has no husband but many offspring. The neighbours move into her house and take care of her kids. When Mrs Morris returns, the neighbours club together and throw her a welcome home party. The tears stream down her face at this act of outstanding kindness.

Consider also East End resident, Jessie. She recalls her neighbours coming out of the pubs at closing time, to sing and socialise on the streets until the very early hours.

'Lovely nights,' she wistfully recalls, 'lovely nights.'

This idea of the East End as a warm and caring area reaches its apotheosis when its chroniclers turn to the Second World War.

For East Enders, the war really started on the 7th of September, 1940, the day when German planes began a 57-day bombing campaign of the area. The Germans were good – 15,000 people killed, 94,086 houses destroyed – yet not good enough to kill off the East End. Many and much survived their ferocious bombardment and at the end of it the *Daily Herald* splashed on its front page in huge type – The Cockney Is Bloody But Unbowed!

For Kay Marriott, Steve's mother, this was the East End's finest hour. She was truly moved by the prevailing spirit of selflessness, bravery and true companionship that she saw all around her.

'I suppose it's a terrible thing to say but I enjoyed the War, I really did,' she confesses. 'Everyone was so nice.'

That same spirit infused all of Britain. In 1941, the playwright Noel Coward, whose work Steve Marriott would remain a lifelong fan of, attended a dance in Plymouth. He wrote in his diary that night, 'The English do not always take their pleasures sadly, at least not when they are surrounded by death and destruction.'

Of course, a myth cannot exist without some truth to support it although it can be equally argued that no one impulse determines the character of any area. Human lives are too complex for such a simple appraisal.

Dark forces live in the East End; they have done so for a very long time. Some of it is harmless stuff, ('Neighbours and friends might help one another out,' Jane Cox writes, 'but there was a good deal of back stabbing in the market place,') but some of it is nasty, violent, propelled by ignorance and bigotry against other cultures, other religions. In the East End, the process of immigration was no different to anywhere else in Britain.

The process starts when a foreign people arrive and settle in. Within days, verbal abuse from a few locals starts. Then come the stares, the threats, the punches and the spittle. The hostility lasts until the next group arrive from a different part of the world. Now everyone turns their spit onto the newcomers – not least those grateful to be removed from the firing line.

'Everyone was fighting for the same crust,' Jane Cox records in her book. The Protestants hated the Catholics and the Catholics hated the Protestants and everybody hated the Jews, as Tom Lehrer used to sing. Little had changed since the days when everybody hated the Flemish, then the Dutch, then the French Huguenots, not to mention the Irish, Scots and Welsh and anyone who spoke 'funny' or ate 'strange food.'

Given this hostility, why settle here, of all places? Why lay yourself open to such viciousness? Because London's East End has always been a magnet for the ambitious poor of the world.

The Irish and the Russo-Polish Jews and the Chinese, the Somalis, the West Africans and the Indians, the Spanish, the Germans and the Italians, the Dutch and the Pakistanis, along with the indigenous Londoners, make up the fabric of its history. The true Eastender comes in many colours, many sizes, just as Steve Marriott's music would.

For centuries, men and women, culled from every part of the world, have worked its factories and its sweatshops. They have prayed in churches which became synagogues and are now mosques. They have drunk in the pubs and fought and fallen hard on the streets.

Some Eastenders have been natural left wingers: staunch fighters against fascism. Others went the other way, towards the extreme right wing of Oswald Mosley and Enoch Powell. Whatever the viewpoint, as long as it's extreme, the East End will sustain it.

Others were not so supine. For them, the East End represented chains they had to break loose from in order to make their name in a wider world. Stanley Holloway, the actor, was born in Manor Park, Alfie Bass in Bethnal Green. The entertainer Bud Flanagan was an East Ender, so were the writers Arnold Wesker, Harold Pinter and Steven Berkoff. Photographer David Bailey hails from these parts and decades later the press still make a song and dance about it. As they do with Terry O'Neill but not the tailor Doug Hayward, the man whose suits Bobby Moore (amongst many others) would wear with such elegance and style.

Of course, not all who escaped ended up in the media or the arts. There was also the thriving underworld in which to find riches and notoriety. In the '60s, the area's most distinguished duo were the Krays, two gangster brothers who for better or worse, remain vital in the preservation of East End mythology.

'I don't care what you say about the Krays,' runs the mantra, drummed into every East Ender since the mid '60s, 'you could leave your back door open when they ruled the manor and no one would take advantage. You were safe with them. (Pause) And they loved their mum.'

At their funerals, thousands of Eastenders packed the streets to pay tribute in the same way as they later marked the passing of the Queen Mother.

Others of a more legal bent made their money and then moved outwards, quick as they could, towards Essex, towards fresh country air. Some stayed in the gutter all their lives, not bothering, or unable, to move.

Steve Marriott's East End was filled with people who played out the drama of their lives in full view of their neighbours. What's remarkable is that within this vibrant area, populated as it was by those blessed with energy and attitude and colour and life, it was he, Steve Marriott, who would stand head and shoulders above everyone else.

'A special kid that one,' his neighbours would coo as he bounced down the street, fair hair to the wind, smile on the go and mischief in his eyes, paying heed to no one and going his own way. It became the echo of his childhood. 'Yes, a special kid that one. Unique. Absolutely unique.'

His mother Kay knew it more than anyone else and because she did she sought to give him a toughness to protect him from those who would rob him of the proceeds of his talents. To her way of thinking, sensitivity was a fatal weakness; the result was that mother and son locked horns, time and time again, week after week, month after month, year after year. Kay protected, Steve rebelled. It was only when he reached thirty and she about fifty, that he sat down and in a rare gentle moment said to her, 'You know mum in all those fights we had as I grew up, you won every one of them. But I never let you see the tears I cried or how scared I was.'

'Yes, I know,' she replied, so pleased that the son had finally understood the reasoning behind her tough ways, her tough love, 'but you never saw my heart break.'

From Bill, the father, came Steve's artistic side but from Kay came the armour, the desire to better himself. For in this East End world of low paid jobs and long working hours, that was always the aim – go better yourself. There was no higher calling. You don't hear it so much these days but back then that was the mantra of the working class all over the country. Go and better yourself. Which is precisely what Kay, Steve's mother, did.

She was born Kathleen Devo on March 14th, 1926, above a Chinese laundry in Mildmay Grove, Islington, 'And I've been cleaning ever since,' she quips. As always, there is a whiff of bitter truth in her humour.

She was the eldest, Sheila was the youngest, in between came Joan who now lives in Australia. Three girls then, which did not please the father. Albert Devo had wanted sons since he was a teenager.

When Sheila, the last of his children was born, Albert came home from work to see the new child. Just as he entered the house, the lights went out. 'Don't bother putting money in the meter,' he said sarcastically, 'I don't need to see what another girl looks like.'

Cruel, but that's how it was. He was a fish man and Kathleen was a chamber maid. That's how they met, Albert delivering fish to a big house one day and catching her eye. The fish man and the chamber maid courted, married and then began to produce daughters.

Soon after Kathleen was born, the family moved to Tottenham, Hillside Road to be exact. There was a zoo in the park down the road which the young Kay liked to visit. But there was also a father who kept a cane at the dining table. If Kay spoke at mealtimes or worse if Kay spoke at mealtimes whilst eating or drinking, the dad would reach for the stick – cracking it upon her fair skin, a flash of pain and red.

To this day, Kay Marriott finds it impossible to talk and drink or talk and eat at the same time. Her mum was of a kinder nature. Once supper was over and dad had disappeared, she would gather her daughters around and they would sit at the table and talk, gossip, be together, be a family. It meant that the three daughters never respected dad as much as they respected mum.

'And that's how I think it was with Steve and me,' Steve's mum says. 'Bill his father adored Steve but they could never get it right. Steve always thought his father was ashamed of him. If they would go to the pub for a drink, his father would say, "Are you going to sort your hair out?" And Steve would get narky and say, "No, I bloody ain't". See it was Bill's Victorian upbringing. He wanted Steve to have a short back and sides and of course Steve would have none of it.'

‡ ‡ ‡

When Kay was ten, the Devo family moved from Tottenham and travelled eastwards, to a gloomy Victorian house, number 302 Strone Road in Manor Park. Kay would live in this street for many, many years. To support his family, her father opened up his own fish shop. At the back was a large hole where he oak-smoked the fish three times a week. On her way home from school that smell would fill Kay's nostrils and she has never forgotten it. Her school was on Shaftesbury Road, opposite her dad's fish shop and close to the Trebor sweet factory.

At home, under her father's strict regime, Kay learnt the art of deviousness, learnt how to get the things she wanted even when her father commanded her, no. Years later when her son Steve pulled a similar trick, Kay would smile inwardly and tell him, 'Steve, there's nothing you have done that I haven't done already. Really, there isn't.'

Three years after moving to Manor Park, the Second World War broke out and the family were evacuated to Norfolk. Their father didn't go with them. Instead, he went into the Territorial Army. A weak heart soon prevented him from continuing his service and he spent the rest of the war working on the buses. When the family returned to London months later, it was not to their home in Manor Park but to Elstree, to stay with their aunt Maud.

Once there, Kay, who had now left school, started work as a tea lady for an engineering company. She proved herself hard working and dutiful, but also young and naïve. One morning someone asked her to go out and buy some red, white and blue spotted paint. Okay, she said and trotted off to the shops blissfully unaware of the giggles behind her back. In the shop the salesman put her right and she blushed so hard she can remember the feeling to this day.

They left Aunt Maud's not long after, travelled back to Strone Road. Their old house, number 302 was now occupied so they moved three doors up to 308, another Victorian style house. It even had a servant's bell hanging in the sitting room.

'But we never used it,' says Kay, smiling.

She joined the Wrens. She wanted to do her bit for the war but more than that, she wanted to please her father. She knew it hurt him to be without a son so she tried the next best thing – acting like one. In truth, the war didn't scare her. The German bombers who took East End lives and reduced large sections of the area to rubble never frightened her in the way they did her mother. Kay would sleep through the loud sirens and then in the evening she would make her own way to dances, walking through streets as bombs exploded nearby, sending shards of shrapnel flying over her head.

'See, life had to carry on or what else are you going to do?' Kay asks. 'And at 13 you are not frightened by anything. My mum was but I wasn't.'

And in 1943, four years into the war, she met the man she would marry.

Kay was out celebrating her 17th birthday in the Burnell Arms pub on High Street North, Manor Park, when she came across Bill Marriott, enjoying a good night out.

'I went past him and we started chatting,' she recalls. 'He said, "What's the celebration?" I said, "It's my birthday". He said, "Funny, it's mine too."

Kay laughed but didn't believe him. He was obviously spinning her a line, the cheeky git. But it was true. Bill Marriott had indeed been born on March 14th, but fourteen years before Kay in the year 1912 at Kings Cross in London. He was the family's eldest child. There was a younger brother and a sister, and Bill's father, a cab driver, owned two taxis. Not a bad living in those days.

One day at school, Bill made a painting of two large eagles and, much to his surprise, it won him a scholarship to the Royal Academy of Art in central London. There, in that illustrious building, he studied still life painting. The student life was not to his liking and he left, never to realise his dormant artistic talent. His son would take on that particular job for him.

Bill now entered into an electrician's apprenticeship, a job that took him to Madam Tussaud's waxwork museum in London's Baker Street.

'He made Sleeping Beauty breathe,' Kay recalls, 'he was proud of his work there.' The work finished and Bill moved on to work for a variety of firms all over London. He was rarely happy. One day at work he had another row with another ignorant boss.

Sod it, he said. And he went and joined the Navy. It was then that tragedy struck. Within four short years, two of the people closest to Bill would be taken from him.

Bill was eighteen when his mum died. His sister took over her role but at just twenty-two, she too departed this earth, leaving behind a two-year-old daughter.

Perhaps this explains the reserve in his character, how he was content to stay in the shadows. Cruel and random blows had decimated his family and maybe now he felt that life was too unpredictable, too treacherous to fully embrace. You gave it your best but still it wounded you. Best not to get too involved, eh? You only leave yourself open. His son would disagree and take for the high road, the other route.

Naturally, Kay knew none of this background detail on March 14th, 1943, as she made her way back to her table.

'Fancy any of them?' Kay asked her sister Sheila, nodding towards the sailors as she settled down beside her.

'Nah, not really,' Sheila replied and that would have been it except for one factor; Kay's father. Spotting the lads at the bar, he rose from his chair and approached the sailors.

'Lads, do you fancy coming back for a ding dong?' he asked them. A ding dong. It was a wartime East End tradition. If you saw any of the armed forces in a pub you offered them a drink at your home. They fought, you didn't. It was the done thing. The sailors gladly accepted Albert's offer. Kay felt annoyed. It was her birthday. Not theirs. But she didn't complain. Not with father sitting there.

The boys came back to the house and Bill, shy, unassuming Bill, couldn't keep his eyes off the attractive birthday girl. Kay was a beauty and she knew it. She had known for some time now that men were drawn to her. But Bill looked at her differently. There was something nice about him, safe. So when he asked if she would like to go out one night, she said yes.

But Kay wanted to make one thing clear to her new suitor: don't let our time together make you think for one minute that is the start of something. The war had smashed everyone's future, reduced life to day-to-day living. Kay and many others didn't see the point of long-term relationships, of long-term anythings in fact. Each day as it came. That's how you got by. How else could you cope? You never knew what might happen next. One night, you might meet the man of your dreams, the next day he might be dead. So let's face the music. And dance.

The war created a new, more reckless social attitude in the British. Death was now a daily presence in everyone's lives and its power made the old idea of living by rules set down by others or regarding the rich and the powerful as superior, instantly redundant. In the East End they said, Get your fun now, for it might be gone tomorrow. And it was this spirit that gathered steam after the War finished and shaped Britain's most fabulous decade, the Sixties.

Kay and Bill kept on seeing each other. She liked him, liked him a lot. She told him so as well and that encouraged him to ignore the rules she had laid down. He proposed marriage very early in the relationship. Strangely, instead of telling him where to get off, Kay now became unsure. So did her parents. Bill was solid, grounded and good husband material. He was older but in their eyes that made him more attractive.

'Getting married,' Kay would say at the breakfast table, 'it all seems so final.'

Yet something about him had got inside of her, something inside told her to put away the doubts. It was the right thing to do. After all, she may never meet another like him again.

There was another compelling reason to accept his offer. Marriage would remove her from the family home. She could now make her own way and that was a temptation too large to ignore.

Six months after meeting, on the 8th September 1943, Bill and Kay Marriott married at the East Ham registry office. She was seventeen, Bill was thirty-one.

Kay's dad gave the newly-weds two rooms in 308 Strone Road under the condition they kept them clean and in good repair. A slightly nervous Kay and a very happy Bill moved their stuff in before departing for their unconventional honeymoon.

At the time of his wedding, Bill Marriott's ship was positioned in the English Channel. The men's mission was simple; it was to build a pipeline on the sea floor to supply petrol to the forces on land in Europe. The line was called Pluto.

'Very famous in its day,' instructs Kay. 'Very famous.'

The closest port was Shanklin, on the Isle of Wight and for his honeymoon, Bill was given permission to come ashore every night to see his wife. They stayed at a friend's house in Shanklin who gave the couple their front bedroom, referring to it jokingly as the bridal suite. After a three-week honeymoon, the couple parted; Bill to stay full time on the ship, Kay to return to Manor Park. Neither knew that disaster was about to strike.

Three weeks later, Kay received an urgent message from the captain of the ship. Her husband, Petty Officer William Marriott, had lost the use of both his eyes. The terrible accident had occurred when Bill started sawing a length of copper and the wire exploded into his face, injuring both his eyes. He had been placed in the Haslar Royal Navy hospital, in Gosport.

Mrs. Marriott would of course be given extended visiting rights to see her husband. The journey was long – Kay had to travel to Portsmouth and then get a ferry over to Gosport – but she made the trip every week to sit by his hospital bed. As she did so, Kay constantly re-assured her husband that everything would be fine. Secretly, she began preparing for life with a blind husband.

Luckily, time and fortune favoured the young couple. A new wonder drug, penicillin, had just been approved for use by the relevant authorities. Kay was asked permission for Bill to be injected with the new drug every four hours. Of course, she said, anything that might help and ease the pain. The medicine was administered every four hours and Kay helped clear away the hateful black stuff that dripped down from Bill's eyes. After a few weeks the pain vanished.

The doctors now proposed an operation that might save one of Bill's eyes. Kay agreed to the proposal. Any chance was worth taking at this particular stage. The operation was long but it was successful. Bill got his sight back in one eye and Kay has never forgotten the surgeon's name. Sir Williamson Noble.

She returned home, happy, able now to turn her attentions upon herself. Since her marriage, she couldn't help but note how broody she was becoming. Each day, the idea of creating a child grew stronger and stronger but how to persuade Bill? She knew him well, knew he would make objections. Not because he didn't want children but because his nature was cautious, uncertain.

'I could see he was frightened to have a child, so I had to chase him,' she says. Two years later, the War ended. Millions were dead, countries and cities were shattered, Britain and its allies emerged victorious. A piano was wheeled into the Marriotts' front garden and all the street and all the people from everywhere around dressed up and, oh how they partied, drinking long into the night and then onwards into the sunny morning.

War was finally over and Kay's wish to bear a child now became her primary mission. Before long she was pregnant.

Chapter Two

Give Her My Regards

On the 29th of January, 1947, Kay travelled to East Ham hospital for her regular check up. She was eight months gone. The examining nurse told her the birth was at least four weeks away and sent her away to return in a month's time.

Outside the snow was falling heavily from the sky, piling up on the pavements. The wind was vicious, quick to cut through your clothing. It was the worst winter since February, 1929, that's what the papers said. Britain was grinding to a halt.

The Thames was frozen and electricity supplies had been cut by 25%. Great parts of London still lay in ruins and people scrabbled upon them to try and make a living. Meanwhile, the Royal Family were preparing to set sail for the warmer climes of South Africa.

In the daily papers, Whiteways were advertising their wines with the slogan, Britons Do Make It – a jibe at Johnny Foreigner's perceived superior wine industry – and a radio in the shops would cost you fifteen pounds. The price was well out of Kay Marriott's reach but it wasn't money or home or husband that concerned her on this day. It was the overpowering feeling that the nurse was wrong, that she was near to giving birth. Her baby was not four weeks away from arriving, it was more like four days.

Bill hadn't accompanied Kay to the hospital on this freezing day. He had caught a vicious flu bug and had been in bed for days. Kay looked in on him when she got home. He was lying fast asleep and vapour seemed to rise off his body. She went downstairs and prepared his medicine, took it back up to him. Then she returned to the kitchen and made herself something to eat and afterwards she settled down as best she could to rest. At eleven o'clock that night the contractions started. She had been right all along. Her child was on the way.

After an hour of enduring the pain, she went upstairs to tell Bill. He was still feverish, still in another world. The flu had drained him of everything. Still, he managed to tell her to put on those thick socks he had brought back from Russia all those years ago so she wouldn't slip on the icy cold pavement and then to hurry next door to the Lewises and call an ambulance. The Marriotts didn't have a phone. Nor did most of the houses in the street.

Bill slipped back into semi-consciousness and Kay, now dressed, went downstairs. She was absolutely petrified. She opened the front door and a rush of bitter cold wind assaulted her. She dropped her shoulders, tentatively stepped out onto the ice and made the short journey next door.

She knocked on Mrs Lewis's door. Mrs Lewis had a grown son who Kay was sure would now help her. She was wrong. Mrs Lewis opened her door, and said no, Kay could not use her telephone. 'Go to Mrs Stone, further down the road, use hers'. Then she closed the door on her pregnant neighbour. The good old East End.

Kay gathered herself against the cold and walked down to number 318. Mrs Stone opened the door in her nightie and pigtails and Kay told her the baby was on the way, could she call an ambulance. Mrs. Stone shrieked, rushed to the phone. After a minute of listening to the receiver, she cried to Kay, there's no answer. Kay had to laugh.

She told her friend, 'they're not answering because you haven't dialled the number yet,' and then Mrs. Stone shrieked again but this time with laughter.

The ambulance soon arrived and Kay was taken to East Ham hospital. She arrived at half-six in the morning. Alone. The night shift was just finishing, the day shift about to start. Kay was told to wait patiently in a room, a small, grey waiting room. She settled down but within minutes the contractions started up again. A nurse walked by and Kay shouted to her for help. The sister quickly examined her and then called for assistance.

Kay is rushed to the labour ward but even there, they refuse to take her condition seriously. She is offered breakfast, a bowl of porridge. She refuses the food. The contractions continue. Finally, the nurses and the doctors agree that action is needed and they make the necessary arrangements.

At eleven in the morning, on January 30th, 1947, Kay Marriott gave birth to a baby boy. A son. Kay is absolutely elated, very relieved and so very tired. She tells the nurse she wants to call her son, Peter Stephen Marriott but the nurse says, 'Oh we had another Peter born today,' so Kay changes the names around. Stephen becomes the first name. She got the names Peter and Stephen from the Bible and if she is honest, it feels slightly scandalous to use such religious names for her child.

The nurse tells her that as Stephen was a premature birth, he must be taken away for a short while. Nothing to worry about. Routine tests, that kind of thing. Not to worry.

Again, Kay is left alone. She hopes no one passing by thinks that she is unwed. 'My husband is ill,' she will tell anyone who asks.

Kay sleeps for a bit and wakes. A little later, the nurse walks back in with her child.

'You can feed him now,' the nurse says, passing him over.

Just as she does so a passing matron rushes into the ward.

'Take that child away from there immediately. I said, immediately,' she shouts out.

The nurse grabs the baby from the shocked mother and rushes out of the ward, back to the nursery. Kay has no idea what is happening.

'What's wrong,' she cries. 'What's wrong with my baby?'

'Don't worry, he'll be fine,' the matron replies and walks out. She will not tell Kay that Stephen is ill, that he must be kept at the same room temperature. In fact, no one will tell Kay about the illness. After all, she is only the mother.

At six-thirty that night, Kay's mum arrives. Thank God, for that. She is the only person in the whole world that Kay wants to see. On learning of her grandson's condition, the mum demands answers from the hospital and they are now given.

Stephen Marriott was born weighing four pounds and four ounces and has jaundice. His weight is plummeting. He cannot leave the hospital until he recovers. Kay can feed him but he must not be taken out of the nursery until he gains the necessary weight.

Mother and son spent a month in that hospital. The first few days were the worst.

Stephen simply didn't look like recovering and Kay felt a deep despair of the kind known only to mothers. Yet this time tragedy let her be. The illness gradually fell away and the boy began putting on weight. After four weeks, mother and son were discharged. The hospital charged them £21 for their stay. That's including the ambulance, of course. It was an absolute fortune but Kay was so happy to go home to Manor Park with her first born that they would worry about the money another day.

Kay knew they had done the right thing in having a child. She knew because when she showed Bill their baby for the first time his face lit up in a way she had never seen before.

Father and son, whatever went on, love would always be present between them.

‡ ‡ ‡

By now, Kay's parents had split up. Her father Albert had re-married and moved out of 308, Strone Road. The house was now divided into two flats and Kay and Bill decided to move downstairs.

'It meant we had to give up the bathroom but I thought it was more important to have a garden for a child,' she says.

Given the energy that her son would soon display, it was a good decision. Meanwhile, Bill was worried. He was finding it hard to find work. The economy was depressed and jobs were scarce. There was only one thing for it. If he couldn't find someone to give him a job, he would make his own.

In September of 1947, he opened a small fish stall called Bill's Eels directly outside the Ruskin Arms pub on High Street North, Manor Park.

'We had jellied eels that we used to get from Grick's in Upton Park,' Kay explains, 'They used to deliver them and a big sack of whelks. We used to sit in the garden and do all the whelks, getting them ready for the evening. We had a tricycle with a big square box like Wall's ice cream had years ago.'

The business was soon thriving. Kay wanted to keep things as they were but Bill was more ambitious. He kept the stall on but he used its profits to take over some empty premises opposite the Ruskin Arms. Not long after, he opened up a pie and mash shop. You could see his thinking. Pie and mash was recession-proof. During the war, eels and pies had survived a bad economy and proved to be one of a tiny handful of businesses to survive. The food was cheap and nutritious. Whole families were raised on this fare. The business couldn't go wrong.

Unfortunately, Bill Marriott's customers thought differently. 'The pies are not like Cooke's,' they would say referring to the famous eel pie makers of the East End. Bill secretly agreed with them. Which is why he went to see the Cooke brothers and struck a deal with them. For a cut of the profits, they would supply him with their pies. Bill now returned to work in a more confident mood. A week later his customers delivered their verdict on his new pies.

'They're not like Cooke's,' they maintained and nothing could convince them otherwise.

Custom dwindled and the local businessmen moved in for the kill.

'They all ganged up on him,' Kay states, the voice still angry at their behaviour. 'and in the end he lost all the disability money he got from the Navy. When he sold up they were all there competing and getting the cheapest stuff. It was all new stuff, new stainless steel stuff. It was lovely. But he lost all that. But I didn't say to him, "I told you so." We still had the stall. For a long while we had the stall.'

As they worked the stall, their baby son Steve would be parked in his pram next to them.

'No wonder he didn't like eels,' she says, smiling. 'He was brought up on them. He used to be outside the stall and we'd give him some jelly from the jellied eels to keep him quiet.'

It would be one of the very few times they would be successful in silencing their son.

‡ ‡ ‡

Throughout his childhood and teenage years, Steve's most significant relationship was with Kay, his mother. It was not the easiest of bonds. It never is when people are forged from the same fire. Both were stubborn. Both were proud. Both would not give way. The arguments therefore erupted on a daily basis. Thus turbulence, agitation and noise became the tenor of his youth.

In later life, be it onstage or travelling in a car or recording in a studio, Steve would recreate those very same elements.

'He was a very, very naughty boy,' his Aunt Sheila recalls, 'In fact, he was wicked sometimes. He was a difficult child and he and Kath [his mother] did not get on because he was so headstrong. So he would come round for a bit of light relief.

'He and I always got on well and he got on very well with my husband, David. But I had to tell him off because Kath would be on the phone crying about the latest bit of naughtiness and how he had upset her so much. So I had to tick him off.'

She pauses. Child development has progressed since her days. 'I am sorry about that now,' she confides. 'He was obviously coming round because he needed a bit of comfort. I was his auntie and I hope I was good to him but I had to give him a ticking off. He upset his mother so much.'

‡ ‡ ‡

It would take years for the East End to heal itself from the war, to right itself, to clear up the rubble and bury the shelters. Broken cities always make for the bleakest of pictures. Steve Marriott's childhood took place amidst piles of bricks and mortar, amidst deformed buildings. No wonder he craved escape. Everyone did.

When he was seven years old, he went to the local cinema to see *The Wizard Of Oz*, the 1939 film which would launch Judy Garland into stardom and onto the road to self destruction. It was the first musical to be made in technicolour. It also took four directors – Richard Thorpe, George Cukor, Victor Fleming (who grabbed the final director's title) and the legendary King Vidor – to bring the film to the screen.

Marriott arrived at the cinema at two in the afternoon. By six that night, he had not returned home. His parents were not worried by his absence. It was a different world then, children could roam around freely.

'You could send your kid to the pictures,' Kay recalls. 'You might get the occasional flasher – nothing worse than that.'

But when the clock said ten, Kay and Bill hurried off to try and locate Steve. As they walked hastily towards the cinema, their son came into view, sauntering towards them, loudly singing songs from the film.

He had loved *The Wizard Of Oz* so much he had stayed the whole day in the cinema, watching it again and again and again. He would never forget its impact. It remained his favourite film of all time, the first piece of art to demonstrate that despite your surroundings for everyone there is a yellow brick road you can follow. You just have to have the courage to do so.

At the same time Steve developed a liking for cartoon films. Aunt Sheila and her husband often took him to London's West End, 'up West', they'd call it, to see the latest cartoon films. His grandmother, who Steve adored because with her he found a sympathy unavailable to him elsewhere, took him at great expense to the Dominion Theatre in London to see the film of Jules Verne's *Around The World in Eighty Days*.

'The trouble was,' Aunt Sheila recalls, 'I had just bought him his first puppy. I got him from Petticoat Lane. He was called Butch. Apparently, Steve spent the whole film saying he wanted to go home and see Butch. I don't think my mother was too pleased with that.'

From a very early age, Marriott was attracted to animals and throughout his whole life would keep them close to him.

‡ ‡ ‡

Listen to the adjectives mother and sister apply to him as they recall Steve's childhood character; extrovert, cheeky, mischievous, protective. Interestingly, the term talented is rarely used. It's as if that is a given.

'Even a woman down the street where we lived, she was a fortune teller and she told us that he would go right to the top in his profession and that we wouldn't have to worry about him,' Bill Marriott recalled in 1996. 'And she was right.'

'He was unique.' his mum concurs. 'You didn't have kids like that then. He was so different.'

Soon, though, little Stevie would have some competition on his hands.

On the 22nd April, 1952, Kathleen Marriott (now known to all as Kay) gave birth to a baby girl. She too was named Kay. Fifty years later, his sister remembers Steve as, 'a great brother,' protective, inspiring, charming and often very devious.

One of her first memories is when she was, what – three or four – and mum giving her sixpence pocket money and Steve, having already spent his allowance, pulling her aside and saying to her, 'Kay, because I am your brother and I love you very much indeed, today I have got a very special treat for you.'

He then pulled out a large brown penny coin and held it in front of her eyes. 'See how big this coin is?' he would say, 'Well I am going to give you this big coin because I love you so much and you can then give me that little silver one.'

Kay remembers saying thank you so much and passing over the sixpence and receiving one penny in return.

She laughs, sounding just like her mother.

'Very mischievous, very cheeky and very protective towards me. I will always remember that protectiveness. When he was in the Small Faces, they were on tour once with Scott Walker who I really wanted to meet. I told Steve this. Then on my birthday they played Romford. He did everything for me that day. Got me presents, made an announcement from the stage, everything, but he refused to let me backstage. Every gig I always went backstage but this time he wouldn't give me a pass in case I saw Scott Walker. '

She stops, adds, 'He could say anything to me, anything – and he often did – but no-one else could. It was like that until the day he died.'

Kay was the flipside of Steve's boisterous nature, took more after her father.

'I was the introvert, he was the extrovert,' she explains. 'Steve didn't have a shy bone in his body but he was never a show-off or nasty with it. He could be that bit withdrawn, and that became aggression in the later years, but he was never rude as a child. Never.'

Kay may have grown into a shy quiet person but in very early childhood, she once displayed a penchant for performing. Which was fine with Steve – until it threatened his spotlight.

‡ ‡ ‡

Every year, without fail, the Marriotts holidayed at Jaywick Sands holiday camp in Essex.

'The children absolutely adored it,' says Aunt Sheila who used to join them on the weekend, 'it really was a carefree happy holiday.'

Here, Steve Marriott started to display the traits which would form the basis of his individual nature. His sister Kay recalls incidents such as her brother insisting on everyone playing a game of cricket, with him to bat first. But when he was bowled out or caught, the young Marriott would simply refuse to leave the crease. Nor would he give the bat to anyone else.

It was as if he refused to acknowledge reality and believed that through stubborn behaviour he could make the world how he wanted. Naturally, the family would remonstrate with him, ask him to be reasonable, but Steve refused to budge.

Finally, after being told no one was going to play with him anymore, he would shout at them, 'Alright then, I'm off,' and angrily throw the bat away and storm off. Half an hour later, he would return to the fold, acting as if nothing had happened.

'Who wants to play cricket?' he'd shout. 'I'll bat first.'

At Jaywick, there were other pleasures. He loved getting up early in the morning and going tadpole hunting with his sister.

He loved the breaking of routine, the air of freedom that he inhaled during this two-week jaunt. And he was unable to stop himself spending as much time as he could in the campsite's noisy arcade with its rows of brightly coloured fruit machines.

For a while, it became a tradition that as soon as Marriott got to Jaywick, straight away he would rush to the arcade, his pockets full of the sixpences his Gran had saved up for him and sister Kay. Within a short space of time he had blown all of his holiday money. The next day, absolutely broke, he would raid his sister's jar.

'There was no malice in him, no wickedness,' the mum quickly interjects, lest anyone get the wrong idea, 'He just didn't see any wrong in what he did.'

All his life, Steve Marriott was a spender, never a saver. His attitude to money was like his attitude to life, carefree and careless.

Yet, even without his holiday cash, Jaywick was important to Steve. For it was here, many years later, that he first fell in love with performing, fell in love with the sound of applause, the sight of people smiling at him, the sensation of mass attention. It thrilled him to be able to entertain people although in later life the act of performing would mutate into a different beast, one which he had to fight hard to master.

'All his life he got himself into a real state before performing,' his mum says. 'He was nearly sick with worry. And then he would walk out on stage and you wouldn't believe it was the same person. You really wouldn't.'

‡ ‡ ‡

From austerity to affluence in a few short years; that was the British people's experience of the Fifties. At the start of the decade, the Labour Government was enforcing food rationing and Stafford Cripps, the Chancellor of the Exchequer, was taking a tax of nine shillings and sixpence from every pound. By the end of it the Prime Minister, Harold MacMillan was telling the country that they had, 'never had it so good.'

Despite the wave of optimism that had seen Clement Attlee's Labour Party swept into power in 1945, soon, everyone was saying the same thing – life was even bleaker than it had been in wartime. By the early '50s, the Government were told that only seventy people in the entire country were known to hold more than six thousand pounds in their bank accounts. The Labour Government paid the usual price.

In October, 1951, the Conservatives, led by Winston Churchill, were returned to power. Their timing was immaculate for as they assumed office, so the British economy finally began to pick up.

In July 1954, food rationing was finally abolished and the following year commercial television was given the go ahead to challenge the BBC.

The Marriott's income at this time was derived from Kay's new job at the Tate and Lyle factory in Silvertown and Bill's work as a printer for the *Daily Sketch* newspaper, now defunct.

Steve had started his education at the nearby Monega Infant and Junior school in Monega Road but on November 5th, 1955, when he was just eight, tragedy again threatened the Marriott family.

Celebrating Bonfire Night with his family in their small garden, a Catherine Wheel firework spun off the garden fence and flew straight into Steve's left eye. He was rushed to Moorfields Hospital in Old Street where he was admitted for an indefinite period. Kay his three-year-old sister stood and cried in the garden.

Life was so unpredictable. Only the day before his injury, Steve had dressed her up as Guy Fawkes and taken her to the High Street in her pram. There he made her hide under her blanket until he he made a sign, at which point Kay would suddenly sit up and startle passers by. The locals took the prank in good spirit and Steve and Kay (well, Steve anyway) made a tidy sum that day.

Now her brother was in hospital and the longer he stayed there, the more his parents' worry increased. Bill, especially, felt the strain. He couldn't help thinking, Had the same curse which had taken his eye now been visited on his son? Thankfully, Steve recovered his eyesight although his left eye did bear some trace of the incident.

'You always knew when he got tired,' Kay the sister recalled, 'because that eye would droop a little bit. But that was all.'

‡ ‡ ‡

The early morning quiet of Strone Road is broken by the rattle of glass set to the rhythm of horses' hooves. Harry Ells, the milkman has just arrived. The two Kays, mother and daughter, can still hear his cart lumbering down the road and the sound triggers off a series of memories from the simpler place and time they once inhabited.

They think of the baker arriving on a cart, delivering hot fresh bread on a Sunday, the children playing out on a street uncluttered by cars, the neighbours coming out of their houses in summertime to stand around – the men in their vests and braces and the women with scarves wrapped around their heads – to smoke, to laugh, to take the mickey and to gossip.

'Hello, Mrs Jones, how's your Bert's lumbago?' Steve Marriott would sing in one of his most famous songs, stealing the phrase off the cleaner in his Pimlico house. He would always remember such characters, those who stood by the fence nattering away to his mum as she hung her washing and he never ever forgot the name Harry Ells.

One hot summer day in 1957, workmen arrived to re-surface Strone Road. Standing outside his house, bored, the ten-year-old Steve observed two things; Ells the milkman was at the top end of the street whilst the workmen were now taking a tea break. A mischievious impulse struck him. He walked over and without anyone noticing, casually picked up a bucket of cold tarmac. He then strolled down the road to where Harry Ells' cart and horse stood.

Making sure no one was watching, he started applying the black sticky substance to Buck, Harry's horse. He couldn't help smiling to himself; it was such a laugh. Having finished the job, Marriott then hid the bucket and dashed indoors to watch events from his front window.

Unfortunately, he had forgotten to take one thing into account. It was a hot day and as the sun bore down on the horse turning the tarmac hot, the animal became more and more agitated until finally, rearing up in agony, he nearly tipped the whole cart over.

The commotion brought Harry Ells running down the street and the neighbours rushing out of their houses. Everyone was appalled. Who could have played such a horrible trick on such a defenceless animal? What wicked mind could dream up such a thing? There was one name that sprang to all their minds, that of little Stevie Marriott from number 308.

Already he was known for such stunts as putting manure through people's letterboxes or stealing milk bottles off doorsteps. Another favourite ruse was to rush out into the street, shouting, 'Quick, quick, my mum and dad are killing each other.'

The neighbours would hear his cries and bolt into the Marriott house only to find Bill and Kay sitting quietly in the kitchen having a cup of tea. 'It was only a laugh, that's all, only a laugh,' the boy would say in his defence.

All his life, he would use that very same phrase. For Steve Marriott a laugh excused everything.

Try as she might, Kay his mother could not quell his ways or curb his behaviour. Most days, mother and son would argue and rage until finally she would order him to his bedroom. God, he made her so angry but an hour later she would relent – as mothers do – and take him a peace offering, usually a plate of food on a tray.

The room would be empty, Steve, having escaped through his bedroom window, would now be sitting in the nearby cemetery, sulking, wondering why the world didn't turn his way and why he had such a strict mum.

Sometimes the world was so unfair.

‡ ‡ ‡

From a very early age, Kay reports, her son was drawn to music: singing around the house; turning on the radio every time he entered a room. Music became such a passion that finally Steve's parents bought their son a ukulele.

Kay can always remember her and Bill walking home with the instrument and Bill, knowing his ten year old son's undisciplined nature, saying, 'I don't know why we've bought him this, he won't bloody learn it.'

But Bill was wrong. After showing Steve some basic chords, he then stood back in amazement as his son diligently applied himself to mastering the ukelele. From that day on musical instruments would never be far from Marriott's hands.

A year later, the family holidayed as usual at Jaywick. As with most holiday camps, a main attraction was the children's talent contest. This year, 1958, Steve entered and walked off with first prize after singing the Buddy Holly hit 'Oh Boy.'

The following year he won again, this time singing Tommy Steele's 'Little White Bull,' a chart hit of that year. He loved performing, loved the thrill it gave him. But the following year, however, Steve suffered an unexpected setback. Inspired by his success, his sister Kay decided she too would enter the contest.

She dressed up as an old man and sang the Cockney standard, 'My Old Man's A Dustman'. She was good, won first prize. Mum and Dad were happy, proud. Their son wasn't. He was beside himself with jealousy. He raged and he sulked – so unhappy at having his thunder stolen. Kay understood the message. She retreated to the shadows and never entered the contest again.

Yet there was a softer, more generous side to young Steve's nature as well. At Jaywick, come the early evening dusk, Steve would take out his ukulele and stroll around the area, passing by the chalets, huts and nearby houses like a little Pied Piper, singing standards like George Gershwin's 'Summertime.'

On hearing him, people would come out of their houses to pass him money and soon, very soon, he understood the power of his talent, understood that people are fascinated by the gifted especially when the performer is a young, bright and good-looking child with a bounce in his step and a smile on his face that suggests he truly believes that the world is his for the taking. And it would be for the next thirty years although if events in that world didn't go as he planned then a burning anger would suffuse his body and he would strike out without care.

‡ ‡ ‡

'Didn't have telly in them days, so we had to amuse ourselves.' Unprompted and separately in both their interviews, the two Kays express these sentiments and do so with a real tinge of accomplishment in their voices. Many of their nights at 308 Strone Road were given over to music and parlour games. When visitors were present, Bill would sit at the piano, Steve would get out his ukulele and then everyone would gather round and start singing.

Christmas Day was the best time. That was when all family differences were put aside and the Marriotts came together as one, to sing Cockney songs with risqué content. You can imagine the young mischievous Steve standing by the piano, his face caught in a permanent smile, relishing the way the naughty words and the vibrant music of each song conspired to crack open people's faces into a smiles.

It was a device he would later use to such great effect on songs such as 'Rene' or

'Happydaystoytown.'

'It was always lovely at Christmas,' Kay recalls. 'Even when Steve was playing in groups he would always find some reason at Christmas so he could come home. We had so much fun.'

In central London, the young were also having fun as they began to create their own form of entertainment. But it wasn't music that opened up London to the young, it was actually an Italian coffee machine that gave birth to British youth culture. The arrival in London of the Gaggia coffee machine led to coffee bars opening up across the city, thus creating a space for young people to come together.

The proprietors of these bars would book groups to entertain their youthful clientele. At the time, skiffle, a music that meshed together folk music and blues, was the most exciting sound in Britain.

Skiffle's most famous venue was the 2 I's bar on Old Compton Street. Here the young congregated to hear artists such as Tommy Steele or Joe Brown who in turn had been inspired by the first true exponents of the sound, Ken Colyer's Skiffle Group, a 1953 off shoot of his band, The Jazzmen.

Colyer's group featured three acoustic guitars, a bass, a washboard and a young musician by the name of Lonnie Donegan. Donegan soon became one of Marriott's earliest heroes. In fact, when Steve discovered where Donegan actually lived, he decided to pay him a visit. He got dressed up, got excited, headed out to meet his hero.

He came home crestfallen. Could you believe it, he told his sister? Donegan had opened the door with boiled egg stains on his shirt and his hair all messy. Marriott was crushed. He had never imagined his idol looking so sloppy. Kay found his attitude highly amusing.

Years later, when she would ask about someone famous, (usually, someone she had a fancy for) Marriott would shout back at her, 'What are they like? They're human. They breathe, they eat, they shit. They're human okay?'

And Kay would turn round and shout back, 'Yeah but you didn't think that when you went to see Lonnie Donegan, that time. You didn't think he should have egg spilt down his shirt, eh?'

A scuffle about skiffle, a music that the Marriott family often came together to play, especially in summertime. That was when they would set up in the garden with Steve on his ukulele, Bill on catgut bass, Kay the mum hitting the washboard, Kay the sister, contributing handclaps. On hearing the music, the neighbours would come out to sing along and enjoy the music.

In this small community, despite Steve's antics, the Marriotts were well liked on Strone Road.

'Kath was a very attractive woman,' says neighbour Rita Hann, of Steve's mother, 'quite a glamorous figure and an extrovert character, very forceful. Sometimes a bit over the top but with a heart of gold. Bill, well he was exactly the opposite, a small quiet unassuming man who kept himself to himself. They were extreme opposites. Kath definitely wore the trousers in that house.'

‡ ‡ ‡

In the Britain of the Fifties, the pre-war notion that you were expected to know your place, expected to know where you belonged in the scheme of things, was still being peddled to the masses by an increasingly powerless establishment.

Steve Marriott could not have played that game even if he wanted to. He would never bow down to everyone for a fierce pride, garnered from his family and locality, refused to let him. He had to go his own way, do his own thing. That's what made him so unique.

It was a quality that he relentlessly displayed at both his schools, especially his second school, Sandringham Road Secondary School, a rough impersonal place where the violence of the children was equalled by the indifference of the teachers.

'At school, the teachers used to leave him to do what he wanted,' his mother recalls. 'If he wanted to hang outside the window, as he invariably did, they would leave him. If he wanted to jump on the milk float and ride around in the playground they would let him. Otherwise, he would just disrupt the whole class.'

Such stories suggest an active brain but one not conducive to study. Wrong, say both the parents, wrong.

'As soon as they had any exams,' Kay says, 'and they had to study, Steve would swot up for a fortnight and then be in the top ten. He didn't do anything for a year and then pass his exams. It used to drive the teachers mad.'

Bill Marriott: 'We went to see his teacher on open day and she said, "There's only one thing I can say about Steve. He's unique." That was it. Later she told us that she had caught him hanging out the window about four storeys up with just his boots showing.'

Steve hated school and he would regularly bunk off for the day, either alone or with friends. Once after a sustained period of non-attendance through a supposed illness, the school inspector came to his house to enquire after his health. Kay informed the inspector that she was very sorry about Steve missing school, that her son had not been ill and that she would now personally make sure he got to school every day.

When Steve discovered his mum's treachery, he was appalled. How could you rat on me he asked her? Round the East End, a rat was the lowest of the low.

But Kay just told him, 'You're going to school and that's it. Think me a rat, I really don't give a monkey's.'

‡ ‡ ‡

Like most children, Marriott went through various obsessions and enthusiasms – his mother recalls a brief passion for model aeroplanes.

'All over the house, they were,' she says, but nothing came close to the effect that music gave him. It had entered his blood and his soul and would stay with him all his life.

Unable to afford a record player, the young Marriott would visit a young couple who lived nearby and ask to use their record player. The first record he ever took there was one his mum bought for him, Cliff Richard's 'Travellin' Light,' a number one hit in November 1959.

The record didn't stay in his possession long. After committing another major misdemeanour, his mum actually smashed it in two upon his head. That'll teach you, she said, knowing full well it wouldn't.

Another early favourite was Hank Williams, the country music pioneer who like many would die before their time. Marriott loved the simplicity of William's songs, their storytelling element, the mournful Williams voice. Later on, Elvis Presley was another to fire up not only Marriott's imagination but the rest of the Western world.

His 1955 debut single on Sun Records, 'That's Alright Mama,' signalled the arrival of rock'n'roll, an exciting blues based music that the young gleefully claimed as their own. The fresh youthful spirit starting to blow away the cobwebs of England's dusty past was not only confined to Britain.

Above all, though, Marriott loved Buddy Holly, the bespectacled American rock'n'roller, famed for hits such as 'Peggy Sue' and 'Oh Boy.'

Marriott responded strongly to the man's fabulous mix of melody and energy, loved that trick he did with his voice, the way he stretched out the words and then made those funny little noises from his throat.

Oh, he loved Buddy, big time.

'He used to go round with the Buddy Holly glasses on,' says his sister. 'They had no lenses. I found them in his bedroom. I also found an exercise book with Buddy Marriott written on the cover. Of course, I teased him about that. I wish I had kept it.'

Another early favourite were The Shadows. Today, their records sound tinny but back then Hank Marvin's use of echo and twang was not only sonically unique but gave Marriott and a million other hopefuls, a good insight into the possibilities of the guitar.

Marriott would store such sounds and ideas away, unconsciously save them for a future date. He would do so because music was in his blood now. It would never ever leave him.

‡ ‡ ‡

Sex lived up the road from Steve Marriott at number 241 Strone Road. This was the home of Renee Tungate, a sex worker who made her living pleasuring a succession of locals, many of whom considered her to be a little off-balanced.

When not working, Renee was not at all averse to spending her time off entertaining Steve and his school mates who found her form of education somewhat more pleasurable than that of the state system they were busy avoiding.

Of course, his mum knew all about these illicit rendezvous. Nothing got past her.

'I didn't like him going round, there, didn't like it at all,' she sniffed.

Later, Marriott would claim that everything he learnt about lovemaking, he learnt from Renee Tungate. No wonder he wrote such a raucous song to celebrate her unique form of instruction.

Fact of the matter was, Steve Marriott was developing into a strikingly handsome man, one who would prove fiercely attractive to the opposite sex. He was good looking, intriguing but above all, he was funny. Women love humour. Along with beautiful eyes and good shoes, humour is one of the essential requisites. So is cheekiness and someone who never hides their feelings, says what he is thinking right away, whatever the consequence.

It makes a man intriguing, makes a girl want to be the one to conquer him. Steve Marriott spent a lot of his time with a lot of women, loving them, hating them, fighting them, charming them and smiling with them. He married three times but he, unlike them, never learnt the most basic lesson about himself.

That he could never be tamed. Not by himself or any of his many lovers.

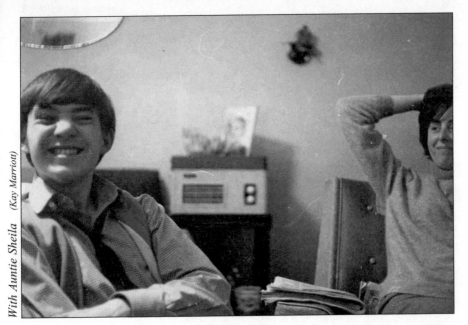

Chapter Three

The Words Of Fools

Steve once told his mother, 'Mum, if I had stayed at Sandringham I would have ended up in prison, no doubt about it.' And he was right.

Like all natural born anarchists, Steve Marriott was never going to take any education system seriously unless it allowed him to do exactly as he pleased. As that was never a possibility, Marriott quickly set himself against the school system. He would go his own way. If they didn't like it, then let them try and stop him. He didn't get too much opposition.

At Sandringham secondary modern school, the pupils were viewed as fodder for the factory lines. The majority of teachers were of the opinion that most, if not all of the pupils, were incapable of gaining qualifications. They would all leave at sixteen and head straight into work. Therefore little effort was required from either pupil or teacher.

'To go there,' confirms Ken Hawes, one of Marriott's classmates, 'was to be condemned to a life of doing nothing and being a nobody.'

The teachers offered the pupils a simple deal. If anyone wishes to study, fine. We will help you. If you don't, make sure you don't bother us and we won't bother you. In the absence of a moral centre, of a collective direction and purpose, bullying flourished at Sandringham.

'I'll never forget that first day at Sandringham,' Marriott's schoolfriend, Ken Hawes states. 'The initiation was for first year pupils to have their heads pushed down into the sinks. The sinks were outside on the playground and the taps would be turned on.

'The bullies would block the sinks with large amounts of paper and literally try to drown you.'

Sandringham was a large and impersonal beast which swallowed Steve Marriott up, denied him the chance to be the centre of attention. Instead, he was surrounded by several tough boys who often picked on him.

To protect himself, Steve Marriott joined the school boxing club. His first fight pitted him against the school champion. It wasn't much of a contest. Steve stood helplessly in the corner of the ring trying to protect himself as his opponent waded into him.

Kay, his mum, sat in the crowd, shouting, 'C'mon Steve hit him back!' but with arms like his, what chance a knockout? Steve was small in height, (he would only reach five foot five inches) and skinny in appearance.

Yet according to Ken Hawes, Steve was not usually the cowering type, quite the opposite, in fact.

'Steve,' Hawes insists, 'was a downright bully, a real hard case. The school had a very undesirable atmosphere and there was an underlying level of violence in the playground, a lot of terrorising going on. I just used to keep out of everybody's way to survive but you got noticed by bullying, younger smaller pupils.'

It's hard to imagine a boy of Marriott's diminutive size throwing his weight around. Equally, hard to imagine a boy as boisterous as Steve, an attention seeker of the highest order, allowing himself to be rendered silent.

More probable is that Steve stood his ground, learnt to use his mouth in threatening ways, learnt in other words to create an aura of toughness. It was perhaps the first flourishing of his talent as an actor.

At the same time, Marriott was busy developing his musical ability. He now had a new instrument to master. In his first year at school, his mum and dad had presented him with a guitar. They then directed him over the road to the house of one Tunky Jordan who played in a band supplying Hawaiian music for the BBC.

It was Jordan who showed Steve the instrument's basic chords.

'Then we got somebody to teach him,' Bill Marriott recalled, 'but they said it was useless because he'd got his own way of teaching. He taught himself. Very good.'

Very good, indeed.

Within three years, Steve Marriott would have his name printed on a record sleeve. He would also have formed his very first band and thrown everything his family wanted for him back in their faces.

‡ ‡ ‡

In 1959, aged twelve, Marriott put together his first band with his school friends, Nigel Chapin and Robin Andrews. They were called The Wheels although they later changed their name to the Coronation Kids.

The band's repertoire entirely reflected Marriott's tastes, the set list full of Cliff Richard and Buddy Holly material. There was also room for one of Marriott's first ever compositions, a song, named after his aunt, entitled 'Sheila My Dear.'

According to the few who heard it, the song was a Buddy Holly style affair played at a jaunty pace. Not surprisingly, the band's nickname for Steve was

'Buddy.'

This youthful beat combo played the coffee bars in East Ham as well as Saturday morning gigs at cinemas such as the Essoldo in Manor Park. Then they changed their name yet again, (due to his overactive nature, Marriott often switched band titles until chart success with The Small Faces made it silly to do so) this time turning into the Mississippi Five when their line-up was augmented by the arrival of Simon Simkins and Vic Dixon.

Soon, though, Marriott's attention would be diverted towards another form of music, one that would allow him to write some of the best songs of his career and help secure his place as one of the great vocal talents.

The story of R&B music in Britain is a fascinating, still hidden history deserving of its own time and space. It is a story of people's obsession, of the beauty that such love and dedication creates. It is the story of entrepreneurs and hustlers, of fabulous lives and fabulous records. It the story of a music that remains underground to this day but has never lost its power to bind people together. It is the story of a music that sings in a million different voices about joy and pain, smiles and tears, ecstasy and delight, speed and love, mohair and madness.

For Steve Marriott, American R&B music forcefully reflected his own inner passions and fires. It moved him like nothing else and soon he would seek to replicate the very same emotions that musicians such as Ray Charles and Bobby Bland had infused their work with.

All his life, until the day he died, Steve Marriott loved, respected and honoured rhythm and blues. It was the music that he would remain the most faithful to, the music he would become a servant of, preaching its glory wherever he went, and it was the music that would serve to ignite one of the biggest rows in the Marriott family history.

‡ ‡ ‡

'*Food, glorious food...*' The weekly diet of the Marriott family, Manor Park: on Sunday, a roast beef dinner; on Monday, meat leftovers with mashed potato; Tuesday, a stew concocted from the final remains of the joint; meat pie and processed peas on Wednesday; shepherd's pie on Thursday; fish and chips on Friday and on Saturday, a great big fry up... *Food, glorious food*!

One day at work, Bill Marriott spotted an ad announcing auditions for Lionel Bart's acclaimed musical *Oliver!*, his ingenious adaptation of Charles Dickens' famous novel, *Oliver Twist*.

The show was being successfully staged at the New London Theatre in London's St. Martin's Lane. However, the law stipulated that after three months performers of school age had to take a break. New cast members were required to replace them – hence the advert.

Bill came home, showed Kay a copy of the ad. That very night, without their son's knowledge, they sent their son's details to the show's producers. A few days later, a letter arrived, inviting Stephen Peter Marriott to audition for the stage production of *Oliver!*.

That day, that momentous day, Steve came home from school to be told by his mum that they were going out.

'Where? I just got in.'

His mum didn't want to tell him where they were going or what they were doing. She didn't want any nervousness to affect him until the very last moment.

'I'll tell you on the train,' Kay replied. 'Change your trousers as well. Put on your khaki shorts.'

'I'm not wearing khaki shorts. I've got my long trousers.'

'Stephen, I don't want any nonsense out of you today. Now go and put on your shorts and your ankle socks. Just trust me.'

'Why?'

'Stephen, please don't argue. Do as I say.'

'But why?'

Oh, that son of hers. He would stand there all night until he got an answer.

'Because you're going for an audition. For *Oliver!*'

'Blimey.'

'Now put your shorts on. I want you to look younger than you are.'

'But mum...'

Still arguing, Steve changed his clothes and he and Kay left, went 'up West,' to London's West End. Throughout the whole journey he didn't say a word to his mum. Why should he? Making him wear khaki shorts. Imagine if anyone saw him. The embarrassment of it all. He would die of shame, right on the spot.

'For my first number, I would like to play 'Who's Sorry Now' by Connie Francis,' he says.

The thirteen-year-old Steve Marriott stands on an empty stage with his guitar in hand. The song he is about to sing was released in April, 1958 and became the second best selling single in Great Britain that year. Only 'All I Have To Do Is Dream' by the Everly Brothers fared better...

'For my first number I would like to play 'Who's Sorry Now,' by Connie Francis.'

The chart both these songs entered was filled with records dripping in cloying sentimentality. They were sung by bland artists like Perry Como, Frankie Vaughan, The McGuire Sisters, raking it in for their manager and record company by successfully selling a world of lightness, a world where lust and sweat and animal instincts had never existed, where sweetness reigned supreme.

Of late, there had been some records which had challenged the status quo. Fats Domino had hit home a few times, as had others. But as far as most people were concerned, including the music industry, the rock 'n' roll revolution of 1956 was finished.

Elvis Presley, the man supposed to lead the battle charge, had swapped his jive clothes from Beale Street in Memphis for US Army fatigues. Chuck Berry and Jerry Lee Lewis had been publicly disgraced for revealing their penchant for very young flesh, Buddy Holly was dead and Little Richard was about to discover God.

If you were young and restless in 1960 musical excitement was in pretty short supply.

'Thank you very much indeed.'

Steve Marriott has just finished performing his Connie Francis number.

Before anyone can say a word, he announces, 'For my next number, I would like to do 'Oh Boy,' by Buddy Holly.'

Nobody on the judging panel is quick enough to stop him, to tell him the rules, that applicants only get to play one number. And if they had pointed out that fact, would he have taken note? Probably not!

Marriott launched into a rendition of one of his favourite songs, written by Holly in 1957.

'Okay Stephen,' said a voice from the stalls as the last Holly chord drifted away into the roof of the St. Martin's Theatre, 'very nice, very nice indeed.'

Marriott, flushed with adrenaline, thanks the panel and walks towards his mum who is standing in the wings. She feels so proud.

'Mrs. Marriott?'

One of the play's assistants is standing next to her.

'Yes.'

'We would like to keep Stephen for a while.'

'Really?'

'Yes.'

A shot of delight such as she has never known before zips through her. She was right. Her boy was special. It wasn't mother talk. She was right. Her son was unique.

'But how's he going to get home?' she wonders out loud.

'Don't worry. We'll see him home alright.'

Bill Marriott was standing at the gate of their house when Kay came home. As he watched his wife skip down the road and then joyfully throw her arms around him. He knew straight away that something momentous had just happened to their lives.

‡ ‡ ‡

A deal was struck; Steve would play different boys throughout the production, singing different songs depending on which character he had been assigned. He would be paid eight pounds a week, (eight pounds a week!) and there would be an enforced break of ten days every three months. A woman called The Matron would supply extra schooling.

The matron. Ah yes, the matron. Steve's mum Kay smiles ruefully.

'Steve would have loved to have played the Artful Dodger and if he hadn't been so cheeky and so rude, he would have got the part easily. But he didn't like the matron because she was posh and she didn't like him because she thought he was cocky and disrupted her boys. He would have been marvellous as the Dodger but there you go.'

Steve Marriott, like Dicken's famous boy character, The Artful Dodger, was a quintessential Londoner. The London spirit was his, had entered him at an early age. It made him, like Dickens' creation, cheeky, sly, flash, talkative, sensitive, humorous, resigned, brusque, but above all it gave him an energy that others simply couldn't keep up with.

Steve stayed with *Oliver!* for twelve months. During that time, his low boredom threshold was partly assuaged by the acting approach of the show's leading actor, Ron Moody, who played Fagin.

'He loved being on stage,' Kay says of her son, 'he enjoyed every minute of it. He said that although they did the same thing every night it was always different because you never knew what Ron Moody was going to say. He changed little things here and there and that made Steve laugh. He kept it spicy, kept it good.'

It was typical of Marriott to warm to someone who bent the rules and didn't stick to the script. And such was the vocal talent Steve displayed in his time in *Oliver!*, it was he who was selected to sing the Artful Dodger songs for the official album of the show, released by the World Record Club label in 1960.

Prior to recording, the album's producer Cyril Ornadale invited Steve and his mother to his London home to assess the boy's vocal talent.

'Can't remember where his house was,' tuts Kay. 'Somewhere posh.'

Steve duly sang and afterwards, Ornadale theatrically exclaimed,

'Why, you're an absolute natural.'

Unlike the other cast members, Marriott's was the true cockney voice, perfect to replicate the Artful Dodger with. The others who had applied for the job were, in truth, singing out of their class.

On the *Oliver!* Album recorded at the famous Abbey Road studios, the first studio to capture the Marriott voice, Steve sings three songs: 'Consider Yourself,' 'Be Back Soon,' and 'I'd Do Anything.' His voice is how you would expect a thirteen-year-old's to be – thin, tuneful and lively and one which displays his Cockney roots. On 'Consider Yourself,' Marriott sings 'the drinks are on the harse,' as opposed to 'the house.'

The Oliver songs were the creation of Lionel Bart, a man who not only shared Steve's East End background but also many similarities. Both were men of wayward ways, both could lay a claim to being the most talented songwriters of their time, both had problems with authority and above all both men's work created a musical line that takes us directly back to the music hall of the East End.

Music halls had risen to great prominence in the early part of the 20th century but the advent of cinema, television and finally pop music rendered this working class form of entertainment absolutely redundant. That said, the genre spawned much memorable music.

'These are songs,' writes London's restless biographer Peter Ackroyd, 'that still retain enormous power and feeling. Who could fail to be moved by verses like 'My Shadow Is My Only Pal', or 'When Those Old Clothes Were New?' Who could fail to be amused by 'Why Don't We Have The Sea In London?' or 'Don't Stick It Out Like That' or 'I Don't Suppose He'll Do It Again For Months and Months and Months?'

Who indeed? Except maybe the Royal Family and the uptight.

'When Steve left *Oliver!* after a year he had stars in his eyes,' his mum simply states. 'He wanted to be in show business.'

The exciting and so thrilling journey to stardom had now begun.

Chapter Four

Almost Grown

'Here's the story of a boy Jekyll and Hyde… a shaggy-haired 14-year-old who leaves his neat council home every evening to join London's worst gang of juvenile cut-throats," ran the *Stratford Express* in 1961. 'Pocket sized Stephen Marriott likes swimming, billiards, table tennis and English…but hates maths.'

'I want to go on the stage when I leave school,' Steve tells the reporter.

The article goes onto reveal 'that Stephen is putting aside a third of his weekly wage to buy a new guitar.'

Oliver! taught Marriott many things, not least that a lack of educational qualifications did not equal disaster. For years, successive generations had been told to pass exams and better themselves. At the age of fourteen Steve Marriott had bettered himself on entirely his own terms. He had earnt good money doing something he absolutely adored and had done so without a qualification in his pocket.

So who's sorry now?

He now knew what to he was going do about school, the place he hated so much. Put simply, he was going to make it vanish. Literally.

'I remember being selected to go to into this art class,' says Steve's classmate Ken Hawes, again. 'I don't know why. I hated art. It was in a large room with large windows. The school was a big Victorian building. The floor was a plain polished floorboard with gaps between them where they had shrunk over the years.

'They were creaky floorboards. The desks were in pairs and in several rows across the room. About ten rows in all.'

'When I walked in for the first time this kid who turned out to be Steve Marriott said, "You're sitting next to me." I was the smallest in the year. I weighed under six stone and people always thought I was ill. I sat next to him. I wasn't at all interested in art and neither was he. I sat there in complete silence and he sat there looking at the art teacher as he got out of his bag several sheets of paper.'

Marriott then proceeded to tear the paper into little squares which he then wrapped around his ruler and stuffed into the floorboard space beneath him.

'Throughout the whole lesson he continued to tear paper and push it through the floorboards,' Hawes continues. 'He didn't do any art at all and of course the teacher wasn't bothered in the least about anybody that didn't want to work. Steve just stared at the teacher all the time and carried on tearing up these bits of paper.'

The following week, Marriott again grabbed Hawes, told him, 'You're sitting with me.' He then made him sit one chair up from where they had previously sat. Again, he spent the whole lesson staring at the art teacher as he stuffed bits of paper into the floorboards. The following week, the same scenario was again played out, the two boys again moving up another chair until as, Hawes puts it, 'Eventually, we had worked our way right across the whole class.'

Finally, after about ten weeks, Marriott was sitting against the wall at the far end. Halfway through the lesson, he dipped into his pocket and pulled out a box of matches. He lit the match under his desk and then dropped it down the floorboards.

'Suddenly,' Hawes says, 'smoke just shot out of the floor. The fire caught on in no time at all and everybody scrambled down the stairs. The playground was right underneath the art room and that's where everybody had to gather and stand in line. Marriott turned to me and said, "You didn't see a fucking thing alright?"'

It was a sizeable fire and the fire brigade had some trouble bringing it under control. All the time, Stephen Peter Marriott stood in the playground watching the proceedings, his face betraying nothing but a huge grin was writ large upon his soul.

'The whole room went up and it demolished that side of the school,' Hawes recalls. 'Nobody spoke to me afterwards. I think a teacher may have just said, "What was that all about?" And I looked at him and said, I didn't know anything about it.

'See Steve was not an academic but he obviously had this sheer determination to make it in show business whether it be acting or music. With the arson thing I suppose in a way I was impressed about how he had meticulously planned the whole thing months in advance, the sheer dogged determination to see it through. He could quite easily have been caught and would have had to face the consequences. There was no danger in anybody getting hurt because we were at the back of the room. We had to be at the back otherwise somebody would have noticed what he was doing. There was no malice against the other pupils, he just wanted to burn the damn school down.'

Fire. The man who would die far too young from being exposed to its fierce properties was a boy arsonist.

Naturally, he never admitted to the crime. Even when Hawes bumped into Marriott many years later, Marriott's immediate instinct was to deny everything.

'In 1984,' Hawes recalls, 'I was working as a sound engineer at the Mean Fiddler pub in North West London when Steve Marriott came in wearing a long herringbone overcoat down to his ankles.

'He was just standing around with his band while a sound check was going on. I crept up behind him and introduced myself, but my name initially meant nothing to him, so I said, "We last met at Sandringham Road school when we were about twelve years old. You must remember the place, you burnt it down."

'He turned round and said, "It wasn't me!"

'I just laughed and said, "Steve I was the one who sat next you."

'He said, "Do you want to have a drink after the gig?"

'Which we did. We went to the bar upstairs. I said, "Steve, there's no one else around. Can we just get over the fact that I know it was you?" He laughed and said, "I hated that school, really hated it".'

He said that after he had lined up in the playground where we all got ticked off by the fire marshal, he nipped off home and as he turned into his road, he heard his mum who was standing at the gate of the garden say, "Steve, that was you wasn't it? I've heard the fire engines and I've heard that the school is on fire. You wait until your dad gets home."

Ken Hawes pauses and then adds, 'Steve Marriott had a pent up passion about him. He was dedicated, concentrated, focussed on what he was doing. But he was very much a loner. He didn't have any close pals back then. He kept himself pretty much to himself.'

The artful dodger as a shy retiring sort is an interesting image – perhaps it went part and parcel with his artistic talents. The nineteenth century writer Stendhal believed, 'Every great poet with a lively imagination is shy; in other words he is afraid of men because they can interrupt and disturb his exquisite reveries, and he trembles for his ability to concentrate.'

His mother disagrees with Hawes' assessment though: 'People just followed him,' she wistfully recalls. 'He always had a gang. He was small and cheeky, not the sort of person you think of as a leader but he just had that magnetism about him.'

One thing's for sure: Steve Marriott hated school and everything to do with it. To survive it, he acted tough and aloof but his irrepressible energy could not be contained and it obviously attracted others. Part of Steve's appeal must have been his growing confidence in his own abilities, bolstered by his time in *Oliver!* and the fact that everything he had attempted so far had been a success. Steve Marriott would not taste failure for a very long time but when he did, it would inevitably hit him much harder than most.

Daines Close flats (John Hellier)

Chapter Five

Call It Something Nice

In 1961, the Marriott family moved from Strone Road to 9, Daines Close in Manor Park. The property was a brand new council flat and compared to their draughty former home, was considered a real luxury.

Bill still worked at the newspaper and Kay now had a job as a bookbinder. But it was not work or money that occupied their minds, it was their son's education. Kay knew that his days at Sandringham were numbered. In all good faith, she could not risk another incident which threatened lives and property.

Another school had to be found.

In 1911, the actress Italia Conti opened up a drama school in Great Portland Street, London. The eponymous school soon built up an excellent reputation and has sustained it ever since. For years now, the Italia Conti has remained the destination for scouts and directors in search of true talent. Steve Marriott's Auntie Sheila worked for an impresario called Jack Hylton and knew the school.

'When Bill and Kay realised he had an awful lot of talent they thought he ought to go to an acting school,' Sheila recalls. 'So I approached the people at the Italia Conti school because I used to deal with them through work.'

Through Sheila, a Saturday morning audition was arranged. Steve arrived at the school, located now in London's Archer Street, accompanied by his mum. He was asked to recite some Shakespeare.

'He loved it. He'd deny it now,' says Kay, talking as if her son was still with us, a verbal trait that exists to this day, 'He'd say it was horrible. But he loved it.'

Again, success came easy for Steve. The Italia Conti offered to take him on for a month. When the four weeks passed they had no hesitation in offering him a permanent place.

'The deal with the Italia Conti school,' Sheila says, 'was that we said we can't pay any fees. They said, don't worry. We'll get him work and we'll take our fees from the work. They were so convinced that he would be employed and they would be able to get their money. That's how he got to the Italia Conti school and he really enjoyed it.'

The family still had to pay for Steve's books and uniform and travel expenses to auditions and this expense placed a big strain on the family finances but Kay was determined to see her son get the best chance. To pay for the additional expense, she found work as the chief receptionist at a photographic studio in Holborn.

Steve's first significant role; a sizeable part in a two-hour film entitled *Night Cargoes*. The film was divided into eight fifteen-minute parts and designed for Saturday morning screenings to a very young audience.

In *Night Cargoes*, Steve plays a local West Country lad involved in smuggling. One of his co-stars was Hugh Janes, a classmate from the Italia Conti.

'The film was shot on location in Devon,' Janes recalls. 'We did a lot of horse riding. Steve was a relatively hopeless horse rider. Neither of us had ridden a horse previously; we just lied to get the job. When we went for an audition we would just say yes to everything and work it out afterwards.'

Prior to filming, the boys were given horse-riding lessons by a Major Henderson,

'Fearsome man,' says Janes. 'Anyway, on the film set, we'd ride all the time. I remember Marriott and I racing along. He had a pony that I used to ride in the film and I was on a horse. Steve would go hell for leather to catch me.

'I also remember Steve always had a guitar with him. He had played guitar from a very early age and was already into rhythm and blues, much more earthy stuff than what was in the charts, although he was always into Buddy Holly in a very big way.'

Janes recalls many hours spent in the school's dressing room listening to Marriott sing and play guitar. He adds that the Italia Conti teachers consistently encouraged Marriott's musical efforts, a far cry from the indifferent treatment he received at Sandringham.

'Even back then,' Janes says of the teachers, 'they knew he was a rare talent both musically and with the acting. There were quite a lot of cheeky Cockney kids there. The school would often send them for elocution lessons but with Steve they just loved his character as it was.'

So did many others. In his time at the Italia Conti, Marriott worked consistently in film, radio and in television. He made four TV appearances. His debut was in *Citizen James*, a half hour comedy starring Sid James, Hugh Lloyd and Patrick Cargill. Marriott made his appearance in December, 1961 and delivered two lines of dialogue.

He even appeared in another West End stage production, this time in the role of Tootles in the Italia Conti production of Peter Pan at the Astoria theatre in Charing Cross Road (the same venue that his memorial concert was staged 39 years later). In April of 1962 he could be seen in *Mr Pastry's Progress* starring Richard Hearne, a job he was paid thirteen and a half guineas for. Then there was a lull and it would be nearly a year before he appeared on television again, this time in an episode of

Dixon of Dock Green, entitled 'The River People' scripted by the veteran writer Ted Willis. Marriott played a character called Clive Dawson. Transmission took place in February of 1963.

'There was a huge vat of water that he had to go into and he used to come home frozen at night-time,' Steve's mother recalls of the *Dock Green* filming. 'It was done in the depth of winter, see.'

Marriott's last appearance as a TV actor came in March of 1963 when he played Bertie Franks in a show entitled *William the Peacemaker*.

Steve was less successful at picking up radio work, but he did get a role in *Mrs Dale's Diary*, a very popular show of the time, playing a pop star named, Art Joyful. He also had a spell reading out the letters for agony aunt Marjorie Proops on her Sunday night Radio Luxembourg show. There was also a television advert voice-over for 1001 carpet cleaner.

The most significant work Marriott undertook at this time, though, was for the cinema. Marriott appeared in three more films and his experiences in making them there helped him decide which path he should follow: music or acting.

Marriott's two most significant roles were in the films, *Live It Up* and *Be My Guest*. Both works were typical of the time and sprang from a genre best termed 'Pop and Cop' films: the plot always involved a band's adventures attracting the attentions of the long arm of the law. Marriott also took a small role in a notable drama entitled, *Heaven's Above*, directed by John and Ray Boulting and released in April 1963. It starred Peter Sellers as a prison chaplain, assigned to the wrong parish. Marriott played a street kid and there were reports from the set of he and Sellers duetting on banjos between takes!

Live It Up appeared three months after *Heaven's Above* and starred David Hemmings and Heinz Burt. This time Marriott enjoyed a far more prominent role playing the drummer in a group. Also on the movie's credits were names that would enter history. John Stephens and Mary Quant worked on the clothes, Joe Meek, the celebrated producer who would shoot his landlady and then turn the gun on himself, supplied the music. Artists featured included Sounds Incorporated and Gene Vincent.

In the follow-up film, *Be My Guest*, released in February 1965, Shel Talmy who would produce the early Kinks and The Creation in the '60s and then Marriott himself in the '70s, replaced Meek and Jerry Lee Lewis took Gene Vincent's spot.

In both films, Marriott played the same character: the cheeky Cockney drummer; the bubbly one with the loudest mouth. His role was symptomatic of a growing trend of the arts reflecting British working class life. This pattern was borne out in John Osborne's breakthrough play, *Look Back In Anger*, films like *Saturday Night and Sunday Morning*, and the books *Poor Cow* and *Alfie*.

Marriott's job in the Pop and Cop films was simple: supply Cockney charm and energy – nothing else. Interestingly the pair of movies also reflected the battle between the young and the old, a generational conflict becoming increasingly prevalent in British society circa 1963. That year, the young were winning hands down. They had now invaded every cultural form in Britain and were busy revolutionising theatre, film, books, fashion, music, television. It was all change and all change for the better.

Naturally, the older generation were not giving in without a fight. When playwright John Osborne criticised the Queen in his work, *The Daily Express* sent a soldier who had fought the Germans to his home to publicly remonstrate with him.

On television, *That Was The Week That Was*, a weekly satirical programme that viciously attacked the Establishment, was still courting controversy. It had been launched in October of 1962, the same month that The Beatles released their first single 'Love Me Do,' yet despite sizeable opposition from the conservative section of the media and public, the programme survived, protected by the firm backing of the BBC chairman, Hugh Carleton Greene, younger brother of author Graham Greene. Greene may have been donnish in appearance but he was smart enough to recognise the growing enthusiasm for innovation, risk and challenge that was sweeping through the land... And one of the most important aspects of that change was the continued development of the Rhythm and Blues scene in Britain.

When Dave Godin wrote a letter to the music paper *Record Mirror* bitterly complaining that Bo Diddley's 1959 album, *Go Bo Diddley* had been overlooked by the paper's reviewers, he could not have known the effect it would have; within a week he received a deluge of letters of support from other R&B fans around the country. These fans soon formed alliances: started to meet up in each other's houses, bringing along their precious records and holding listening sessions long into the night.

'That shared worship of Black American music bound us together,' Godin told authors Mike Ritson and Stuart Russell. The efforts made by these young soul pioneers set a standard of music appreciation that endures to this day.

Back in the early sixties though, supplies of this fabulous music were low. According to Godin, the only place to hear loud raw R&B was in 'low life juke joints and, strangely enough, the funfair.'

But the demand for these sounds grew larger by the week and soon the more astute record companies began to take interest. Dedicated R&B Record shops opened too, the first being Dave Godin's own Soul City operation in South London. Devotees of the music could also visit Transat in Lisle Street, or order their records direct from their local record shop, although this would involve a wait of a few weeks before their arrival.

Presswise, it was *Record Mirror* who first smelt the vinyl and began running in depth reviews and news on the R&B scene. Hip London clubs also felt the musical sea change. The Flamingo Club in Wardour Street had opened its doors in the 1950s and had initially established itself as a premier jazz club. But by the early '60s, The Flamingo management were sharp enough to give a young organist and singer called Georgie Fame a Saturday night residency. His renditions of US blues and R&B songs brought a sizeable crowd of black American servicemen into the club.

The soldiers loved Georgie's interpretations ('it's like being back home,' they would tell him) and many of them would come armed to the club with the latest American imports. The next week, Georgie would have the tunes down pat and be blowing them out from the stage.

When a serious knifing incident at The Flamingo saw the GIs indefinitely grounded on their base, a new London youth cult moved in to colonise the club. They were the Mods and Steve Marriott was now one of them.

Italia Conti colleague Hugh Janes remembers Marriott's first stab at establishing an identity through clothes. He recalls Marriott arriving at the drama school dressed in winkle picker shoes, straight trousers and a cotton Woolworths' shirt. There was little money around, he explains, so when it came to dressing, they all did the best they could.

By the time of 1963's *Live it Up*, Marriott's look was starting to evolve. Sartorially, his best scene occurs early on in the film when he is seen in an open roof car wearing a stingy brimmed hat, a cotton Harrington-type jacket with stripes on collar and sleeves, a leather jerkin, a button-down shirt and dark trousers. David Hemmings rides up alongside him on a white scooter – thus creating one of the first ever cinematic representations of the Mod style.

Marriott was not just looking good for the sake of the camera. With some money coming in, he was now able to start assembling an eye-catching wardobe, able to go up West, visit Carnaby Street, look in at the highly expensive American clothes in Austin's on Shaftesbury Avenue, walk down to Cecil Gee's on the same road.

British mens' clothing had not been left unaffected by the mood of change swirling through the country. A shift in attitude towards menswear which was spearheaded by the likes of John Stephens, Cecil Gee and John Simons, gave London's youth the chance to create their own colourful identity. No longer did son have to dress like Dad, as had been the tradition. Now son could put together his own style.

'He was a little bit outlandish, you know,' recalls Kay. 'His white trousers – you never saw boys in white trousers. We're talking, what? 1963? And his jazzy jackets. Lovely jackets. But you had to be brave to walk out and wear them because everyone else was in dark suits and short hair.'

For the next seven years, Steve Marriott would sport a staggering array of clothes and secure himself a prestigious place in Mod history.

Mod was a secretive London cult that began sometime in the late '50s, had its roots in Soho, in London jazz clubs such as Club Eleven on Archer Street where clued up musicians such as Ronnie Scott began dressing in the style of their American heroes, the be bop men such as Miles Davis and Chet Baker.

This was a sharp formal look, one of suits and button-down shirts, ties and cufflinks. At the same time, clothes entrepreneurs such as Cecil Gee were introducing a more vibrant, casual look as they returned from countries like Italy, laden down with colourful tops and new ideas.

Mod was an amalgamation of these American and European influences and was also inspired by the cool dress sense of Caribbean 'Windrush' immigrants, who had started to arrived in great numbers, just after the war, from Jamaica, Barbados and other islands.

It was also a subtle sect which gave its participants an identity that could only be truly appreciated by other initiates. To the mainstream world, to the outsiders, Mods were invisible and that was precisely the point.

In return, Mod demanded of its disciples that they live the life every day, every night, the first youth cult to make such demands upon its members. In laying down this rule, Mod made men obsessive about their clothes. By 1963, the London boys had never known such a variety to be available to them. Bright casual tops, colourful shirts, smart jackets, trousers with creases, patterned socks, elegant but striking shoes, the choice was enormous, the potential to transform yourself, endless.

Steve Marriott gravitated naturally towards these colourful, striking clothes. He had a great body for clothes – the very small and the very tall always do – and he wore his clothes with natural style and panache. In every photo taken of him in the Sixties you would be hard pressed to find him not looking clean and colourful and totally right. His use of colour was always spot on. He put blues with browns, white with black, even made orange tops go with striking Prince Of Wales checked trousers. He became expert at making his clothes grab people's attention.

As his dress sense grew more outlandish, more challenging, so his feminine side became apparent, especially when he adopted a hairstyle that put together a middle parting with a slight bouffant at the back. The girls really took notice then. To them, he was a little boy doll, an intriguing male with a feminine sense of dress. And by the mid '60s he was a style icon in the very best sense of that much abused phrase..

‡ ‡ ‡

The family were so thrilled. Their son, their Steve, was in films. It was wonderful. It was fantastic. It was also bloody boring. Steve Marriott, that ebullient ball of pure energy, did not have the patience for film-making: the continual waiting around, the endless takes, it drained him. He itched for excitement, for adventure, itched for the thrill that performing music gave him.

Having to play the same cheeky Cockney role again and again didn't help either. Nor did the chance to play alongside one of the great actors of his day.

Marriott's last audition as an actor took place at the National Theatre in London. The prize was a year's worth of work performing with Laurence Olivier. The tour was due to start in Bristol. Marriott auditioned but in truth he didn't want the part. He wanted to play music. So he came home and brazenly lied to his parents.

He told them, 'Nah, I didn't get the role,' and then went upstairs to throw himself into his records.

Hugh Janes, his Italia Conti friend, recalls Steve's growing collection: 'Not a big one,' he says, 'but he had lots of records that I had never heard before, fairly obscure rhythm and blues stuff like Bobby Bland and Ray Charles.'

A week later the Marriotts' phone – they could finally afford one – rang. It was the National Theatre. Where was Steve? He hadn't shown up for rehearsals. But he didn't get the part, his mum replied.

What are you talking about? asked the caller, of course he did.

The lie revealed, Marriott's parents angrily challenged their son. What on earth was he playing at?

Thence came the bombshell. In no uncertain terms, their son told them that he had made his mind up. The acting life was not for him. He was going to be a musician. That was it. Like it or lump it, full stop.

Kay and Bill were dumbfounded. So were the rest of the Marriott clan. No one could understand the boy's attitude. All the sacrifices they had made, all the effort and you walk away because you want to be a flaming pop star? You have the chance to tour with Laurence Olivier and you give it all up for pop music? Are you out of your tiny mind?

The argument raged for days, threatened to tear the family apart. When it did finally quell itself, mum and dad and sister, they were so disappointed. They knew their Steve, knew he wouldn't change his mind even though he knew he was smashing every one of their dreams. Oh the hurt of it all! The waste!

Even today, some family members bristle at his decision.

'I loved him being an actor,' Kay the sister states. 'I didn't want him to be a pop singer. I wanted him to be an actor. He was so talented'

'His relationship with his parents was always fiery,' Manon Piercey, Steve's nearby neighbour recalls, 'especially when he gave up the acting to concentrate on the music. They were very much against that.'

‡ ‡ ‡

…Another fight, another row between mother and son… In his teenage years Steve had taken to leaving home and staying away for weeks on end, sometimes months. Once he ended up in Finsbury Park, 'in a mud hut,' he later told journalist Keith Altham. Kay, as ever, stood firm when he vanished like this.

'One time he came home, he'd been away for a week. He was only about sixteen and he said to me, "You never asked me to come back." I said, "I never asked you to go." It was awful when he came back with his tail between his legs. He'd go to his auntie's or to friends.'

The family were still hurting over Marriott's decision to quit acting. Even the understanding Aunt Sheila thought it a terrible waste. 'It was very sad for all of us,' she stares. 'I was upset because I thought there are so many pop people and he is just going to go down the same road as them. I really thought he was naturally gifted as an actor. But you see he didn't have the discipline. And he would never have been given a stage role because he was so badly behaved. You have to turn up on time every night for weeks on end' – a small laugh – 'he would never have done that.'

There is a touch of regret in the voice. Aunt and nephew shared a lot. Had done so since his childhood when Steve would sit at the kitchen table and recite recent sketches from the Goons show, mimicking all the silly voices to make his aunt shake with laughter.

Bill the dad would tut loudly, rustle his newspaper. Finally, he would tell them to shut up. Steve just ignored him, carried on playing the goon. Marriott's humour was mainly robust and ribald, but he had a liking for the surreal as his later love for *The Goons*, *Monty Python's Flying Circus* and *Fawlty Towers* would demonstrate. Such humour appealed to his vivid imagination as did books such as Tolkien's *Lord Of The Rings*. He also adored any biography on Noel Coward, a man he admired right up until the end for his stylish individual stance. Coward was a working class boy who with talent, class and style, had effortlessly lifted himself up into the highest strata of English society. His style appealed to the dandy lurking inside of Marriott.

(Jason O'Brien)

Chapter Six

Donkey Rides A Penny A Glass

It was 1963, the year The Beatles took over Britain, the year of The Ronettes' 'Be My Baby' and The Beach Boys' 'Surfin' USA', the year Steve Marriott's mother and father and his auntie and uncle, Sheila and David, began attending the Manor Park Social Club every Saturday night.

'When the social club closed,' Sheila recalls, 'we would go back to Strone Road for sandwiches and coffee. Steve would be up for waiting for us, guitar in hand. Bill would get on the piano and they would all sing songs.

'This particular night Steve sat quietly and then he played a song he had just written called 'Imaginary Love.' I thought it was very good. I said to him we have to do something, this is nice. We all agreed it was. He said, "But what do I do, Aunt Sheila?"

'I clearly remember the conversation. I said, "What you do Steve is that you go up to Denmark Street with your guitar and you bang on the doors of the publishing house, and say 'I've got a song I would like you to hear'."'

Sheila breaks into laughter at the memory.

'George Gershwin and Irving Berlin used to do that. I thought Steve could go and do it in London. This was Saturday night. I went to work on the Sunday. My office was in Panton Street then. Half past five came and he called me from a phone box. He said, "Auntie Sheila? It's Steve."

"What's up? Where are you?"

Marriott was in Denmark Street. He had spent the day knocking on the doors of various publishers but either no one was in or no one was interested. What should he do?

'I said, "Stay there Steve and ring me back in about ten minutes." That was when I rang my friend Lily who worked for Jack Hylton at the same time as I did. I explained the situation and said: "Lily what can I do about my poor nephew?" She made a couple of calls and rang me back. When Steve called I told him what to do and at six o'clock he went to this office in Savile Row, it was Cliff Richard's agent, Dick Reagan. Steve got the Decca contract from that.'

Reagan spotted the talent. On the strength of 'Imaginary Love,' within a short space of time he had secured a deal as a solo artist for Marriott with Decca Records. Quite a sizeable achievement for a fifteen-year-old to secure a record contract, especially in 1963.

The business Marriott was about to enter and make a living from for the rest of his life was dominated by a small coterie of companies. The main players were Decca, EMI, Pye, RCA and Phillips.

Pye and EMI also had a cluster of off-shoot labels to their names. According to Andrew Loog Oldham, the Rolling Stones flamboyant second manager who would later set up Immediate Records, British pop music's first independent label, these companies were hardly hotbeds of creativity when it came to pop music.

'They did not even appear to like or listen to pop music,' he explained in the first volume of his autobiography, *Stoned*, 'they could have been selling baked beans for all they cared.'

Such was these companies' domination of the market, however, they could afford to be lax, lazy, uninterested. With Dick Reagan's help, Steve Marriott had just broken through this seemingly insurmountable barrier. He was now contracted to make a proper record.

Seemed like everything Steve touched became a success.

Marriott's first solo single was a Kenny Lynch song, 'Give Her My Regards,' backed by his own first composition 'Imaginary Love.' The record, produced by Franklin Boyd, was released in 1963 and is a typical example of early Sixties pop. It has a brisk pace, rumbling drums, a clean and very clearly enunciated vocal that leans towards Elvis Presley's ballad style.

Marriott's Buddy Holly infatuation is also apparent. When he sings the word 'go' he does it Holly style, in other words as if he has a fly buzzing around the back of his throat – 'go-oh -oh -oh-oh.'

On 'Imaginary Love' the pace slackens a little but the vocal is again to the forefront. Marriott sings with such care that he sounds, like most young British vocalists of the era, much older than he really is.

'As fragrant as a wild rose in spring / Her voice is sweeter than a nightingale can sing,' are Marriott's opening lines. No wonder the record company thought they could sniff a hit and naturally, they didn't have a clue. The single appeared in July of that year and promptly vanished. But having a chart hit wasn't the point here.

The point was that Steve Marriott had made a record. Who else for miles and miles around could boast such a thing? Surely now, everyone could see that music was the right path for him to follow. Sod 'em, if they don't.

Steve's next move was to put together a new group. He named his new band, Steve Marriott and The Moonlights, the name both reflecting his leadership as singer and frontman and perhaps inspired by the style of moniker adopted by numerous American doo-wop outfits.

As with all of Steve's bands during this time, the name was always under constant review. They soon became Steve Marriott and The Frantiks, a name more befitting of the group's musical energy.

The band consisted of Johnny Herve, Tony McIntyre, Colin Green, Marriott and Dennis Thompson. Their first gig was in a coffee bar on the corner of Colchester Road, a stone's throw away from the Marriott family house in Daines Close. The ever loyal Manon Piercey was at that show.

'He had his Buddy Holly glasses on with no glass in them,' Manon says of Marriott, 'and he played a lot of Buddy's songs. Onstage he put on a confident front, he was a confident boy and of course he'd already trod the West End boards in *Oliver!*.'

'We did not have much in the way of equipment,' band member Dennis Thompson recalls, 'but finally my dad bought us some stuff including a van to get around in…

'We toured extensively around England and Steve even lived at my parents' house for a few months. He had some issues with his parents so he moved in with me and that lasted three months. He was a very boisterous and energetic young man and it was amazing how quickly he learnt how to play guitar, harmonica, drums and piano.

'He was a perfectionist about the music and sometimes we would all get in a big fight. But he was not obnoxious and would give you the last penny in his pocket. He also never stopped talking or chatting up the girls. Oh and he loved wrestling.'

'I used to go and watch the Frantiks regularly all over London,' says Hugh Janes, his friend from Italia Conti. 'They were only playing small clubs and their repertoire at the time was mainly rock 'n' roll classics by the likes of Chuck Berry, Bo Diddley and Little Richard.'

Steve's girlfriend at the time was the actress Adrienne Posta who he had met at Italia Conti. At some gigs, she would make a guest appearance and boyfriend and girlfriend would duet on 'Twist and Shout,' a song he would remake ten years later to much better effect with The Blackberries, an American vocal group.

'I didn't like her at all,' Kay says of Posta with a shiver typical of the disapproving mother. 'Very cheeky, terribly spoilt girl.'

Janes disagrees. A great catch, he says admiringly. Well, he would, wouldn't he?

As was the norm for most bands of the time, The Frantiks leaned towards rock'n'roll although they had also begun incorporating some R&B music into their set. They had been inspired to do so by a local outfit called, Scrooge and the Misers, an energetic band from Romford, Essex, fronted by singer and harmonica player, Pete Harper.

The Frantiks often shared a bill with The Misers and when they did, Marriott would place himself as near the stage as possible and soak up Harper's wild performances. Harper remains an important person in his early musical development.

'Steve absolutely idolised him and a lot of Pete rubbed off on him,' says Hugh

Janes.

Songs such as Bob Troupe's classic '40s song 'Route 66' (and they say Elvis 'invented' rock'n'roll) Chuck Berry's 'Talking 'Bout You' and early James Brown material were now added to the Frantiks' set list of Shadows and Buddy Holly numbers.

The Frantiks even cut a record, a version of Cliff Richard's 'Move It,' but it was never released. (In a 1983 interview with an Australian magazine Steve would boast with a smile that the record came out in Malaysia and was that country's first ever number one. It wasn't.)

The recording session the band undertook had been arranged by their new manager, Tony Calder. Calder was an intriguing shadowy character in the sixties pop world. Unlike Andrew Loog Oldham, his later partner in Immediate Records, Calder's drive was not fashioned through a need for fame and notoriety but for money and success.

Calder hailed from Southampton and as a young man had helped pioneer the idea of the DJ as an entertainer in his own right, (he credits Jimmy Savile as the first proper DJ) an attractive proposition for club owners, who now only had to pay one wage as opposed shelling out for an entire band.

One of Calder's earliest DJ'ing engagements was at the Ilford Palais in Essex, the venue he says he first lay eyes upon Steve Marriott. It was 1962. 'This kid pops up and says, "Hello Tone, I'm Steve. Can I play the records?"' he recalls, 'I took one look at him and said, "Yeah, carry on." He used to come down every Saturday afternoon and make my life easier.'

Having witnessed the Frantiks live, Calder approached the band, taken by Marriott's energy – his charisma and his obvious talent. Marriott was Calder's target. He was the first to try and manage him, arranging a meet in 1963 with the Marriott family where he presented them with a contract. Bill Marriott didn't trust him, refused to sign. Calder said fine and bided his time.

For the 'Move It' session, Calder brought in some much needed experience in the form of ex-Shadows drummer Tony Meehan, needed to help out his young charges. The song was recorded in a day and then hawked around the labels.

No one was interested.

Not long after, Dennis Thompson and Johnny Herve quit the band for other outfits. Marriott again changed the band name. The Frantiks now became Steve Marriott and the The Moments, the band no doubt believing their new moniker was more in tune with the times.

This band would prove to be Marriott's most successful venture, to date. Yet more importantly, The Moments project would see Marriott exploring further his love for rhythm and blues, a musical direction which he would pursue to a higher level with his next group, The Small Faces.

'I remember going to a Moments gig at Gidea Park near Romford,' recalls the ever-loyal Manon. 'He took to the stage looking very young and spotty and went into the Animals song, 'House Of The Rising Sun.' He started off singing very twee and the yobs in the audience were literally laughing at him. Then he got to the chorus and his voice suddenly changed. He hit notes nobody else could and these yobs looked on in awe. They even came backstage to apologise.'

The band's heavy live schedule allowed Marriott the chance to develop his voice onstage into something truly special. He knew he had been vocally gifted and worked hard to realise his voice's potential.

Manon recalls him telling her to go to the top of the stairs of the council block where he lived whilst he stayed below and sang powerfully up to her. It was then, she said, as the neighbours came out to tell him to shut up, that she realised he had 'the voice of all voices,' and what's more it emanated from such a tiny body.

'The Moments worked as much as six nights a week,' says Janes of the group, 'and they covered a much wider area geographically than the Frantiks. The repertoire was much wilder R&B, more in keeping with rising bands like the Pretty Things and the Yardbirds.'

The Moments line-up featured Barry Hewitt on bass, Tony McIntyre on drums, Steve Marriott on vocals and rhythm guitar, Johnny Weider on lead guitar and Allen Ellett on keyboards and vocals.

Ellett was a Manor Park boy, born and bred. He had previously worked with a singer called Jackie Lynton and had seen Steve around Manor Park many times, not least in their local music shop, the J60 on Manor Park's High Street North.

Two days after his return from a German tour, Ellett found the young Marriott waiting for him on his front doorstep.

'He was looking for a piano player for a new group he was putting together,' remembers Ellett. 'He impressed me because he already had a lot of good ideas.'

Marriott told Ellett he had a bass player and drummer already lined up. In that case, said, Ellett, yes, I'll join.

Marriott's next mission was to persuade Johnny Weider to come on board. Weider was a local sensation. He played lead guitar for Johnny Kidd and the Pirates – one of the most exciting live acts of the day.

Marriott was a big fan. He had avidly watched Johnny Kidd and the Pirates on several occasions at the Wykeham Hall in Romford and was keen to secure Weider's services.

After a fruitful discussion, Weider agreed to sign up and then found the band a rehearsal room in a studio near his Shepherd's Bush home. The band practiced there every day. At lunchtime, Weider's Polish father would appear with bowls of soup, urging the boys to 'Eat! Eat!' Steve liked the man immensely but he was no fan of his cooking. He would often wait until Weider's father wasn't looking and then chuck his soup into a nearby plant.

As he hailed from the East End, Marriott soon tired of the long journey across town to rehearsals. He soon put his charming nature to good use and persuaded the manager of the local Essoldo cinema to allow the band to rehearse there during the day.

'It was marvellous,' Ellett recalls. 'They had a stage and a piano. I also remember rehearsing upstairs at the Ruskin Arms pub. We quickly built up a big repertoire of numbers, mainly rock'n'roll and R&B covers. We also did loads of Chuck Berry stuff and Steve would turn the lyrics around so they involved all the band members. I do remember us learning 'Zip A Dee Do Dah' (from the Walt Disney film, *Song*

Of The South,) that was actually very intricate chord wise.'

The band's repertoire was no longer restricted to covers. Steve was now writing a lot of songs himself. Indeed, Ellett describes him as 'prolific,' citing the American rocker, Jerry Lee Lewis as a major influence on the budding songwriter:

'One of the songs in our repertoire was Jerry Lee's 'I'm On Fire' and Steve and I wrote a song ourselves which was very much in that vein. It was called 'A Touch Of The Blues.' It was also similar to Dave Clark's hit of the day, 'Glad All Over.' You know the middle eight when the drums go bump, bump, bump and they sing, glad all over? Well, ours went, bomp. bomp, bomp, a touch of the blues. We were just moving along with the times.'

It was this song that the band took a stab at recording one night in Denmark Street with Calder's friend, Andrew Loog Oldham producing, though the session has never seen the light of day. Oldham had first met Steve on a London street. Marriott and Calder were walking through the West End when they bumped into him.

At the recording session Loog Oldham, who had already produced his own band, The Rolling Stones, was very impressed with Marriott's musical ability.

After the recording, he approached Steve and asked if he would play harmonica for his band, a loose outfit called, The Andrew Loog Oldham Orchestra. Steve agreed and soon they were back in the studio to record two instrumental songs. One of them, '365 Rolling Stones,' was released as a single.

This alliance was furthered when Oldham was given the production job for Steve's second solo single for Decca, a cover of the Rolling Stones song 'Tell Me,' backed with 'Maybe.' The record was delivered to the company, approved and given a catalogue number. An advert was booked on the front of the *New Musical Express*, but for reasons never made clear, Decca withdrew the record at the last minute. It must have been a disappointing blow for the young performer.

Analysing the music Marriott was writing at this time but not able to record as yet, Ellett describes it as more Chuck Berry than Ray Charles: 'I suppose he was serving his song-writing apprenticeship. He would always be turning up with lyrics that he had just written on a small scrap of paper and then bandy ideas around with other group members. Sometimes when we were on tour he would wake in the middle of the night and jot down ideas for a song on a piece of paper that he always kept handy.'

Regular live work allowed Marriott to develop a stage presence. At the time, live presentation was an important part of every band's armour. The hangover from Britain's show business traditions still lingered on. Marriott had no time for such niceties.

'Steve Marriott was always a supreme showman on stage,' Janes reveals of these early gigs. 'He'd developed this thing with the lip, a shake of the head and, of course, the finger in the ear and he was already using the 'Come on children,' thing, a phrase he nicked from an old James Brown record.' (Or maybe, according to ex-squeeze, Adrienne Posta, from a teacher's phrase at Italia Conti.)

In fact, the Moments played a number of James Brown songs such as 'Please Please Please,' 'I Don't Mind,' and 'Night Train,' the song that Marriott would have lifted his trademark 'C'mon children,' shout from, if that was the case...

Thus Steve Marriott and the Moments joined a growing list of London bands, the aforementioned Pretty Things, The Yardbirds, The Rolling Stones, Steampacket, and many others, playing R&B and blues standards albeit in a youthful, energetic manner.

This burgeoning live circuit acted as a springboard for the likes of Eric Clapton, Mick Jagger, Keith Richards, Rod Stewart and Jimmy Page, lauching them towards worldwide fame, leaving behind contemporaries such as Brian Auger, Long John Baldry, Jeff Beck, Duffy Power, to find other, more modest degrees of success.

‡ ‡ ‡

In 1964, Steve borrowed some money and bought a second-hand van. The band stripped the van's interior, fitted an additional six seats, painted the back-door windows black and then wrote The Moments across the back. It was a sound investment. Over the next year it would see plenty of action.

Tony Calder had, meanwhile, employed an agent called Arthur Howes to find the band gigs and Howes secured them slots on package tours supporting the likes of Billy J. Kramer, The Hollies, Freddie and The Dreamers and The Kinks. They also played support for a number of other musicians, including strict R&B outfits such as Georgie Fame, Graham Bond and Zoot Money. Watching these pioneers strengthened Marriott's conviction that R&B was where he should be heading musically.

In March of 1964, according to Beatle chronicler Mark Lewisohn, Marriott again changed the band's name, playing a Surrey gig under the moniker, Steve Marriott and the Wondering Ones. In April 1964, he changed the name back to The Moments and they played The Flamingo and London's prestigious 100 Club. In June they were at another Mod hotspot, the Birdcage in Portsmouth and on July 28th they played the Albion public house in Rainham, Essex. It is a gig worth noting for this is the night, Steve Marriott met his first songwriting partner and future brother in Mod, Ronnie Lane, who was now playing guitar with support band, The Outcasts. At the time, both young men thought nothing of their meeting. It was only later that their destinies would cross.

Later on that summer there was a gig with The Animals, another fiery R&B outfit from Newcastle just starting out towards fame, at the Attic Club in Hounslow, Middlesex. A live recording of the show was made but unfortunately the tape went missing. As did guitarist Johnny Weider. The band's music was not to Weider's liking. He quit and was replaced by one John Trelawny, a posh guy who was a bit la di da but he could play and that was all that mattered.

Calder kept the The Moments on the road for most of 1964, with gigs in Hounslow, Ramsgate, Golders Green, Nottingham, Manchester, Peterborough, Kingston, Putney and many other towns and cities. Calder insisted the band wore uniforms on stage and they kept their hair neat. It worked for The Beatles, boys, look at them, he would announce. Marriott just sneered at the comparison...

‡ ‡ ‡

Life on the road runs in fits and starts – great adventures mixed with hours and hours of boredom. With Marriott on board, though, anything could happen.

'I remember travelling down to Camborne in Cornwall,' Ellett says, 'to play a gig in the local skating rink. It was then that we realised we hadn't taken the piano. In our quest to find one we went into a church. There was a funeral taking place but Steve just walked in wearing his leather jacket and leather cap and had the cheek to ask the vicar,

"Can we borrow your piano?" We were quickly shown the door.'

'We went from there to the local cinema and an elderly woman that worked in the box office rather stupidly told Steve that she had a piano at home that he could borrow. We waited for her to finish her shift and then drove her home. She lived near the top of a hill on a rather shabby council estate.

'We got there and loaded her piano into the back. Part of the instrument was hanging out the back of the van and the doors were tied with a towrope. As we started to move away, the rope broke, the piano fell out of the van and started to roll down the hill.

'We stopped, jumped out and chased it down the hill. It was like something out of a Buster Keaton film. We actually recovered it without any damage and eventually got it to the gig at the skating rink.

'At the end of the gig all I could think about was getting the piano back to the house. All to no avail because Steve had sold the piano to the guy at the skating rink!'

Meanwhile, the work kept coming in. Tony Calder was proving an efficient manager. The band members were now earning about £30 a week each – a sum far above the average wage. Even so, this was the music business and there were a million traps being set for a million bands.

One such scam was for promoters to book a band and then at the end of a long evening's work, inform them that their performance had actually been an audition, not a paying performance.

'Promoters such as Ron King and Pat Meehan,' Ellett says, 'would fill your head with promises of work and recording contracts and bands like ourselves being young and naive would fall for it hook, line and sinker. You could only hope that being seen at shows they put on would open other doors for you. We just loved playing and of course people took advantage of that.'

Another music biz ruse, was to get bands to record versions of contemporary UK hits and then release them in other countries, particularly the States, before the original arrived.

For The Moments, their chance came when they were asked by the World Artists label to record the recent Kinks' hit 'You Really Got Me' for American release only. A number two hit in September 1964, the song had exploded into Britain's consciousness with its distinctive guitar riff and compelling vocal. In that same month, The Beatles had 'A Hard Day's Night' at number six, The Beach Boys had 'I Get Around' and The Zombies were in at sixteen with 'She's Not There.' Pop music really was getting interesting.

The Moments' take on 'You Really Got Me' was perfunctory. Its B-side, however, specifically Steve Marriott's vocal, makes this single of interest. On the flipside's 'Money Money' Marriott for the very first time brings his R&B influences to bear, attempting to push his voice into the kind of territory occupied by singer, Richie Barrett on his great record, 'Some Other Guy.'

It was all to no avail, though. The single went to America, disappeared and soon after so did another band member, Allen Ellett.

'The thing I remember about Steve,' Ellett recalls, 'is that he must have been the first person in the country to use the word 'gig.' He was using it back in 1964 when everybody else referred to a date as a booking. I suppose he was a loveable rogue really and definitely a bit of a "tea leaf". I remember going to the BBC studios with him once and he nicked a professional microphone complete with stand. It must have been worth hundreds of pounds. He could also be very cruel with his tongue.

'If he passed somebody in the street with a disability he would wind the window down and give it the whole spastic bit. But Steve Marriott definitely had something about him. He could walk onstage or into a room and command attention without doing anything, A great singer, musician and songwriter.

'Sometimes, when he was lugging equipment from the van he would wear an old pair of jeans with rips in the knee,' adds Ellett, a smile now crossing his lips. 'One night in Sheffield we were running very late and Steve just for once went on stage with these jeans. We returned to the same venue about a month later and there were dozens of fans in the audience with jeans with no knees in them. Incredible, eh?'

Through their extensive live work, the band had picked up a loyal following: small but committed. There was even a fanzine, *Beat 64*, dedicated to 'Steve Marriott's Moments', started by Stuart Tuck who also played in David Bowie's Lower Third, a group Marriott would audition for the following year. The publication didn't last long though.

In October, 1964, the band suddenly decided that Marriott was not right for the job. They needed an older singer. Marriott was given his marching orders, sacked from the group he had put together. As Ellett points out it couldn't have been for musical slackness. Marriott's skill as a front man had given him a good reputation within the business and he was also viewed as a singer of real talent.

'Officially, the band was The Moments,' he says, 'but lots of promoters would advertise us as Steve Marriott's Moments because Steve was known as such a good vocalist. Also he had a good head for business back then. Many times after a successful gig that had been booked through an agent he would arrange a return visit under our own steam.'

Ex-Frantik Dennis Thompson believes the sacking was because Marriott was 'maturing and getting far more bluesy,' and his band simply didn't want to follow that route. Also. Marriott was a chatterbox, a ball of pure energy that eventually wore down all who came into contact with him.

Marriott did meet up with the Moments again shortly after his dismissal. Stuart Tuck, the Moments' fanzine editor, had recommended the band to his friend Maurice King purely on the strength of Marriott's talent.

King ran the Starlight Rooms in Paddington and asked the band to play two Sunday afternoon sessions on the 8th and 15th of December not knowing that

Marriott was no longer in the line-up. Meanwhile, Marriott had been invited to guest at the very same show by the marvellously named Johnny B Great and the Quotations, which featured a certain Phil Collins on drums.

On the 22nd December, Marriott entered the Ilford Palais talent contest where he sang The Animals' hit, 'House Of The Rising Sun.' He came first. It was like Jaywick Sands all over again. Afterwards, Tony Osbourne, father of Jan who would later marry Small Faces drummer, Kenney Jones, told Marriott he would get nowhere in the business.

On January the 2nd, after a great Christmas, Marriott found a job at the J60 music shop in Manor Park. It was a temporary number but perfect for his needs. Now he was off the road and the Decca contract had run out, he needed a source of income and what better place to earn it than in a music shop?

Plus, Steve Marriott badly needed a new band. He was now a seventeen-year-old Mod who knew exactly where he wanted to go musically. A sound – a wild, R&B-based sound – was starting to take shape in his head and was making him impatient for the action to begin.

One day at work the shop doorbell rings. Marriott looks up, sees a Mod entering the shop. He recognises the dark-haired man straight away. He is a face, a well-known local lad who is older and far flashier than Marriott. Steve greets the twenty-one-year-old respectfully. He has just saluted Jimmy Winston and the Small Faces are about a month away from realising both of these boy's dreams.

PART TWO

THE WIZARD OF MOD

(Hutton Pictures)

Chapter Seven

Grow Your Own

Listen to mother. 'They looked lovely didn't they?'

It is the first time in Kay Marriott's lengthy interview that the Small Faces are mentioned and immediately her mind flashes up their collective beauty, present and correct in a million photographs.

The Small Faces wore the Sixties. Mohair, cotton, leather, PVC, Prince of Wales check, striped shirts, silk shirts, tab-collar shirts, bright neckerchiefs, Madras jackets, suede jackets with large buttons, suede jackets with small buttons, wide belts, striped jumpers of all colours, straight leg trousers with sharp creases, and then there are the shoes.

Good dressing begins with the shoes and the Small Faces might well have invented that rule. Their shoes were always on the button: crocodile skin, basket weave, suede, two-tone, loafers, brogues, always patterned, always striking. Marriott even wore white plimsolls to one photo session. He put them with brown mohair trousers and a green striped jumper, turned to the camera with his shades on and his hair centre parted and posed immaculately.

Clothes play a huge part in this group's legacy. Clothes made the Small Faces look and act like a tight gang; like brothers in Mod bonded by colour and style.

Consider the footage of Steve, Ronnie and Mac, shot in 1966, coming out of their Pimlico abode, jumping onto a jeep and riding through Victoria.

The camera catches them disembarking from the vehicle, standing outside a clothes shop admiring the goods.

They start mimicking the '60s comedian Harry Worth's one and only trick by fooling around with shop window reflections, then, as one, they turn and strut down the street in their Mohair suits and in that one magical moment they look for all the world like the princes of London town.

'From 1965 to 1967,' says John Hellier who was there at the time, 'Steve Marriott was a style icon. You waited to see what he would wear and then you'd go off and try and get it before anyone else.'

'Steve Marriott turned heads,' one magazine would later proclaim, 'when he walked down Carnaby Street wearing a blue silk shirt and white trousers.'

Yet clothes were also the band's Achilles' heel. When they signed to Don Arden's Contemporary Music he put them on twenty quid a week and softened the blow by opening up accounts for them in clothes shops up and down Carnaby Street. On that rare occasion when they weren't playing or recording or shopping or smoking spliff and taking pills, and they asked how much money they had, they were shown figures, which shocked them. When they complained they heard the same old story – 'What do you expect? You have spent it all on clothes.'

Indeed, a teen idol magazine reported that in one year alone 'The Small Faces spent £12,000 on clothes,' a small fortune.

Don Arden their first manager said it. Tony Calder and Andrew Loog Oldham who took over in 1967 said it too.

'Ronnie Lane,' Calder says, 'would walk into a shoe shop, see a pair of shoes he liked and buy every pair in his size and in every colour. He would wipe the shop out and then he would tell them, send the bill to my record company and the shoes to my house.' (Small Face Ian 'Mac' McLagan disputes this, says Lane was not a big shopper.)

Not that Marriott was too fussed about his bank balance. Throughout his whole life, the anarchist in him kept the same attitude towards money.

'Steve wasn't too bothered,' stated Jenny Rylance his first wife, 'he just wanted to play and write music, the money or lack of it was totally irrelevant to him. As long as he had enough money to pay the rent he was happy.'

'He said to me once,' says Steve's mother, 'that as long as I can just keep playing and making music I am the happiest bloke alive,'

From such attitudes do others grow rich.

Like so many musicians of the '60s, The Small Faces lived in wonderland. They had girls and drugs on tap, clothes shops they could raid without paying, their faces in the papers, classy accommodation, a chauffeur-driven limo, celebrities popping around to see them, TV companies asking them to perform, the radio blaring out their records – why bother with money when you're so young and everything you want is yours for the taking anyway?

Thus the band and hundreds of their contemporaries paid in full for their time in the magical garden. When it was time to leave many did so without a penny to their name. Yet other legacies remain.

The Small Faces story reflects the changes in music, clothes and drugs that took place in Britain in the last half of that decade of magic, the Sixties.

At first, the band dressed smart, adored amphetamines and played furious R&B with attitude. So did many others.

Two years later they discovered LSD, applied their Mod sensibility to the prevailing hippie fashions and began adding psychedelia to their music. So did many others.

During their time, the band made three albums. One of them was a near classic, one is regarded as one of the greatest records of the era. Time has not harmed their music. In fact, time has enhanced it. Will we ever hear a record as unique and as powerful as 'Tin Soldier' or 'Afterglow (Of Your Love)' or 'Green Circles' or 'Get Yourself Together' or 'Rollin' Over' or 'I'm Only Dreaming' from a group barely out of their teens? Doubtful. The odds are long and getting longer by the year.

By the time each member of this band was in their very early twenties, they had notched up over ten top ten hits, spent months in the album charts. It was not bad going for a group whose main struggle was to be taken seriously. And when they failed in that task the Sixties ended and so did they.

‡ ‡ ‡

It began in the J 60 music shop, second day of January 1965, halfway through the decade of magic. Jimmy Winston, like most working class kids of the Sixties was a Mod. He was tall, moody, had a penchant for the girls and a taste for rumbles.

He was older than Marriott by four years and it showed. After all, the gap between the ages of seventeen and twenty-one is so much bigger than the one between thirty-eight and forty-two. He also hated his surname – changed it around a lot.

Marriott smiled at his pretentions. 'He actually used to call himself James Moody before he started using Winston which was probably in honour of Winston Churchill,' Marriott would tell John Hellier in 1984. 'James Moody gives you a picture of the guy; collar up, coat on, shades. But we were too busy being lunatics to take things as seriously as he was.'

At first, Steve looked up to Jimmy who was worldly, dressed well, had respect. On the street these factors matter. But within a band situation different dynamics apply. Leader comes first or he dies. Marriott would quickly rise to Jimmy's level and then he would topple him. He would topple him because Jimmy Winston threatened to move into his spotlight and as Kay his sister will tell you, that's the one move you do not make against Steve Marriott, not without expecting a fight.

Originally, Winston wanted to be an actor. He had spent a couple of years at drama school without achieving anything of note. In the week he left, he decided to turn his attention to music.

His family ran the Ruskin Arms pub in Manor Park and Jimmy began compering musical evenings which featured him singing with the resident band. Jimmy was also handy with a guitar – played it well in fact – which is why he was in the J 60. He was on guitar business.

Marriott noticed him straight away.

'I suppose I found Jimmy Winston,' Marriott told John Hellier. 'He used to come to the J 60 the same way as Ronnie but he was more of a regular. I didn't know him except from there… The Ruskin Arms was a great pub. I went round the pub once and he was mucking around on guitar. He was proficient on guitar, more so than me at the time. His family were much more well off than mine so he had some decent equipment.'

Music brings the like minded together. Steve and Jimmy talked, shot the breeze.

'Then, one night, while I was singing in the pub,' Winston continues, 'in walked Steve and Ronnie.'

Steve and Ronnie. Marriott and Lane: the heart and soul of the Small Faces; the Yin and the Yang; the one and the two which makes three – the magic number. As local musicians, their paths had crossed many times and they had now drawn close. Both were young musicians, Mods and in love with R&B.

Where Steve was garrulous, a thousand words a minute, Ronnie was laidback, quieter, more reflective. Where Steve was action, Ronnie was thought. Where Steve rushed in, Ronnie strolled. He was a dreamer, a searcher and he adored the little bundle of pure energy known as Steve Marriott.

Consider their TV performances. Every time Steve pulls a funny face or yelps out in sheer joy, Ronnie's face automatically breaks open and it is a lovely smile, a smile of love.

The other members of the band sometimes grin at Marriott's behaviour, sometimes grimace. But Ronnie always smiles. Understanding.

'Ronnie was a lot less aggressive,' says their later engineer and producer Glyn Johns, 'he was a milder individual although he wasn't all bells and whistles. He had an unpleasant side too.'

Ronald Frederick Lane was born on April, 1st, 1946, son of Stanley and Elsie Lane. He went to school in Plaistow, East London, an area thought by many to be upmarket. 'Don't believe all that guff about Terence Stamp being a cockney. He was brought up in Plaistow...'

That was Sixties photographer Terence Donovan mocking Stamp, revealing the pecking order within the East End.

At five years old, Lane could strum a ukulele. At sixteen he enrolled in the Lister Technical College in Plaistow. Afterwards, he briefly worked on a fairground in Battersea, South London, and the nomadic lifestyle he was exposed to there would never lose its grip on him.

By the time Ronnie had started visiting the J 60 music shop, he and Marriott had already been in some scrapes. Lane worked for Selmers, the music equipment people. One day, Marriott had shown up at his workplace unannounced, looking to blag some free equipment. Lane was amused by his friend's chutzpah. He picked up a microphone and started announcing to his colleagues, 'Free PA for Marriott, Free PA for Marriott.'

Lane's boss was not amused and handed the young Mod his P45. Lane wasn't that bothered. He had high hopes for The Outcasts, the group he was playing in.

Lane's closest friend in the band was drummer Kenney Jones. Kenney was a little bit like Ronnie. East End boy, quiet as well, not one to crave the limelight. There was an essential goodness that shone out of Kenney. Still does to this day. He was born a year after Marriott, 16th September, 1948, started playing drums at an early age. He had been introduced to Ronnie via Lane's brother Stan. They discovered that they had both served in the territorial army. Now Kenney Jones was a little drummer boy.

After his dismissal from Selmer's, Ronnie Lane figured that his friend Marriott owed him big time. He and Jones went to visit him one Saturday morning, Lane hoping that Marriott would help make amends for his role in Lane's sacking by selling him a guitar at a good price.

His plan failed.

The first thing Marriott did was to tell Lane to forget guitar playing. Since The Beatles had crash-landed in the UK from who knew where and turned the world upside down, everyone wanted to be a guitarist. It was a far sharper move to play bass. That way you were never out of work. He then showed Lane a Harmony bass, offered it to him at a really cheap price.

Ronnie said that his father would have to return and sign the HP forms. Marriott said cool and suggested Lane try out the instrument first. Lane plugged in, Jones went behind the drum kit and Marriott pulled out a guitar. The trio played for a bit and Lane agreed to buy the bass.

Soon after this meeting, Lane got back in touch with Marriott. His group The Outcasts had a residency at a pub called the Earl of Derby in Bermondsey, South London. Why didn't Steve pop down and have a play, a blast? Can't hurt, can it? Of course not.

'We got paralytic,' Marriott recalled. 'I don't know if it was nerves or friendship or both but we got paralytic and went onstage. I can't remember much of it but I think I smashed the piano up or something. I was banging the shit out of it, jumping on top of it.'

After the gig, Ronnie and Kenny and Steve sat outside the Earl of Derby. All were drunk, exhilarated.

The Outcasts were finished. The landlord had sacked them. Marriott's drunken behaviour was the reason.

For the second time running, Marriott had cost Lane a job.

'So we said let's form a band of our own,' Marriott recalled. Lane happily agreed. So did Jones when he was asked.

'I know someone else we can get in,' Marriott told them. He was thinking of Jimmy Winston.

The next day, January 24th, a Sunday, Lane went to Marriott's family house in Daines Close and Steve Marriott played him Ray Charles and Bobby Bland records.

The boys sat there, captured by the music they were hearing. The thrill of the new ran through both of them, made them shiver with delicious delight.

Now, it was Steve's turn for a dismissal. After selling Ronnie the Harmony guitar at such a low price, Marriott was given the sack from the J 60. Both boys were square now.

Marriott started using his days to travel up West and hang out in the Giaconda café on Denmark Street, where all the major music publishers had offices.

'I'd hang out there because it was like Tin Pan Alley,' Marriott explained. 'If people wanted demos made they'd come in and say, "Can anyone play drums?" and someone would say, "Yes, I can." At least it was a few quid in your pocket. I'd do anything; drums, vocals, harmonicas, backing vocals, guitar, bass, anything. I'd play anything. I don't really remember any of the things that I worked on, most of it was foul.

'There were some good writers around like Clive Westlake and another one called Barry Norman who became a producer. They favoured me for singing on their demos so whenever they made them I'd be there. I think these were publisher's demos, not recordings as such. At the time it didn't enter my head.'

Marriott was also readying himself for the release of his second Decca single, 'Tell Me' c/w 'Maybe'. It was February 1965, but the disc never appeared and Marriott never mentioned it again. In truth it was a knock-back, a swift kick to the kidneys.

It meant that any dreams he had of making it alone were now over. Still, there was always the band. Or was there?

After a few rehearsals, Marriott began to have conflicting feelings about the other band members' abilities. Put baldly, Ronnie and Kenney were not up to scratch. They were too young, too inexperienced. Jimmy Winston though was ideal. He not only had good guitar technique but he also brought valuable things to the table. He owned an organ, his parents ran a pub whose upstairs landing they could rehearse in, plus Jimmy's brother Derek had put his black Mariah van at the band's disposal.

Yet Marriott had other ideas for the elder man. One day, he suggested that Winston switch to the organ whilst Marriott stayed on guitar.

Winston agreed and Marriott smiled to himself. He had achieved his first ambition. He now played in a group with the exact same line up as the band he so revered, Booker T and the MGs, writers of classics such as 'Green Onions'.

'There was no conflict at all at that early stage,' Winston recalls. 'What I liked about that time was that we would get together and just sit around and play acoustically. We didn't have to set up with 2,000 watts of power. Within just a couple of weeks we were doing a very raw set. There were only about five songs in the set. Apart from our own song. 'E Too D,' there was stuff like 'You Need Love', or 'Baby, Don't You Do It.' They all had a certain kind of feel about them.'

That feel Winston refers to is the product of the band's full-on immersion into rhythm and blues. 'You Need Love' was a Willie Dixon composition performed by the blues legend, Muddy Waters. It would later inspire Led Zeppelin's 'Whole Lotta Love.'

'It was fantastic, I loved it,' Marriott said of the song. 'Muddy Waters recorded it but I couldn't sing like Muddy Waters so it wasn't that much of a nick. I was a high range and Muddy was a low range so I had to figure out how to sing it. So I did and that was our opening number for all the years we were together. Every time we were on stage that was our opening number, unless we had a short set. That's where Jimmy Page and Robert Plant heard it. Robert Plant used to follow us around. He was like a fan.'

Meanwhile 'Baby Don't You Do It' was a Tamla Motown classic written by Holland, Dozier and Holland and recorded by Stevie Wonder and Marvin Gaye, the crème de la crème of Tamla. 'Shake' was a classic Sam Cooke song, written and performed by the R&B pioneer who would later be murdered in a motel.

Rhythm and blues. All over Britain groups were using R&B as the bedrock for their music. The Stones, Them, The Animals, the desire to sing like an R&B man and play fiery music was irresistible.

In March, Marriott was still not convinced of the band's worth. He secretly auditioned for a group named, The Lower Third. His indecision was hardly surprising.

'What you have got to remember,' Winston states, 'is that when we first met we had no pre-history. Steve and Ronnie had not known each other for too long. It's not as if you've known somebody from school, it was all absolutely fresh. My energy was with Steve because he was very similar to me in a way. He had a lot of drive, a lot of attitude and there were a lot of things he wanted to do. With great respect to Ronnie and Kenney they were slower and just coming out of their shell. Me and Steve had both been at it for a few years to find something that would carve into a career. Our energies were definitely higher so in a way we fascinated each other.'

The Lower Third were unable to see Marriott's potential. They gave the spot to a young singer-songwriter called Davey Jones who would later became David Bowie and, just for good measure, he too would plunder 'You Need Loving' by The Small Faces, nicking the distinctive rhythm for his huge 1972 hit single, 'Jean Genie.' On a recent VH1 documentary called *Storytellers* David Bowie tells the tale about himself and his good friend Steve Marriott's plans to form an R&B group in 1964 to be called 'David and Goliath'. Bowie was presumably David leaving Steve as Goliath!

‡ ‡ ‡

One grey weekday Ronnie Lane popped into the Giaconda café on London's Denmark Street, to see Steve Marriott. Lane was now running errands for the Home Office and that day carried with him a brown tube. Naturally, Marriott had to see what was inside it.

'We opened the tube and it was stuff like intricate diagrams of a nuclear submarine,' he revealed, 'Polaris submarine bases is what it was. Of course, it had brown sauce all over it by the time we had rolled it back up.'

Later both musicians briefly shared the same day job at a Lyons Corner House café in Baker Street, central London.

'I was only there a couple of days,' Marriott said, 'four I think. I got pissed off with it. My hands went all brown and the skin started falling off them because of the bleach they used to wash up with.

'I used to have to wash the plates and Ronnie would rack them and push them through a shower. It was a nightmare – a conveyor of eggs and bacon. I think we got eight quid a week. Ronnie stayed on to get his weeks wages but I pissed off. I couldn't handle it. There was this mad Scotsman who used to go round with a knife all the time and this other mad woman who used to turn on all the gas taps and just giggle. The Scotsman would pick up a carving knife and yell, I'll fucking kill the bitch and go after the one who turned on the taps. It was fucking mad.'

Despite his acute resistance to mindless work, Marriott needed money. He had again left home and was now living in a flat in Loughton, Essex, with friends including one Mick O'Sullivan. He was also seeing a girl named Annabella who Winston had first introduced to him.

Despite the age gap, Jimmy and Steve maintained a friendly relationship. The pair would often visit Winston's girlfriend Annie at her a flat in Kensington. She shared it with a girl named Wanda and the boys would spend the night smoking dope, listening to music or spoken comics. It was here that Marriott first heard the work of the comedian Lord Buckley whose comical stories were filled with hip druggy references. One of his pieces was called 'Here Comes Da Nazz'. In later life, that phrase would be plundered for a record entitled 'Here Comes The Nice'. Annie proved useful in other areas.

'I don't know if she had the readies or not,' Marriott said of her, 'but she signed the HP agreement for me, God bless her, which allowed me to get a Marshall amp – the old ones with the big cooker knobs on it. It was massive for those days. We were notoriously loud – if you can't play, play loud.'

It was Annie, too, who gave the band their name after watching their very first show at the Kensington Youth Centre in East Ham on Thursday, May 6th. 1965.

'You've all got such small faces,' Annabella said to the band after the gig. She had been in the front row watching them and that was her strongest impression of the band. Small Faces. The phrase had a contemporary resonance. 'Faces' was a term applied to the Mod elite, those who rigorously kept themselves above the rest in terms of attitude and fashion. The small part of the title provided a nice humorous angle.

Small Faces? All agreed? All agreed.

The band's debut show had been arranged by Marriott. He had experienced little problem in persuading the hall's owner to let them perform there – mostly because youth nights were run by fan and former Moments fanzine editor, Stuart Tuck.

After watching their debut gig, not only did Tuck invite the group to play the next night at the venue but he also asked them to perform at his wedding reception.

'Basically,' Marriott recalled, 'we formed for bar mitzvahs and weddings. Any chance to play. Not trying to make it, just to have a laugh.'

It's an important quote. Twenty-five years later he would be using it to rigorously defend his position as the leader of a pub band.

As the band's equipment was stored at the flat in Loughton, and the van wasn't available that day, the band persuaded Tuck to move his reception to their flat in Loughton. The resulting reception was a rowdy drunken affair. The band played like demons and at some point in the night the bride managed to throw herself over the first floor balcony. She escaped serious injury.

It was that kind of night.

Before departing on honeymoon, Tuck again phoned his friend Maurice King at his Starlight Rooms club in Paddington. On Tuck's strong recommendation, King agreed to book the Small Faces for two afternoon shows on Sunday, May 16th, 1965.

The group spent the preceding week rehearsing at both the Kensington Youth Centre and The Ruskin Arms. On Tuesday and Thursday night they performed for the Ruskin Arms regulars as a warm up before travelling to Paddington on the Sunday to play the Starlight Rooms, nerves running through them, excitement crawling up the spine.

Chapter Eight

It's Not What You Do

Two sets, two shows. Once more, the band impresses and once more the baton is passed on. Maurice King now picks up the phone and calls a friend of his in Sheffield. The name of the friend is Peter Stringfellow. His club is called, The Mojo. It is Mod central in that city.

King insists to Stringfellow that he should book this new act he's just worked with. They would be perfect for his club.

A date is arranged, Saturday, May 22nd. As the band is travelling north, a couple of other dates are also put in, one in Manchester, one in Sheffield.

Their first ever tour.

The band rehearse all week. On Thursday, they pack the van with guitars, amps, bags of clothes and bags of nerves, then they travel to Manchester. With them is roadie Terry Lucas, known as 'Terry the Egg'.

'I don't know where Terry the Egg came from,' Marriott said. 'He must have been an acquaintance of mine but he wasn't a friend.'

The band's first date is at Manchester's The Twisted Wheel. It is a landmark club.

The Twisted Wheel started life in the early '60s, mainly playing beat music. In 1964 it booked one Roger Eagle to DJ and he turned the club on its head. Eagle was an apostle and a missionary for the R&B music that was revolutionising Britain and changing young people's mindsets forever. On his first night at the club Eagle played tunes such as 'Help Me' by Sonny Boy Williamson, 'Wednesday Night Prayer Meeting' by Charlie Mingus, 'Tell The Truth' by Ray Charles and 'Road Runner' by Bo Diddley.

Within six months, soul crazy kids were travelling from all corners of the Isle to hear him play. Most of these kids were Mods. They dressed smart, dropped pills, chewed hard and danced like dreams. Black music was their religion. It articulated their thoughts and it swayed their groins. Sometimes it achieved both feats simultaneously. That was R&B at its very best and the Twisted Wheel was the Small Faces kind of club. Souled up and Modded out.

So how devastating was it for them to be turned down and turned away by this Mecca of northern Modernism? Because that's exactly what happened, according to Philip Adabi, one of the club's owners.

He told Keith Rylatt and Phil Scott, authors of the book, *Central 1179*, that the Small Faces were 'the worst band we had ever seen at the Wheel.'

Adabi added that he walked out after hearing just two songs at a Friday afternoon audition. He remembered he gave them a pound for petrol and then packed them off to Sheffield.

Marriott remembered things somewhat differently. He told John Hellier, 'In Manchester, we played the Twisted Wheel – that was the first gig on the trip. Some bastard lent our black Mariah van for an hour and came back with a load of fucking leather coats in the back – done a job. Me and Ronnie and Kenney all got leather coats out of it. Done a job like when we were playing and we really enjoyed playing there.'

'I think it was Terry who suggested that these people use our van. I think he was driving it, said he wouldn't be gone long, probably got paid a bit of whack. Anyway we finished the set and the van still wasn't back and we were out there waiting for it when it screeches around the corner and someone yells, "Get in, get in!" So we piled in the back and it's up to here in leather coats. We screamed around to some bird's house and they were getting the coats out and bundling them up. They said. "Take a coat, anything you want." It was a great coat, had a belt and buttons.'

Kay, his sister, would remember the garment years later.

'I remember [Steve] bringing it home and stuffing it under the bed and laying on it to crumple it up 'cuz [he] said it looked like plastic, it was so new and thick.'

The band travelled to Sheffield. The venue was a small working man's club, the gig a disaster. The crowd were the elderly bingo brigade and for some reason, not particularly fussed by the idea of four groundbreaking young London Mods fusing together raw R&B with a powerful attitude. There were exceptions, though.

Steve Marriott: 'While we were playing, all these old members were shouting out at us. But I do remember this one old girl. I said, 'I'd like to do a number by James Brown,' and this old woman – to me she seemed old, she must have been about forty – started screaming. She loved it. She was hip so we kind of played to her, the only one in the audience who knew what we were doing. And the manager just slung us off after three numbers, paid us off and told us to piss off. That was Sheffield.'

No, it wasn't. That was the first night in Sheffield. The second day the band were told by the Mojo club that their date had been put forward a night but extra accommodation would be paid for. The band hung around town all day and then as early evening arrived, went down to nearby the Esquire Club, asked if they could perform there.

'The Esquire was a very sort of trendy blues club,' Marriott states. 'It was where American blues acts would play when they came through. The audience was sort of ex-beatnik still had the shades and the plastic macs.'

The band did themselves a kind of justice in front of this more demanding crowd and the next day went on to play the Mojo, a gig which would put all bad memories behind them.

'It was a great club, 'Marriott says of The Mojo. 'Really was. It was like *Ready Steady Go* or something, a very appreciative crowd. I think we only played the one gig until we had a hit record. It wasn't very long after that we hit. Suddenly, we were their band. It was like they discovered us so they went crazy when we went back there. It was a special place for us because of the crowd. They gave us an even break which no one else was willing to do. Fond memories of Sheffield.'

He's not the only one.

'They went down an absolute storm,' says Stringfellow, 'One of my first memories of Stevie was that I used to live above the Mojo club and after their gig we went upstairs to my apartment as it was called in those days, and we played to them music that had been written by Mark Townsend from one of the local groups, The Cadillacs. Anyway, after that night I put in three bookings on them at pretty low prices. The second time they came they had a record at near number one and they packed the place solid. Steve was very much a people's guy. He would talk to the audience which is what they wanted. He wasn't just going, here's the next number but he would talk to them in his Cockney accent which they loved and therefore they took to him and the rest of the boys. He had a phenomenal voice. Out of that little frame came this huge voice. He was unique. Then as they became massive they kept this friendliness about them which is why everyone loved them.'

The Wheel fiasco now forgotten, Marriott and his boys returned to London in a positive frame of mind. They rehearsed all week long and then on the Saturday, Marriott travelled across town to appear at the *New Musical Express* stand at the Battersea Park Festival Gardens where he signed a few autographs.

Then, later that day, as arranged, he and Terry The Egg met up in the West End and went to see the manager of the Cavern In The Town Club in Leicester Square, (now the Notre Dame Hall).

Their mission was to convince the manager to book them, a tricky task given that he had never heard them play before. The turning point in the discussion came when Marriott was asked how many songs they performed in their act. Five came the reply.

Not really enough, the manager opined. We would need at least two more songs. No problem, came his eager, lying reply, we actually have a few numbers as back up.

Good, said the manager, you can play tonight. Marriott rushed back home, returned with the three other Small Faces. It was Saturday, May 29th, 1965.

Maurice King came down that night to see the band play. He was not there for kicks. He was there to ascertain the band's management status.

When he came backstage after their performance and asked if they had a manager, Marriott played him beautifully.

'Yeah, we're still kind of sussing it out,' the up and coming songwriter replied. 'Here, any chance of using your rooms for rehearsing this week?'

Put on the spot like that, King could hardly refuse. It would prove to be a significant rehearsal. During it, The Small Faces shot up to a whole new level and it was drummer, Kenney Jones who took them there

'I never thought Kenney was that good up to that point,' Marriott revealed. 'He was okay but I didn't realise that it was the material that he was playing. He set his drums up and he went berserk. For about half an hour he made me and Ronnie kill ourselves laughing. We were giving him the encouragement, "Go on my son," and he really opened up. It was like a different drummer. It really was an eye opener and after that there was no looking back. Every song we did swung like Hanratty. It was like a revelation. We just couldn't believe it.'

Marriott and Jones maintained an easy-going relationship for most of their time together. Jones was a quiet man, the most reserved member of the band, and in some senses easy pickings for Marriott's brand of send-up humour.

In truth, Marriott felt an affinity with the drummer, had done so since the day they met and Jones took one look at him and told him that they had already met in a dream of his. In it, Jones explained, Marriott and Lane performed on the TV show, *Thank Your Lucky Stars.*'

'It sounds ridiculous,' Marriott pondered, 'but Kenney's too sort of straight to make anything up like that. The Small Faces were a fated group.'

They were a fated group but not always in the benevolent way that Marriott refers to here. Senseless deaths, unpaid royalties, the history books tampered with, all this and more would play a large part in the band's history.

In the early days, however, luck came to stand by their side for just as Kenney Jones was shedding all inhibitions and taking the band up a gear with his powerful assaults on the drums, into the Starlight Rooms walked a young woman, there to see Maurice King. The woman worked as a secretary to a manager called, Don Arden.

'A chick from Arden's office spotted us, his secretary. She just happened to be around,' Marriott said. 'I'd seen her before at the Starlight Rooms. King might have been managing Elkie Brooks 'coz she used to be there a lot. I used to get up and sing with her sometimes and that chick had seen me down there too.'

As the girl waited for King, her attention was increasingly diverted towards the four good looking boys rehearsing. On returning to Arden's office at 55, Carnaby Street, she went straight to his office to alert him of a new talent in town. Don Arden listened with his usual interest and then followed his usual pattern. He sent his henchmen, Ron King and Pat Meehan to check it all out.

‡ ‡ ‡

Where there's gold, there's rogues.

Rolling Stone guitarist Keith Richards once said of the music business, 'I'd rather deal with the Mafia.' You can see where he is going. With the Bada Bing boys, at least you know what the deal is. At least, you know where you stand. It is the pretence of the music biz to be a business of fair and scrupulous practice that is the most painful for those whose work in it.

For the musicians, the best-ever record company was Frank Sinatra's Reprise label. Artists were signed for one album whose copyright they owned, not the record company. The royalty rate Sinatra set was laughed at by the music business but was in fact fair and proper. Plus, the costs were evenly divided.

Apart from Reprise and a couple of other labels, the music business remains unparalleled in its constant ability to crack open human lives and leave the blood on the doorstep, dripping outside their black windowed buildings for all to see.

The suited and booted sharks first moved in with the arrival of rock'n'roll in the mid-50s. They called themselves managers but acted like minor gangsters. They would take talent and exploit and exploit and exploit and then they would steal and lie and cajole. They would realise for so many young working class people the dreams they never thought would be theirs but they would make sure to take their slice of the action before anyone else. And what a slice it was.

In their abject gratitude, singers allowed the shysters to take massive advantage. Soon the pattern was set. You did things their way or you simply didn't do anything: your choice.

For Steve Marriott, Don Arden was inevitable really. Marriott recognised his game from the start but he didn't really give a fuck. He told the *New Musical Express* in 1984, 'Look, you go into it with your eyes open and as far as I was concerned it was better than living on brown sauce rolls. At least we had twenty quid a week guaranteed. In those days it was great, you could hold your head up with your mum and dad.'

Arden certainly knew the ropes, knew them back to front in fact. By the time he had been alerted to the Small Faces, he had cut his own records, worked as a comedian/compere, tried to save Gene Vincent's career from alcoholic abuse (he failed) and taken The Nashville Teens into the charts. His acts didn't sign to record companies, they signed to him. His company then did the deal with any interested record company.

Arden was a first in pop management. Before managers had merely been slimy, pretended to love their act. Arden was never that. He was a brusque, no nonsense guy who told his acts he would exploit them for all they were worth. Literally. He could do so for he knew the value of angles. That's why he sold himself to the world as the 'Al Capone of Pop.'

Under that very title, he told the *News Of The World* in 1966, 'I'm a success. Because I found out that a clenched fist can settle an argument faster than wrangling in court. And I've even had my men waving guns about to scare the daylights out of a business rival and produce quick results. That's how I came to be known as the Al Capone of pop. Let's get it straight right from the start. I am damned proud of my sumptuous Mayfair office and my Georgian mansions. In an industry riddled with drug addicts, homosexuals and hangers-on, I'm one of the few real men left.'

After receiving fave reports from Meehan and King, Arden came to the Cavern Club to see for himself if his boys were on the case.

The night before he arrived at the Cavern Club, The Small Faces rehearsed at the Ruskin Arms. Afterwards, to save money, Steve and Ronnie decided to walk from East Ham to Loughton.

'We got on a bus for the last mile or two as we were a bit exhausted and it was freezing cold,' Marriott recalled, 'We were standing on the platform at the back of the bus and there's this guy standing next to us – we don't know him from Adam – and he's telling someone who's following him to fuck off. He gets off the bus and runs away and we get off the bus carrying on talking and this van follows us with six or seven chaps in it who must have been twenty years old or something – which was old to us.

'They were like the skinheads. There was us, the Mods and then as they got older they became these car-driving skinheads with bovver boots. They jumped out of this van and beat the shit out of me with this bottle. They did Ronnie with a piece of wood with a nail in it so he had a hole in his forehead. I've still got a scar from the bottle, which I use as a parting. I got into using it as a parting in the front when I had bangs.

'We were covered in blood, really badly beaten, kicked to bits. Eyes out to here, lips, ears, everything. We found out later that it was some boys from Loughton who had gone down to Tottenham and smashed up a few cafes so this was a return visit. We didn't know, we had no idea.'

As the boys were being beaten, a concerned couple pulled up in their Volkswagen car. The man wound down his window and shouted at the mob to stop. They turned, took one look and then rushed over to the car and began jumping all over it. The couple drove off in sheer panic and the mob returned to finish off Marriott and Lane.

'Ronnie by this time had disappeared up the road while they were jumping on this Volkswagen,' recalled Marriott. 'So they only had me to beat up. They left me for dead.

'I remember Ronnie coming back to see if I was alright. I was floored, on the ground and he's got this hole in his head, blood spouting out everywhere and in the shock, we couldn't stop laughing about it to each other. The shock of being that badly beaten, nothing but blood and we were blowing bubbles and laughing about it. This Volkswagen came back and they took us off to the Woodford hospital.

'We were covered in blood and we were still laughing from shock and this nurse came out and I'll never forget the line, she said, 'Be quiet, this is a hospital,' which hurt us that much more because we couldn't stop laughing again.

'They were saying it was a maternity hospital and we didn't have any right to be there. That was really bad. If anyone's that badly beaten they need a bit of attention. the least they can do is clean me up for fuck's sake. So this man and woman – I'll never forget them either – took us to their own doctor.

'We used to wear these little polo necks under our shirts. We used to call them bring me downs 'cos if you stripped off in front of a chick they were a right bring me down and I remember me and Ronnie wringing our bring me downs under the tap and they were full of claret.'

'And the next day we were playing the Cavern Club and Don Arden was going to be there. It was fucking hilarious. Every time Ronnie hit a high note, his stitches would open and the blood would be running down. My face looked like a gargoyle – two black eyes, very fat lips, stitched up head. [Pause] They liked us apparently.'

In fact, Arden thought the boys' wounds were part of their stage act.

The Small Bloodied Faces, what a great idea.

I'll sign this bloody lot.

‡ ‡ ‡

The Cavern Club gigs marked the turning point in the band's career. They played the club five Saturdays running and in doing so established the group's name and earned themselves a much-valued recording contract.

'We had that place packed after the first time,' Marriott explained, 'It was like there was a new band in town. Kit Lambert came down to see us and got a lot of flak from The Who because he was going to take us on at one point. I think every organisation must have come down at some point.'

After their debut at the club, Ronnie Lane had drawn a picture of a mod on a scooter with the band's name behind him on a small blackboard and placed it outside the gig. The club was soon packed with Mods. Marriott meanwhile was busy creating his own bit of mayhem.

'I can't remember if I hit the traffic warden or not,' he told John Hellier, 'or if I had just words with him. I think I hit him or shoved him. We were trying to load up the van,' he explained, 'and he was telling us to piss off and eventually we had to push his ass out. See, by the time you had walked up all those stairs carrying a Marshall cabinet you didn't feel like arguing about anything.

'The Cavern was a nice place,' Marriott continued. 'Curtains, nice high stage, the whole fucking gear. It was one of the nicest places we played. I don't think it had a bar in those days. I remember when we were down there we thought we had invented words like "spliff," because we had heard it off the guys we got our stuff off, Nigerians or Jamaicans or whatever. We had a number called, "Pass The Spliff," and all these guys in the audience would crack up. We thought it was our word, our "in" word.'

Yet not everyone was enamoured with the band's performances. Lloyd Johnson, a man who would later make his name significant in the rag trade, was a Mod who worked at Cecil Gee's large shop on Charing Cross Road. The branch was just up the road from Covent Garden and the hip shoe shop, Annello and Davide.

'All the bands used to go there and get their boots,' Johnson recalls, 'and then get a lot of their gear either from Cecil Gee's or a place called David's on Shaftesbury Avenue. The bands always used to give us tickets because we were the same age as them and that's what happened with the Small Faces. I can't remember who came in but they said, We are playing the Cavern club, do you want to come?

'I remember going there and they looked absolutely brilliant but I left the gig early. I was with a mate of mine, a Dutch guy I was working with, and the band had a Hammond organ and the sound was just hitting the absolutely shambolic so we just went home.'

‡ ‡ ‡

Stuart Tuck, Maurice King, they had all put themselves forward in their own little way as prospective managers. But Marriott knew the business and knew it better than most seventeen-year-olds, including his band.

Don Arden was their man. He knew how to blow life into dreams, turn that which only existed in the mind into reality. For Steve Marriott, there was no contest. Arden was their man. Matter closed.

'He was an excellent manager,' Marriott told Hellier in 1984, 'excellent.'

'He was a friendly sort of rogue in his own way,' Jimmy Winston recalled to John Hellier. 'We were very young and gullible and he kinda looked like what we were looking for.'

Arden, in turn, would grow to like his new protégés.

'And just to prove that the Al Capone of the pop world has a soft spot,' he boasted in the *News of the World* sometime later, 'let me tell you I felt these kids should have at least one year of enjoying the very best in life. After all, they had been hungry in their time.'

One year of the very best in living. At eighteen years of age, to be given a year of the very best was amazing,

As Marriott himself would say, Nice, extremely nice.

Or so it seemed.

‡ ‡ ‡

1965, it was a very good year.

The writer Richard Williams states simply, 'In 1965, things changed fast.'

Author Simon Wells fully agrees with him.

'What takes a year to change now took a day in the Sixties,' he says. Even *The Times* writer, Bernard Levin couldn't ignore how life had speeded up to almost unimaginable levels.

He wrote of this epochal decade, 'Fashions changed, changed again, changed faster and still faster: fashions in politics, in political style, in causes, in music, in popular culture, in myths, in education, in beauty, in heroes and idols, in attitudes, in responses, in work, in love and friendship, in food, in newspapers, in entertainment, in fashion.'

Music led the way. The Beatles, Dylan, The Stones, all of the top boys were making audacious moves, taking on risks, all of them hell-bent on seeing where their art would lead to them to.

A different sensibility dominated Sixties music. Where today an innovation is relentlessly copied, back then an innovation was the spur for the others to take similar leaps of faith and imagination. They used a sitar on their latest record? Shit. I know, we'll go for feedback.

Thus pop progressed in so many new and exciting ways.

Yet pop is also a hard taskmaster. It does not always reward the talented, the risk takers. It establishes a hierarchy, creates a history that many abide by. There is a line that can be taken with the Sixties, a line which takes you through the usual names and careers of those who have become synonymous with the decade of magic.

John, Paul, Mick, Keef, Bob, Quant, Bailey, Stamp.

But there are deeper seas to trawl, others of equal importance to meet and greet.

Just for starters, Lindsay Anderson, Berry Gordy, James Brown, Jim Stewart and his sister Estelle, Hayes and Porter, Freddie Scott, the writer Joan Didion, the film *Bronco Bullfrog*, the clothes man John Simons, the actor and writer, Patrick McGoohan.

These men and women of creation were just as important, just as vital to the spirit of the time as anyone else but like the Small Faces they would find their work hidden, their stories misrepresented.

Mod was no different to this process. Mod finished in 1963. The originals saw *Ready Steady Go* and decided too many seven and sixers knew the game. Time to mourn the Mohair. Yet to this day mention Mod and people's mind instantly flash to 1965 and fights with rockers on Brighton Beach.

In his book, *The Sixties*, the academic Arthur Marwick pinpoints 1954 as the year the Sixties started, 1974 as the year it died. In *The Neophiliacs*, Christopher Booker goes further; he states that during this period Britons actually experienced a mass hallucination. This was the only explanation for the eruptions that took place almost daily as the country was turned on and then turned on its head.

For the first time, the young were allowed to take the spotlight. There was talk of a meritocracy, the Lords mingling with the loud as all of them got high, got laid.

The Prime Minister (Number Two) gave The Beatles (Number One) medals. Bailey the working class boy started working at *Vogue*. Caine and Stamp made their names at the cinema. Gritty working class dramas became all the rage. The illusion that all the barriers were down was created. Everything was up for grabs and anybody could make it...

That's what Harold Wilson, the PM said. Funnily enough, Tony Blair is still saying it today.

In the '60s everyone was talented but not everyone was lucky.

And luck, said Steve Marriott, was exactly what was shining on The Small Faces the day Don Arden got involved in their affairs.

Chapter Nine

Something I Want To Tell You

On Monday June 7th, 1965, The Small Faces gather at Don Arden's office at 52-55 Carnaby Street. Typically, Arden gets straight down to business, makes them an offer. Money-wise, you have a choice, he tells them. You can be given a straight wage or a cut of the profits. That's the deal. Take it or leave it.

The group ask to go out to the reception area. Five minutes later, they return with their answer; we want both.

Arden smiles. Okay, no problem, he replies. I'll give you twenty pounds a week, a cut of the records and I'll also open up accounts for you at every clothes shop in Carnaby Street. Deal? Done.

You are eighteen years old. You are a Mod and you are in a band. You have just done something many of your schoolmates never will: you have escaped the factory line. You do not have a boss breathing down your neck taking out all his bitterness on you. Instead, you are being paid to do something you absolutely love, which is make music. In turn, you will also get clothes, drugs, fame and girls.

1965, it truly was a very good year.

Four Small Faces, together now for just, what, five months? Playing a five-song set and already they have top class management? After only five gigs? What's their secret?

Steve Marriott: 'I think it was our energy, we had a lot of energy, a lot of push and a little bit of flair which was missing off the scene at the time. We were little Mods and by that time devout Mods. We were arm flingers, feedback players and I think we had a lot of charisma because of the size of us and the kind of music we played.'

At the time of The Small Faces' emergence, the London they inhabited was in parts, a place of great danger. Gangs were commonplace, gigs a great place for violence.

Hugh Janes, Marriott's mate from Italia Conti:

'From early 1965, I followed Steve's career with the Small Faces. This was before their first hit record came out. I remember a gig at a church hall in Shepherd's Bush. There was an almighty punch up because the crowd there felt we were in the wrong manor. The London scene was getting very territorial.

'After that particular gig, myself and another pal of Steve's, Colin Spall, were picking Steve up in Colin's yellow Triumph Herald convertible and we were mob attacked as we got in the car. I remember Colin knocking a guy over as he reversed the car in panic. That obviously made the situation worse and we were lucky to get away with our lives that night. That wasn't a one-off incident, there was a lot of that in the early days.'

Those who had attacked them probably supported a young West London band called The Who. That year The Who had released their debut album and were now busy smashing up instruments onstage, fighting endlessly amongst themselves and creating a music full of attack and spite and beauty. Rivalry and friendship between themselves and The Small Faces was inevitable although the little East Enders could certainly claim the moral high ground when it came to matters of Mod authenticity. The Who were a band that turned Mod.

Their manager, Pete Meaden was a top Mod and he had persuaded his band to adopt mod clothing, write Mod style music. The Small Faces on the other hand were Mods who became a band.

That's no la la la lie but a sha la la lee truth.

‡ ‡ ‡

After signing with Arden, the band were quickly exposed to their new manager's devious behaviour. Arden's first move was to appoint a Ron King as their agent. King immediately booked a gig for them at the Wykeham Hall in Romford.

Marriott should have seen what was coming. The year before he had played the same venue with The Moments. At the end of the night the group were told by the venue's manager that they had been auditioning in front of a live audience and therefore were not eligible for payment.

The very same scam was now being played upon the Small Faces. They even complained to Ron King their agent when they realised what had happened but it was a pointless gesture. He was in it as well.

'We did a gig for him,' Marriott said of Ron King who also owned the Galaxy Entertainment company (in which a certain Don Arden was a shareholder) and he wouldn't pay us. He said, "You were too loud." Our own agent wouldn't pay us. We thought, "What have we got ourselves into?"'

What indeed?

Right from the start, Kay and Bill Marriott expressed their suspicions of the band's new management.

'Steve reckoned Arden was a good manager,' Bill Marriott told an American TV crew in 1996, 'but I didn't like him very much. I don't like any managers very much I'm afraid and I told Arden so. I said to him that I had never met a straight manager yet and suddenly I've got a couple of big chaps behind me, so I kept my mouth shut.'

The encounter Bill refers to took place on Thursday, June 10th, in Don Arden's office, the day the band, with their parents in tow, signed a contract binding them to his company, Contemporary Music. For three years.

Not long after, Arden secured a recording contract for the band with Decca Records. One of Arden's main contacts there was the A&R man, Dick Rowe. Having famously turned down The Beatles by telling their manager that 'guitar groups were out,' Rowe was now extremely eager to avoid making the same mistake.

His new attitude meant that he was far more likely to sign a band than not. If they succeeded, great. If they failed, great. As long as they shone or fell on Decca and didn't prove to be a huge success on another label, Rowe was happy.

‡ ‡ ‡

By now, Steve Marriott and Ronnie Lane had agreed to set up a songwriting partnership, à la Lennon and McCartney. Both musicians would take equal credit and royalties for every song no matter what their input.

For those around the group it seemed a strange decision. Marriott, the hyper bundle of nervous energy was the band's main songwriter. Lane was a beginner, slower and, at that point, not nearly as creative as his partner.

Kay Marriott: 'I said to him, Why is it both your names, Steve? And he said, 'Without Ronnie's help keeping me awake and being there I wouldn't do half of it. He keeps me going.'

Bill Marriott: 'They helped each other out with writing but I think it wasn't so much that Ronnie did a lot but that Ronnie encouraged him to work and kept him happy. Because Steve was very prolific. He used to write things in half an hour.'

That Marriott should give Lane such a generous deal speaks volumes about his generosity and the depth of the boys' friendship.

Four years later, there would be a different story to tell. This very same agreement would split the friendship, split the band and push Steve Marriott into spending years ignoring his friend, Ronald Frederick Lane.

‡ ‡ ‡

At rehearsals in the Ruskin Arms, Marriott had taught Jimmy Winston a little riff that he had 'borrowed' from the Solomon Burke record 'Everybody Needs Somebody To Love.'

Marriott later used the riff as a springboard to create a vibrant instrumental. Now, after signing to Decca, the band were keen to record a single. Their thoughts turned to this song. It was certainly bouncy and catchy enough. The only problem was that it needed words and needed them quickly.

Arden turned to the songwriting team Samwell and Potter to help out. Samwell was a respected name in the music business. He had composed 'Move It' for Cliff Richard, widely regarded as one of the first and very best British rock'n'roll records.

The team returned with a set of lyrics entitled 'Whatcha Gonna Do About It.'

In early July, the group entered the Decca recording studios at 165 Broadhurst Gardens, West Hampstead, to record two songs: 'Whatcha' and a cover of Timi Yuro's 'What's A Matter Baby' for the flip side.

The recording went smoothly. To celebrate, the band agreed to support the Stan Foster Big Band at a reception in Newham Town Hall for West Ham football club, recent winners of the European Cup Winner's Cup.

It was the summer of 1965. David Bailey was in *Vogue*, Bobby Moore was captain of England, Terence Stamp was a major film star, the Krays were in the headlines and the Small Faces were about to hit big.

Blimey, the East End had never had it so good.

Chapter Ten

E Too D

That rise to the top, always the high spot, always the best part of the journey. Palates are not jaded but eager for success. The soul is itching to savour all the delights now made real by your glorious talent. Money, fame, girls, drugs, clothes, such are the gifts made available to the famous.

The only problem is that no one ever warns them of the following fact – that which entices you is that which will enslave you.

The Small Faces had spent two days recording 'Whatcha' and 'What's A Matter Baby?'

The following week, over another two days, the songs were given their final mixes and then delivered to Decca. On receiving them, the company arranged a photo shoot for the band. Pictures were needed for press, promotion and artwork. The photographer chosen was Decca man, David Wedgbury; the location, London's South Bank

Wedgbury and the band arranged to meet in a car park.

'I watched in amazement as the band circled the car park once and then began to drive off,' Wedgbury told the authors of *Quite Naturally*, the second Small Faces biog to appear in the '90s. 'I frantically ran after the car waving and they eventually saw me and stopped. I found out they were too broke between them to afford the car park.'

For the session, Marriott wore a white shirt with cufflinks, white trousers and a Madras jacket. His shoes, unfortunately, reflected his financial status although the resulting photos caught the band's Mod image nicely. Their haircuts were right, their clothes smart and suggestive. Only Winston with his larger frame and face seems slightly at odds with the photo's composition.

In mid-July, an advance cut of the band's debut single was sent to *Top Of The Pops* producer, Johnny Stewart. Two weeks later, at the start of August the Small Faces travelled to Birmingham to fulfil Kenney Jones's dream and perform on a summer offshoot of the TV show, *Thank Your Lucky Stars*. Also appearing was Marriott's former actor friend, Heinz.

At the show, the band ignore the blond haired actor but strike up a rapport with the American act, Sonny and Cher. Jimmy Winston moves in on Cher's sister, ends up back at her Knightsbridge flat. (Marriott might have been a little put out by his organist's success. Didn't the lead singer get the goodies first?)

On August 6th The Small Faces' debut 45 is released. It is a fresh, jaunty single built around a commercial structure, which is then peppered throughout by intriguing possibilities – the feedback from Marriott's guitar, Jimmy Winston's organ playing. Above all, it brought out of Steve a nicely controlled vocal that hints at his power but that's all.

A good rule – less is better.

The voice is so self-assured, however, it is hard to believe the singer is just eighteen. For the flip side, Marriott less successfully attempts to negotiate a musical landscape usually inhabited by crooners.

Ray Pollard's vocal on 'The Drifter', is a good example of the sound that Marriott is trying emulate on 'What's A Matter Baby,' but his voice is slightly overwrought and he heads for the big notes far too soon. The backing from his band is nothing special.

Immediately after the single's release, the press react predictably: the band are compared to The Who.

Record Mirror make the first accusations. At an interview held in a café, the writer Richard Green asks Marriott 'How about the feedback on 'Whatcha Gonna Do About It?' or the drumming of Kenney Jones, rather after the manner of Keith Moon.'

Not fair, cries Marriott.

'I'm not saying I can play guitar,' he responds, 'but I admire the playing of Pete Townshend and I admire the playing of Dave Davies and I admire the playing of Eric Clapton. The easiest of those styles for me to follow was Pete Townshend's so I did.

'But we just don't copy The Who. We don't use feedback now,' he continued in defensive mode, 'and Kenney has been playing like that ever since I've known him. He doesn't copy Keith Moon.'

Green moves onto the band's influences. 'They like numbers like 'Ooh Poo Pah Doo' [by Ernie K. Doe] and things by Wilson Pickett and Bobby Bland.

'I'm not too keen on Solomon Burke though,' puts in Marriott. [Clever man! Cover your tracks best you can.]

Meanwhile teenage girls constantly interrupt the interview, unable to stop themselves hugging the baby-faced star.

It is a taste of what is to come.

'This music is great,' Marriott tells Green in between kisses. 'It gets hold of you

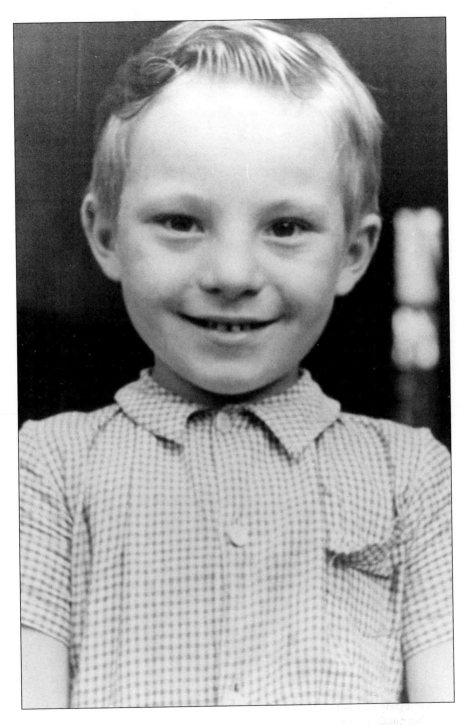

Steve aged 2   (Kay Marriott)

Steve aged 4   *(Kay Marriott)*

Jaywick Sands with Mum and sister 1957   *(Kay Marriott)*

MONEGA JUNIOR MIXED SCHOOL

REPORT on *Stephen Marriott.* for School Year *1956/57*

3rd Year No. in Class *39*

A B C D *B* Stream Position *9d.*

SUBJECT	Grade in Stream	REMARKS
ENGLISH Composition	C	During this school year,
Comprehension	B	Stephen's main aims have
Reading	B	been to do as little work,
Spelling	B –	and be as great a nuisance,
Usage	B	as possible. He does not
ARITHMETIC	D+	seem happy unless he
HISTORY	B –	is the centre of attraction.
GEOGRAPHY	C –	He has achieved 9th
LOCAL STUDY	C –	position in class by not
NATURE	B –	even trying. If he applied
RELIGIOUS INSTRUCTION	C	himself to his work, he
WRITING	C –	could be at the top, or
PHYSICAL EDUCATION	C	perhaps in the A stream.
MUSIC	.	I hope that next year
ART	C –	he will reverse his
CRAFTS	C –	outlook, and make a big
		effort to improve his
		standard of work and also
		his behaviour.

SCHOOL CLUBS & OTHER INTERESTS

Member of Boxing Club.

GENERAL REMARKS

W. A Beech.

Signature of Parent Class Teacher

Steve's school report 1957 (Kay Marriott)

THE

UNCLE KEN SHOW

JAYWICK SANDS

This is to certify that

was adjudged the

WINNER of the TALENT COMPETITION

held on

Signed

Holiday Talent Show winner 1958   (Kay Marriott)

Steve and first guitar 1958   (Kay Marriott)

On holiday in Jaywick Sands   *(Kay Marriott)*

Artful Dodger in Oliver *1960*   *(Kay Marriott)*

Steve aged 15 *(Kay Marriott)*

Steve in The Frantiks 1963 *(Kay Marriott)*

Live It Up *film set 1963*   *(Leanne Read)*

Steve Marriott's Moments at QPR football ground 1964   *(Monitor Press)*

onstage. You want to yell and leap about. It's part of you and you just do whatever you like.'

Green knew what he meant. At the gig the writer attended at the Cavern, during 'Come On Children' the band had spontaneously broken into the old standard 'You Are My Sunshine'!

It was a precursor to the kind of drunken, amiable onstage behaviour that would play a significant part in The Faces' success in the Seventies.

The interview is dated September 1st. The very next day 'Whatcha Gonna Do About It' entered the charts at number fourteen and stayed around for a further twelve weeks.

Success breeds many things, amongst them press interest. *Melody Maker* ran a 'Ten Week Trip To The Top' article detailing the group's rapid rise to fortune whilst their rivals, the *New Musical Express* responded with a piece detailing the likes and dislikes of all four members.

The article was run on the 17th of September. In it, Marriott cites James Brown, Garnet Mimms, Bobby Bland and Ray Charles as his biggest musical influences. His fave bands/instrumentalists are Charlie Mingus and the organist, Jon Paton; his most thrilling experience was 'falling over my wallet,' and his personal ambition is to play jazz.

(A typical comment. At some point all talented songwriters want to move into foreign musical areas such as classical or jazz. Most are dissuaded from doing so when they see the wages on offer.)

On the very same day of the *New Musical Express* piece, the Small Faces made their debut on *Ready Steady Go*, the nation's hippest music show. *RSG* purveyed a Mod sensibility. In the week before transmission, their scouts scoured London's clubs looking for the best dancers and the best looking, inviting them all to peacock in front of the cameras.

When the show began, it tended to feature the major pop acts of the day but, after producer, and R&B lover, Vicki Wickham came on board, a surfeit of R&B acts started appearing. Their importance was gauged by the *RSG* specials made with James Brown, Otis Redding and the Motown label. Meantime, Marvin Gaye and Kim Weston and The Isleys and The Marvelletes all regularly performed on the show.

The show had other functions. By broadcasting nationally, the show brought London Mod fashions to the rest of the country. Neat and dandy. But in doing so, *Ready Steady Go* popularised Mod and in the process killed it off.

'I think the original Mods were quite happy to see themselves emulated on television,' an original Mod named Robert Hall says in the book, *The Soul Stylists*, 'but when that spread nationally it was finished.'

Even so, *RSG* remained the hippest show around thanks to the likes of Wickham.

'I first met Steve,' Vicki Wickham says, 'at *Ready Steady Go*. He came down when we were filming it for Rediffusion. The studio was on Kingsway but right on the corner where Kingsway goes into the Aldwych. The show was all mimed so the Small Faces did it mimed. I remember him being a little sweetheart, a cheeky little kid. Cathy McGowan and I loved him.'

The Small Faces would hardly have been nervous about appearing before TV cameras. They had already made their TV debut on *Gadzooks*, a BBC music programme on the 6th of September and then, as the single charted, made it onto the big one, *Top Of the Pops*, recorded and transmitted on the 16th.

Mum and Dad Marriott were so thrilled. Especially Bill. He was now working at the *Evening News* and had placed placards advertising his son's single all around the office. After two weeks of the single's chart inactivity, his workmates had started to turn on him.

'Everyone said about Steve, "Who is he?" and "he's a nobody," he recalled in 1996, 'but then he went right up the charts. I think they played it on *Top Of The Pops* and it was exciting for us.' He pauses. 'He always made our life exciting.'

Always made our life exciting, that phrase remains the father's finest testament to the son whose nature he never quite got to grips with.

For the band, performing on *Ready Steady Go* was a landmark, tangible proof of their growing popularity.

'Before we formed the band,' Winston recalled, 'I used to watch the show and think, "Cor wouldn't it be great to play on there." All the different shows that we did were exciting in their own way but the *Ready Steady Go* ones stand out in my mind the most. They had Gary Glitter moving the crowd around and I remember Eric Burdon introducing us as The New Faces. I never liked him after that. Silly really.'

Marriott didn't bear a grudge against the Animals frontman. Burdon's vocal power impressed him. Their paths would happily cross over the coming years.

'He's quite a one,' Cathy McGowan the host said of Marriott, after watching him perform 'Whatcha Gonna Do About It' and then joining the audience for a dance at the show's conclusion. 'He's a real little Mod!'

Fittingly, it was their dress which first suggested the gap opening up between the band and Winston. On *Ready Steady Go*, the organist chose to present himself to the nation wearing a black see-through t-shirt. It bore little relation to the threads his teammates had on – white Levis, button downs, sharp shoes. No doubt Marriott noted the discrepancy. He was already finding himself irritated by the elder man's actions since they had started performing for the cameras.

Marriott was the front man, the visual centre of the Small Faces. That was his turf, his job. Yet Winston's stage movements suggested otherwise. Every time Marriott turned around it seemed the organist was playing to the cameras or the audience.

Enough was enough. He had to go.

That then is the story of why Jimmy Winston was sacked from the band just months after joining, a tale that has steadfastly held firm since it entered the public domain.

Yet Steve's mother Kay puts forward a much more intriguing take on the sacking of Jimmy Winston.

She alludes to 'the business thing,' the fact that Winston was much older than his band mates and far less acquiescent. Winston questioned Arden about their money on a regular basis. In doing so, a power struggle started to take shape. Arden saw it coming straight away. He started suggesting to Marriott that maybe Winston wasn't right for the band.

It was a good time for the manager to make his move.

Fame had served to drug the band, given them its first rush. Suddenly, they were no longer nobodies. Girls screamed at them in the street, strangers recognised them, stared hard, made them feel uncomfortable. Marriott was disorientated, one step out of kilter with the rest of the world he once knew and he didn't like it, not at all.

'It was scary mate,' Marriott told the *NME* in 1984, about this period, 'Our nuts went and we all went a little mental.'

To cope with it, the teenagers in a trance, Marriott, Lane and Jones, huddled closer together. Winston, four years older, had no need for such protection. He was wiser, more sussed. That's why he was dangerous. That's why the knives were sharpened behind his back.

‡ ‡ ‡

For fourteen weeks, The Small Faces debut single stayed in the charts. Fourteen weeks! No-one had foreseen this level of success, no one except Don Arden who would have been absolutely furious had the single not charted. He had, after all, paid a significant amount of money to achieve that very aim.

'I knew that for certain sums any record I was associated with could be elevated to the charts,' he quite openly told author Johnny Rogan in his excellent study of British pop management, *Starmakers and Svengalis*.

'It got to be a habit. I paid out anything from £150 a week to £500 a week to people who manipulated the charts and who in turn shared the cash with people organising other charts so as to ensure they tallied... Neat little swindle, wasn't it?'

Arden itemised to Rogan the outlays involved. £5,500 to two individuals to buy contemporary records from the shops. £2,750 to chart fixers such as Tony Martin at the *NME* to tamper with the paper's authoritative chart and between five and six grand to gain extensive airplay on Radio Caroline.

'Of course,' Arden added, 'the Small Faces had no idea what went on.'

Didn't they?

In 1984, Marriott claimed to John Hellier that not only did they know about the hyping, they took part in the swindle themselves.

'Ronnie and I used to go in and order a dozen of our records at a time,' Marriott stated. 'Very suspect. They had promotional pictures and people used to look at us and say, "Hold on a minute." We had a list of record stores that Don Arden's office had supplied so we did that but only for about two days – we got tired of it. After it charted then the rest of the machinery went to work.'

Kind of reminds of you of the sort of thing Fagin and the Artful Dodger might have got up to had they landed in the '60s.

Part of the machinery Marriott refers to now required the setting up of a Small Faces fan club. Although a Mod band with serious intentions of bringing sacred R&B music into everyone's life, the Small Faces were also four good looking, sharply dressed guys with baby faces. Compared to their gritty, serious looking, slightly unwashed British contemporaries such as The Animals or Them, the Small

Faces looked clean and gorgeous and beautiful, the only R&B band of their day to do so. Their handsome look gave them a head start over all their rivals.

In such matters, the young girls, they understood. Just one look, that was all it took.

'We used to get a sackful of mail – sometimes a couple a day,' Fran Piller revealed. Fran was friendly with Jimmy Winston's parents. Her husband ran the betting shop next to their pub, the Ruskin Arms and the families got on well. Sensing their impending success, Derek, Jimmy's brother, had approached Fran about the possibility of her setting up a fan club for the group. Fran was happy to accept.

'It was so exciting to be involved with a band really going somewhere,' she said.

In fact, the band were not going somewhere, they were going everywhere! Between Thursday the 23rd September and Sunday the 26th they played eight shows, two apiece in Epping, Trowbridge, Brighton and London. On the 30th there's a second *Top of The Pops* appearance to film and then on the 3rd of October they return to the Mojo club in Sheffield for two sold out, ecstatic shows.

More good news. An audition tape they had submitted to the BBC, containing their versions of the R&B numbers 'Jump Back' and 'Think' plus 'Whatcha Gonna Do About It' has been given a thumbs up by a three man panel quite taken by 'the band's driving imaginative sound.'

The BBC will now accept the band for 'broadcasting generally.' The company had instigated the auditions as a way of filtering the thousands of groups now hammering on their doors demanding airplay.

In 1965, thousands of youngsters yearned to be pop stars. Innocent times. Today, they just want to be celebrities. Undignified times.

Two days after their show at the ever welcoming Mojo club, the band play High Wycombe and the following day made their way to the Pinewood Studios in Buckinghamshire to appear before the cameras. Don Arden has made some calls, got persuasive with some, angry with others and landed his boys a spot in a feature film. The band is impressed.

Excellent manager, Marriott says, excellent.

Unfortunately Marriott falls sick with laryngitis and so on the Thursday the band reconvene and film their part for another Cop and Pop film called *Dateline Diamonds*.

(It was the usual formula, a crime story set in the fab pop music world of teenagers where all comes good at the end. Marriott knew this shit off by heart now.)

For the movie, the band perform at the Top Rank in Watford and play a new song, 'I've Got Mine,' dressed in blue suits that they were forced to wear. The date is the 7th October, 1965.

'We wanted to be ourselves,' Marriott recalled, 'but they wouldn't have it and we wore the blue suits. Looked like policeman.'

Actually, they look pretty cool. Winston plays guitar rather than organ and throughout the performance, there is a kind of knowing look on Marriott's face as he takes the band through the song.

He looks like he knows that his ship has come in and he is going to savour every moment of his impending success...

(Unknown)

Chapter Eleven

Here Come The Nice

Steve Marriott was now living back at his mum's, back in Daines Close. It was a move prompted by several reasons, not least the need to have something solid and familiar to wake up to. Yet even here he could not escape fame's claws.

Girls had started gathering outside the flat, screaming his name. They were clever as well. Many of them acquired the flat's phone number.

'We had to go ex-directory in the end,' Kay the sister recalls. 'The phone never ever stopped. I loved it but we had a dog at the time, Steve's dog, and we got complaints because she'd be left on her own all day and she used to howl when the phone went.

And the phone never stopped.'

Mother Kay: 'He always said, "Never forget your roots, never." And he never did. He might send me and his dad up and take the mickey but he always wanted to be here.'

In their own way, Kay and Bill had now started accepting the winds of change that had blown into their lives, for they too started taking risks.

In late August 1965, they forgot Jaywick Sands and holidayed abroad in Ibiza, the fancy Dans. Commercial travel in Britain was now opening up to the working classes.

For Kay and Bill, a foreign trip was another sign of the family 'bettering themselves.'

On the beach in Ibiza, Bill and Kay heard a young kid singing 'Whatcha Gonna Do About It' and couldn't help themselves. That's our son they proudly told the youngster, that's our Steve, he wrote and sang that song.

On the flight home they opened up a national newspaper and discovered that 'Whatcha Gonna Do About It' had hit high in the charts. They gasped in pleasure.

'He always made our life exciting.'

He did. Even on a dull plane journey home.

‡ ‡ ‡

On Sunday October 10th, the band travelled to Manchester to play two shows at the Oasis club in Lloyd Street. Working the cloakroom was a young girl named Sue Oliver, ambitions to be a model. She loved horse riding (Marriott would actually purchase a horse, Petite Fisage through her father's connections but only kept it for a short while) and wore a ring that in later life would remind Steve's mother of Princess Diana. 'Blue and white, you know, blue and diamonds.'

Sue's family lived in Shaw, a town near Oldham and over the next eight months, Steve Marriott and Sue would fall in love, get engaged and then finish because Steve couldn't stand her mother's interference.

'Lovely girl,' Kay recalls, 'but the mother was there all the time. I often wonder what happened to her. Lovely girl. And then after that it was Eva, Swedish girl. She was lovely. We were upset when that broke up. She did his ironing and looked after him, beautiful girl.'

In Sixties pop, rule number one; never ever let your audience suss that the band do not exclusively belong to them. Within a second they will dump you for another group. It was Don Arden who took Marriott aside and made it absolutely clear that all his and the band's relationships remain top secret. Only The Beatles got away with breaking this law of pop.

On their return from Manchester, The Small Faces went into the studio to work on four songs they have been asked to supply for the film *Dateline Diamonds*.

One of the songs, 'I've Got Mine,' was selected as the follow up to 'Whatcha Gonna Do About It.' The other three tracks were 'It's Too Late,' 'Come On Children,' and 'Don't Stop What You're Doing.'

More gigs follow. The best one is at the Flamingo in Soho, the club that Georgie Fame made his own by recording his groundbreaking debut album there. Marriott knew the place back to front. When not working he was often to be found in a variety of Mod clubs – the night usually ending at The Flamingo's legendary all nighter session.

'Took pills and stayed up all night,' he told the *NME* in 1984. 'The Scene club until midnight, The Flamingo for the all-nighter. It was just a case of all me mates were Mods and I was a Mod. It was as simple as that.'

Like the majority of young working class kids, Marriott had been attracted to Modernism for many reasons. Colour, style, expression and individualism.

There also existed within Mod fashion a dandy element, one which liberated the young, allowed them to take all kinds of chances with their appearances.

Marriott is perhaps the prime example of this look. As time progressed, he stepped out of his dark mohair numbers and started wearing all kinds of colourful items; silk shirts, snazzy belts, straight leg trousers in all kinds of material – Tonik,

Prince of Wales, Mohair, and always amazing shoes. Like all pioneers, he encountered huge resistance at first.

'I liked the attitude,' he explained to Hellier. 'It was certainly a lot different than my mum's, that's as blatant as I can put it. I was starting to turn Mod when I was still living at home, trying to be an individual and having terrible rows with my dad for looking like a poof. But I liked the idea of being an individual. It felt secure yet you could say what you wanted.

'It's down to the individual as to what they want to wear within some set rules to do with the hair, the trousers length and the shoes. Mod is an individual expression but as soon as it becomes a mass expression its no longer individual and it's wasted.'

Which is precisely what happened.

In the year Mod expired on the beaches of Brighton, the Small Faces' audience was still heavily male. The band attracted them with their Mod image and their rough but adventurous musical style.

They used R&B as their marker but then added twists along the way – the use of feedback, the dropping in of pop style chords into certain songs, the occasional strange sound wrought from Winston's keyboards, and always Steve Marriott's powerful, beautiful voice, kept at the central focus of all their musical endeavours.

In these early months there was an aggression about the band, an East End aggression that, like the music of their counterparts The Who, mirrored the mood of the times. Street violence in the mid-60s was a tough reality. Young men beat each other bloody. They did it at clubs; they did it on the streets. They did it at football matches. They did it with knives and they did it with iron bars.

The Who had tapped into this violent maelstrom, this angry mood, and their audience became a prime target for the Small Faces.

Here's well known Who man, Irish Jack describing for the very first time, the night The Small Faces played The Who's stronghold, the Goldhawk club in Shepherd's Bush:

'It was sometime in winter 1965,' he reports. 'There was a special buzz in the air because they were a top twenty band but I can also recall a definite tension down on the dance floor because let's face it, the Small Faces were not a local band, not like The Who.

'We felt they had invaded our sacred turf coming to the Goldhawk and bringing with them their unmistakeable Cockney swagger all the way from the East End... It was alright to see the Small Faces playing up west in Soho where West London Mods mingled freely with East End mods but playing at the Goldhawk? Come off it.

'I'd never seen them before,' continues Jack, 'and they sounded to me like they were more evenly presented than The Who. I couldn't put my finger on it at first and then it occurred to me that it was their organist playing the Hammond, which filled out their surge of sound. It was very danceable, not at all the guttural guitar chords produced by The Who.

'What hit me was the sheer power of Marriott's voice. It was almost like if you closed your eyes for a second you'd think he was black. I pushed nearer the stage and I couldn't keep my eyes off him. The veins in his neck stood out like they were ready to pop.... I remember going into the toilets before the band went onstage. The usual clique were gathered there selling pills and there was that tell-tale ring of spittle around everyone's mouths.

'I wanted to score some blues and noticed there in the middle was the bleeding Artful Dodger himself, Steve Marriott. He was small, jumpy, bony, his hair like a creation parted in the middle. I thought, "Is this really him, is this the bloke everyone's talking about?"

'He moved over to the urinal and while I waited to use it, I stared into the back of his head at that wonderful hair. I noticed how thin his shoulders were, he was like some geezer who had mitched off school... I realised in a rush of excitement that this bloke was the genuine article, a true little Face.'

Consider some of Jack's statements. Watching Marriott sing, Jack sees the veins in Marriott's neck popping out. Kay the mum will say the same thing later on. The man pushed himself hard every night, got lost in music. His all or nothing performances would remain the central energy point of the Small Faces live.

Ten minutes before he is due on stage and where is Marriott? In the toilet chatting away with a potentially hostile audience, maybe scoring pills that make you shine for hours.

Obviously, the word was out and the word was favourable. Marriott had the respect of his Mod peers, his people. After all, he was the bloke everyone was talking about.

Final point. Isn't 'mitching off school' a wonderful phrase?

‡ ‡ ‡

All were agreed, manager and band together, Jimmy Winston was finished. Time to go. Thirty years later, after much mis-speculation that flourished in the absence of hard fact, Winston comes forward to put his side of things.

Kay had been right all along, it was a business thing. In pop, these things always are.

'It was the combination of a few things,' he revealed to John Hellier in the mid-90s.

'There's the notorious story concerning my brother and his van. He loved the band and he was keen. Like the rest of us he didn't have a lot of money but with the few hundred pounds that he did have he offered to buy a van and do the roadying for us. We were earning virtually nothing at the time and agreed to give him ten per cent. He was going to buy the van, insure it, tax it and do all the driving. Everybody agreed that was fine.'

Winston reveals how after every gig he would be told to collect the money. He was the tallest, most threatening of the group. On receipt of the cash, Winston says, he would automatically pay his brother first, then the band.

'The rest of the band got a bit grumpy about this,' he says. 'I don't know why. It was one of those incidents where I got stuck in the middle. I did get into conflict with Ronnie and Steve over this.'

Grudge number one. Now enter, Don Arden who certainly wasn't happy with the

10% deal.

'Don Arden saw it as 10% of his earnings and I think right from the start he was trying to do something about it.'

He certainly was. And he succeeded in turning the whole band against Winston.

On Sunday, October 31st, the band travelled to Stockport for two shows. Throughout the whole stay, Jimmy was deliberately ignored by his fellow band members.

The Small Faces froze Winston out. When not playing, the three of them spent time studying that week's music magazines. One of them was *Beat Instrumental* and on a page in the review section, they came across a picture of Ian McLagan, organist with the band, The Boz People – though, in fact, the caption was incorrect, the picture was actually of Boz, not McLagan at all.

Looks interesting, says Ronnie Lane, oblivious to the caption error. The band agree.

A discreet phone call is made. Arden is asked to contact McLagan. Arden rings back later on. Transpires, he's perfect. McLagan has just left The Boz People and he's willing to talk.

He's coming to the office tomorrow. You guys play the gig, come home, get some kip and then make your way over here.

And don't forget – make some money!

On returning to London, Arden called him into the office and delivered that which had been asked of him; he sacked Jimmy Winston. Did it nicely, though. Told him he was out but then suggested that Winston form a group, which, he, Don Arden, would then manage, and record. This Winston did. His final comment now.

'In retrospect I'd have been better off leaving Don Arden and going somewhere new.'

Which is precisely where Ian McLagan was heading, straight into the new.

Ian McLagan shows up at Don Arden's office bang on twelve o' clock. He settles down to wait. Five hours later he is still waiting.

Finally, he is allowed into Arden's presence. The manager apologises for the wait, says to him that what he is about to hear is for his ears and his ears alone. Okay?

Okay, probably wondering why you're here, here's why; congratulations, you are now a member of the Small Faces. For a month. If you prove to be suitable you will be asked to join the band. If not, you'll be shown the door. Alright? Alright.

Now come back to this office at six sharp. There are some people I want you to meet.

An hour later, in Don Arden's office, situated above the John Michaels clothes shop, Ian McLagan is introduced to three men who are and will remain an integral part of his life.

Steve Marriott, Ronnie Lane, Kenney Jones, meet Ian McLagan, born May 12th, 1945, in Hounslow Middlesex, educated there, ex-member of The Muleskinners and The Boz People, blues and R&B man, but above all the same height as you guys.

Mac later said of the meeting that it was like 'looking at a mirror of myself... We all looked alike.'

They went to a hotel and drank and did other things, but above all, they hit it off straight away, bonded like long lost brothers. Amazing. Like it was fated.

The next day down to Carnaby Street for a haircut and then they show Mac the best part of the job by going into every shop on Carnaby Street and buying up a ton of shirts, trousers and shoes, safe in the knowledge that they don't even have to pay for it. They can just put everything on account.

'It was still good down Carnaby Street then,' Marriott wistfully recalled to Hellier. 'I haven't been down there in years but it was still good then. Stuff like Granny Takes A Trip and all those stores ruined it for Carnaby Street because the good shops had to go into competition with them, start selling the kind of clothes they never sold before. It sort of ruined the purist shops.'

That night, there was a gig: Mac's first. At London's Lyceum venue, he is handed a Telecaster guitar and told to mime the guitar part from the band's new single, 'I've Got Mine,' for the benefit of Radio Luxembourg's new *Ready Steady Radio* show.

Before the show begins, the band has a visitor. Name of Jimmy Winston. Probably wants his stuff back. 'He came to the radio show where you had to mime,' Marriott said, 'and was asking why and he got very upset about it. I said, "Sorry mate, it's just not working out between us all and we've got a new kid and everything." I tried to be as honest about it as possible.'

A week later the new single, 'I've Got Mine' c/w 'It's Too Late,' is released. As far as Marriott is concerned this is the start of the journey.

Unlike 'Whatcha' the new tune is moody, built on musical tension, a tension the band only relieve with its explosive chorus. It's a Marriott and Lane song, the first proof of their talent.

Meanwhile, the gigs keep coming. Mac makes his debut at Swindon's Locarno Ballroom. Then it's Colchester, Cleethorpes, Bishop Stortford, Birmingham, Harlow, Llanelli, Morecambe, Rawtenstall, Guildford, Herne Bay, Great Yarmouth, Crawley, Bath, Leicester, Torquay, Plymouth, Sidcup, Romford, Peterborough, Stevenage, Chesterfield and finally Christmas Eve at the Wilton Hall in Bletchley.

Throughout this period, the band make two TV appearances to promote the single. First *Crackerjack* and then the real triumph, playing live on *Ready Steady Go* (Mac again on the Fender guitar, nerves jangling) and singer Wilson Pickett is also there.

The Christmas *NME* appears. The Small Faces have been voted sixth in the best new band category. Above them, stood only The Seekers, Walker Brothers, Yardbirds, The Who and The Fortunes.

But there is a problem, a sizeable one. 'I've Got Mine' has stiffed, failed to reach the charts. The news momentarily stops them in their tracks. What's the problem? Many answers. The song is too moody: not enough colour? Maybe not enough enough money has been put behind it?

Arden may have neglected to hype it reasoning that the band's high profile would be enough to see this single through. He was wrong and now knew he had to kill the growing idea that his boys were just one hit wonders.

To that end, he again went outside the band, this time to songwriters, Kenny

Lynch and Mort Shuman. Write me a hit, boys, he told these two professionals. They returned with a song entitled 'Sha La La La Lee.' The band heard it, didn't dig it but knew after the failure of their last single, they had no choice in the matter.

They would have to record it and record it as best they could.

'It was like the vacuum cleaner coming round your house with a bunch of songs,' Marriott said of Kenny Lynch and his pal, Mort Shuman.

'I admired Mort Shuman for the work he did with Elvis, I was totally knocked out that he performed it for us sitting down.'

But that was all. Marriott hated the finished product, especially Lynch's high falsetto voice on the chorus. Totally ruined what good there was in the first place. Worse, months later when the record was high in the charts, Long John Baldry, one of Marriott's heroes since he was fifteen, walks into the Scotch of St. James Club, sees his protégé and laughs. 'Look,' he sneers, 'it's Steve Marriott, soul singer.' Then in a ridiculous high pitched voice he sings, 'Sha La La La Lee.'

Marriott was mortified. He would carry the scar of that putdown for months and months. He would also temporarily lose a good friend over this wretched song.

'One day in 1966,' Manon Piercey recalls, 'Steve turned up on my doorstep in a smart suit and wanted to play me an advance copy of the new Small Faces single, 'Sha La La La Lee.' I told him I didn't like it very much and he got quite shirty and said, "Well what do you know about it?" He was furious. I told him I know what I like and that record is not you. We had a big argument and I didn't see him for ages after that. When we got together many years later he told me, "I didn't like it either but I didn't need you, who I trusted, to tell me the truth."'

A more subtle sign of the band's unease at this new poppier direction can be detected in the four hours it took them in the studio just to get the intro correct.

So what better time for Arden to step in and nix any thoughts of rebellion by bestowing upon them a magnificent gift. He had rented for the band a four bedroom house in Pimlico, all theirs, no expense. Arden would be looking after that side of things. They could move in when they liked. And by the way, there's a housekeeper, German lady name of Liesel who comes with the house and a chauffeur-driven limo put at your disposal.

Merry Christmas, all you Small Faces.

The band were ecstatic.

On Boxing Day of 1965, Steve Marriott and his Small Faces moved into 22, Westmoreland Terrace. It was a four storey house set in the run down area of Pimlico. In the basement was a kitchen where the band also put some of their equipment. On the ground floor were two smaller rooms, located on your right as you entered the house. Upstairs was a large sitting room. At the top of the house a bedroom and a bathroom which of course Stevie Marriott took straight away.

Kenney Jones opted to stay at home with his parents. He had to, his dad made him.

But Jones was relieved in a way. He knew exactly what was about to occur in those four walls and although he loved his band like no other, he was not about to place his sanity in any kind of danger, not even for them. He liked his eight hours kip, did our Ken.

The other three called him a poof, then accepted his decision with a knowing smile. They knew his reasons before he did.

Happy times, then, for the band. Not so, for others.

Kay Marriott for one was aghast at Arden's present and her son's taking of it. In a stroke, the manager had taken that which was most precious from under her wing and flown him to a far away part of town. Her son now rested under Arden's roof, not hers. She was livid.

'Out of our control,' she snaps, 'we didn't know what was going on, did we? He was still under age, in those days it was 21. I felt that terribly. Although he'd walked out a couple of times in temper, he came home. But this time, I thought, no this is arranged. This is management. I didn't like it.'

The hurt behind her admission – 'I felt that terribly' – is there for all to feel.

And her instincts were right. In 1965, Steve Marriott left home and did so for the very last time. He would only ever return for visits. He was out and about in the free world now.

1965, and for Kay Marriott, maybe not such a good year, after all.

Later on she did have one good thing to say about Don Arden. 'He said to us in the early days, and I agreed with him, he said, "At the moment Steve is trying to find out where he's at and he's copying everybody else. But once he finds it, he'll be that." And he was right. Very astute.'

But don't be fooled. To this day, Kay Marriott never leaves a sentence hanging in Arden's favour. 'I didn't like him, though. Crook, crook.'

The Small Faces entered 1966 as the toughest R&B band on the circuit. They had a handful of songs to their name, a couple of chart hits, had learnt how to improvise now, learnt how to keep the excitement flowing by jamming hard and fast.

It was exhilarating stuff. For many of the songs, Jones and Lane would set up a basic powerful rhythm, Marriott would then assault his guitar, hitting huge ringing power chords, or squeeze out angry feedback. Mac's organ would be primed to intrude at crucial points. On the top of this dark mix came Marriott's powerful voice, Mac and Lane adding to it with their chanted slightly haunting backing vocals.

The band were producing a music way ahead of their collective ages yet within a year, they would have changed this music beyond recognition and arrived at a sound partly inspired by creativity, partly by chemicals.

‡ ‡ ‡

1966 began with a New Year's Day show at the Wimbledon Palais. The next day they took off on their first European adventure: a six-day tour of Holland, Belgium and Germany. They go on the 5th, are back on the 11th.

On the 12th, they are in Bristol, the next night Worthing. Friday they are at the BBC, Saturday in Redhill, Monday in Kent. The days dissolve, the machine grinds on.

Friday January 14th, arrives. It is the release date of their third single, 'Sha La La La Lee' backed with 'Grow Your Own,' an instrumental that according to the *NME* took five minutes in the studio to compose.

No doubt, Arden made some 'arrangements,' to ensure the single's success in the charts and no doubt the band's hectic promotional schedule – gig, gig, TV, gig, gig, press – played its part. The single sailed to number three in the charts and stayed around, as singles did back then, for weeks and weeks.

Success regained, mission achieved, but this song and its follow up was to have a massive affect on the band's career.

Those two singles would bring them a whole new audience, one of young girls who would totally alienate their original audience. Through their behaviour, Steve Marriott would discover that fame was a bogus friend and perhaps one he should avoid at all costs…

‡ ‡ ‡

In mid-February 1966 The Small Faces enter the IBC studios in Portland Place to start recording their first album. As they do so, The Who's landmark single, 'My Generation' is slipping down the charts and Spencer Davis's 'Keep On Running' is in the ascendancy. Otis Redding is singing 'My Girl,' and Stevie Wonder has the monumental 'Uptight' hammering up the charts. Working with The Small Faces is a young Glyn Johns, he's engineering.

'Marriott had more energy and he was more blinkered,' Johns later recalled. 'He was determined to do what he wanted to do with the music. Booker T. may well have influenced him but he took that like a little terrier and hurled it around the room a few times. Ronnie was the same although they were very different characters. Marriott was a bolshy little bugger. I never really liked him very much. I got on all right with him but he was cocky. He was obviously very insecure and he had a huge ego but he couldn't have been the artist he was without it.'

They spent five days in the studio, Mike Leander producing. In that time, twelve songs were mixed and recorded, a feat beyond the reach of the musician today thanks to technology. Then it was back to the concert halls where slowly but surely the band's audience had started changing.

On Monday, March 7th, 300 Small Faces fans descended on the Ideal Home Exhibition in London's Olympia in the hope of seeing their heroes play.

They are victims of a bad rumour. The band were never booked to play in the first place. The disappointed fans start chanting: 'We Want The Small Faces.' A door is kicked, then another. Boys start jostling other boys, another door goes. The girls start screaming. The police are called. The crowd disperses.

We want the Small Faces. So did America.

Nine days after this mini-riot, the group are filmed playing two of their singles outside the Royal Albert Hall for American TV.

'Whatcha Gonna Do About It' is performed with disinterested ease although the band snap into life for 'Sha La La La Lee.' Marriott's shoes – white with crossover straps – Ronnie's Prince Of Wales check trousers and McLagan's dogtooth jacket provide the sartorial highlights.

At the end of the month, the film *Dateline Diamond* is released. Two weeks later, following their performance at the Streatham ice rink, Steve and Kenney are overwhelmed by eager fans. Marriott is knocked half unconscious, Kenney dislocates a shoulder. The gig attracts the biggest crowd ever seen at the venue. It's full-on stuff, from now on.

At a gig in Harlow ('Harlow, Harlow' Ronnie quips as an opening on stage greeting), the band's driver and two young girls, one of whom is Fan Club secretary Fran Piller, are left in the dressing room after the band go onstage.

'All of a sudden this horde of girls stormed in,' Fran recalled. 'Bill, their manager (actually their chauffeur, Bill Corbett, ex Beatle driver) was there and he just pushed us into this cupboard. It was terrible because when we finally came out they had rifled through everything. All the boy's bags, clothes, everything.'

At first, the band dug the new breed of audience. The power to excite these girls to wild extremes of public behaviour, was intoxicating. Had to be. The sex of it all was great, so was all the attention.

But the thrill wore off.

It became a real drag to be assaulted by girls, thrown around like a rag doll. They say they love me, Marriott mused, but all they do is try to rip me to bits. They're fucking crazy, the lot of them.

Steve Marriott: 'There weren't really any labels when we started doing what we were doing and getting screamed at. It was just called excitement, that was the label. So the louder you got screamed at the better you supposedly were. The Who got screamed at, The Stones got screamed at, Spencer Davis got screamed at – that was how you gauged how popular you were. There was no other way. Later on, they started to label everything and if you got screamed at you were a teenybopper group. We didn't want to be a teenybopper band.'

A teenybopper band. That was how the band was now being viewed. Thanks to their good looks and chart success, these tough R&B Mods had gained an image that they had never sought and would now find nigh on impossible to shake off. It explains why their talent was never fully recognised at the time. The press simply couldn't see the band for the screams.

As those screams got louder, so the band were forced to withdraw inwards. Wild nights in at 22, Westmoreland Terrace now became the norm. Raving in public was a near impossibility given the commotion they caused everywhere they went.

Hugh Janes was still in touch with Steve Marriott in 1966. He often popped round to see him in Pimlico.

'It was known as party central,' Janes recalls. 'Steve and the others loved the adulation they were getting by then. By 1966 they had the whole world at their feet and Westmoreland Terrace was one non-stop party. One room was set aside for a giant four track Scaletrix set. No chairs in there, just cushions and in the middle of the track was all the drugs, food and drink. They took their racing very seriously and during pit stops they'd take the opportunity to roll a joint or whatever.

'Steve and Kenney in particular would spend hours on end racing Scaletrix and eating baked beans. During the daytime there would always be dozens of girls outside and, of course, certain hand-picked ones were invited in. But to be honest, Steve was much more interested in Scalectrix and music. (In fact, Ronnie's brother Stan made the toy cars they used, the original Scalectrix models didn't go fast enough for the boy's liking.)

'None of the band at that time were doing heavy drugs, mainly dope and a few tablets. Other pop stars of the day such as Georgie Fame and Marianne Faithfull would be seen here regularly.'

So would the likes of Eric Burdon and Steve Winwood and many other singers whose vocal aims were that of all R&B artists – true salvation through the voice. Chaotic scenes occurred thanks to the copious amount of chemicals and alcohol available to all.

'I remember Marianne Faithfull screaming a lot,' Marriott said. 'Sometimes there'd be so many people there I would have to go in the toilet and write.'

Steve Marriott liked this location as a songwriting location. In fact, he would write one of his most popular tunes sitting on his aunt Sheila's toilet thinking about the neighbours who made it very clear they had no time for ravers. Stan Lane, Ronnie's brother, visited them regularly at Westmoreland Terrace. 'I used to go round in my lorry,' Stan remembers, 'see if they were alright. They never had any money so me and my wife at the time used to go round there weekends and do them something to eat. Georgie Fame used to come round and eat beans on toast.'

Pimlico was a gas but it also drew out a more reflective side to Marriott. Not every night was party night for there were other evenings, spent stoned after coming back from a gig, where he and the group would play the latest records, start talking deep. Some of those discussions now started showing up in the teen mags.

'What makes you tick? '*Rave* magazine writer Dawn James asked Marriott.

'Sometimes I think I know the answer,' Marriott replied, 'other times I'm not so sure. Who knows themselves? Do you?'

'No, but I try to,' James replied.

'Oh I try. I wouldn't be so happy if I didn't know something about myself. The laughing I do comes from inside. I have my roots, one of them is my own ideas on religion. It forms the basis of my way of life. I don't believe in a God sitting in a chair in the sky, but I have a faith.

'I believe we came from the earth and we go back to it when we die. The earth gives you and the earth takes you back and you become the bark of a tree or a cluster of grass. That accounts for the desire in people to get close to the earth. Haven't you felt such emotion from the scent of a flower that you wanted to crush it in your hand? Sometimes the smell of the country air makes me gasp because I just can't get enough of it. I think that is the body trying to get back to where it came from.'

And they say the drugs don't work.

Later on in the same interview, Steve stated, 'I believe in honesty because I'm too lazy to be dishonest. I think you are put on earth to live, and live you should. I really enjoy my life. I get a kick out of everything I do. Really, I'm very easily amused. I don't need to spend a lot to enjoy myself. And it takes a lot to make me really miserable.'

On May 11th, 1966, the band's debut album *Small Faces* was released. It sold extremely well. The band became the eleventh biggest selling artists of the year. The album is a raw R&B experience, its sound an amalgamation of Lane and Jones's tough rhythms, flavoured with Marriott's angry guitar and the organ work of Jimmy

Winston and Ian McLagan. It featured the band's singles to date except 'I've Got Mine,' and was augmented by the band's live set plus newer songs such as 'Don't Stop What You're Doing,' 'It's Too Late,' and 'Own Up.' Kenny Lynch donated two songs, 'Sorry She's Mine' and a co-write with Jerry Ragavoy called 'You Better Believe It.' The album was designed to reach and reflect the angry young Mods of the cities but its cover – the boys clean cut and smiling and youthful – went straight to the girl's hearts.

‡ ‡ ‡

Steve 4 Bridget, Ronnie 4 Marilyn, Mac 4 Maria, Kenney 4 Joy. That's how these four young London schoolgirls divided their affections for the band. The girls were Small Faces obsessed and determined to meet their idols. In 1966, the four of them marched into the offices of *Fab 208* magazine and asked where they could find the Small Faces. You're in luck the girl replied, we're doing a photo shoot with them on Carnaby Street right now.

The girls rushed down to the location but the band had just left. Dispirited, they returned to the *Fab 208* offices. There, a girl took pity on them. 'Look,' she said, 'I never told you this but 22 Westmoreland Place in Pimlico might be a good place for you to go…'

So it was that Marilyn, Bridget, Maria and Joy came to travel over to Pimlico during the day to stand outside the house, try and get a glimpse of their idols.

'We never wanted to bother them,' Marilyn says. 'We would stand outside and watch and if they came out they would wave to us but if we ever knocked on the door we had to have a reason for doing so. I remember I had some money once and I bought Ronnie a St Christopher medal because it was his birthday. That gave us a reason to knock on the door. But we didn't want to associate ourselves with the girls who stood out there and harassed them.'

The girls usually spent an hour or so in their lunchtime standing by. They also collected every article and cutting on the band. Because money was tight they would buy one copy of a magazine and then the other three would write the article into their scrapbooks.

'I think it was their characters,' Marilyn explains. 'The music as well hit the right note but their faces, the way they looked, it was Mod, the cockney thing, and they did seem very normal, you could identify with them.

'They were not that much older than us so you could think well one day he'll go out with me. There was something school boyish about them as well. It wasn't like The Who. There was never a sense with the Small Faces of the drugs, the alcohol, the smashing up the hotel rooms. I'm sure it went on in the background but it didn't come out into the open like it did with The Who.'

If he had heard that statement at the time, Don Arden would have bristled with pride.

Chapter Twelve

Shake

On Friday, May 6th, 'Hey Girl' c/w 'Almost Grown' went into the record shops. The following week it was in the charts, eventually peaking at number twelve. The song was a jaunty sing-along, the sound of compromise between band and management. Arden had told Steve and Ronnie that he would only consider their own material if they were catchy little numbers with mass appeal. 'Hey Girl' was just that song.

As with 'Grow Your Own,' the B-side to 'Sha La La La Lee,' the band placed a vibrant instrumental on the flip side to 'Hey Girl,' a signal to their Mod audience that they had not left them or their influences behind. 'Almost Grown' is distinguished by Ian McLagan's keyboard playing, its dramatic intro and the chant the band come in with halfway through, reminding the listener of the famous Lowell Fulsom song, 'Tramp,' covered by Otis Redding and many others.

A week later the band's debut album appeared and reached number three in the charts. It stayed around for weeks confirming the band's increasing popularity.

The album is short on melody and defined by its dense, wildstyle R&B music.

'Come On Children,' 'E Too D,' 'You Need Loving' and their cover of 'Shake' – these are the songs at the heart of the album, designed to reflect the band's musical roots.

Their musical structure, created from lengthy jams at the Ruskin, allows for many things; Marriott to show what a great singer he was, Kenney Jones to display a playing style he has rarely been called up since to replicate. The spirit of adventure within the band was reflected by their inventive use of feedback and dissonant noises.

There are poppier songs there – 'It's Too Late,' 'Sorry She's Mine,' 'One Night Stand' – and they serve to balance out the album. But it is the R&B aspect of their playing which satisfies the most.

Marriott knew that, as well.

He told the *New Musical Express*, 'We ourselves prefer our LP tracks. We never thought "Sha La La La Lee" would do so well and "Hey Girl" we thought would do well but not shoot up so fast.'

'I'm not saying that the singles we have had out are exactly what we want to do,' he told another reporter. 'But the album is. Anyone listening to the album will know it was exactly what we wanted to do at the time.'

Actually, Marriott would have done better to point out the mixes used for the French market. Released as an EP, the record carries the best recorded versions of 'Shake,' 'Come On Children,' 'Whatcha Gonna Do About It,' and 'E Too D.'

The instrumentation has more attack and to hear Marriott scream-shouting that he can't stop his brain running wild, going wild, can't stop it, is absolutely electric.

It was a natural talent, his voice. It had range and soul and emotion and no one but no one could figure out how he got it so powerful. Close your eyes, like Irish Jack did at the Goldhawk, and you will hear a voice that in no way whatsoever suggests that the owner is a five foot five Cockney geezer from Manor Park. No way.

But that's precisely what he was and in terms of talent he was the leader of the pack, a pioneer.

The art of white musicians convincingly singing R&B has since been termed 'blue eyed soul.' But Marriott was too powerful for that category, always has been. By using R&B as his guide, his base, he, along with his contemporaries – the ones who gathered at Westmoreland Terrace – were now making sturdy bridges, musically and otherwise.

After the success of their first album and the 'Hey Girl' single, an employee of Robert Stigwood's management company decided to contact the band, see where they stood as regards management.

Don Arden heard about the call, blew up into a massive rage. He contacted four well muscled friends, took a trip to Stigwood's London office where he barged into his office, picked up an ashtray and smashed it so hard upon the desk that the wood split into two.

He then lifted the impresario from his chair, dragged him onto a balcony and held him face down. Arden then asked his 'friends' out loud if he should drop the unfortunate man or not?

Drop him, came the reply. Stigwood went rigid with shock. Arden pulled him back into his office.

Don't ever interfere with any of my bands ever again, he told Stigwood before marching off. Within days the story had done the rounds of the music industry thus cementing Arden's tough man reputation.

'I don't believe this story about Stigwood getting in touch with us,' Mac states.

Excellent manager, said Stevie Marriott, excellent.

‡ ‡ ‡

Towards the end of May, The Small Faces played at the Top Rank Ballroom, Sunderland. *Rave* magazine asked Marriott to write about the gig and his report also appeared in *Beat Instrumental*. It begins with Marriott waking up early but leaving the house late.

'We stopped off once or twice on the route,' Marriott wrote, 'and of course when we went into transport cafes, we got the usual wise-cracks and whistles; but we're used to them by now. We finally arrived in Sunderland at about 6.20 p.m. so we went for a quick meal and then decided to go straight on to the booking. Trouble was, we didn't really know where it was. We looked round for someone to ask and stopped a couple of rocker types. They looked at us, then at each other, then turning back to us one of them said... well I can't really print what they said, but it was rather rude. "Charming," said Plonk, "but what can you expect from these Elvis Is God types. Finally a little old lady told us how to get there. Funny how we always seem to meet them."'

Marriott now describes the dressing room before a gig.

'This is always when the nerves start playing you up...we all show our nerves in a different way. Take Kenney for instance, he comes over all exuberant, he runs about punching people and playing on your head with his sticks. Plonk just laughs all the time, you can't shut him up, he keeps on laughing. Mac goes very, very quiet, won't say a word. Me? Well, I don't know, it's hard to tell what you're like yourself. All I know is that I get very panicky.'

The band are taken to the venue's revolving stage which they climb on to, waiting for the records to finish and the lights to come on.

'At last the records stayed off and the bloke at the side of the stage gave us the thumbs up,' he stated, 'and round we swung into a deafening wall of shouts and screams and hundreds of people clawing the stage.

We went straight into 'Ooh Poo Pa Doo' and I got that great feeling that everything was just fine. The amps were giving us a beautiful sound and I was really pleased with my guitar. After 'Ooh Poo' we went into 'You Need Love' (*sic*) and whoops – all of a sudden the whole crowd came screaming at us. We just ran over the back of the stage, amps were going down, wires tripped us up.'

The band retreat to the dressing room whilst the stage manager and his assistants run on stage and try and hold back the screaming hordes. Eventually, after order is restored, the audience is told to sit on the floor or the band will not re-appear.

'Surprisingly enough,' Marriott notes, 'they did what he said and we went back on stage. It was a scream seeing everyone on the floor but off we went again. We did a few more numbers and everyone seemed to be ok but when we got to 'Sha La La La Lee,' they all went mad, they got up and came after us again. We finished up pretty smartish and ran off.'

The group return to the dressing room and according to Marriott pat each other on the back and then swig down several cokes. Nice. The girls are kept back from the band and for that Marriott is grateful. He then relates how at one gig in Warrington he came off stage, entered the dressing room and saw a girl peeping through the adjoining toilet door. When the door was opened thirty girls fell out.

'I counted them.' Marriott said 'and I almost collapsed laughing.'

It was a typical scene from the concerts of that time. Band comes onstage, plays a song, the girls scream, the girls attack, chaos ensues, gig finishes, everyone home by ten.

In June, in East Kilbride, Scotland, Marriott would be knocked unconscious when fans invaded the stage. Later on, Mac and Ronnie had similar experiences. Yet there was an upturn to all this craziness. Success puts you in the driving seat.

In mid-May the band felt strong enough to turn down the popular *Thank Your Lucky Stars* show after being told they could only perform one song.

'We'd been opening everything,' Lane complained to the *NME*. 'They were beginning to call us the Small Openers. We had a number in the top ten at the time.'

They even argued for a week with the prestigious *Top Of The Pops* show after again being asked to be show openers.

Surprisingly, they win the fight and go on to triumphantly perform 'Hey Girl.'

‡ ‡ ‡

The album is still top three. More gigs, more mayhem.

On Friday, June 10th their hectic schedule claims a victim. Steve Marriott. At the *Ready Steady Go* studios the Small Faces began playing 'Hey Girl' for the cameras. Just as they are reaching the song's end, Marriott moves back from the microphone in obvious distress. Sensing an upset, the director tells the camera to pull away as the band stop playing.

Their frontman had collapsed, fainted.

Major fan Marilyn Einsor was watching the show at home on television. 'Oh I went into floods of tears when I saw Steve like that,' she reveals. 'I phoned Bridget straight away. I said, "Did you just see what's happened?" She said, "I can't talk to you I'm too upset".'

So was Vicki Wickham, the show's producer.

'I did not know that he was on whatever he was on,' she recalls, 'but he passed out in the studio. We were all concerned, thought he had flu or something and it was only then did someone say. "Oh you know, he's taken too much" whatever it was.'

Marriott was taken back to his Pimlico abode where he spent a couple of days recuperating. His actions had no affect as far as future appearances on the important *RSG* show went.

'I just remember him being a real sweetheart,' Wickham says. 'If we liked somebody we could book them whenever we wanted and the Small Faces were perfect for *Ready Steady Go*. They were a Mod group, they were cute, they had great music, they were right up our street.'

Marriott went back on the road.

There was Burnley, Sheffield, London, Purley, then onto Reykjavik in Iceland, back after two days, a quick BBC interview Saturday, off to Germany on Sunday, a week of gigs there and then back to England and up to Hull, back to London, onto the Isle of Man, then Maryport, Luton, Nottingham, Blackburn, London, Coventry, Plymouth and at the end of July, the Sixth National Jazz and Blues Festival held at Windsor racecourse.

'The first time I saw the Small Faces was at the jazz festival. Everybody in the business was talking about them,' says writer Chris Welch who would cover Marriott in *Melody Maker* for years to come.

'I first met Steve at *Top of the Pops* in 1966. He was just a ball of energy. I remember him being very raucous and very rude to a girl reporter from one of the music weeklies.

'Steve and Ronnie were mercilessly taking the piss out of her and she went off in a huff. If somebody upset him, he could be really nasty. He saw himself as the Small Faces spokesman and he was never very comfortable with the other guys doing interviews. In that way he was a total control freak.'

The Small Faces' press had been assigned to an agent named Tony Brainsby. He too had something of the Ardens about him. Welch recalls him making up all kinds of silly stories to get the band exposure.

'I remember him announcing that the Small Faces were going to appear in a film with Brigitte Bardot. Steve read this and got quite excited about the prospect until he realised it was just a publicity prank. He was really gutted.'

When that story faded, Brainsby then announced another film project, this time starring the band and the actress, Jayne Mansfield .

'I have never met Jayne Mansfield,' Ian McLagan said in a press release, 'but I'm looking forward to filming. It will be a new experience altogether.'

I'm sure it won't be.

‡ ‡ ‡

At Tony Brainsby's office worked a young secretary, name of Jenny Rylance. She was a London University student who was friends with the young designer, Ossie Clark. Jenny was an intriguing character. She was studying philosophy, she was gorgeous and she was dating a young London singer called Rod Stewart.

In Paul Gorman's book, *The Look*, she is described as 'the ultimate '60s rock chick.'

When Steve Marriott walked into Brainsby's office and saw her for the very first time, he flipped, despite his ongoing relationship with Sue Oliver.

'I liked him straight away,' Jenny reveals. 'He was very funny and we got on very well but that was all it was for quite a long time.'

That's not surprising. Time always moves differently after you meet the woman who will be your first wife.

What a summer and what a great time to live in London. Everywhere you look, all is bright; all is energy. New shops here, new club there, all fantastic.

That's of course if your daddy is rich, your wage packet full and you live on the King's Road or in London's West End.

Otherwise, much of London was not bright, was not inspiring. Notting Hill, Hoxton, Camden, if you had told their 1966 residents how desirable their property would become in the not so distant future, they would have laughed until they dropped.

In 1965, US magazine *Time* had dubbed the capital 'Swinging London' but that was only the young and the very well heeled they were describing, the elite. For a large family stuck on the top floor of a tower block in East Ham, the Sixties was a different game altogether. No room to swing a cat and mouths to feed, bills to pay and every morning waking up to another day on the sweat line.

'The Sixties are as much a state of mind as a chronological concept. And like all states of minds they are open to many interpretations,' writes Jonathan Green in his book, *All Dressed Up*.

For Steve Marriott the Sixties were 'marvellous.' That was the word he used to describe his time there when he spoke to the *NME* in 1984, 'marvellous.'

Well, he would say that, wouldn't he? He had escaped school, factory and office. He had made his life exciting for both himself and those close to him. He had pursued his yellow brick road and he hadn't tripped up yet.

The wider euphoria of the sixties reached a fever pitch in July 1966, when England beat West Germany to win the World Cup.

A month later, The Beatles released their groundbreaking album, *Revolver*. Again, new ideas, fresh, exciting.

But what really caught people, was that the record was the first to show off the effect of taking LSD. And in 1966, LSD was the drug everyone was talking about.

The ingredients for LSD had been accidentally discovered by one Dr. Hoffman. In the '50s, his discovery made its way to the CIA, the American secret service, of all people, who tested it on their own people to assess its potential value for warfare.

Enthusiasts such as Dr. Timothy Leary and writer Ken Kesey latched onto LSD in the early '60s. Their public support for the drug gave birth to the American hippie movement and switched the focus on youth away from Swinging London over to San Francisco. Now LSD was available in London. No wonder everyone was excited.

Pills and dope, that was the Small Faces at the time. But in 1966, they would be exposed to LSD and it would markedly alter their lives, their music and their direction.

The band had been introduced to the drug by the Beatles' manager, Brian Epstein. On May 11th, he and the Moody Blues drummer, Graeme Edge, turned up at the front door of the band's Pimlico residence. The boys had met Edge at the Decca studios in West Hampstead, got on well with him and invited him to an all night rave at Westmoreland Terrace. He brought along his friend, Brian Epstein, who had with him oranges spiked with LSD. These were soon offered around on their arrival.

'I didn't take the stuff,' Kenney Jones says, 'but the others did. The only time I took it was down at Portland Studios when Marriott spiked my drink.'

In his book, *All The Rage*, Mac recalls Ronnie Lane and he wandering out to sit by the Thames whilst Marriott stayed behind at the house and began packing his bags to go to Manchester and visit Sue Oliver at her parents. When they finally return to the house, their perceptions still all at sea, they go to Marriott's room, see how their leader is faring.

'He was not what I'd call a particularly balanced person,' Mac writes, 'and he was rarely relaxed, and in the same way that acid can lead you to the heights of illumination and wonder, it can also take you down to the depths of your darkest fears.'

Marriott was not enjoying himself.

To help him through the bad trip, Mac, Ronnie and friend Mick O'Sullivan escorted Marriott to Euston railway station where he caught the train to Manchester. The boys returned to Pimlico and fell asleep.

The next day, Marriott is back in the house. He had spent the previous day arguing with Sue's parents who demanded proof of his commitment for their daughter. In the midst of a brutal comedown, whilst still on acid, Steve Marriott finished the relationship for good.

'He only wanted to get laid, not married,' Mac notes.

Despite Marriott's bad time with the drug, LSD was quickly added to the weekly shopping list.

'We took acid very seriously,' Ronnie Lane announced in 1993. They certainly did. The drug changed their songs, their clothes, and their characters. By 1968, the bassist would be a devotee of the mystic, Meher Baba and endlessly ruminating on life and the universe. Marriott would soon complain that his friend was fast disappearing up his own cosmos.

Ronnie had forgotten the unwritten Small Faces rule about life; everything is or can be reduced to a joke. Even mystics from India who tell you don't worry, be happy.

‡ ‡ ‡

Around this time The Small Faces added a new song to their live set, 'Good Lovin'' by the Young Rascals.

'Good Lovin'' suited the Small Faces. It was built around a 'La Bamba'-type rhythm, enlivened by organ stabs and a suitably energetic vocal – strange they only played it once then.

But then Marriott was always more of a lover of records than a follower of groups. Music inspired him in a way people never could.

'I get lots of ideas for songs from noises on other records,' he told Dawn James of *Rave* in 1966.

'I listen to all kinds of music, and the things I conjure up in my mind's eye spur me on to write my own sounds about them. Music makes more music.'

Asked whether it mattered if groups were unable to reproduce their records on stage, he firmly stated, 'I think it would matter if the group were poor musicians and played dud chords and sang flat. But to have lots of interesting mechanical sounds on records that are part of the songwriter's theme, especially when the writer is a member of the group, doesn't matter at all. I call that progress. Records must be made more and more interesting and you can't allow yourself to be limited and not use the equipment and the gimmicks available.'

He didn't have to for 'All Or Nothing.'

It was their fifth single and to date, their best. According to Marriott it was created in the studio. He told Richard Green as much when he was interviewed by him in early September for *Record Mirror*. It's an interesting article. Green arrives at the Pimlico house where a line of girls are loyally keeping guard outside. Steve meets Green wearing nothing but shorts and a housecoat. In a separate room, Green can hear Plonk messing around on an amplified guitar. Marriott and Lane take the writer to a room upstairs, the girls briefly see them at the window, and scream. Marriott goes off, gets changed walks back into the room with Mac in tow.

Marriott then puts on a John Patton album and settles down to talk.

'It's great,' he says of 'All Or Nothing'. 'This is the first proper record we've done instead of all that Mickey Mouse stuff like 'Sha La La La Lee'.'

'We take writing far more seriously now than we used to,' he reveals of the single. 'I don't think there is anything the Small Faces could do to improve "All Or Nothing." With some of the other numbers we could have done a much better job if we could spend more time on them.'

Marriott adds that the group currently work in blocks of two-hour recording sessions and these time constraints are starting to bother them. In fact, if it wasn't for Arden visiting the studio, their new single may never have seen the light.

'When we were doing a session, Don [Arden] came in to watch us. Don gets the hump if he doesn't hear a hit. You can play him the melody but he can't hear the end product right away. We could see he was fed up.

'So I just played him an idea I had. The organ hadn't played it, the drum hadn't played it, the bass hadn't played it, but I'd thought about it so I let him hear it. He liked it so we re-wrote it on the spot and it turned out to be 'All Or Nothing.'

'We can't have a go at him.' Marriott continued, 'because he turned out to be right. The record has been accepted far more than any of the others.'

The pride in their single is obvious and justified.

For the first time they have managed to produce a record which meets everybody's criteria – commercial enough for Arden to sell, serious and inventive enough for the boys to feel proud about.

Furthermore, 'All Or Nothing' displays, apart from the usual Small Faces elements – Marriott and Lane's unquestionable talent for creating unique arrangements.

'All Or Nothing' begins with a loud drum roll, an idea maybe taken from The Young Rascals' song, 'Baby Let's Wait.' The song then hits a tricky guitar riff which cleverly acts as if it is actually winding the song down, not introducing it. The effect is disorientating until Marriott's vocal enters, soft, controlled.

Quickly, his voice and the music gather pace, both delighted to know that a powerful chorus awaits them. Later on, a touch of the band's humour when the backing vocals switch to a chanting style and then are suddenly disrupted by Marriott's voice and guitar. Heady stuff.

Marriott and Lane were a great, often sublime songwriting partnership (whatever the nature of the relationship) but their strength also lay in how they constructed their records, giving them an ever changing pattern which bestowed upon them a style of their own; no mean feat in an age dominated by song-writing talents whose work still reaches us to this day.

In all the interviews the band conducted around the single's August 5th release, the same mantra is to be heard. We must progress, we have to change, we're onto something now and new. Now and new, that was the '60s for you.

Kay Marriott: 'He wrote "All Or Nothing" for Sue Oliver.'

Jenny Rylance: 'He told me that he wrote "All Or Nothing" as a result of my split with Rod Stewart.'

And both stories are absolutely true.

‡ ‡ ‡

Work to do. Promotion. August 5th, a Friday, 'All Or Nothing' is released. That same day, another *Ready Steady Go* show to perform on.

The next day, the Imperial Ballroom in Nelson. Then its Sunday in Blackpool, Monday in Bath, Tuesday in Southport. Wednesday, more TV. On August 10th the band record a TV special at the Granada Studios in Manchester. They play nine songs, the singles to date plus various album tracks. They also perform a version of Little Richard's 'Bamalama Bamaloo'. Unfortunately, Granada decide not to transmit the show.

The group journey back to London for their eighth appearance on *Top Of The Pops* and on the Friday night they start a package tour alongside minor talents, such as Crispian St. Peters

The tour begins at the Lewisham Odeon. The *NME* reported: 'Certainly one of the most exciting stage acts I have ever seen was presented by the Small Faces... Steve Marriott is the vocal and focal point of the group and as such never stops his full power delivery. When he's not actually bawling into the mike, he cavorts about the stage with his guitar, often spinning backwards on one leg like an out of control top....Hundreds of girls chanting, "We Want Steve," held buses up for twenty minutes after the show when they blocked the road behind the theatre.'

The next week another writer for the very same paper calls the show 'one of the most mediocre packages I have seen for a long time.'

The press, eh?

Kay Marriott attended a lot of the gigs. Had done so from the early days and was witness to the screams and the turmoil.

'I used to get quite concerned when the bouncers were being unkind to the girls, because they were rough, you know,' she remembers.

'At some stage you'd see the girls being passed over their heads while they were performing, all these bodies going over. But a lot of them hadn't passed out. Really it was just a way to get onstage. They just used to go hysterical. Stand up, scream. It was quite frightening, really. And all I could see was the veins on Steve's neck standing out because he was giving it his all and you couldn't hear him because of the screaming.'

The serious pop collector, Dave Fowell tells me, 'I was speaking to a female assistant in our local Spa shop who is 51-years-old and still has a perfect c.1966 mod/Small Faces hairstyle. She saw them live, said that they wore matching white shirts, were very good, very loud, as were the screaming girls and that the crush downstairs was so great that she and her friends had to escape upstairs to the balcony! A female friend of my wife, who at the time was living in Knutsford,

Cheshire, also saw them in Manchester with her girlfriends and only remembers the screaming and crying girls.'

John Perry who would later play guitar for The Only Ones, recalls seeing them at this time. 'Even in a medium size provincial town like Bristol there was always a minimum three gigs a week in the mid-60s. The Who, The Creation, The Byrds, Downliners Sect, Graham Bond, Cream, Steampacket, Mayall, all were regularly playing the Locarno, Top Rank or the Corn Exchange. The thing people always seem to leave out when they talk about the Small Faces onstage is how funny they were, a bit like the Pistols when Glen was still in the band. They put a lot of energy into the show – and Marriott sung like a dream in those days before he developed that overdone "Humble Pie voice" – but they put just as much energy into trying to crack each other up. I saw Marriott and Lane reduced to hopeless giggling; it was only the volume that allowed them to ride it out. Their onstage patter was VERY funny. Dry. Spare. A matter of little knees-ups, sly glances…corner of the eye stuff that I, as a kid trying to form groups and interested in how members interacted, watched real closely. They were a riot. Later on, the Faces did a similar routine but it was more self-conscious. Great band.'

Ann Moody, now appeared on the scene, following the band all over the country with friend Rita Fox. Her devotion to the band resulted in the band nicknaming her 'Mad Ann'. They liked her chutzpah, the strokes she pulled to get into sold out gigs and then get backstage. They liked her so much they started leaving her free tickets at every gig she came to. They even visited her in hospital after she accidentally put her hand through a glass window.

'The gigs were just like The Beatles, it really was,' she confirms. 'You couldn't hear them on stage at all for all the screaming. They could have been playing anything.'

At the end of every gig, a road crew member would come out, ignore all the waiting lovelies and give her and Rita the first backstage passes.

'A lot of the girl fans couldn't believe it,' she says. 'They were all done up beautifully and looked just like models from a fashion magazine. They were amazed that ordinary fans like myself and Rita were shown favour by the band. A lot of girls tried just about every trick in the book to reach the dressing room but very few were successful. They loved all the female attention at first, especially Steve, but it soon became a nuisance.

'Steve was a bit of a Jack the Lad but he was lovely with the fans and always looked after them with autographs and the like. He was difficult to get close to, though. We were both the same birth signs, Aquarius, and we would fight and argue quite a lot. Nothing too serious just differences of opinions on things like music. He could also be very moody at times and I recall back then arguments with Ronnie.'

Arguments with Ronnie, they were kind of inevitable really. Marriott was strongheaded, stubborn, knew where he wanted to go and always relied on his instincts, it is what gave his music a unique flavour.

Ronnie sometimes disagreed with his views and said so as well. And that's when the Marriott mouth would snap open and attack.

Keith Altham: 'Steve was the boiler room of the Small Faces. He did all the hard work and although the Marriott-Lane partnership was a clever one, it was never anywhere near 50-50. It was Steve who supplied the backbone to all the hits. When he took new songs into the studio the rest of the band would chip in with ideas – even Mac and Kenney but Steve always had the last word. Even Ronnie's ideas would have to be bloody good for Steve to accept them.'

Yet, fights aside, the band's personal camaraderie remained unaltered. Richard Green, again for *Record Mirror*, visited them backstage after a gig.

'Steve and Plonk,' he told his readers, 'frequently use the word "nice" in their conversation. "This sounds nice, she's nice" and so on. It seems to be an in word with them.'

It was. The band used it as drug slang. Good pill. Nice. Good smoke. Nice.

'If that's what they're like in public,' Green mused, 'goodness knows what goes on in the seclusion of their house where they all live together. Must be a sort of Mod's satirical palace.'

The Mod's satirical palace, what a fetching phrase! Mind you, Green was not above taking liberties with the English language himself. Describing his entrance into a dressing room covered in marijuana smoke, he reports, 'There was a very strong smell of asthma cure in their dressing room when I went in and through the fumes I could just about make out the figure of Steve Marriott sitting on the back of a chair playing a guitar...'

‡ ‡ ‡

'All Or Nothing', it was an appropriate title for their first number one. And thanks to a change in the way the charts were compiled, the week they hit the top spot they shared it with none other than The Beatles and their flimsy single 'Yellow Submarine.' On *Top of The Pops* that week, the show blended two pictures of the bands together.

That year, Steve would add the Lennon and McCartney song 'Paperback Writer' to the band's live set list and come out in defence of John Lennon after his statement that 'The Beatles were bigger than Jesus,' blew up in his face.

'He was right to think it,' Steve told *Melody Maker*, 'but not to say it. Religion is dying in this country...'

To celebrate their chart topper, the band were taken to Carnaby Street and photographed sipping champagne. Mods and Moet, surely, no picture could be more appropriate.

‡ ‡ ‡

Fame. It was his now. He was the centre of attention, every day, and that was good, felt great. But somehow it didn't because Fame didn't make him feel how he thought he would feel when he lay awake in Manor Park all those years ago and imagined himself famous.

Steve Marriott was starting to realise that Fame has many many faces and you have to be very careful which one you choose to wear. Or which chooses you. Fame was also hard work. On Thursday August 18th, the band tape a version of 'All Or Nothing' for *Top Of The Pops* and then dash up to Glasgow for two shows. After the gig, fans catch the band outside the hotel. Mac ends up in a police station for his own protection, Lane is rushed to hospital. It was his turn to be knocked unconscious by the hysterical fans. Friday, Newcastle, Saturday Liverpool, over to Blackpool for Sunday, two shows in Manchester Monday, two in Cardiff on Tuesday, two in Exeter on Wednesday, Southampton the next night before back to London for another *Ready Steady Go*.

Lincolnshire on Saturday, Blackpool on Sunday, Hersham on Monday, radio on Tuesday, TV on Thursday, Northwich on Saturday, Blackpool on Sunday, two shows in Manchester on Monday, over to Cardiff for Tuesday, dash to Exeter for Wednesday night, final night of the tour in Southampton on Thursday. There he would meet a young promoter, name of Laurie O'Leary who eleven years later would become his personal manager.

'Steve Marriott appears at the soundcheck,' O'Leary recalls, 'and from this little guy came the loudest voice I'd ever heard. It was so loud I asked him if he could keep it down a little and he replied, "How the fucking hell I can I keep it down? I gotta hear myself sing."

'The gig was jam-packed, absolute chaos, a superb evening. We all made a lot of money. This young kid with the larynx like you've never heard in your life before made an enormous impact on me. The others in the group were good but it was this boy that done it for me.

'His language though...we didn't like swearing in the place but there was young Stevie breaking every rule in the book. He managed to swear often and loudly but nobody would take any notice or exception to it. It was almost like being down at Millwall.'

‡ ‡ ‡

The short tempers created by their work schedule are reflected in the press.

To *Rave* magazine, Marriott finally lets loose.

'Doing TV can be a real drag. If you're not prepared for it, it can be depressing, especially when you have to hang around doing nothing. Glamour in TV? It doesn't exist.

'You get in about 11 a.m. then wait around for your call – maybe for hours. Then you rehearse for about an hour, over and over again, the actual broadcast is over before you know it.

'We were playing Leeds one night and we had to record a Simon Dee backing track in London. We flew down to London, recorded the track and were then driven back to Glasgow for the night's performance.

'When you're travelling round all the time, you just lose all resistance, and you just crack up. If you can go on some kind of sporting kick then you'll be all right.

You don't get any time to sleep, except in the car, and that's quite hard enough... Long tours are also killers. You've got the same thing every day, routine and all that, plus the fact that you're travelling. It can get on top of you.'

‡ ‡ ‡

In the September 10th *Melody Maker*, proof of the wonders of LSD as Marriott enthuses about the band's plans to use glasses of water as rhythmic instruments for their next album, a device they discovered whilst waiting at Manchester Airport. 'We've got a whole lot of confused ideas that have got to be sorted out and put into their slots and boxes,' the band leader stated. His sergeant in arms was right behind him.

'We've gotta do something different now,' Ronnie Lane was telling *Record Mirror* at the same time.

'We'd get left behind if we kept on with the same thing all the time.'

Everybody else was feeling the same way, determined to put out singles that radiated quality, ambition, newness.

That autumn alone there was 'Sunny Afternoon' by The Kinks, the achingly beautiful, King and Goffin song 'Goin' Back' performed by Dusty Springfield, Phil Spector's last studio gamble, the titanic sound of Tina Turner on 'River Deep, Mountain High,' and there backing them up, Brian Wilson's 'God Only Knows,' one of the greatest love songs ever committed to vinyl and at the time, maybe the most revolutionary piece of music to be spilling out onto sunny London streets. In the middle of all this, the mercurial, Bob Dylan ordered that 'Everybody must get stoned,' and it seemed like the whole of London town was taking his advice.

That new music, those new drugs, no wonder Steve Marriott now began talking about getting more time in the studio and spending far less time onstage.

'What we really want to do,' he told *Melody Maker*, 'is hire a studio and work in it night and day until everything is exactly how we wanted it.'

He had had enough of seeing his musical ambitions unrealised. 'All Or Nothing' had brought that frustration to the surface.

Arden was not amused by his boys' artistic intentions. In fact, they made him very edgy. Work all day on a song? In a studio? You off your rockers?

All Arden required was the band to keep coming up with chart songs which they could then take on the road and play to their loyal and devouring fans. Records and gigs, money, money, money.

Arden believed the new drugs made the boys lazy, slowed them down. LSD didn't propel you out into the night air, brimming with confidence. It stopped you in your tracks and then opened up another universe for you to experience. At least those French Smith Kline pills the band swallowed gave them energy, allowed Arden to work them that much harder. LSD merely gave them silly ideas about recording.

Arden knew he had to get to grips with the band's drug use. How to do it, though? If he ordered one of his employees to guard them full time, say Mad John, it would be four against one and they would run rings around him. Who could he turn to?

He got his answer the day he got a phone call from the band's parents requesting an interview to talk about money.

Arden saw his chance. Of course, why didn't he think of it before? If he couldn't get them off the drugs, then he knew some parents who could.

‡ ‡ ‡

In one of the John Stephens shops in Carnaby Street, 1966, on sale, Steve Marriott wigs priced three pounds, nineteen shillings and sixpence.

'They never seemed to have much cash but they always had new clothes,' Fran Piller, their fan club girl recalls. 'They always had new clothes for the concerts.'

Keith Altham: 'Steve was a natural clothes horse, unusual for a guy of his height. Back in 1966, Steve was really up for the male modelling lark. It paid a good fee and got your face on the front cover.

'There would be a really cool pic of Steve and down the page it would say things like, Shoes From Ravel, £19.00, Trousers From Lord John, and so on. Although it was good fun the problem was it didn't help Steve's desire later on to be taken seriously.'

That year, the band would proudly announce that they had spent some £12,000 on clothes alone. In 1966, that was a fortune and one of the reasons why Marriott's friend Hugh Janes, loved visiting him. He too got to share in the bonanza.

'Steve and the others would buy enormous amounts of clothes in Carnaby Street,' he recalled. 'If they liked a particular shirt he'd buy one in every colour that it came in, same for jackets, jumpers, etc. After wearing something just once he'd throw them on a pile in his bedroom and invite me to help myself. I've had literally dozens of shirts and some nice leather jackets from Steve in that way.

'Ronnie was also very free with his clothes but not Kenney and Mac. They were more careful with their belongings. Steve never kept specific items of clothing for stage wear. He would go on stage in whatever he was wearing at the time. Obviously he would change after a gig as invariably his clothes would be soaking with sweat.'

That's of course if he got to finish the show.

‡ ‡ ‡

On that very same Carnaby Street, four sets of parents belonging to the band walk past the Marriott wigs and the stripey jumpers and the patterned shoes and the flashing neon lights, wincing at the loud pop music blaring out and they exit left from Planet Teenage and enter the office door numbered 52-55 Carnaby Street.

They go and sit down in front of Don Arden and they say, 'Where's our boys' money? Two shows a night, album in the charts, singles in the charts and they're still on twenty quid a week.'

And Don Arden looks at them all innocently and he says, 'Money? Gone, they've spent it all on drugs.'

And in that one moment every misgiving Kay Marriott ever had about Don Arden was unforgettably crystalised; she had been right all along, the man was a wrong'un.

'I said to him, "You took them away from home. This is what you wanted."

Steve's quote to Dawn James about being too lazy to be dishonest now bears fruit. Marriott never hid his use of marijuana from his parents. Instead, he admitted to it and then argued with them over the matter.

'When Steve first spoke about it,' his mum remembers, 'I was absolutely horrified and terribly upset. He said to me, "Don't be frightened; there's books and things. Read about it and you'll realise that smoking cigarettes and things like that are far more addictive." At the time it was frightening. We had never dealt with it or heard about it. So that was worrying.'

Therefore, when Arden made his move, he hadn't counted on the Marriott's foreknowledge of the subject.

Bill Marriott: 'Steve had already come clean with us some time before and said he was smoking joints. We didn't like it but he said it was a social thing. He doesn't smoke them all the time but he goes to a party and they pass it round, so it's a social thing. Of course, the other parents didn't know and they were really shocked. The way Arden put it, they were on drugs. Not that they are smoking a joint which is very different. I said to Arden, "That's alright we know." And that shocked him then.'

One up to the Marriotts. At least Kay and Bill had that satisfaction. What made it funnier was Ronnie Lane's later comment on the matter.

'Well my old man smoked a bit of hashish himself so he wasn't too worried either.'

Still for the band's manager to play such a trick behind his boys' back was unforgiveable.

Don Arden's grip on the Small Faces had just been considerably loosened.

Chapter Thirteen

Talk To You

With Britain under their control, the Small Faces now fixed their gaze on America; began dreaming about conquering it. Arden kept making promises about the group touring there but all his statements on the subject never bore fruition.

Instead, they stayed rotting on the news pages of the music press.

Ian McLagan believes that Arden never had any desire for the band to visit the USA in the first place.

The brusque manager's hectic schedule would prevent him accompanying the band for such a long period of time and Arden always got scared when his bands were out of his sight. Producer Glyn Johns, believes their failure to tour the States was their biggest mistake.

'That was the key,' he said in 1994. 'If they had gone to America they would have absolutely cleaned up. When English bands went to America in the Sixties and made it, immediately their standing in Britain was tripled. That never happened with the Small Faces.'

Outside the UK, Germany was the band's biggest market. At the end of September they would make their German TV debut by performing four songs, Marriott resplendent in a magnificent silk shirt with great collars. They would also find favour in Sweden, embarking on a nine-day tour of the country at the start of October.

Before they departed, Steve Marriott went to Arden's office and gave him a demo tape of new material to reassure him that the band were still on the case as far as recording went.

Recently, both Arden and Decca had been putting pressure on them to quickly follow up their recent number one, both parties anxious that the momentum built up by the group did not falter.

Marriott's delivery of a demo tape was the band's way of assuring everyone that everything was in hand. No need to worry.

‡ ‡ ‡

On the day The Small Faces began recording a new song – provisionally entitled 'Mystery' but subsequently changed to 'Have You Ever Seen Me?' – Don Arden was interviewed at the IBC studios at 35, Portland Place for a BBC documentary entitled, *The Managers*.

As the band ran through the song, Arden told viewers that 'if I've ever exploited anybody it's for their own benefit. If they don't want to be exploited there's no point to it.'

Sporting a shirt and tie and resembling a burly bank manager, the contrast between Arden and the programme's other main interviewee, Andrew Loog Oldham, manager of the Rolling Stones and head of Immediate Records, is striking.

'I take something,' the polo necked, sunglassed and pop visionary Oldham revealed, 'and put it into a shape. Anything that has some kind of image to it, I get involved in.'

No one, least of all Oldham, could have known that inadvertently he was talking about the Small Faces .

Saturday, October 15th, and the start of another package tour featuring The Hollies, Paul Jones, the brothers Paul and Barry Ryan, The Nashville Teens and Peter, Paul and Mary. Great, thought Marriott, enough bleeding Pauls to last you a lifetime.

The first gig is at Aldershot. When the band discover they are not the headline act, they simply turn around and go back to London. They don't rejoin the tour until the Tuesday when matters are settled in their favour.

Six days later, on the 21st, the band are placed third best band in the *Melody Maker's* Readers Poll. The Stones and Beatles are in front; makes sense.

In *Record Mirror*, better news. They're at number two, just behind the Beatles in front of The Stones. Next year, chaps, next year.

The roll call of towns played becomes a blur to them, but history for us. Cardiff, Taunton, Wolverhampton, Peterborough, Hull, Ipswich, Northampton, Cambridge, Lincoln, Chester, Coventry, Wigan, Manchester, Leeds, and all the time Arden is shooting off at the mouth to the press about his plans for the boys; two week Christmas show at London's Hammersmith Odeon! Big USA stars to support! Huge tour of the States in February! New single out soon! Film with what's her name? Brigitte, Jayne, Diana Dors…

The boys trudge on with the tour which mercifully ends in Newcastle. They have a final rave up after the gig, (nice), and a bit of a kip, (nice), and then it's all into the Roller for the Monday morning trip down the A1 and don't forget your passport for Pimlico.

At lunchtime, with London still a dream away, Steve Marriott asks that the car radio is switched on. His former girlfriend, Adrienne Posta is being interviewed on the BBC and he wants to hear what she has got to say for herself.

Towards the end of the interview, the interviewer, Barry Aldis, unexpectedly mentions Marriott. Steve shuts up everyone in the car, leans forward to catch what is being said. Countryside speeds past his window.

'By the way Adrienne,' Aldis announces in his best BBC voice, 'the Small Faces have a new single out this Friday, entitled 'My Mind's Eye.'

Aldis then plays the song from the demo tape Marriott left at Arden's office prior to the tour's commencement. Neither manager or record company had told the band about the record's release.

Aghast, the band immediately order their driver to take them straightaway to 52-55 Carnaby Street. Fuck going home.

They want a talk with their manager, Mr. Don Arden. The meeting doesn't go well. Afterwards, the band agree they no longer want Arden involved.

The *Melody Maker*: 'A mystery developed this week over the future handling of the Small Faces. Rumours of changes in their management and agency…'

In the beginning the pop group were shiny and smiley and dumb and their job was to go onstage and sell, sell, sell. Their music was written by professional outsiders, their career guided by managers or other interested parties. The band had no say in anything.

Not any more.

Not after The Beatles. They changed the rules. They were the first to write their own songs, the first to ditch soul sapping tours and the first to spend their working hours solely in the studio.

After that, the man was right: the artists had taken over the asylum.

The Small Faces were desperate to be cast in a similar light. They wanted credit for their skill and talent as well as money to sustain their lifestyle.

A manager not sensitive to the changes occurring in both music and the world at large was a manager still stuck in the past, one liable to hold them back forever. Arden had completed his job. He had bought them success, turned their dreams into reality and Marriott for one would always be grateful.

Even after it transpired that Arden owed the group a whopping £12,000, Marriott was still keenly defending him.

'Without Don Arden there would not have been a Small Faces,' he insisted back in 1984. 'I think he managed us very well, money regardless. Fuck money – money only gets in the way but what he did was that he put us over very well and opened a lot of doors.

'It's all very well to scream "rip off" and be bitter and belligerent – ain't no good to ya. Without those people you'd never get anywhere,' he stated.

Marriott the realist.

As for Arden, how did he feel about the band's decision to drop him? And why did he let his most profitable act walk away so easily? After all, this is a man who had hung rival managers out of windows when they'd made approaches to his boys.

The suspicion is that he felt they simply were not up to the job. He had begged them for a great follow up to their number one and what had he got in return? A demo tape. Not good enough. The Beatles wouldn't have done that. They would have had three songs ready and waiting the day after they went to number one.

This lot were too lazy, took too many drugs. Arden had heard the new music they were producing and no doubt about it, the band had gone soft on him. Songs about dreaming and green circles and wooden hills and suchlike. Not one number one amongst them. Best to cash in now while the going was still good.

Arden liked his boys. They were funny little herberts but in terms of staying power, of talent? Forget about it. Marriott obviously had something about him but he was uncontrollable, had to go his way whatever the cost. Too dangerous, too time consuming. The others? Do me a favour.

Business is business. There's plenty more out there. He saw them through to the end, though.

On November 11th, out came the single 'My Mind's Eye' c/w 'I Can't Dance With You.' The record went to number four in the charts and very nice, too. For the fans the record certainly didn't sound like a demo. It sounded fine, a touch psychedelic on the lyrics with a catchy little riff to see it through.

On the B-side, just to show that the group still retained their tough edge, came 'I Can't Dance With You,' a spectacular workout in which the highlight is the mix of Marriott's tough vocals with Jones's powerful drum-work. The production here is certainly not of a demo standard, not by a long chalk. This is tough, swaggering music, not tentative or restrained.

According to some, the A-side was a direct lift from an unlikely source; the Christmas song, 'Gloria In Excelsis.'

Melody Maker asked Marriott directly about the similarity in an interview to promote the record.

His reply?

'It's great, fabulous…Someone said somewhere that the bloke who wrote the song would be turning in his grave if he heard 'My Mind's Eye' – but I'm sure he'd be leaping about. I'll certainly be chuffed if someone revives one of our songs in a couple of hundred years. (English church hymns were a constant source of 'inspiration' for the band.)

A few paragraphs later he calls the single 'very pretty but it's very near boredom.'

Had The Small Faces changed as people *Melody Maker* now wondered? Course they had, Marriott stated, but not too drastically. He admitted that when he started out, he absolutely loved live work. Now, he just wanted to stay in the studio.

'I would have a bed there if I could,' he stated.

By Christmas, the word was out. Arden and the band were no longer in love. For a while, confusion reigned. On December 7th the band had been booked to appear on the children's show *Crackerjack*, hosted by Leslie Crowther.

Either no one told the band or they simply couldn't be bothered to show up. That afternoon, the BBC rang Arden. The band had not arrived at the studio yet. At this point, Arden didn't care one way or another. He simply told the caller he didn't know where the band was and then blanked all the BBC's subsequent and very desperate phone calls.

The band meanwhile spent the day recording at the Olympic studios in Barnes whilst on TV Leslie Crowther performed 'My Mind's Eye' on the piano for his audience of kiddiewinks.

The very next day Marriott told the BBC that they had a new manager, Harold Davison. The relationship did not survive the holiday season.

'We didn't get out of the contract with Don Arden, it was sold to Harold Davison who then sold it in turn to Andrew Oldham,' a Marriott tinged with bitterness recalled. 'We were sold – that's what we felt like, pounds of flesh. Like a cattle market.'

On December 15th, The Small Faces headlined a charity concert to raise money for the victims of the recent disaster in Aberfan, South Wales, where 144 people, 116 of them children, were killed when a tip of coal waste slid onto the village. The tragedy dominated the news.

No doubt, it was this gig that Marriott was referring to when he told Hellier how his relationship with Chrissie Shrimpton, sister to Jean, a key model of the time, started.

'I'd seen her a lot in the office at Immediate,' he recalled. 'She was like Andrew's secretary for a while, doing odd bits and bobs at reception. I'd also seen her at Adrienne Posta's flat and I always thought she was beautiful. We did a gig that New Year's Eve, maybe at the Albert Hall and she was there but I didn't know it. I went back to my home and Greg Phillips brought her around and she flung herself at me – it was great! It was terrific. I don't know what she was on, but go ahead.'

New girlfriend, new manager, new direction, new career, new ambitions and soon a new home for the New Year.

1967. The year of the new.

Big Ben sounded the chimes and the world listened, caught its breath and then started up again, as if from scratch.

Chapter Fourteen

Patterns

It was a dove-grey Mohair suit with nipped waist and covered buttons. There was an inverted pleat placed at the back of the jacket and the draped trousers had slanted pockets as well as a paisley lining. It was a thing of rare and true beauty and it belonged to a precocious teenager called Andrew Loog Oldham. He had awoken one day and decided to wear this suit instead of his school uniform. Predictably, he ran into trouble.

'I don't know why you bother, you only wore it for a day,' his teacher scolded him as he changed back into his uniform.

And the Mohair boy looked at his teacher and he said to himself with a smile, 'Yeah, but what a day.'

And that, in essence, was Mod.

‡ ‡ ‡

In 1965, the British recording industry did not understand pop music. For those that ran the show, pop music was a bright tricky little creature whose ways remained a mystery. It was only the young who understood and thus it was only the young who could make it work.

Andrew Loog Oldham was young, also brazen and fearless and very sharp. He was, in author Johnny Rogan's words, Britain's 'first teenage tycoon.'

One of Oldham's favourite films was *The Sweet Smell Of Success*, starring Burt Lancaster as a powerful newspaper columnist and Tony Curtis as a conniving PR man. In both their characters, Oldham saw himself.

By the time he was eighteen he had already lived double the life of his peers. He had worked with two of the decade's greatest lights – Mary Quant and Pete Meaden – and handled press for another, The Beatles.

He wanted to be a pop star but had had enough self-awareness to realise he would never attain his musical ambitions. Nondescript guys in glasses rarely make it into teenage beds or bedroom walls.

Instead, Oldham blazed his own trail, became the star behind the stars. He found a group, the Rolling Stones, took them over, persuaded John and Paul to write them a hit, then insisted that Mick and Keith now write their own music.

He indulged his Phil Spector fantasies by producing the resulting music and then used the media brilliantly to sell the group as the dark alternative to the sweet Beatles, the guys who had given them a hit in the first place.

'Anything that has some form of image,' he told the TV cameras and therefore the nation, 'I get involved in. I'm a terrible user and a thief.' Andrew Loog Oldham understood the potential of the media. He dreamt up the headline 'Would You Let Your Daughter Marry A Rolling Stone?' and would place ads in the music weeklies extolling the virtues of songs he adored but had no business connection to. The Mamas and the Papas and The Righteous Brothers were just two groups that gained from his enthusiastic benevolence.

In August 1965, again following his hero Spector's example, he launched his own record company, Britain's first major independent label. He called it Immediate, a very '60s word.

The company operated on the classic good-cop-bad-cop principle. Oldham was the good cop, the man with the ideas, the creative soul who could mingle and sympathise with disgruntled musicians.

The bad cop was none other than Tony Calder, the man who had asked to manage Steve Marriott in 1963 and did so with The Moments in 1964. Calder, who had learnt his trade at Decca and so knew the enemy well, was assigned to look after the finances.

Both men wanted the same thing, to establish a company that rivalled the success of the American music publishers, Neven and Kirshner who operated out of the now legendary Brill Building in New York.

'They had Carole King and Gerry Goffin, Mann and Weill, Phil Spector and Neil Sedaka,' Calder says. 'They would say to the writers, write a song that is between that song and that song. It was absolutely on the button pop music and that was what we wanted. We wanted a music room where people could come and sit down and write with each other.'

In all their offices, a room containing a piano and a revox amp was always maintained. Many would write there, including Steve Marriott.

Oldham and Calder's initial business strategy was simple. The company licensed American hits for the UK. At first, the policy worked well. Their first release, The McCoys' 'Hang On Sloopy' went to number one in August

The next two singles came from the group Fifth Avenue and an intriguing vocalist named Nico. Neither charted, however.

Oldham now developed a separate strategy, persuading Mick Jagger and Keith Richards to write and produce songs for his artists. The duo dutifully began work with new signing, Chris Farlowe, who had a hit with their 'Out of Time'. It would take a year for the idea to really pay off when the band Twice As Nice took the Jagger-Richards song 'Sittin' On A Fence' into the charts, but a year is a long time to wait. By the end of 1966, the company was not in great shape. Great ideas, little chart action. It was at this time that in his office at 63-69 New Oxford Street, Tony Calder took a call from the agent Tito Burns. The company had moved from their original Ivor Court offices some months previously.

Burns came straight to the point. Did Calder want to buy the Small Faces? Arden wanted them off his hands. They were going cheap. Calder said No, they're going off the boil. Plus, I don't want to work with Don Arden. Not that Calder didn't admire Arden's methods. He just didn't want to find himself subject to them.

Burns persisted. With Arden no longer their manager, Immediate could even fulfil that role. Would he at least see Arden? Calder agreed to meet and within ten minutes, Don Arden was sitting in his office. To his surprise, Calder claims, he discovered that the band were not actually signed to Decca but to Arden's company, Contemporary Records. That made life a whole lot easier. Calder told Arden he would ring Oldham who was recuperating from his excesses in a nursing home in the country.

'I said to Andrew, "I don't want to say anything but they have no direct contract with Decca". He said, "That means we can put them on Immediate." I said, "Yeah and the price is twenty-five thousand".'

Calder goes back to Arden. He needs the band's signed agreement to the sale. 'Not a problem,' Arden replied laughing, 'That lot will sign anything to get away from me.'

Arden then added an extra proviso; he wanted the money in cash and in a brown paper bag.

'I remember sending the contracts girl to the house in Pimlico to sign the paper,' Calder recalled, 'and she came back and said, "There's your piece of paper and never ask me to deal with that band again." I said, "Why not?" She said, "I went to the house and there was marijuana smoke everywhere. I go to the upstairs bedroom, knock on the door and the first thing that Steve Marriott says to me is, "Do you fancy a shag?"'

Phase two of the band's career had just kicked off.

‡ ‡ ‡

Tony Calder says that Immediate gave the band the best deal of their career to date. For the UK, they were given ten per cent of monies earnt from record sales, five per cent for those sold abroad. Andrew Loog Oldham assumed all managerial duties although he was in no way the band's first choice.

'Me and Ronnie did a bit of teamwork on the shopping for a new manager,' Marriott revealed to Hellier. 'We flitted around to a few different things. We were with Robert Wace but that didn't work out because a band like us needed a lot of attention and they couldn't give it to us. We also saw Chris Blackwell at Island but he pointed out that he wouldn't have the time to give us. Andrew said he could and did.'

It was a fortuitous time for all concerned parties. Here was a band desperate to compete with their contemporaries, to win respect for their creativity. Here was a company amenable to realising that vision.

To do so required a huge scaling down of their concert commitments and much more time spent in the studio. For Loog Oldham and Calder that scenario was perfect.

'See,' Marriott explained, 'since Oldham had a record company, he didn't have to work hard as a manager because we were in the studio, we were on his label and under his management. So it suited his purposes much better to have us turning out records he just had to market rather than manage us on the road and have to worry about all that kind of shit.

'As for us, we loved the opportunity to use all the facilities of the studio.'

Last word goes to the ex-journalist turned PR man, Keith Altham. 'Andrew did care,' he states, 'and he was an enthusiast. See, Don Arden was just like a puppet master. He pulled the strings and the artists danced to his tune. If he got it wrong, he got it totally wrong.'

'Basically, he was a strong-arm man and he used that reputation, sometimes to good effect and sometimes to extremely bad effect. His artists were just a means to make money for him. He certainly didn't care about them at all. Andrew could relate to what his artists were doing and for a while the Small Faces loved the freedom he gave them in the studio. Unfortunately, after a while Andrew just lost the plot, probably one too many substances and Immediate just went down the pan. It is of my opinion that Andrew did care and meant well. After all he was a very good manager for the Stones but by the time he took on the Small Faces he was a truly fucked up guy.'

‡ ‡ ‡

The year 1967 begins with the group entering the Olympic recording studios in Barnes for four straight days. On the 6th there is a kind of homecoming gig at the Upper Cut in Forest Gate and then it's back again into the studio on the 7th until the gig at Purley on the 11th. The band make a hectic dash home to catch new guitar sensation Jimi Hendrix perform at the Bag 'O' Nails club.

Hendrix remained a fan of the band, could see the cleverness and liked the unexpected touches within their music. More recording follows, then gigs at Chelmsford, High Wycombe, Stevenage, Hull and Stockport.

Meanwhile, the first fruit of the liaison between band and record company is made apparent when Immediate issue singer Chris Farlowe's version of the Marriott-Lane song 'My Way Of Giving' on January 27th. (Rod Stewart would later cover the song.) The record was produced by Mick Jagger and featured Steve and Ronnie on vocals and guitars. Marriott was a huge fan of Farlowe's strong voice.

PP Arnold, a fellow Immediate artist Marriott had befriended recalls that, 'Steve loved his American soul roots but I remember vividly the day he first heard Chris Farlowe. He completely flipped and thought he was the greatest thing England had ever produced. There were even plans afoot [for Steve and Chris] to do an album together. During 1967, Chris Farlowe was Steve's favourite singer in the whole wide world.'

Marriott was also a great fan of Arnold's voice as well as her other attributes. In 1967, they would start a relationship which would enable him to write one of his greatest ever love songs.

With the popularity of LSD, the switch of focus to the hippie lifestyle of San Fransisco and the birth of the well heeled Chelsea set who now said they too wanted to come out and play, the working class Mod look of '66 gave way to the hippie look of '67. The brilliance of Steve Marriott was to take these two opposing fashions and blend them together.

Yes, his hair grew long but never in a scruffy or unruly manner. Yes, he wore flares but velvet crushed ones with frilly shirts and waistcoats. He also wrapped colourful scarves around three button down Grandad vests.

No other band of the time looked like his group. The Beatles had opted for an Edwardian hippie style – round glasses and uniform jackets, moustaches – The Stones had gone for a wasted image that would eventually define the term 'outlaw chic,' The Who remained the same, as did The Kinks.

The Small Faces, however, pioneered and developed a new Mod look, still strong today, and one in parallel with their musical ideals. The shape those ambitions took were hinted at when *Melody Maker*'s Nick Jones attended a December Small Faces recording session.

In the article, Jones meets the band at their Pimlico house. Outside, the occasional screams of young girls huddled by the front door can be heard. In the kitchen, Jones noted, 'tape recorders, miles of tape all over the place, guitars, speakers and the old piano in a corner. Onto a tape recorder whirled a rough backing track – just drums, bass, piano and guitar.' The song in question was 'Green Circles,' a mini psychedelic masterpiece written by Marriott and destined to become one of the jewels in the Small Faces canon.

At eleven, the team depart for the studios, carrying bottles of Napoleon Brandy, 'guitar cases and other oddments of mystery and imagination.' As they walk into the studio, Jones quotes Marriott as saying, 'I love this place.' The band commence recording. When they take a break, Marriott sits next to Jones and tells him 'Our outlook is one of happiness and well being and this must come through with your music. We are living and we want our music to live as well.'

‡ ‡ ‡

With Arden gone, so too the Pimlico abode.

'When they moved out of Westmoreland Terrace they left everything there,' Stan Lane recalls. 'I've never seen so many shoes in my life.'

Steve would now find trouble settling anywhere in London. His habit of listening to music at extremely high levels any time, day or night, would see him ejected from flats all over town.

His rowdy reputation soon spread amongst letting agents. In the end he was forced to use an alias, Fred Smith, when applying for property.

His inability to please his neighbours was picked up by the *Daily Sketch*. They reported that the pop star had been asked to move house three times within a month. 'Some people apparently had complained to the agents about noise late at night,' he told the *Sketch* reporter, 'but nobody said anything to me about it.'

Maybe that was because he couldn't hear them.

‡ ‡ ‡

In late January, a reminder of the risks involved. On Saturday the 28th the band played two shows at the Gilderdrome in Boston, Lincolnshire. Nearing the end of the set, Marriott broke a guitar string. He bent down to fix it and a host of objects thrown from the crowd sailed above him.

One was a heavy glass ashtray which hit Kenney Jones full on the head. The drummer fell to the ground: blood everywhere. Marriott shouted, 'That was a fucking nice thing to do,' and the band walked off stage. Jones received six stitches. 'There were a dozen boys who started jeering when Steve broke his string,' Jones told the press, 'they must have been jealous of us.' Actually, they were hard mods, displeased by what they perceived as the band's lame R&B renditions.

In February, more gigs, then recording at Olympic followed by a welcome mid-month holiday. Despite Jones's injury, the band had much to look forward to, a feeling bolstered by their healthy standing in the recent music press polls. In *Disc and Music Echo* they scooped Best Single for 'All Or Nothing' came fifth in the best album category whilst Marriott himself was voted eighth top singer, third best dressed boy, third Mr Valentine and sixth Top Boy Singer.

In the *NME* a similar pattern was repeated, whilst on the 24th of January they were made winners of Radio Luxembourg's 'Battle of the Bands' competition. Record wise, however, the band remained in a state of limbo. Such were their contractual obligations with Decca, Immediate had agreed to produce and then licence the records back to them until everything was resolved. The first offering would be their seventh single, 'I Can't Make It' c/w 'Just Passing.'

It came out two weeks after Marriott and his girlfriend, Chrissie Shrimpton were arrested and taken to the Gerald Road police station in Belgravia. The taxi they were travelling in was stopped by plain clothes policemen. While they were detained in custody, their flats were raided by other police officers. Marriott's abode yielded nothing, Shrimpton's some pills prescribed by her doctor. Shrimpton's take on the matter was probably nearest the truth. The police had recognised Steve and thinking that he was probably carrying, pounced on him.

Marriott meanwhile quickly put out a press statement. Part of it read, 'I have never taken drugs in my life. There is nothing to this at all. My conscience is clear.'

No further comment.

‡ ‡ ‡

On Thursday, March 9th, Decca Records issued 'I Can't Make It' c/w 'Just

Passing.'

The band refused to promote the single but were stunned when the BBC banned the song from their airwaves. The title was 'too suggestive,' they announced.

Today, their action seems absolutely archaic but in 1967, there was a real fight taking place between the forces of conservatism who worried loudly about the onset of the permissive society and those who wanted to see British society freed from all constraints. Caught in the middle of this battle, the BBC sometimes acted very inappropriately.

'I know how you're feeling,' sings Marriott on 'I Can't Make It,' a great example of pop/soul, 'I felt that way too / But don't get hung up because it's healing / And I'm going to help you through it all... I can make it if you can.'

The subject was left up to the listener. You decide. What is not in doubt is that 'I Can't Make It' yielded from Marriott one of his most sensual vocal performances to date (check his little yeahs! halfway through) and that was what the man from the BBC was running scared from, not the words but the sound of the words. By the time of the ban, the band were on tour, undertaking another lengthy package tour, co-headlining with the American singer-songwriter, Roy Orbison, supported by Paul and Barry Ryan, Sonny Childe and the T.N.T, the Robb Storme Group, Candyman and the Settlers and guitarist Jeff Beck, although Beck left the tour after the first show citing sabotage as a reason. He might have had a point. The *NME* review stated that the guitarist, 'looked unhappy and sounded diabolical.'

Marriott hated the tour, hated it. A cock up from start to finish, he complained. Every night, the band looked out at the audience, Mods, on one side, the middle aged Orbison fans ('the beehived barnet brigade,') on the other. However well the band played, the gigs never really took off. To liven things up, at one show the band secretly tuned Roy Orbison's guitar to a much higher key.

When showtime came, Orbison walked onstage, picked up the instrument, strummed it once, realised what had happened and without missing a beat, sang the opening song perfectly.

'Didn't miss a note,' Marriott admiringly recalled. 'Then he looked at us all standing in the wings waiting for the fuck up and he called us cunts.'

'Untrue,' Mac says. 'It was his backing band who tuned his guitar up a tone, and it happened on the last night. Roy said something like "You bastards," not "cunt".'

On the day 'I Can't Make It' entered the charts, where it would reach number twenty-six, the band pulled away from the tour to play a gig in Hull's Skyline Ballroom with The Jimi Hendrix Experience. Naturally, Marriott adored Hendrix.

He told reporter, Pat Saville, 'In this business you often wonder if anything new and exciting will happen and then from nowhere someone like Jimi appears. He's fantastic and when I saw him I stood and cheered.'

Five days later, the band rise early to meet film director, Peter Whitehead at Cumberland Terrace, near London's Regents Park to film a promo for their new hit single's B-side, 'Just Passing.' (For what reason remains a mystery. The song is barely a minute long and is but the B-side. Later on, their song 'Get Yourself Together' would be dubbed onto this footage) .

The film featured Marriott being chased down the street by the band who are dressed as policeman. The band catch up with Marriott and there is a mock fight, some of it filmed in slow motion.

In light of his recent scrape with the law the press quickly picked up on the reference points but Marriott angrily refuted their suggestions of the group attacking the police. 'Even though I came out of it clear (the arrest with Chrissie Shrimpton who he had now stopped seeing) other people painted me black,' he lied. 'It was a drag. But then we had an idea to do something to make people laugh at the whole thing for what it really was. So we shot this tele-film. We wouldn't want to make the police look stupid…'

Three days later Steve Marriott went down with gastroenteritis. The arm of the law is indeed long.

'Just Passing' was very short, full of whimsical words, the odd laugh, careful little chord changes and as a nod to its inspiration, a car horn nicked from the Beach Boys' 'You Still Believe In Me,' issued on their groundbreaking concept album, *Pet Sounds,* a timeless work which along with *Revolver* by the Beatles and *Blonde on Blonde*, by Dylan had provided the soundtrack for 1966.

The song was a snatch of the dream to come. The band were changing fast. Their growing confidence as songwriters, their desire to experiment, and their new found studio freedom, had taken the band away from the dense sound of their R&B roots and into a new pastoral period. Apart from The Beach Boys, black music had acted as a springboard for all of the above to explore their own creativity. Dylan sang the blues, The Beatles sang Motown.

The Small Faces's ability to replicate the sound of the R&B records they loved so much, had been enough to satisfy them. Not anymore.

Pop music in the mid-60s was at its most fertile, regularly throwing up new sounds, new styles, new techniques which would then be the talk of the town until the next little explosion came along. The word 'progressive' was heard a lot. Every song, every single had to be a progression from the last.

Move forward. Progress. Your ability to do so defined your talent, your standing amongst your peers. For the Small Faces to be accepted into this world, they would have to find the same levels of ingenuity and inspiration as their contemporaries. It was as simple as that.

Otherwise, they really would be just passing.

‡ ‡ ‡

Steve Marriott was living in Baker Street now, beneath the flat of Cilla Black, of all people. The woman that Brian Epstein believed he could turn into the 'Edith Piaf of pop,' but who would end up presenting *Blind Date* instead, had quickly made known her distaste for her new neighbour. 'You'd think she would understand,' Marriott stated to a journalist, 'but she has been complaining the most. I'm sorry I make so much noise but I am only having fun. The guy who owns the place came to see me and said, "No noise after midnight," and I'm paying £40 a week. It's a joke.'

Marriott was speaking on a day he had been persuaded to hold a press conference at his flat. One of the writers present, the *Melody Maker* man noted a stereo in the hallways blasting out a 'spirited bossa nova.' Later, Marriott jigged around to Steve Cropper and some Bar Kays music.'

In his interview, Marriott explained that the last single had not done so well because of the BBC ban. It didn't help either that at the time the band had been managerless and there had been no one to promote the record on the radio. As for the idea that the title had been 'too sexy for consumption,' he stated, 'You've got to have a disgusting mind to think like that.'

On his brush with the law, Marriott was unequivocal in his summing up. 'They busted me just because I'm a name. As far as I'm concerned there should be a distinction between hash and pot and hard drugs. If you read any dictionary they are not even classified as drugs. Pills are a bad scene and so are hard drugs. The only thing against hash and pot is that people can say they are a stepping stone to hard drugs but that's only because the public are under the impression it's all the same thing. Why don't the newspapers wake up and give the people the facts?'

With The Beatles and their manager having admitted to taking LSD, with the ongoing saga in the press concerning the private habits of The Stones, Marriott's public defence of marijuana use was the first sign of his attempt to join ranks with his contemporaries. Yet such was the huge media fuss generated by The Beatles and The Stones, his voice got lost in the commotion.

He retaliated by writing and issuing two singles that year which would be laden with drug references. Both of them would be hits and one of them you can still hear on TV thirty-two years later, a song that is regularly called upon by advertisers when selling the Sixties back to us.

‡ ‡ ‡

The name of the band caught their attention – The Little People. It was a deliberate nod to the Small Faces and came from the band's drummer, Jerry Shirley. He had first seen the Small Faces on *Ready Steady Go* playing 'Whatcha Gonna Do About it,' and Kenney Jones's playing in particular had gripped him.

'I became a psuedo-Kenney,' Shirley would later tell Hellier. 'I did just about everything I could to be like him.'

Shirley travelled to a lot of their gigs and made contact with his heroes. He was eventually rewarded with a support slot for his band at a Small Faces show at the Wolsey Hall in Cheshunt.

'After the gig,' Shirley recalls, 'Steve actually asked me if I would be their stand in drummer for Kenney in the event of Kenney being sick or unavailable. It was probably just friendly chat on Steve's behalf but of course it made me feel ten feet tall.'

The pair became good friends. Shirley would often visit Marriott at his new flat in William Mews, Knightsbridge and Marriott reciprocated by offering his band a new song he and Ronnie had written called 'Tell Me Have You Ever Seen Me.'

For Shirley it was a dream come true, Marriott and Lane taking his band into the studio to produce the song along with a vibrant instrumental entitled 'Madame

Garcia.'

At the session, according to Shirley, Marriott was far keener on the job at hand than his co-writer.

'Ronnie was always a bit distant,' Shirley recalled, 'I think he had some resentment about us coming in and recording one of their songs. Ronnie was at the recording session but he left halfway through.'

Immediate Records agreed to release 'Tell Me' as a single but they wanted The Little People to change their name. Marriott suggested The Nice – the band's phrase for good gear. Loog Oldham turned the name down immediately, said it was rubbish and instead christened the band The Apostolic Intervention.

Three days later he announced that he has signed PP Arnold's backing band and given them a name. He called them The Nice.

Despite being a fine 45, 'Tell Me Have You Ever Seen Me' c/w 'Madame Garcia' did not propel the Apostolic Intervention into chartland but it did solidify Marriott's relationship with Shirley, creating a friendship that would last for many years.

Chapter Fifteen

Happy Boys Happy

Fran Piller had gone now. She had made the mistake of asking Don Arden for money to cover the fan club's expenses. Arden's reply was succinct. Fuck off. One of the last things Marriott gave her was a toy rifle for her son, Edward, bought from Hamleys. Pauline Corcoran now took over and began issuing fan club letters. In issue seven, she railed against the BBC for banning 'I Can't Make It,' and she also drew up a list of honorary fans of the band.

They included, Sonny and Cher, The Hollies, Paul and Barry Ryan, The Move, The Amen Corner, the Walker Brothers, The Nashville Teens, David Garrick, Lulu and Jimi Hendrix.

The news she didn't mention was that plans to send and sell the group to America were alive again. According to music press reports the band were considering an invitation to appear at the Monterey Jazz and Pop Festival in June.

They never made it and that was a real shame. That year, soul man Otis Redding appeared before a mainly white hippie crowd and he tore the place up, his music and passion crossing all boundaries. The band had already witnessed Otis's potency as a live act when on March 17th of that year, they attended the Stax Volt revue at the Hammersmith Odeon and also witnessed their all time heroes, Booker T and the MG's in action.

'I was in heaven,' Ian McLagan recalled, summing up their night.

At the time, Soul was experiencing one of its greatest ever phases. That year, 1967, Aretha Franklin issued her feminist anthem 'Respect' ('Goddamn it,' said Otis when he heard her version of his greatest composition, 'that woman has gone and stolen my song,') whilst James Brown, Dyke and the Blazers, Lee Dorsey,

Allen Toussaint, The Meters and Lowell Fulsom were busy edging and shaping the music we now know as funk.

Sly and the Family Stone's amazing potpourri of music and creed and colour and clothes was starting to gather pace in San Francisco, Holland Dozier and Holland were getting itchy feet at Motown and were about to launch their own Invictus label, whilst a young producer named Norman Whitfield was readying himself to take The Temptations out of their sharkskin suits and into flowery shirts and bell bottom trousers, ushering psychedelia into Motown's second great phase.

Many of these great strides forward were never afforded their rightful dues in these artists' homeland, mainly due to America's segregated radio system. Marriott himself held forthright views on the American penchant for categorising music.

'You know what happened to us in America?' he asked Keith Altham, then with the *NME*. 'They released 'All Or Nothing,' 'Sha La La La Lee,' 'Whatcha Gonna Do About It,' and decided we were a R&B group. So we got restricted airplay on the coloured radio stations. I mean R&B – own up! We're more a Walt Disney sound.'

A Walt Disney sound. Marriott was never one to take credit where it didn't exist. He always championed the original source rather than the cover version. He always heard music not personalities.

'Records are what he liked,' Tony Calder informs us, 'records. He didn't like bands as such, he just heard records he liked. He would come into the office raving about a record and then about a week later he would play us a new song of his and I would say, that sounds like that record you were playing last week. "No, it doesn't," he would shout back, end of conversation. But it did.'

Keith Altham recalls hearing, 'mainly James Brown and Rufus Thomas records,' in the Pimlico house as well as Marriott raving about The Lovin' Spoonful's music, 'and perhaps, quite surprisingly, The Association. He was very switched on to new things happening. You always felt like you were getting the latest news with Steve. He was always looking for change.'

Chris Welch vividly recalls Marriott's enthusiasm for the debut album from Blood Sweat and Tears, released in 1967:

'Somebody had sent him their first US album and for a time it never came off his turntable,' he recalled. 'A little later on it was the same thing with The Band's *Music From Big Pink* album. He was always listening to new stuff, especially American.'

Yet it would be years before Steve Marriott would finally get to walk upon the soil that had brought forth so much of the music that he loved.

And by that time he was a completely different man to the one who led the Small Faces.

‡ ‡ ‡

The process that took the band away from the concert stage and into the studio was a gradual one. Although 1967 saw the band spend more time recording, they also fulfilled some live engagements. End of March, start of April, saw them finishing off their package tour. On the 10th of April, they flew to Italy for one day's promotional work then moved on to Scandinavia.

They returned and on the 16th entered the studios for a week. During that time, the band took a day out to appear on the hugely popular *Morecambe and Wise* show where they played 'I Can't Make It' and 'All Or Nothing.'

Marriott looked fantastic. He wore white shoes, black trousers, a big button down collar and a Paisley style jacket. Six months later the show was transmitted on national TV. At the end of the month they departed for a week long tour of Holland. On May 7th, they again played the prestigious *NME* Poll Winners Concert at Wembley Arena along with Dusty Springfield, their old friend Georgie Fame, Lulu, Jeff Beck, The Move, Geno Washington, Paul Jones, Cat Stevens, The Troggs, the Beach Boys and Steve Winwood. A mouth-watering list of artists whom the band headlined over, finishing the show, according to the NME, 'in fantastic style.'

A week later, another reminder of the risks that are ever present.

The band agreed to make a personal appearance at a charity football match at the Odsal Stadium, Bradford. The event was a sell out. The band arrived and were met by the organisers who argued that the security risks of letting them onto the pitch were too high. The band disagreed and had their chauffeur, Bill Corbett drive them onto the field in a Vauxhall car. Within minutes the car's wheels had stuck in the mud at the centre of the pitch and was surrounded by screaming fans.

'I remember Ronnie laughing hysterically as the car's wheels spun wildly in the mud,' Ian McLagan would later write in his biography, *All The Rage*, 'the girl's bodies pressed against the car, their sweaty excited faces squashed hard against the windows.'

Such is the pressure of the fans piling on top of the car the vehicle actually starts to sink into the ground. Eventually the band is rescued and they are quickly driven away from the ground of screams. Steve is the first to react.

'The minute Bill parked the car,' McLagan writes, 'Steve jumped out, climbed over a low wall and started running for his life across the field. Without a word we followed and ran screaming after him for all it was worth, until we were exhausted.'

Despite the cheery persona and the dream of a life he led, Marriott always hated falsity and pretentiousness, the two elements that fame induces both in those it enters and those who are exposed to it.

Marriott's East End upbringing, the no nonsense approach of his family and his own need for that which was true, as evidenced by his adoration of soul music, meant that he found it hard to deal with people's perceptions of him. Pop stars at that time were a relatively new phenomenon. Many, especially The Beatles, were seen and treated as magicians. Marriott was no exception.

After all, he had been on television, an enormous achievement in the Sixties, especially for someone his age. Yet the way people acted around him frustrated the singer terribly.

'His mates did treat him different,' his mum confirms. 'They were very shy and didn't know what to say. He used to say, "I wish they would just be normal." I said, "They can't," and he shouted back, "But I'm the same."'

Bill Marriott concurs. 'Steve hated the big star thing,' he stated, 'always has done, right from when he was number one. He would walk around the corner to avoid crowds. He wanted to mix with ordinary kids. It was so difficult when he went back to the East End and met his little mates that he knew before he was a star. They treated him like a God and he said, "I don't want that, they're my friends and I don't want to be a big star." I liked him for that. He was never toffee nosed or big headed.'

As far as Marriott was concerned, as long as he was allowed to go onstage and play his music, then life was as it should be. Everything else that went with his work, contracts, royalties, deals, lawyers, he simply ignored.

'I said, "Steve you should have all the money you want in the bank",' Bill Marriott recalled in 1996. 'He said, "I know but my job is on the stage, playing the guitar. I've got to leave it to somebody else to do my money and to be honest I've got no interest in money, dad, no interest in money at all".'

'He never pushed himself,' his mother says, 'He was a softie underneath. That's not a mum talking either, that's someone that knows her boy. See, you have to build a wall around you when you're meeting all these people, make out that you're tougher than what you are.

'He once said to me when he was in his twenties, If I die tomorrow mum, I've done everything, I've loved it, I've enjoyed every moment of it and I've done things that other kids of my age would never do and enjoyed every minute of it.'

'Underneath that cocky, tough nut image of his,' PP Arnold concurs 'he was a big softie.'

A big softie who like all true musicians craves respect but not cheap applause, a big softie who took several big risks with his career because fame scared him so, a big softie who was granted his wish and did get to play his music onstage, right up until the day he died, in fact.

But in doing so, Steve Marriott paid the price in more ways than one.

‡ ‡ ‡

Two days after the Bradford incident, the band left for a tour of Europe. Germany first, where they and The Beach Boys made appearances on the country's top rated TV music show, *The Beat Club*. Outside of England, Germany would always prove to be fertile territory for the band. As would Scandinavia – which is where they now travelled to for gigs in Sweden, Denmark and Norway.

Meanwhile, unknown to them, Decca Records had determined to cash in on the band by putting together an album of b-sides and unreleased material. They also scheduled a single, 'Patterns' c/w 'E Too D' to promote the work. The group were furious.

In June, their new Immediate single and album was due for release. The single was called 'Here Comes The Nice,' and along with the album had been designed to herald a brand new phase for the band. Worse, 'Patterns,' the song that Decca were putting out as a single, was not only a very ordinary song, it was in no way whatsoever representative of the band's new style. Put frankly, it was beat group bullshit and the group publicly made known their decision not to promote its release.

On May 26th 'Patterns' was released. On June 2nd, the song they did believe in, 'Here Comes The Nice' c/w 'Talk To You' was sent out to the shops. 'Patterns' failed to chart, 'Here Comes The Nice' reached number twelve.

On the album battlefront, a similar story.

The Decca album *From The Beginning*, was issued on June 2nd and reached seventeen, the band's debut Immediate album, *Small Faces*, was issued three weeks later on June 24th and climbed straight to number twelve.

Rounds one and two to the band.

‡ ‡ ‡

Although there had been plenty of drug references in their previous work – the title of 'Grow Your Own,' for example – never before had Marriott been so explicit as he was on the first Immediate single.

He sings, 'Here comes the nice / Looking so good / He makes me feel like no one else could / He knows what I want / He knows what I need / He's always there when I need some speed.'

To return with such an explicit pro-drug song after the banning of their last single can only be construed as a stroke of absolute defiance, a real two fingers up to the establishment. Under Arden, the single would not have seen the light of day, let alone made it onto vinyl. Under Oldham, the band had a manager cheering from the sidelines.

The title had been filched from Lord Buckley's monologue, 'Here Comes Da Nazz' (musician Todd Rundgren nicked the last two words for a band name) which was still a favourite amongst the band.

Amazingly, the BBC allowed it onto the airwaves. Perhaps feeling guilty over their behaviour with 'I Can't Make It,' they added it to their play list without a murmur.

When they realised their mistake they would try to extract revenge by banning the band's next single. Instead, they would be brilliantly outplayed by Steve Marriott.

Musically, 'Here Comes The Nice' was another example of the swaggering soul-pop the band was becoming expert at. The single featured many of the band's distinct musical trademarks – a soft guitar intro which also served to close the song, several changes of pace from fast to slow and back again, and above all, Marriott's ability to sing in a number of different tones, effortlessly switching from assured to passionate. His phrasing was now like his music: natural, instinctive, often masterful – and he never neglected to add those little shouts of 'Yeah!' and 'Hey!' so reminiscent of the American soul singers he adored.

The flip side, 'Talk To You' was more straight ahead than its companion but equally as dynamic. The song's subject matter sounds as if it was inspired by Marriott's relationship with model, Chrissie Shrimpton. In the song, the singer wants to talk to his girl but such is her fame he can't get past the doorman outside her flat who mistakes him for a fan. Marriott created a contagious groove for these words and then inserted several shouts and chants to lend the song a distinct sexuality.

It was a solid start to their Immediate career but gave no real clue to the musical direction that was finally unveiled on their second album, *Small Faces*.

The year 1967 demanded creativity on every level from its artists, from song to album covers. On their second album, the Small Faces had forcibly met that challenge, had done so by creating a batch of songs that blended their disparate influences into a satisfying whole. Yet that whole made them impossible to pigeonhole and therefore created a vacuum around the band. No one could figure them out or what they stood for.

Who else was dropping East End humour into a mix of soul, psychedelia, folk and rock and making it sound absolutely organic? No one. Who else could go from the organ-led instrumental 'Happy Boys Happy,' to the pop brilliance of 'Get Yourself Together?' No one. Who else could lead off their album with the hard acoustic edge of '(Tell Me) Have You Ever Seen Me,' and then produce one of the great psychedelic songs of all time with 'Green Circles'? No one. Who else could begin the song 'All Our Yesterdays' with a loud Cockney accent announcing, 'And now for your delight, the darling of the Wapping wharf launderette, Ronald Leafy Lane', and then mix in blaring horns with a such a playful vocal? No one.

It was by achieving this synthesis that Marriott and the band believed they had now met the criteria expected of them.

Ronnie Lane had certainly played his part. His predilection for a softer, pastoral and more psychedelic sound was heavily evident on songs such as 'Show Me The Way' and 'All Our Yesterdays.' Yet on many of Lane's songs, Marriott could not help asserting himself.

Every time the music even suggests a drifting off, Marriott quickly inserts a change of pace or an impassioned vocal line to jolt the listener – keep the energy levels high. Although this album weighs in at less than half an hour's playing time it feels so much longer thanks to the band's inventive melodic shifts and turns in nearly every song.

'During the Decca period,' Kenney Jones reveals, 'most of the self-penned stuff was 99% Steve. It wasn't until Immediate that Ronnie became more involved. The first Immediate album is made up of 50% Steve's songs and 50% of Ronnie's. They didn't collaborate as much as people thought. In fact, when they did, they often ended up arguing and fighting.'

The album was released in early June of 1967, the summer of love as it was named. Its great misfortune was to be followed into the shops by none other than the album which would change so much in such a short space of time: The Beatles' *Sgt. Pepper's Lonely Hearts Club Band.*

It was the work that would dominate the summer of 1967 and overshadow all other music. Inadvertently, it would help kill the single as a creative medium and make the album all important.

Ironically, *Sgt. Pepper* was not prime Beatles. Compared to other works of theirs, such as its predecessor *Revolver*, or its successor *The White Album*, artistically it comes a pretty poor third. No matter. With songs such as 'A Day In The Life,' The Beatles had signalled their support for the drug counter culture and perfectly caught the spirit of experimentation and risk that pop music and the decade demanded.

The Small Faces album did respectable business but it was *Sgt. Pepper*, that effortlessly achieved the twin goals of commercial and critical success. Marriott and his boys had perfectly welded together all their yesterdays into a unique shape, but in doing so had created a kind of ambivalence about the band. People simply couldn't get a handle on them.

Were they hippies? Were they Mods? Were they teenyboppers?

'Its an ok album,' the *NME* said. An ok album? Just ok?

One thing was for sure, Steve Marriott now knew where he had to go to gain the respect he craved.

Keith Altham; 'While the Small Faces loved the freedom that Andrew Oldham gave them in the studio, The Beatles were the flagship for everybody back then. I remember Steve being totally knocked out by *Sgt Pepper*. *Sgt Pepper* was the influence behind the band's next album, *Ogden's Nut Gone Flake*, very definitely.'

The presence of the Decca album didn't help anchor the band's image either although it did contain a few great moments. In essence, the album reflected the band's musical journey to date. It contained R&B covers in the form of The Miracles 'You Really Got A Hold On Me,' and the Motown staple 'Baby Don't You Do It.'

There's a romp through the Del Shannon hit 'Runaway' and then, bang, we're into psychedelic territory land with the second rate 'Yesterday Today And Tomorrow' placed just before the startlingly powerful 'That Man.'

Missing from the collection, however, is the sense of playfulness, the air of fun that the band could never resist from displaying. Not that life was all light and smiles for the boy Marriott. There was a serious, sensitive side to him which he occasionally allowed to surface in interviews.

In summer of 1967, journalist Bill Harry visited Marriott at his Baker Street flat and noted the books on his shelf. They were a mix of the surreal and the serious. Colin Wilson's *Beyond The Outsider* nestles next to Spike Milligan's *The Little Pot Boiler* and *Silly Verses For Kids*. (LSD's ability to reduce the user to a state of childlike wonder was reflected by songwriters such as John Lennon raiding the work of children's authors such as Edward Lear for inspiration. Marriott seems to have taken a similar track.) *The Rubayiat Of Omar Khayyam*, is placed next to four red leather bound volumes of Hans Andersen's *Fairy Tales* (and it is worth noting here that this was the year that Marriott would write one of his best ever songs, 'Tin Soldier' whose lyrics would directly refer to the Andersen fairy story of the same name.)

Marriott had also bought or been given four James Bond stories. Anya Seton's *Avalon*, and a book entitled *Classical Dances and Costumes Of India*.

Harry asks Marriott about music. 'I like everything, really,' he replies, 'there's no limit. I've got every sort of record from *The Planets Suite* to Mingus. It's just a matter of opening your mind up to it. Music is music, you can't hate a particular kind. Those people who say they dislike a style of music probably haven't really listened to it.'

He spoke of his ambitions. He didn't want to be in a band all his life. It's okay at first, especially when you taste success. But then you want to go on and experiment, become successful in other fields.

On his own song writing, he said, 'Some of the songs I write are true experiences that I feel strongly about. I also like to put myself in someone else's position. It's like character acting. I imagine I'm someone else, create situations and then wonder how I would react to them. This approach to songwriting is interesting.'

'Record producing, songwriting and arranging are much more interesting,' he concluded. Attractive also. If he did follow that particular path it would mean creating but staying out of the spotlight. Perfect.

Yet live the hysteria still showed no signs of abating.

On May 20th, 1967, *Record Mirror*'s Mike Adams published his review of a Small Faces gig, the location unspecified. When Adams arrives, the hall is already packed, 2,000 kids at least. The band is then announced.

'Before I knew it,' Adams writes, 'hundreds of hysterical teenagers surged towards the stage...muffled guitar chords could just be distinguished beneath the terrific screaming pitch and the Small Faces smashed into their first number...it was too much for 87 girls who passed out within the first ten minutes. True!'

After the show, Adams goes backstage where Marriott talks directly to him.

'The kids don't want us,' he states. 'They don't want to see or hear us really. They come for what the night is – a rave. They probably don't realise it but it's themselves who make the night. We wouldn't be anything without them but that would not make a difference to them. They'd have just a good a night with any other name group.'

Marriott will not directly attack his crowd. He can't. If it wasn't for them the band would be nowhere. But it must have been exasperating. All that work in the studio, all the dropping of hints to the drug heads, all the hip references in songs and interviews, and still the screams come, blanking out their sound and thus denying the band what they believe to be their rightful place on the podium of pop.

What a bitter pill to swallow.

‡ ‡ ‡

Since the release of 'Here Comes The Nice,' the Small Faces had not jumped off the promotional wheel. Every TV appearance, every interview, none were refused. All were undertaken.

'With all the promotion they intend putting in on this one,' the *NME* reported, 'it should see them in the top ten.'

They had returned in early June from their Scandinavian tour. Now there were gigs in Norwich, Cardiff and in between TV performances of the single and its B-side for shows such as, *As You Like It* and *Dee Time*.

They also gave a series of press interviews. Nothing was being taken for granted. Now that the BBC had failed to react to the single's pro-drug stance, band and label pushed the song wherever and whenever they could. Europe was no exception.

In late June, the band, along with PP Arnold (who Marriott was now seeing) and Twice As Much, set off for a quick promotional tour of the continent. These trips allowed the band to meet a country's media in just a few days. Tony Calder and Loog Oldham would often accompany the bands.

'Our whole thing was to promote in Europe with junkets,' Calder remembered. 'You'd get Small Faces, the Nice, Pat Arnold, Chris Farlowe all going over. The only thing Andrew would ever say to them or teach them was this: "Right, everyone listen up. The words 'fuck off' in this language are as follows." I remember one conference where Steve got the needle with this German guy and started on about the war. This was the biggest German press crew I have ever seen. They were all big fellas and he's coming up trying to hit them. Ronnie says, "What the fuck are you doing?" and Steve goes, "This one tried to kill my father." So Ronnie joined in. It was hysterical.'

End of June, the band return from Europe to play a festival in Blackheath along with The Kinks and Georgie Fame. Marriott showed up wearing a moustache, a look that has always, along with the deerstalker hat, proved troublesome for the true stylist. Some had the right faces to pull it off, The Beatles, for example. Marriott, despite his best efforts never did. Face was too small.

In the first week of July, a clean-shaven Marriott along with the band booked into the Olympic Studios in Barnes for a week of recording.

It was during these sessions that Marriott phoned Tony Calder. The new song he wanted him to listen to was called 'Itchycoo Park.'

'He said, "Tony, you better come down." I said, "I don't go to studios, Steve, I don't like them." He said, "Tony – come now. There's a tape op here called George Chkiantz and he has done something amazing."

'I went to the studio, listened to the song and told him straightaway that it was a number one record, a classic piece of pop music. Andrew then came down, the next lunchtime it was. He had with him a parcel and he said, "Boys, this is what I want you to do. We're going to get you a mobile studio and a country house and I want you to go down there and take this with you but don't open it until you get there."

'He gives them this huge square parcel and the boys are itching to open it. It's like a Christmas present. Steve pulls back a bit of the paper, sees the hash, looks up and says, "Can we start recording now?"'

It was Ronnie's song, really, ('Never happened,' Mac retorts), lifted from the music the band always liked to plunder.

'It is a hymn,' Marriott confirmed some years later. 'We were in Ireland and speeding out of our brains writing this song. Ronnie had the first verse already written down but he had no melody line so what we did was stick the verse to the melody line of 'God Be In My Head' with a few chord variations. We were going towards Dublin airport and I thought of the middle eight. I was in the car in front. We pulled up and I ran to the car behind where Mac and Kenney were and sang them the middle eight. When we got to the airport we mapped it out. We wrote the second verse collectively and the chorus line speaks for itself.'

The song's opening lines concerning the 'bridge of sighs' had been lifted from a pamphlet Lane had read in a Oxford hotel room.

Using that image as a springboard, Lane had started the realisation of a great song. Marriott contributed to the song's creation but in later interviews Lane sounded as if he wasn't too impressed with his partner's contribution.

'It wasn't me that came up with, "I feel inclined to blow my mind, get hung up, feed the ducks with a bun / They all come out to groove about, be nice and have fun in the sun." That wasn't me,' he snapped, 'but the more poetic stuff was.'

The song remains a classic. Starts off with an acoustic guitar, is joined by a piano and a drum flourish and then we're into Marriott's sweet vocal, which will, as usual, soon take on a different timbre and change shape and colour. Noticeable again is the band's R&B influence, evidenced through their use of call and response backing vocals.

'What did you do there?' ask the band, 'I got high,' Marriott sings back at them with tremendous power.

The song has swagger, is filled with great musical hooks provided by Mac's organ licks and Lane's rich, deep bass lines. But the icing is tape op George Chkiantz's contribution. By playing two tapes simultaneously but at differing speeds he was able to create an effect called phasing. The sound brilliantly reflects the altered consciousness the band were attempting to replicate for their audience.

Calder was right, it was a classic piece of pop.

It was also a classic piece of pop that nearly didn't see the light of day had it not been for Marriott's quick thinking.

Tony Calder: 'I must hand it to Steve. That morning, it was a Monday morning and I came in early to the office. Marriott was sitting there. I said, 'What are you doing?' He said, 'They've banned the record.'

I looked at him. 'When did you last go to bed?' 'Couple of nights ago.'

So we scammed up the story together. We told the BBC that 'Itchycoo Park' was a piece of waste ground in the East End that the band had played on as kids. We put the story out at ten and by lunchtime we were told the ban was off.'

The band's biggest selling single to date should have established the band as true psychic warriors, radical proponents of chemical use. After all, they had just placed in the top three of the charts a song that told the listeners not to go to school 'to learn the words of fools' but to head for the Itchycoo Park and get high instead. It was much better for you. They had been much more overt and blatant than the Beatles or The Stones when it came to drug references and equally as strident as Bob Dylan.

That message was blared out from radios and TV sets all summer long yet still the band were seen as teenybopper fodder, or at best, intriguing Cockney charmers.

England is built on hierarchies. The rich unemployed live at the top, the poor unemployed die at the bottom. The music business was no different. Bob Dylan, The Beatles, The Stones were placed top three.

The aura of absolute cool that they surrounded themselves with was instrumental in their ability to change direction at a whim and issue songs that reflected their spiritual insights (The Beatles) or decadent lifestyle (The Stones).

The Small Faces, despite issuing two of the decade's most radical pro-drug singles had not been able to create such an aura. Their raw humour and inability to take life seriously negated against such a move.

Who would ever believe that the darlings of the Wapping Wharf laundrette were the ones to storm the barricades of conservatism? No one! It didn't help that in the press, Marriott had to play things cautiously when asked about the 'I get high,' lyric.

'They mean anything you want them to,' he told journalists. 'We wrote it so that its nothing specific otherwise you're asking for trouble.'

Immediate meanwhile issued a statement that the line referred to nothing more than kids swinging high on park swings. Classic Oldham.

‡ ‡ ‡

Two months later, testament to the song's chart staying power, the band shot a famous promotional film for the single at Chiswick Park. The director was Peter Whitehead who would later direct an acid-drenched documentary entitled, *Let's Make Love Tonite In London* featuring music from The Small Faces as well as newer groups such as The Pink Floyd.

The set up for the 'Itchycoo Park' film was simple. Steve Marriott and Ian McLagan's wife to be, Sandy Serjeant, enter a park where the rest of the band appear as garden gnomes and entice the couple to places such as The Amazing Grotto. On the day, Steve Marriott elected to go in front of the cameras wearing a patterned kaftan with a straw panama hat. Amazingly, he pulled it off. He should have looked stupid. Instead, he pulled off an outrageous fashion statement.

During filming, a middle-aged woman did. She saw Marriott and shouted out, contemptuously, 'Is that a girl or a fella?'

Steve lifted his straw hat and retorted lasciviously, 'Not half lady – come and have a go.'

Often overlooked about the 'Itchycoo Park' single is its superb B-side, 'I'm Only Dreaming,' one of the best ever blends of Lane's dreamy nature with Marriott's vocal power.

According to songwriter Billy Nicholls, also signed to Immediate, the song was all Marriott's work.

'I'd be working in my office at Immediate, New Oxford Street, most days between nine to five,' he recalled, 'and Steve would often pop in around lunchtime and play new songs to me on an acoustic guitar. He was very prolific in that area. He came in one day with a very rough sketch of a song and within literally sixty minutes he wrote 'I'm Only Dreaming'. The song was credited to Marriott and Lane but there was no Ronnie input at all. Steve had the ability to deliver an amazing solo vocal against a huge brilliantly constructed sound and that explains why it still sounds great today.'

Neither this gem of a song nor 'Itchycoo Park' appeared on any of their Immediate albums and nor would their next single. At the time, singles were very separate from albums. They, above everything else, gauged a band's popularity. When Engelbert Humperdinck kept The Beatles's magnificent song 'Strawberry Fields Forever' off the top spot, the papers immediately read it as a sign of weakness and rushed to run 'Are The Beatles Finished?' articles.

On July 8th, Marriott returned to Olympic Studios to re-record some vocals. There he bumped into Charlie Watts and Bill Wyman of the Stones and agreed to supply backing vocals for their song 'In Another Land'. The result can be heard on The Rolling Stones album, *Their Satanic Majesties Request*.

Marriott was a fan of the Stones and got on best with their guitarist, Keith Richards. Both men were serious guitar players, adored blues music, came alive when they heard it. Both men also shared a great propensity for holding their own when it came to serious partying. The relationship would hold for many years.

Two weeks after lending his voice to the Stones album, actress Sally Foulgar filed a paternity suit against Steve Marriott. She claimed he was the father of her fourteen-month-old daughter. A week later she dropped the case.

‡ ‡ ‡

In the Fan Club letter, dated September, October and November 1967, Pauline Corcoran writes, 'Since The Faces have switched to Immediate I have never seen them looking so happy! And also Immediate is taking great interest in the fan club. Tony Corder (*sic*) has promised to really give you all your money's worth. He is going to start sending you American record sleeves in colour of the Small Faces.'

In 2002, Tony Calder said, 'I fucking hated that fan club. All they were good for was buying records,' and then revealed their true worth to him and Immediate.

He confessed, 'See, we had a whole team of record buyers. Little ladies all over the country. We had these two guys, Mick and John, they were the original Afghan carpetbaggers.

'They used to go and buy the carpets and bring the hash back when you could buy it from Afghanistan. They had housewives all over the country and the name of the game was, get it over the counter. You couldn't rely on your fan club handouts – tell them to go to this shop in their area and buy the record. So we had little old ladies doing it. 'Oh, have you got "Itchycoo Park," it's for my daughter.'

We were smart enough to have local women. We didn't have someone from Manchester going into a Glasgow shop. It was all local. And we did it with every record. Didn't matter if it was a number one or a hit. If we loved it we worked it. That's what the fun was.' He pauses, 'When you put a lot of money into a band you want a hit.'

A hit, a hit and nothing but the hit, that was all Calder required, pure and simple. And hit records is what Marriott spoke about to *NME*'s Keith Altham, as he continued promoting 'Itchycoo Park.'

'All our discs were being misunderstood,' he complained. 'I Can't Make It' was labelled obscene. 'All Or Nothing' was more obscene than that one. I mean, I own up to that one. That was a groove. It even got me going. We split from our manager, our agent and our record company. They make me laugh these big companies. All these forty or fifty-year-old executives sitting around big tables deciding what is a good pop disc and what is not. What do they know about pop singles at their age?'

(Privately, Marriott was a little bit more direct in his criticism of the likes of Decca. 'Pipe-smoking cunts,' was his take on the matter.)

He then extolled the virtues of Immediate, how Andrew digs the people he works with and how they dig him and made reference to the BBC's dislike of 'Itchycoo'. 'We're in for a good old banning from the BBC,' he stated, 'until we get into their top twenty then it's alright. What the devil is psychedelic anyway? I read somewhere there are psychedelic socks. What's that? A sock that takes Acid?'

He poured scorn on that summer's fashions.

'Long hair, beads and flowers doesn't mean a thing now,' he stated before falling into a discussion about writers such as Shelley, Byron, Keats and Coleridge, artists who used drugs as opposed to those who let drugs use them.

The implications were very clear.

August began with a trip to the BBC Broadcasting House in Portland Place for an interview with journalist Chris Denning. The next day, two shows at the Locarno Ballroom in Streatham. On Sunday it was Bristol, Monday Cheltenham, then back to town for two shows at the Upper Cut Club in London's East End. On the Friday they were due to play the California Ballroom in Dunstable but elected to miss the gig and again headline the National Windsor Jazz, Pop, Ballads and Blues festival. They began their set just before midnight with a cover of The Beatles' 'Paperback Writer,' then went into 'All Or Nothing.'

Just as they reached the third song, the clock struck twelve and, this being England, the power was cut.

A few days later, a frustrated Marriott commented, 'We opened up with 'Paperback Writer' the other day and then we got stuck on the riff while we listened to electronic tape sounds. It was too much. We all got hung up listening to the tape and just backing it – but I doubt if it got through to the kids.'

Sunday it was Greenford, Tuesday, Southport, and at the end of the week, the band began a four-day tour of Scotland, performing in Nairn, Aberdeen, Montrose and Perth. On the 23rd they travelled back to London and mimed a performance of 'Itchycoo Park' for the *Top Of the Pops* show. Since their formation, they had now appeared on the show over twenty times and knew many of the people who worked there. Some they liked, others they actively despised.

'I thought this particular producer, Johnnie Stewart, was leaving the show and this other guy, Colin Charman, was taking over,' Marriott recalled. 'Anyway, after we had done our bit, this producer [Stewart] comes to the bar and he was doing this thing of, 'That was wonderful, lads, it was a gas, it was wild.' Really full of shit. I knew he did it with everyone whether he liked you or not. So I turned round and said, "You're a cunt, a real two-faced cunt." And he wasn't leaving the show at all.'

The DJ, Tony Blackburn, also aroused anger in Marriott. He couldn't stand his sunny nature, false optimism. During one conversation, Marriott handed the Blackburn a cabbage ('just to let him know what I thought of him') and throughout the conversation kept calling him different names. The unsuspecting DJ finally caught on.

'He was shouting, "You little cunt, you'll never work at the BBC again." I was crying with laughter.' The indiscretion saw the band briefly banned from the show, the first group to be bestowed with such an honour.

This kind of disrespectful behaviour towards those who held key positions within the industry convinced many that the band was unmanageable, not at all serious about their career. In some ways such a reading could be construed as spot on. Marriott was never any good at endearing himself to those who he suspected were false, or wouldn't have given him the time of day had he not been a musician.

Whatever the cost to both the band and himself, Marriott could never bite his tongue and play the game. He appeared on a live pop quiz, hosted by the radio DJ Ray Moore to promote 'Itchycoo Park'. Asked how the unique phasing effects on the single had been achieved, Marriott replied, 'I pissed on the tape.'

‡ ‡ ‡

In mid-summer, Marriott took the *Melody Maker*'s Blind Test in which a writer from the paper played a musician a number of singles whose identities were hidden from him. The musician then gave his opinion.

Marriott was positive about the majority of records played him. Not surprisingly, he adored the Four Tops 'Seven Rooms Of Gloom' and Ramsey Lewis's version of 'Function at the Junction.' ('More of this is what I say.')

He had a lot of time for PJ Proby's 'You Can't Come Home Again,' Kenny Ball's version of The Beatles' 'When I'm Sixty Four,' Del Shannon's 'Mind Over Matter,' The Four Seasons' 'C'mon Marianne,' and The Piccadilly Line's 'At The Third Stroke.' He reserved criticism for The Association's 'Windy,' and Nancy Sinatra's 'You Only Live Twice.'

'It's terrible but there you go,' he sniffed.

‡ ‡ ‡

In their attempt to create the UK equivalent of the Brill Building, Immediate sought to build a camaraderie amongst all their acts. Cross fertilisation was the name of the game.

Tony Calder recalls himself, Oldham, the Small Faces and singer PP Arnold getting bombed on pills and then jumping into two cars and driving to Camber Sands at dawn to shoot an Immediate promotional film with Peter Whitehead directing.

'We were tripping our heads off,' Calder recalls. 'We didn't have a licence to film there and some little guy, a Mr Plod from the beach started giving us an argument. I'm telling him to fuck off and Marriott is saying, "Okay Tone, we'll do it in the sea. We'll hold back the waves, like Jesus." All day he just kept saying, "I'm the nazz, man." Today it's classic footage.'

The rest of the band disliked Calder. He was the money-man: the tough one who denied them many requests. They were fond of Oldham though, after all he supplied them with several types of goodies plus they found his camp ways amusing.

'Andrew was a larger-than-life character,' writer Chris Welch recalled. 'You could never imagine him sitting in an office doing the accounts and saying to the boys, "You gotta pay your tax." He just wasn't that sort of manager. They all had so much energy and they lived the life.'

But Calder, whose job did not entail having to be admired by his employees, was the enemy.

'They never liked me,' he confirms. 'Ian McLagan slagged me off in his book so much that I never even bothered to answer it. For me, it was all about Steve. He had a heart of gold. He'd come into the office. "Tone, I got to get a new guitar." "What happened to your last one?" "I saw some bloke and I gave him my favourite guitar." "Why?" "Because he didn't have one".'

With wife, Jenny (Unknown)

Chapter Sixteen

If I Were A Carpenter

End of September, the band flew to Germany to participate in a special edition of the *Beat Club* TV show. On their return, they blew out a BBC radio show, ('too tired,') although they did appear at the Mecca Royal in Tottenham before departing for a short tour of France, accompanied by a young group called The Herd whose young guitarist went by the name of Pete Frampton.

The following year *Rave* magazine would vote Frampton "The Face Of '68," bestowing teenybopper status upon a band that sought no such honour. The Herd saw themselves as a serious musical force. After all, their first chart hit, 'From The Underworld' had been inspired by the classical myth of Orpheus which formed the basis of Offenbach's opera *Orpheus in the Underworld*.

Frampton would play a crucial role in the story of Steve Marriott but Kenney Jones remembered the French trip for other reasons. He recalls that on arrival at the studio, the band and the show's French producer argued so badly that the group walked out in anger. Whilst exiting the studio Marriott apparently stole the master reel of the show.

'There's Steve running down the road in Paris with this big reel under his arm laughing his head off,' Jones recalls.

On their last day in Paris, Marriott and Oldham missed their flight home, and got a later flight together. There was much to talk about. Immediate Records was now Oldham's only concern. His management of the Stones had been terminated and he was looking to Marriott and Lane to replace Jagger and Richards as the company's main songwriters. The signs were promising. Although the company had released some quality music, 'Here Comes The Nice' and 'Itchycoo Park' had been their first hits in a long time. The welcome news that the latter single had just cracked the American charts, rising to number sixteen on the *Billboard* chart, added to Oldham's belief in the pair. Next year, he envisaged the band making their debut in the States. Oldham knew America well, had tasted success there with the Stones and liked it, liked it a lot. Now he wanted more, wanted to push forward his vision of creating a modern day Brill building in London that would produce world class music.

That was one of the reasons he favoured package tours that featured his acts. It allowed them the chance to get closer, create, and swap ideas. Calder liked them as well. They were extremely cost effective and a great chance for him and Oldham to experience life on the road.

Thus, the Immediate head honchos accompanied The Small Faces, PP Arnold and Chris Farlowe in Europe for two weeks in October.

On their return from the jaunt the band were forced to cancel their one-week tour of Ireland. Steve Marriott had gone close again, been diagnosed as suffering from nervous fatigue and exhaustion. It was time to slow down. His mum of course went mad, then worried herself sick:

'I said to him, yeah, you might be doing what you want but the rate you're going it will only be for two more years.'

She had a point. There exists TV footage of Steve where you can clearly see the ravages, his face unnaturally gaunt and pimply. A holiday was arranged. Portugal, Steve and Ronnie together for a week. Worked a treat, as well.

'This is the first time we've had a holiday this year,' a fresh Marriott told journalist Bill Harry. 'Last time, I went to Manchester. This time I spent a week in Portugal and I'm going back. It was so good that I have made my mind up to have more than one holiday a year. I forgot completely about the whole business. I suddenly realised I was on a deserted beach and there was absolutely nothing to do, nothing to think about except, "this is it!"'

(Later on, he would discover the island of Ibiza and holiday there when he could. Given its current image as one of the rave centres of the world, that was kind of appropriate.)

Marriott was talking to the press to promote the band's new single, 'Tin Soldier,' c/w 'I Feel Much Better,' released at the start of December. The single remains a prime example of the Small Faces at their very best. Made up of great poetic images, ('All I need are your whispered hellos,') and a music that brings forth from Marriott one of his greatest vocal performances, it is a record brimming with power and style. Not only are the arrangements and the sound spot on but Marriott also delivers a performance that must rank as British soul singing at its very best. Which isn't too surprising. After all, the song itself was written for a beautiful, young American.

'Steve originally wrote 'Tin Soldier' for me,' PP Arnold confirms. 'He liked it so much he kept it himself and gave me 'If You Think You're Groovy,' which was nice but not in the same league as 'Tin Soldier.'

The single powerfully signalled the band returning to their R&B roots, a glorious response to those who had made known their unhappiness at the band's new direction, their use of psychedelia, their various musical twists and turns.

Poster for first Small Faces single 1965

First Ready Steady Go *appearance 1965*   *(Tony Gale)*

Small Faces 1966   *(Tony Gale)*

Steve 1967   *(Unknown)*

Evicted again! Steve (alias Fred Smith) 1967   *(Unknown)*

Steve 1967   *(Unknown)*

Small Faces 1968   *(Julia Noble)*

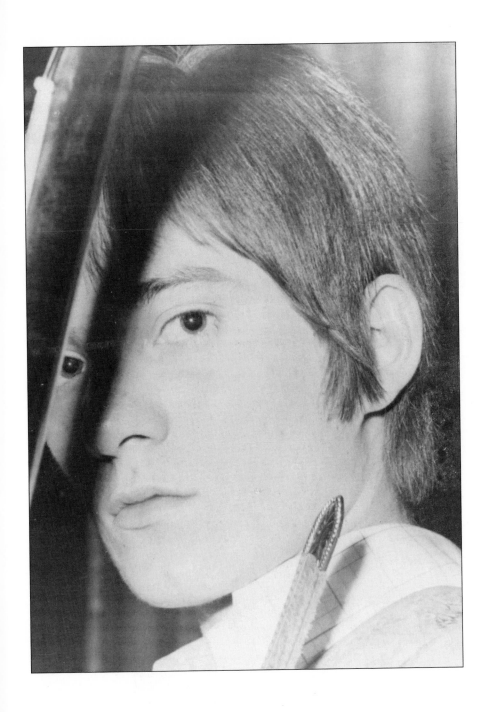

Steve 1966   *(Unknown)*

With Mum 1966 (Kay Marriott)

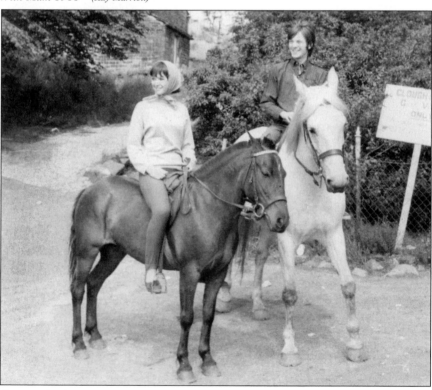

Steve on his horse, Petite Fisage, with fiancée Sue Oliver 1966 (Brian Taylor)

Small Faces in Germany1968   (Warner Roefen)

Steve and wife, Jenny 1968   (Ted Tyler)

Small Faces 1968   *(Unknown)*

Small Faces 1968   *(Unknown)*

'We wanted to make a record that was really us,' Marriott told Keith Altham, 'Tin Soldier' is really us and 'Itchycoo Park' was really a nice kind of send up. Some of the kids were saying that we were not so wild as we used to be and we thought, 'yeah,' and we came up with 'Tin Soldier.'

We can play this one live but we could never get the same effects as 'Itchycoo.'

He added that if the single followed 'Itchycoo Park' into the American top twenty it would be the incentive they needed to tour the States. He forgot that during November, Mac had married dancer, Sandie Serjeant and at the airport been caught carrying some hashish. The arrest of the keyboard player not only made the newspapers but his subsequent conviction would effectively bar him from entering America under their immigration laws.

The Small Faces would never play the States although they would spend one night there, collectively. That was due to a stopover they made in San Francisco as they returned from a tour of Australia, filled with drama. It was the tour that Marriott later claimed robbed him of all his confidence, the tour that would serve to push him into decisions whose consequences would prove absolutely fatal to the band's existence. Again they find themselves fighting the forces of darkness. The BBC inform the band that the last line of their single 'Tin Soldier' has to be removed from all TV and radio broadcasts. Marriott exploded. 'I actually said, sit with her not sleep. The meaning of the song is about getting into somebody's mind – not their body.'

God almighty, if it wasn't the press misunderstanding them it was the fucking authorities needling them. Fuck's sake.

‡ ‡ ‡

It was December, 1967 and Marriott was on the promotional merry go round, talking again to Keith Altham. The singer had a lot on his mind.

'We've been through that phoney scene of being the Four Little Mods for the public. We'd turn up for a TV show and they would say, "Where are all the trendy clothes you're supposed to wear?" We were just four ordinary geezers having to pretend we're pop stars. Now we've stopped pretending anything. We recorded rubbish like 'My Mind's Eye' because we knew it was commercial and it would sell. Now we can afford to do what we like. I feel sorry for groups such as The Herd who are capable of doing things much better than 'Paradise Lost,' but they do it because they want to sell. No one wants to own up, that's all. Take today.

'We are down here to back PP Arnold on her record because we want to do it. In the old days they would have probably have stopped us because it might look bad for our image. Well to hell with that – we played on her backing track, we produced the disc and we like Pat. You don't need any other reasons.'

The band were backing PP Arnold for the TV cameras. They had already worked together on two TV shows, promoting 'Tin Soldier.' One was for a TV show called, *New Releases*, the other, *Top Of The Pops*.

'That *Top Of The Pops* where we were all on stage together with Pat dancing behind us was the seller,' Marriott claimed. It certainly was. The single climbed to number nine in the charts, spent twelve weeks doing so. And Britain wasn't the only country showing its appreciation. In Australia, 'Itchycoo Park' had reached number one. In January, the band were due to fly out there and tour with The Who.

All in all it would be a great way to open the New Year.

‡ ‡ ‡

On January 16th, the Small Faces arrived at Sydney airport. Jetlagged, exhausted, disorientated, the band disembarked from the plane and were met by an aggressive press pack. At the time, Australia was experiencing a downturn in their economy and their had been much fuss made about pop bands visiting the country and leaving with suitcases full of Australian cash.

The first question directed at the group was this, 'How do you feel now that the pound's been devalued?'

The next question was, 'Do you take drugs?' No and fuck off were their replies. The band stayed at the Sheraton Motel Hotel in Macleay Street. On the Friday, The Who arrived from England and after joining up, the entourage flew to Brisbane for the first concert. According to Andy Neill's excellent account of the trip, *A Fortnight Of Furore*, The Small Faces played 'Sha La La La Lee,' 'Itchycoo Park,' an unnamed instrumental, 'All Or Nothing,' 'Tin Soldier,' and two covers, Brenda Holloway's epic soul ballad 'Every Little Bit Hurts,' followed by a heavy version of Tim Hardin's 'If I Were A Carpenter.'

'Dullness was the only big thing about the Small Faces' began one of the next day's reviews, a piece that was unrelenting in its dismissive tone. On Sunday the band flew back to Sydney, played there Monday night. The gig was held at a stadium that utilised a revolving stage so that all of the surrounding audience could at some point view the band playing.

The Small Faces arrived onstage half an hour later than advertised and the crowd grew restless. Towards the end of their set the stage's equipment broke down and refused to turn. Coins started being thrown at the stage. Marriott who was at the piano at the time singing 'Every Little Bit Hurts,' threatened to come down into the audience and 'clip some bleedin' ears if it don't stop.' At the song's finish he announced the band's final number. The stadium was instantly filled with loud catcalls. The band ploughed through the song and then quit the stage to huge waves of booing. On Tuesday the 23rd, the press joined in.

'Filthy Words By Star' ran the *Sunday Mirror* report headline. 'The behaviour of these pouting princes of popdom,' wrote Jeff Wells, 'had me squirming in my seat with embarrassment for the girls of 12 and 13 who had paid $3.30 to be within earshot of them.'

The matter of Marriott's swearing was even raised in the Australian parliament with the then New South Wales Premier, R W Asking, ordering a police enquiry. Marriott was indignant at the bad press he and the band were now receiving.

'My piano wasn't working properly and I was trying to fix it,' he retorted. 'One shorthaired geezer with glasses spent the entire evening flicking pieces of paper at my eyes as I played the organ. I shouted at him that if he didn't pack it in I would thump him. It got in the papers that I had yelled at the entire audience and walked off in a temper. Rubbish, man!'

To add fuel to the fire, tensions now arose between the two rival British groups. At one of the shows in Sydney, The Who had borrowed equipment belonging to the Small Faces. At the end of their set Pete Townshend smashed his guitar into most of it. Marriott expressed his annoyance as well as his conviction that his group should be given co-headlining status with Townshend's.

On the 24th they landed in Melbourne. More press, more attacks.

'Do you take drugs?' 'Have you brought some with you?' 'Why is your hair so long and dirty?' 'We saw you scratching your head earlier. Have you caught fleas from a dog?'

The Australian fans that visited the band's hotels bearing gifts of weed and suchlike provided the only respite from this aggressive niggling. At the Festival Hall shows, Marriott was stopped by security from bringing two girls into the hall. Marriott refused to accept the bouncer's orders, Oldham was over quickly to smooth things out.

'All our real trouble came from these adult males with big body complexes,' Marriott later told the *NME*'s Keith Altham.

In Adelaide, more aggro. To the anger of the waiting crowd, the show was delayed for an hour. The audience booed, slow handclapped the GoGo competition hastily arranged to placate them.

The Small Faces finally took to the stage. Before 'Itchycoo Park,' Marriott made public his frustration at not being able to replicate the song properly. The audience misunderstood him, thought his anger was directed at them, and started booing again. It must have been a nightmare, Marriott stuck in the glare of attention, publicly struggling with himself, the band and a large, angry audience.

That night, the end of the first leg of the tour now completed, the tour party celebrated until the early hours. At 5.00 p.m. they left their hotel in Adelaide to fly to New Zealand. Most of them with varying degrees of intoxication. Some were wiped out, others just wanted to keep going.

'I remember on the bus from the hotel in Adelaide, Stevie Marriott showing me this big bag of dope,' Doug Parkinson, vocalist with the support group, The Questions told Andy Neill.

'It was the first time I had ever seen grass, which was really scarce in Australia at the time. He was sitting in the back busy rolling joints before we got to the airport.'

It would be some flight, ending with the whole tour party being arrested. The press reports of the incident suggest a bunch of dishevelled young men fighting to stay awake and a group of hostesses, primed by the media attention to expect the very worst.

One thing's for sure, Doug Parkinson's actions started the row. He brought out a beer, passed it around. The hostess noted his action and refused to serve the party coffee. Voices were then raised, anger expressed. The hostess now bursts into tears and rushes to the captain's pit.

He in turn diverts the plane to Melbourne and there the whole party is placed under arrest. They are forced to wait hours before the whole thing is sorted out.

Finally, they fly to Sydney, catch another plane and by eight that night they are on their way to New Zealand and the 21st birthday party of one Stephen Peter Marriott. No charges were ever pressed against the touring party.

‡ ‡ ‡

The first show in Auckland was a disaster, ruined by a poor PA system.

The Who meanwhile had had enough and were close to blowing out the final two shows. The next day, the 30th of January, 1968, Marriott's 21st, they flew to Wellington.

The band booked into their hotel and then booked straight out again. There was no available room to hold a party for Marriott. Hours later, they booked back in again. EMI, Marriott's record company, had hired a club down the street for the party. They had also bought Marriott a portable record player and a selection of albums to play, including Stevie Wonder's *I Was Made To Love Her* album – 'Which was sweet of them,' noted Marriott.

The arranged party, however, did not go with a swing so Marriott, Keith Moon and a Who roadie, Wiggy, decided to head back to Marriott's hotel suite. They cracked open the booze and put some music on, loud and hard. Marriott then switched records to Stevie Wonder singing 'Baby Don't You Do It,' at which point the record player started to feedback on itself and break down. Moon picked it up and calmly threw it over the balcony and down towards some fans who had been waiting for autographs.

Wiggy rushed downstairs, picked up all the pieces, wrapped them in a towel, rushed back to the room and then emptied the lot over the balcony again.

'Before you know it,' Marriott chuckled, 'there were chairs, TVs, settees, everything was over the balcony and through the windows – mirrors, everything, the whole fucking deal. There was quite an audience watching it all come down. It was ridiculous, I was hurting with laughter, it was so funny at the time, [we were] pissed as newts.'

Eventually, the destruction stopped. The boys surveyed the room. The scene was one of complete devastation. They needed a plan.

The Artful Dodger had not lost his touch. Marriott tells Keith Moon to phone reception and say their room has been smashed up in their absence. The hotel respond by calling in the police. They interview Marriott who tells them he has been at a party down the road and returned to find his room smashed up and half his belongings stolen. Given the band's bad image in the press, such an attack would sound entirely plausible.

The police accept their story. The next day, as the tour prepared to play Wellington Town Hall, the builders moved into Marriott's suite and put it back together again.

After the gig, Marriott and Moon and Wiggy returned to their newly refurbished quarters.

'Done a good job,' Moon said admiringly of the builders. Then he picked up an ashtray and hurled it right through the window. Within minutes, a thousand other objects followed.

They didn't get away with it a second time. Not even the Dodger could figure a way out of that one. The cops told them they had caused $780 worth of damage and would have to pay the entire sum if they were not to be arrested.

On hearing this, Wiggy, picked up an armchair and hurled it over the balcony.

'Fuck it,' he said, 'make it a grand.'

‡ ‡ ‡

Marriott returned home from Australia a worried man. The tour had convinced him that the band's live performances were not up to scratch. Although the press in Australia had been gunning for them, there was no escaping the fact that when it came to performing The Who had won outright. Thanks to their incessant touring, they were now a dynamic live act.

The Small Faces had seen many changes during the preceding year but the loss of their power as a live act, really got to Marriott.

'That's the drag of having a front man,' he explained. 'When the front man falls, it all falls. And I had fallen. I wasn't a good front man on stage at all after that. I think Australia did it to me. I didn't feel comfortable there and I never felt comfortable again. Lack of confidence. When the screaming stopped and you actually heard what you were playing we went, "Jesus Christ, it's a bit bad, innit."'

Pointedly, he and Ronnie Lane had not spent that much time together in Australia. Due to a shared interest in spirituality, Lane had grown very pally with Townshend whilst Marriott linked arms with Keith Moon.

Andy Neill quotes Lane as telling journalist, Jody Denberg, 'I was reading a couple of Sufi books, and he was reading this book about this guy called Meher Baba that had this thing called Sufism Reoriented. So I started to learn about Baba and he seemed like an alright guy and Pete and I had fun.'

Lane and Townshend had actually been in the room when Moon chucked the record player out but had quickly left. 'This one ends with the police,' Townshend was reported as saying.

At the same time, Marriott was keen to return to the studio. He had a few song ideas but not enough for what he now had in mind, The Small Faces' very own concept album, designed to kill off the screaming fans and let the band finally realise their artistic potential.

Ian McLagan recalls, 'We rented three boats and cruised the Thames with our girls and dogs, writing all day and every day.'

To that end, they set sail in February just as PP Arnold's version of their song 'If You Think I'm Groovy' started slipping from the top forty. The disc had not performed well despite its epic sound and PP Arnold's impassioned vocal. That it should have received more attention added to Marriott's frustration.

‡ ‡ ‡

His fling with PP was over, finished because Steve Marriott had finally landed the woman he had chased for years, Jenny Rylance. It had been a torturous time for all concerned. First, Jenny had split with her boyfriend, Rod Stewart, and spent a lot of time with Marriott, although on a friends-only basis. Then she and Rod got back together and Steve was broken in two. He didn't speak to her for a very long time yet he couldn't shake her from his heart.

'Eventually Rod and I split up after a stormy relationship and Steve must have heard about it because he came to see me at my place of work, Quorum in the Kings Road,' Jenny recalls.

'He started bombarding me with presents, flowers, the whole romantic bit. The last thing I really wanted at that time was another musician boyfriend. I just wanted to get on with my own life and my own career but Steve wouldn't let up.

'A little while later I was very ill and Steve literally cancelled everything to look after me for a couple of weeks in the most delightful way. I had never been looked after like that before and I guess it was then that I fell in love with him... At that time, he was lovely, a lovely man.'

Jenny moved in with Steve. He had now settled in a terraced house in Ewatt Green, Chiswick. On the walls was painted a picture of the cartoon character, Thor. With Marriott was his dog Shamus who had been taken by Jenny to meet him off the plane from New Zealand. Shamus would father thirteen dogs and make an appearance on the Pink Floyd album, *Meddle*, barking away to Dave Gilmour's blues guitar.

Marriott adored Shamus but was terrible at cleaning up the mess he caused.

'He would invite me round to his cottage,' Calder recalls, 'dog hairs everywhere, in the sitting room, in the kitchen and he'd say, "Do you want something to eat?" and it was always, 'No, Steve I had something to eat before I came out.'

Strange that someone so meticulous in appearance did not maintain similar standards with their living quarters.

'He was having a lot of hassle with the neighbours, the Hasslewaithes,' Rylance recalls, 'and ended up writing 'Lazy Sunday' about his time there. Mind you I didn't blame them. It must have been hard living next door to him. They complained continuously about the noise and rightly so. Steve had installed Wharfedale speakers from Olympic Studios in the living room which measured approximately fourteen feet by twelve feet.'

Not long after the contretemps, they moved again, this time to a cottage in Marlow, Buckinghamshire. Lane and Mac also moved in. It was Pimlico all over again but with a difference; they too had girls in tow, Sue and Sandy respectively and they were surrounded by nature not the city.

Rylance accompanied Steve on the boat trip. She confirms that most of the next album was written in this period although the lyrics for the aforementioned hit, 'Lazy Sunday,' were written in Aunt Sheila's bathroom. Marriott had gone to visit his aunt one Sunday, appropriately enough, and during the journey there had been hit by inspiration. On arriving at his aunt's house, he grabbed pen and paper, rushed upstairs, locked himself in the loo and scribbled away.

One of the lines he wrote reads, 'I'll sing you a song with no words or no tune / As I sit on the khazi and suss out the moon.'

Furthermore, Steve had now devised a plan to help the band perform better in a live situation. His solution was to bring in an extra member into the fold. His name was Peter Frampton.

At first the band were mystified, soon they became annoyed at the thought of adding someone to the line up. Ian McLagan; 'We constantly had to shout him down because he often had bad ideas like this.' Effectively, Marriott was saying that they were not up to the job. Who the fuck did he think he was?

'I don't know why they didn't want Frampton in the band,' their leader told Hellier. 'Maybe they thought he was wimpy or something. The kid had come around the cottage and played some real good guitar so I knew he was capable of playing some really tasty stuff. He'd never heard of Booker T. and the MG's or any of those things that I had. Once again, it was like opening up a flower – they hear this music and they go crazy 'cos they have never heard it before. So he wanted to play that kind of stuff and I thought, "Well, the time is right."'

He paused.

'That's my role in life, turning people onto R&B. That's what I have done all the time.'

Turning down Frampton dealt a telling blow to Marriott but despite this, he would not let go of the idea. Later on that year, Frampton bumped into both Marriott and Lane at the Immediate offices. During their short chat, Frampton told the pair how unhappy he was, how he wanted to leave The Herd, since being voted 'The Face Of '68', his group were now seen as a teenybopper band and he hated the accolade.

'I'd been pushed to the front,' Frampton recalled, 'and had become a "mini sensation". But it wasn't the audience that I craved.'

If anyone could relate to a musician being misunderstood by the public it was Steve Marriott. A month later, Frampton got a call from him. Would he be interested in forming a band with fellow Herd member, Andy Bown and drummer Jerry Shirley who was now playing in a band called Wages Of Sin? The group would be signed to Immediate Records and work exclusively with Marriott and Lane.

'As they were the brightest stars on Andrew's Immediate label,' Frampton explained, 'they had long assumed the role of house producers and they saw in the Herd an ideal opportunity to further everyone's career. Anyway we went along there and really hit it off with Steve and Ronnie.'

Much later in the year, Marriott would again call Frampton, this time with an even better offer. Would the Face of '68 consider travelling to Paris to be in the Small Faces for a week?

Frampton didn't make Marriott wait too long for an answer.

‡ ‡ ‡

By 1968, the album had assumed a much greater importance within rock culture. Singles were still important but the album, post-*Sgt Pepper*, was now the medium to conquer. To reflect its lofty position, the music press began running lengthy stories about such events as the band Traffic moving to the country to write and record their debut album. Marriott thoroughly approved of this shift in music. Bands would now be judged by artistic standards not the size of their pop stardom. By creating an outstanding new album he firmly hoped that the band could now achieve two goals in one; lose the screamers and gain respect. He got what he wanted.

In March they worked abroad, Italy and Scandinavia. In Sweden, Marriott was interviewed on TV and asked, 'Do you believe in rock'n'roll?'

He replied, 'I've just trod in some.'

They returned home, their new album now half-completed. A single was now needed to bridge the gap. Marriott wanted a new tune called 'Song Of A Baker.' It was not a pretty song. It was loud, verging on heavy metal, full of crashing guitars and drums. But for Marriott the song had a definite purpose. It would clearly signal the band's intentions and kill off any remaining teenybopper fans. The release was denied him. Instead, a song destined to dog the band throughout their whole career was put on the radio and into the shops.

'Lazy Sunday' began life during the band's time in Australia. All bands create their own private language, their own private lingo – phrases peculiar and understandable only to them. In Australia they had dreamt up a chant to accompany their shouts of 'reeb, nuf, nis,' (beer fun and sin backwards) and it was that chant which Steve Marriott inserted into a slow bluesy song he had written about his trouble with the neighbours.

'I hated that song,' McLagan says of 'Lazy Sunday'.

'It was only when he started doing all these stupid things in the studio that it got any good.'

To emphasise the storyline, Marriott sang the song in his most exaggerated cockney accent, his vocal and the song's intrinsic humour instantly conjuring up the communal spirit of the East End music halls. Once finished, it presented itself as a natural choice for a single. Bill Marriott certainly thought so.

'When he played that one, 'Lazy Sunday,' Kay Marriott recalled, 'Bill said, "that's going to be the A side isn't it?" Steve said, no. Bill said, "Well that's a cert," and that is the only time Bill said, "You listen to me."'

His son did listen but no argument would sway him. Sharp cookie that he was, Marriott saw straight away that 'Lazy Sunday' would colour his band badly, frustrate them in their attempts to be treated as a serious artistic force.

'I had an awful fight with Andrew [Loog Oldham] when he said 'Lazy Sunday' was the single,' he told writer Dave Thompson in 1982. 'It was an album track, it was me taking the piss because I'd had this fight with The Hollies about never singing in me own voice, and they were right because me own voice is Cockney and I'd never sung in Cockney. So I did it for a laugh, for an album track, because it cracked everybody up. If we had done the song straight, like it was written, it would never have been a hit. But because it was this funny, jokey, novelty thing, we were stuck with it.'

On April 5th, 'Lazy Sunday' c/w 'Rollin' Over' was placed in the shop racks. It proved an instant success, quickly rising to number two in the charts and becoming one of the most famous songs in the Small Faces' canon. The group were invited onto *Top Of The Pops* three weeks running as well as taking a day out to shoot another promo film with Peter Whitehead, the location naturally enough, the East End of London at Kenney Jones' family house.

At the end of the month, with Ronnie Lane now a married man, the band travelled to Germany and Belgium, arriving back on May 1st and resuming recording duties on the 6th. By the end of the month the album was finally ready.

'He rang up about four in the morning,' Kay Marriott recalled, 'and he said, "Listen to this." I thought, "What's he on?" He said, "You've got to come here because you can't hear it on the phone."

'I said, "I can't get up there at this time of the morning." His father was laying next to me grunting. Steve said, "You've got to come." So I rang my sister, she lived round the corner and I said, "Do you feel like going to the studio?" "What," she says, "Do you know what time it is?" Anyhow we got there about six and we stayed until we both had to get to work at nine and we were just blasted with it. It was wonderful. I thought it was the best thing they had ever done. But our ears did take a pounding that morning.'

The creativity didn't stop there.

Tony Calder: 'Everything he did he did quickly because he had such a small attention span. We were still in the New Oxford Street office when he came in and said, "Do you think we could do the sleeve like a tobacco tin? Can we do it like an Ogden's?" who were tobacco tin manufacturers. I said, "Yeah, I'll have a word with them."

'They sent over a book of every tobacco tin they had ever made. I looked at it and it came to one called, Ogden's Nut-Brown Flake.

I said, "Steve get your arse in here." He said, "You're right, *Ogden's Nut Gone Flake*." He said, "Do you think we could put a packet of skins in there?" So I called the guy up and he said, Mr Calder, we would be delighted.'

Immediate went further. To advertise the album they created a parody of the Lord's Prayer which ran. 'Small Faces, Which were in the studios, Hallowed be thy name, Thy music come, Thy songs be sung, On this album as they came from your heads, We give you this day our daily bread, Give us thy album in a round cover, As we give thee 37/9d, Lead us into record stores, And deliver us *Ogden's Nut Gone Flake*, For nice is the music, the sleeve and the story, For ever and ever, Immediate.'

When the ads ran in the music press the predictable fuss erupted.

'We didn't know a thing about the ad until we saw it in the music papers,' Marriott stated, 'and frankly we got the horrors at first. We realise it could be taken as a serious knock against religion. On thinking it over we don't feel it is particularly good or bad. It's just another form of advertising.'

Certainly was. He got a whole page in the *Melody Maker* out of it.

Because of its unique packaging and use of a spoken word storyline, *Ogden's Nut Gone Flake* is regarded as the band's classic album. Yet it remains their most uneven – the first of their albums on which they deign not to enter new musical fields but instead play to their strengths. The album showcases all their influences, all their yesterdays. Everything is here – brooding psychedelia, epic pop soul, cockney-tainted tunes, English folk music, and blistering guitars. But the sum of the parts does not add up. Side one alone features the epic psychedelic instrumental title track, moves into the soulful 'Afterglow' contains two raucous Cockney pop tunes in 'Rene' and 'Lazy Sunday,' and has time for the heavy metal-touched 'Song Of A Baker.'

The second side doesn't fare as well in terms of quality and as if in recognition of the lack of cohesion, the band invited the comic, Stanley Unwin (second choice, first was Spike Milligan who turned the offer down) to narrate the story of one Happiness Stan (name of Ronnie Lane's father) and his search for the other half of the moon. It was an inspired move.

No other album, let alone a concept one, had thought to use the spoken voice in such a manner, the songs always told the story. Moreover, Unwin's speciality lay in remaking the English language with linguistic twists and turns unique to him. He called it Unwinese, provided a lot of clever humour.

'I'd had a call via my agent and I considered it a compliment to be asked,' Unwin told John Hellier in 1998, shortly before his death. 'My agent said that this group called The Small Faces are recording somewhere in London and if they gave you a straight script would you transfer it to Unwinese. I thought I'd give it a go and I drove down to Barnes in South West London. When I arrived I first met Ronnie Lane with their producer, a chap called Glyn Johns, and they gave me the script. I read it through once and I said, 'What about giving me some phrases?'

'They gave me 'where you at man?' and 'stay cool,' so I popped those into the dialogue… It was a very warm relationship. Everyone was in tune with what was going on. There was lots of laugher, chuckling and replacing of words. I couldn't understand all of what they were saying as they had their own sort of language themselves'

The comedian spent time with the band in the studio, grew to like them quickly, especially Marriott. Unwin says he was closest to him and that his narration was completed in one take.

'It was a good story, a little weird story which one has to listen to again and again to get the best out of it. I still don't know whether it was worked out by any individual or whether it was all of them cooking up the story. Ronnie was the one who seemed to jump about a bit more than anyone else. I remember getting a lovely card from Ronnie saying something like, "thanks for being such a groove, we're knocked out with it, hope you like it." Ronnie said that he had heard me saying the Sunnyglow and Purimost on a TV advert for Gales honey. He said they had cottoned onto that.'

'It made us laugh,' Marriott later commented. 'Anything that made us laugh we liked.'

Moreover, they had again worked with producer Glyn Johns who, while not a fan of Marriott's personality, was certainly taken by his talent. The chasm between musician and producer can partly be explained by Johns non-use of drugs. As he later explained:

'It got a bit boring sometimes because people would drift off and become unintelligible but the fact of the matter was that everyone I worked with during that period pushed me to come up with new sounds and ideas that I probably wouldn't have done without them. I got the benefit of their drug-taking without the risks to the brain.'

Despite its unevenness, *Ogden's* does contain some of their best sounding songs and Marriott's growing mastery of the studio should not be underestimated. Today most of his Sixties work both in and out of the Small Faces still sounds absolutely contemporary.

'I think Ronnie and I felt that if we got a good drum sound and a good bass sound the rest was cream on top,' he explained to Hellier. 'If the bass and drums are sounding punchy and clear then the rest would produce itself. That's what we went for every time. These days it's synthesisers but then you had to have the drums. The drums were everything. Everything should be behind the bass not in front of it. The Wall Of Sound thing [the title given to producer Phil Spector's epic productions] didn't really affect us. I didn't want to be The Ronettes. We were looking for a Tamla sound which was bass and drums basically, same as Booker T. That's why we opted for our line up.'

The album was released on 24 May, 1968. Intriguingly, the week before, Keith Altham had previewed the work in the *NME* and stated that side one would end on either a version of The Ronettes 'Be My Baby' or a band version of 'If You Think You're Groovy.' Neither song has ever appeared. Never mind. The album stayed at number one for six weeks.

Record Mirror said of it, 'This puts them in the really big league, not just a collection of pretty small faces.' *Melody Maker* considered it 'incredibly, unbelievably irresistible – just so groovy and quite indescribable. You must hear this LP – and buy it!'

Marriott had achieved his aim. The album gave him that which he most desired – respect and success.

Ironic really. It would be the last album he would make with the Small Faces.

‡ ‡ ‡

To promote the album, the band agreed to appear on a special edition of the BBC show *Colour Me Pop* on Friday June 21st, 1968. Songs featured were 'Song Of A Baker,' 'Happiness Stan,' 'Rollin' Over,' 'The Hungry Intruder,' 'The Journey,' 'Mad John,' and 'Happydaystoytown.' Although the band mimed to recordings they had made that afternoon, the microphones were left on to capture nice little ad libs between the boys. Stanley Unwin also took part, delivering his monologue whilst sitting on a throne wearing a crown. In the afternoon, the cameras started rolling and the band, Marriott especially, turned in a riveting performance. Wearing a waistcoat, white shirt, red flares, his hair now shoulder length, Marriott's enthusiasm, his obvious need to communicate, literally stole the show. Yet for Tony Calder, the fact that Marriott was the only focal point of the band was a problem.

'In the Sixties, all the top bands had two leaders. With the Beatles, Paul and John, Mick and Keith for The Stones. Maybe that was the problem with Ronnie. They were meant to be the two front guys but by the time we got involved – and some of it is down to us – it was all Steve. To me he was the leader of the band. He did have a problem about his height as any short person does and I think the physical height of the band put them in a situation where on TV no one took them seriously. They were seen as more of a comedy act.' ('No way,' Mac says. 'That's bollocks!')

This was a perception that the huge success of 'Lazy Sunday' had served to strengthen. To kill it, Marriott started work on a song which he would later state was one of the best he had ever written. Its failure to shake up the world would prove disastrous to all concerned.

‡ ‡ ‡

They got married, he and Jenny. The date was May 29th, 1968, the location Kensington Registry Office, the ceremony kept secret. He had chased her for two years and she had danced in his brain all that time. Now, they were wed.

The designer Ossie Clark supplied Jenny's dress, came to the ceremony as well. Ronnie Lane turned up for the night's party.

A week later the news broke in the press and the fan club mail doubled overnight.

'I got lots of really nice letters from fans wishing us good luck,' Marriott told the press. 'Some letters came that weren't so nice and others came with all our records broken up and scratched across with a nail file. "Oh he's married, there's no chance for me." As if there ever was a chance. I mean – what's all that about?'

It's about girls and pop stardom, it's about fantasies and dreams, it's about posters on bedroom walls and swooning and having someone to live for when you hate the rest of the world because he and only he understands. It was also about making Steve Marriott feel very misunderstood.

In the same interview, Marriott revealed that the band had wanted to work with singer-songwriter, Donovan who Marriott had twice been to see at London's Royal Albert Hall. Management and record companies had quashed the idea.

'The monsters take over and stop us,' Marriott complained in the *NME*. The Beatles who had just started their own Apple record label had shown one way around such obstacles.

'One day the groups will take over the business,' Marriott hopefully predicted. (Yet Marriott does as Marriott does. Business difficulties or not, he still got his way by guesting on the Donovan song 'There Is A Boy For Every Girl' on Donovan's Loog-Oldham produced *Essence To Essence* album. Throughout his whole career, Marriott guested on a huge amount of records. A full rundown of these appearances is available at the back of the book.)

Marriott was talking on the day he attended a private screening in Wardour Street of the band's performance on *Colour Me Pop*. He wore dark red satin trousers, a Fair Isle pullover, green shirt and white shoes. Whatever else was going on, he was still fighting the sartorial wars.

'People often shout, "Oi Ginger!" [term for homosexual] when I walk around Shepherd's Bush market,' he revealed, 'So I thought, right – I'll wear a collar, tie and a nice dark suit. But they still shouted out. It's me barnet [Cockney rhyming slang for hair, Barnet fair – hair]. They just don't like long hair.'

In the sixties and seventies, hair was the chosen battleground which the young and cool and the old and straight fought on. Marriott's hair at this stage was just right, a mix of the Mod style with the hippie fashion. Just like his band, in fact.

Soon, they started rehearsing and in an attempt to bolster their live sound brought in a six-piece brass section. Meanwhile, Arthur Howes, their agent, made clear his intention to send the boys on a package tour of America, Europe and even some Iron Curtain countries such as Russia and East Germany. The band would fly out with The Who, Marmalade and PP Arnold. They would then return and in the Autumn tackle Britain with The Union Gap and singer Bobby Goldsboro in tow.

'It's a groovy idea,' Marriott told the magazine *Disc and Music Echo*. 'For the past two weeks we've been working with a six piece brass section as an experiment. It's worked so well, we'd like to take them with us too. Obviously we'd take Pat Arnold because we dig her so much. She has a really together stage act. I think she's too good for British audiences.'

The proposed tours never happened. In summer the band played just a handful of gigs. They played Exeter and Oxford in June with The Move and The Marmalade. In July, they appeared at a festival in Northern Ireland. That was it. For all his talk of 'groovy ideas,' Marriott still felt that the band were nowhere near cutting it live.

'As I said before,' he said, 'it suited Andrew's purposes to keep us in the studio and so the road thing horribly suffered. By the time we came out of the hole, after being in a studio for a year, the road sounded terrible to me. That's when I thought it's got to be over.' It was a bad time for such thoughts to be surfacing. Marriott and Lane had together bought a cottage called Beehive in Moreton, Essex. There were two buildings on the land, Marriott and Jenny occupied one, Ronnie and his wife Susan (who had appeared in Camay soap TV commercials) lived in the other. This is where they locked themselves away.

They hid – only venturing out from their country hideaway to appear on radio and TV. In retrospect, Tony Calder says, their inactivity was a big mistake.

'They really tried their best with that album,' he told me. 'It was a work of pop art. If we had broken it in America and if Andrew and I had gone on tour they would have been alright because it would have opened up the next stage of it. But it was like here is my masterpiece, it is appreciated in England but the other English-speaking people over the water don't appreciate it. On reflection, I think Steve would have felt that he hadn't achieved what he wanted to achieve.'

Keen to keep the album's sales alive, Immediate asked the band for a single. Marriott had just the song for them. It was called 'Hello The Universal.' Part-recorded on a tiny tape recorder in his garden, the first half of the song features Steve playing a quasi blues riff on an acoustic guitar, the sound of traffic, his dog barking and his wife coming home with the shopping, audible. In the second part of the song the band come in, playing a country style riff which is then augmented with trombones and other sounds.

The song's lyrics were oblique, playful, and conversational in their delivery. Amongst other things, Steve sings of bumping into Mick Jagger. The song, backed by a new heavier sounding track called 'Donkey Rides, A Penny, A Glass,' certainly had no intention of trying to charm anyone. It was far too rough, unusual and raw for such niceties.

In the studio, Steve attempted the song many times but could never match the feel and authenticity of the first taped version. Eventually, he opted to use that version for the record. 'Makes sense doesn't it?' he said in 1984 before adding that the song was 'a right piss take.' Released in June of 1968, as simply 'The Universal', the press greeted this idiosyncratic song with some scepticism and initial sales were hardly encouraging.

To promote it, Keith Altham was called to the band's country hideaway where he met a defensive-sounding Marriott.

'The song was supposed to be called 'Hello the Universal,' Marriott told him, a fact he would repeat again and again in every interview. 'But it escaped before we could put that right. That would have given the impression we wanted. The whole idea of the song was a kind of 'Good Morning' to life. The secret of nearly all our records now is that we are really just being ourselves, that's what it is all about. Our biggest hang-up now may be in trying to follow *Ogden's*. If the next one does not go to number one then a lot of people will start crowing that it is not as good as the last one. You feel a little musically washed out after putting in as much effort as we did into that album, but down here you soon come round.

'All the worries about the tax man and the bills don't seem to matter down here and then along comes an album from America like Dr. John's *Night Tripper*, which gives us a tremendous boot up the backside.'

Other interviews at this time refer to Marriott grooving to the Mason Williams *Classical Gas* album and The Band's debut *Music From The Big Pink*. In the *Melody Maker*, Marriott also went on the defensive. In the piece, writer Chris Welch refers to the bad reviews given the single, one calling it 'an ill-timed catastrophe.'

'You were right,' Marriott agreed. 'It is a catastrophe – musically. It's a weird follow up which we recorded because we liked it and because it's different from anything else. We wanted it to be the most terrible production. We wanted a really evil sound and as far as we are concerned we've got it perfectly – and it's good. But I wouldn't say it was meant to be a send up of Don Partridge at all. We all like him too much to do that. He's a gas…it's supposed to be what I sound like when I wake up in the morning. A lot of people have thought I was trying to sing like Don Partridge or Bob Dylan and a lot of people won't play it. I suppose that is because we didn't put a long enough intro on it for deejays to talk over. But listen to it a few times and it'll grow on you. Anyway Ringo (Starr, Beatles drummer) likes it and Keith Moon said some nice things about it in *Blind Date* so it can't be all bad.'

Despite its erratic character, 'The Universal' stayed in the charts for eleven weeks, peaking at sixteen. A respectable showing. But not good enough for either band or management.

Tony Calder: ''The Universal' was the end of the band. We had got them to a level where the pre-sale was big. We were coming off 'Lazy Sunday,' a number one record but the band wouldn't promote it. I can't remember what happened but they didn't do the TV stuff plus radio didn't like it.' A video for the band was shot at Beehive Cottage. It was directed by Alexis Kanner, an actor who had just gained fame for his role in *The Prisoner*, Patrick McGoohan's enigmatic TV show. The show had gripped the nation. The video for 'The Universal' was aired just once, on an ITV programme called *Come Here Often*.

The band's contract with Immediate was now up for renewal and Marriott for one had problems he needed attending to before signing anything. The allusion to the taxman in the *NME* interview was just one financial worry on his shoulders. Normally, such problems were eased by earning cash from playing live. Now, not even that option was open to Marriott.

'I asked Andrew to lend me £1,200 so I could finish the completion of buying this house,' Marriott told Hellier. 'He said, "Yeah, but only if you get the rest of the band to sign for two more years and I can keep your publishing." Soon after we left, we had totally lost confidence in them.'

The band appointed a new management firm, a company that specialised in making TV commercials. It was a bizarre, hasty decision but one typical of those desperate for cash.

In July, more evidence of the Small Faces' skill as producers and arrangers emerged with the release of Skip Bifferty's 'Man In Black' single. The band had personally asked Steve and Ronnie to work with them even though they were managed by Don Arden.

'Neither they or us were on very good terms with Arden. We had that in common,' Marriott later said. 'They were getting calls at midnight with shotguns and all that crap. They got very heavy with Graham Bell, the kid singer. They were a good band, I thought.'

On the 11th of September the group performed 'The Universal' for *Top Of The Pops* and on the 20th Marriott failed to show up for a live Radio One interview. He was busy writing, though, and hanging out more and more with Peter Frampton. On October 13th at Manchester's Belle Vue club, Frampton joined the Small Faces live on stage where he sang on 'Tin Soldier' and 'All Or Nothing.'

The next night he did the same at the Bubbles club in Brentwood, Essex. The club had just opened and was large but dimly lit with no stage as such, just a small platform in the corner.

John Hellier was in the audience the night the Small Faces played there. He recalled Marriott striding on stage with a ciggy in his mouth and greeting the audience with the words 'fucking cold out there, innit?' Marriott kept his ankle length overcoat on for the whole of the gig.

'Unlike previous concert tours that I had seen, they didn't feature any of the hit singles,' Hellier states, 'and the only numbers I recognised at the time were 'Rollin' Over' and 'Wham Bam Thank You Mam.'

After twenty minutes, Marriott announced that he wanted to bring on a friend. Cue Peter Frampton who stood at the back contributing lead guitar solos. By the end of the ninety-minute set the audience were vigorously applauding, shouting for more and totally vindicating Marriott's belief in the young guitarist. Still, the band would not yield. Frampton could not join.

The press picked up on this growing alliance and both Marriott and Frampton were forced to release bland statements about just being good friends and nothing more. No mention was made of the fact that Frampton had already worked with the Small Faces in the studio. But not in England – in Paris.

Johnny Hallyday was a French singer who every year would recruit a band from London to record with. Glyn Johns recommended the Small Faces to the French vocalist and Hallyday readily agreed to working with them on part of his album. An extra guitarist was needed so Jeff Beck and Eric Clapton were approached. Due to other commitments, both guitarists passed on the offer. Marriott then suggested Pete Frampton. Both Johns and Hallyday had no problem with the suggestion and invited the guitarist over to Paris

'I was on that plane in a shot,' said Frampton. 'I joined the Small Faces for a week and it was unbelievable.'

Of the three songs that Marriott gave to Hallyday, one was old, two were unrecorded. Their old number, 'That Man,' suddenly became a 'new song' entitled 'Amen,' whilst 'Regardez Pour Moi' would turn up on Steve's next album as 'What You Will.' But it was on the third song, 'Reclamation,' that the future would be heard. This was a heavy dense guitar led workout that presaged the sound of Steve's next project, Humble Pie.

The weeklong session, according to producer Glyn Johns, was not a happy experience. He recalls the band constantly bickering at each other until, 'something happened. I don't know what the argument was about but it had obviously been brewing and this was the last straw.'

The band flew home with their once solid bond badly fractured. Marriott was apart from the other three members now. Worse, he was obviously losing his grip and interest.

‡ ‡ ‡

In November, the band finally embarked upon a proper tour along with old buddies The Who, Arthur Brown, Joe Cocker and Alan Bown. They took along their horn section and visited Germany and Holland first before returning to start off in London, Birmingham and Newcastle, a gig where their six-song set was recorded.

Then it was up to Glasgow, down to Liverpool before being allowed a month off. 1968 would finish with a gig on New Year's Eve at Alexandra Palace and it was the concert that would break the band in two.

‡ ‡ ‡

Alexis Korner's unofficial title as the daddy of the blues was well earned. Korner had been absolutely crucial in popularising blues music in this country after the war. Born in 1928, Korner came up through the skiffle scene before working with a wide variety of musicians, from Cyril Davies to Mick Jagger. His musical ability was highly regarded by fellow musicians, Marriott included.

Korner had first met Steve through the TV show *The Five O' Clock Club*, and had been impressed by both his voice and musicianship. He called Immediate Records, set up a meeting. The result was that in September, 1968, Stevie agreed to accompany Alexis on a low key tour of Scotland.

Damian De Korner, Alexis's son, provides the memories.

'What a fabulous player and what a great singer,' the record engineer and Korner archivist says of Marriott. 'If you are a real musician's musician you would always have Stevie along. He was amazing to jam with. Stevie came from that era of players who would listen to what someone was playing and play with them and not fight them. Stevie and my dad came from an era where music was socially more important and everything else was secondary. We've lost that nowadays, such a shame.'

'Alexis admired Steve a lot,' his wife Bobbie told me, 'He thought he was a great guitar player and a fantastic singer.'

On tour in Scotland with Korner, Marriott revelled in the luxury of playing for appreciative audiences. These gigs were a million miles away from the concert circuit Marriott had trodden for years. Where once there were screams and chaos, now genuine, appreciative applause splashed over Marriott, he lapped it up.

'Just standing in the background playing the blues in small venues,' says Keith Altham, 'this was miles away from the Small Faces. Fans at Alexis's gigs listened intently and cheered with appreciation, just what Steve had always wanted. His friendship and admiration for Alexis went a very long way towards him leaving the Small Faces.'

On his return from the Korner tour the band began work on the follow up album to *Ogden's*. The work was provisionally entitled '1862,' the title lifted from a sign that hung above the front entrance of the derelict church hall next to Beehive Cottage. Steve had applied to the council to buy the building, turn it into a recording studio but his request had been denied.

The material they recorded at Olympic included, a version of Tim Hardin's 'Red Balloon' as well as demos of new songs entitled 'The Autumn Stone,' 'Collibosher,' 'Call It Something Nice,' 'Wide Eyed Girl On The Wall' and 'Wham Bam Thank You Mam.'

After completing this studio work, the band made the journey to North London and Alexandra Palace, the gig which would break them in two.

‡ ‡ ‡

Just two hours into 1969, Glyn Johns' home phone rings. It is Steve Marriott, looking for Johns' guest that night, Pete Frampton.

'We were playing records,' Frampton recalled, 'and I remember Glyn saying to me, "I've just done this new album in ten days with a band called Led Zeppelin. I'll play it to you." We had just finished side one and the phone rang. It was Steve calling from backstage at Alexandra Palace.

'He said, "Well, mate. I've done it, I've left the Small Faces. Can I join your band?" I said , "Of course you can!" and then we put on side two of Led Zeppelin.'

In the week, leading up to the Alexandra Palace gig, tensions between Marriott and the band had risen to new levels. The reason, simple. Marriott again wanted Frampton to tour with the band. Again, the band stayed firm. No way.

'He had been throwing wobblers all week,' Kenney Jones recalled. By the time they got to Alexandra Palace no one was smiling.

Keith Altham saw it all:

'I was at the Alexandra Palace the night Steve walked off stage. He was in a foul mood that night. The sound was poor and there were some new numbers in the set that were under-rehearsed. Although they had recently had the *Ogden's* album at the top of the charts, he still felt as though he wasn't being taken seriously as a musician and what really brought that home to him in 1968 was the fact that he had become very close friends with Alexis Korner.'

Of the night, Marriott said in 1984, 'It was a shambles really. Alexis Korner got up to play. It was my idea, I must admit, but I didn't think it was going to be that much of a shambles. I thought this is terrible. I slung my guitar down and did a very unprofessional thing and walked off. I just thought this is horrible.'

'If we'd had any gumption at all,' Marriott later told Dave Thompson, 'we'd have booked Stanley Unwin, hired a string section, and gone out on the road with it, instead, we carried on fucking around, just crashing about on stage and putting up with the screaming. It was horrible. Andrew was losing interest in Immediate, so he didn't give us any pointers; all we had was this awful formula which had been successful for years, and was now an albatross which wouldn't fly away.'

In the dressing room the band tore into Steve, especially Mac.

'He went mad,' Kenney Jones said of the keyboard man, 'but Steve just simply said he couldn't do it anymore. He felt he couldn't cross over from being a pop band into heavier music. He felt it was too difficult.'

And with that The Small Faces came to their end. The lines had been crossed, there was no going back.

'You grow apart for chrissakes,' Marriott stated in 1984. 'You're talking about people living together from the ages of seventeen to twenty two and that's a growing up part of your life. We got to hate each other, no doubt about it.'

They certainly did. Immediately, this closeknit band divided itself into two; Marriott over there, the other three over here. Neither camp would speak to the other for a mighty long time.

Frampton, again:

'The following day after the Alexandra Palace gig I was back at home and I got a call from Ronnie Lane who said, "Me, Kenney and Mac would like to come round and see you." I thought, "Hello, what's all this about?" Anyway they came round to my horrible little flat in Earls Court and asked me to join the Small Faces. All I could say was, "Well, it's a bit late now. Why couldn't you have asked me while we were in Paris? We'd all be in the same band together and Steve wouldn't have left."' (Mac vehemently denies this story.)

If Frampton's memory is serving him correctly then it seems incredible that the remaining three members should make him such an offer. For months, they had resisted taking him on. Now, with their leader gone, Frampton had been the first person they had turned to, suggesting that they were just as enamoured of his guitar skills as Marriott.

A handful of possibilities now appear. Maybe by resisting Marriott's wishes the band knew that eventually he would walk. Maybe that was what they wanted. After all, the man was a handful. Hyper here, hyper there, non stop chatter, on and on he went, centre of attention at all times.

Maybe they were tired of taking Marriott's orders, worried by the erratic song writing direction their man was taking.

In all the interviews around 'The Universal' single it was only Marriott who spoke openly and lovingly about the song. The others just rued putting out 'Lazy Sunday' as a single.

In a moving interview given by Ian McLagan for Channel Four's 1996 documentary on the band, the keyboardist spoke wearily of the levels of exhaustion that Marriott's hyper nature would drive him to. He revealed that when Marriott showed up in his hometown for a gig in the late '80s and called him, McLagan heard the message and declined the chance to meet up.

He never called him back.

‡ ‡ ‡

They couldn't just split up. There were gigs to fulfil, contracts to honour. Germany, always a good place to play for the band, was first. Five dates there, an Austrian show as well.

'That tour,' McLagan recalls, 'was the only time we made any money playing live and that was because I took over the finances. Everybody was ripping us off but once I took care of the cash we made some money. As for the tour, I don't remember it being strained or anything.'

Damian De Korner does though. His dad Alexis was the co-headlining act for the final German jaunt and he brought along his son.

De Korner recalls at most gigs there were two dressing rooms – one for the band, one for interview purposes. But as the tour wore on, Marriott soon co-opted the interview room, made it his own private space. Immediate's wooing of Steve and their refusal to entertain keeping on the rest of the band also caused friction. The tension was palpable.

'Stevie was a fabulous person, he was so up, always so bouncy,' Damian De Korner recalls, 'But you didn't want to get on the wrong side of him. You really didn't. He had a viper's tongue. Seriously.'

In Dusseldorf, Damian recalls Marriott in a foul mood as they arrive at their hotel, 'a weird castle cum hotel.' In the main dining room a banquet is being re-enacted, all the guests clothed in fancy Victorian costumes.

'The Small Faces, the road crew and my dad walk in,' Damian recalls, 'and you know straightaway this is not going to be a good blend.'

Marriott checks in and starts asking if they can go and eat in the dining room. The hotel say no. Marriott (who in Damien's words, 'believed that any hotel he stayed in belonged to him') begins berating the manager. Meanwhile, the road crew slips upstairs. They were on a mission.

On tour, says De Korner, Marriott had stipulated that he be given a suite in every hotel. On arrival, members of the road crew would carry Marriott's bags up to his room. In Dusseldorf, the suite allotted Marriott was entered via a small anteroom.

Fed up with Marriott's black moods, the road crew pulled in the bed from the bedroom, blocked off the door to the suite with a wardrobe and left Marriott's bags just inside the front door. Then they hid in their respective rooms on the same floor.

Marriott came upstairs, opened his door and stepped into what he thought was a tiny bedroom not the expected suite. His temper exploded. Swearing profusely he rushed downstairs to get the manager. At which point the road crew entered the room and quickly put it back to normal.

Two minutes later, Marriott arrived with the manager, flung open the door, realised what had occurred and shouted at the top of his voice, 'YOU FUCKING BASTARDS!'

The manager meanwhile had no idea what this angry, tiny man was going ballistic about.

After unpacking, Marriott now decides he wants to eat. He calls room service. Room service is closed. He slams down the phone, heads out of his room to go to reception. As he marches down the corridor a cleaning maid walks towards him. Marriott starts shouting, 'you can get me some food, I know you can, I know you can.'

The maid tries to ignore Marriott, Marriott won't allow it. In a flash of red, he grabs a painting on the wall and brings it down on the maid's head who runs down the corridor with the painting swivelling around her neck.

The next day the party was banned indefinitely from the hotel.

Meanwhile, back home the papers had got wind of the band's internal problems. *Disc and Music Echo* reported that The Small Faces had been recording without Marriott. For the session, Pete Townshend had taken his place.

'We recorded at my studios at my house,' Townshend confirmed. 'Ronnie asked me to play lead guitar for them as a favour. They don't quite know what's happening. They were making the discs to see how things would work out without Stevie.'

The report also revealed that Marriott 'had been raving about a new group he was forming with Frampton.'

He had already named the band Humble Pie, and was busy rehearsing with them out in the country. By the time they had been announced to the world, the band had been playing for months.

Frampton himself recalls how desperate Marriott was to get working.

'The Herd by this time had finally collapsed and the Oldham/Calder thing had failed to work out. I was now going to throw all my time and energy into preparing for the new band with Steve. The Small Faces still had a handful of live dates to play at home and in Germany but their hearts weren't really in it. Everybody was pondering over their futures and although they had been a very successful band, they were all broke.

'Steve was itching to get home and start rehearsing with our new band which by then was called Humble Pie and featured not only Steve but ex-Spooky Tooth bass player Greg Ridley and Jerry Shirley, of course.'

They were all broke. Once again, Marriott and the band had delivered hit after hit; once again their pockets were empty.

Tony Calder: 'Everyone's account was in the red. That was the problem. The company was carrying too many unrecouped losses on recordings. They were earning the money but they were always taking money, which we would put on their royalty account. In the end we couldn't afford it. One year, we got a bill for dog food for four hundred quid.' Mac disagrees with Calder's assessment. 'Absolute lie,' he fumes. 'They were always taking money. The only advance Immediate paid out was for Beehive Cottage.'

That the band's anger at their parlous financial state would be forever directed at Calder and not Oldham is in no way surprising. That's what happens when you play the 'good cop, bad cop' game.

'I liked Andrew's flair,' Marriott told Hellier, 'we all did, thought it was great. He had a lot of style. They wanted us involved with all their artists, the whole thing so at least we were involved with it. We came in very handy but I can't slag Andrew. He was a very nice man. He had his moments but we all did. I think Tony Calder ran that company, him and the massed band of Tasmanian accountants. I don't think Andrew knew what was going on.

'I think he knew up to a point but only up to a point. Don't think he really wanted to know. Sort of hid from it. Then everybody did a runner – zoom. Men overboard!'

With the band now broken in two, the friendships quickly fell apart. The worst fallout occurred when Marriott and Lane clashed over ownership to Beehive Cottage. Jerry Shirley remembers the spat well.

'They had got an advance from Immediate Records in both their names to buy Beehive Cottage,' he reveals. 'Ronnie left Beehive Cottage after splitting the band and when Ronnie tried to get some compensation for it, Steve just turned around and said, "You'll get nothing, this was bought with money from the hits that I wrote, not we wrote." Steve actually produced a PRS [a statement of publishing royalties] that showed a list of all the hit songs they had with the Small Faces. He underlined all the biggest hits – 'All Or Nothing', 'Tin Soldier' – and whatever in red ink and said, "I wrote these so you get nothing".'

Ronnie and Sue, who by now had moved out, retaliated by sending Marriott an angry five page letter which consisted of nothing but the phrases, 'blah blah blah, waffle waffle waffle.' The bassist then ended with the sentence, 'Steve, forget it, that's what you're best at.'

The brothers in Mod, the brothers in blood, were now the brothers at war. The feud would last for years.

'I never really knew Ronnie that well,' Shirley says, 'but I felt bad for him, he was ripped off big time. Shame because they were so close a few years earlier.'

So close.

‡ ‡ ‡

The final Small Faces gig took place at the Springfield Theatre, Jersey on the Channel Islands, March 8, 1969. The last song The Small Faces played together on a stage was 'Tin Soldier.'

Prior to the gig, Immediate had rushed out a new single, taken from *Ogden's*. It was called 'Afterglow,' another epic pop-soul tune, Marriott's powerhouse vocal is again the central force, placed at the centre of a blitz of organs, guitars and drums. As for the B-side, 'Wham Bam Thank You Mam,' Marriott explained it thus.

'I played Ronnie 'Wham Bam Thank You Mam,'' he recalled, 'and he said, "Cor, it's a bit heavy innit?" and I said, "Of course it's fucking heavy," y'know, giving me the needle; but we still recorded it and in a way it was getting into Humble Pie direction.'

It certainly was the Humble Pie direction. 'Wham Bam' was full of loud raucous guitars, a song lyrically filled with allusions to sex and women of the night. It was a preview of Steve Marriott's music for the next five years.

The single, which reached 36 in the charts and then dropped away, also signalled something else. Marriott was now determined above all else to kill that which bugged him every day of his life since he could remember: fame.

'I don't think he ever got to grips with the fact that he was famous,' muses Tony Calder. 'When people come out and they want to touch you and get a piece of you and you're eighteen years old, it's not like playing the theatre or being in a TV studio. It's real life, it's your life and if you don't like it, you've got big problems.'

With The Small Faces dead, Stephen Peter Marriott would now do all in his power to evade fame's seductive touch. He would resist many of its enticements, shun the cameras, avoid the limelight, try and hide in the shadows.

And of course in doing so, he would become more successful than ever before.

PART THREE

HEAVY MAKES YOU HAPPY

Beehive Cottage, Moreton   (Kay Marriott)

Chapter Seventeen

What You Will

Steve Marriott sits in Tony Calder's office at 11, Gloucester Place, the two men discussing the sleeve for the first Humble Pie album, *As Safe As Yesterday Is*. It is hoped that the album will shake up an increasingly moribund albums chart. That year, 1969, music was badly faltering. The year's best selling album was the *The Best Of The Seekers*, followed by the film soundtrack for *The Sound Of Music*. *Abbey Road*, by The Beatles was at four but then look what's behind it at numbers twelve and fourteen; *The World Of Mantovani* and *The World Of Val Doonican*. It was like the late '50s all over again. Only the singles charts, with 'I Heard It Through The Grapevine' by Marvin Gaye, 'The Israelites' by Desmond Dekker, 'Harlem Shuffle' by Bob and Earl, 'Honky Tonk Women' by The Rolling Stones and 'Time Is Tight' by Booker T and the MG's gave any cause to celebrate.

Meanwhile, Marriott and Calder have differing views on how best to present the debut Humble Pie album. Calder tells Marriott that Immediate want to make a big splash with the group, really push them. You're an important band he tells him, massaging his ego, and elaborate record sleeves are one way of reflecting that.

Marriott vehemently shakes his head, is firmly against the idea.

One, it will further delay the album's release.

Two, he is absolutely determined that the band will be presented in the most low-key fashion possible. That means no fancy designs for the album sleeve, à la *Ogden's*, no band photo on the cover. And he is serious. In an industry where public recognition is required to sustain a career, Steve Marriott now wants to remain as anonymous as possible.

Sod being a pop star, sod screaming girls who send you letters of hate and broken records and sod the bands and the critics who won't give you respect.

So, he tells Calder, let's fuck all their heads up. Let's put each album in a brown paper bag and wrap it with a length of hemp. The listener can untie the goods and then smoke the hemp whilst listening to the music. That'll fuck their heads up.

Marriott is still a keen psychic warrior, still up for advertising the joys of the high, but these inclinations have been superceded by his desire to stay out of the spotlight.

That's why his taste in clothes has now significantly changed. No longer will Marriott dress like a dandy, stand out in the crowd. No longer will he dress to be regarded as a 'Face' around town. Mod is gone. So has his youth. New rules now apply.

Today, he favours a smart hippie look, dark jeans and simple cotton style tops, the kind of clothing he wore for the inner photo of the album that is under discussion.

Calder is in favour of Marriott's sleeve ideas. He loves controversy. Makes lots of lolly, doesn't it? But he has a problem. The logistics of putting every album in a paper bag are impractical. He puts forward a compromise idea. The album should be designed to look like a paper bag with hemp tied around it. That way, you get what you want and your audience still gets the message.

Marriott ums and ahhs, sees his point and finally agrees. He'll have to think of another way to fuck up people's heads, he tells Calder. Both men laugh, both men unaware that in a year's time their lives will be flying off in totally different directions.

By April the following year, Immediate Records will be no more. Cashflow problems will finally bring this mercurial label to its knees. The end had already been signalled in February of 1969 when Oldham announced plans to launch a subsidiary of Immediate called Instant. 'Natural Born Bugie' was to be the first single to appear on the label. It would give the enterprise a much needed early cash boost.

Then Calder showed Oldham the books and such was the bleak financial picture they painted, the single was moved back to Immediate, the idea of Instant quietly forgotten.

The stark reality is that there had been too many groups on Immediate, not enough hits. Despite Oldham's charm and Calder's toughness, the label had not pulled through.

Which is why, in late 1969, in an attempt to hold back the inevitable, Calder and Oldham made one last throw of the dice and issued a double Small Faces album entitled *The Autumn Stone*, featuring a selection of hits, live tracks, cover versions and the new material taken from the aborted '1862' sessions.

In Germany, a similar Small Faces album, *In Memoriam,* was also released, another desperate attempt to find cash, stave off the inevitable. Their efforts are in vain. Immediate Records stopped trading in April, 1970, five years after their birth in August, 1965.

Theirs had been an outrageous adventure, an inspired journey through the staid UK music business. It had been a gas, a provocative and inspired period of time with never a dull moment. Immediate had demonstrated that with wit and skill mixed with an iron willingness to do anything to survive, the monopoly of the big three major companies could be overcome, that anyone, high or low, could gatecrash the party. It was what the '60s had supposedly been all about.

Immediate now became the yardstick, the great role model for a whole new generation of musical entrepreneurs. Would Stiff Records, to name but one, have been half as adventurous in their marketing without the example of Oldham's erratic trailblazing? It's doubtful.

Immediate had a downside, though. A big one, as well. They left their musicians skint. The Small Faces were no exception. Despite the success of their records, especially the chart-topping *Ogden's*, when the group finally fell apart in March 1969, all four band members were broke. Now came the arguments, the onset of bitterness.

'Immediate wanted us to re-sign,' Marriott told Hellier. 'We were saying, "No, we want this much dough to re-sign," and they for some reason decided not to pay us what they owed us let alone what we were asking for.

Jenny Rylance remembers this time well but does so with fondness. Yes, she and Steve were broke but what the hell? They were together, away from the madness, living in the country and discovering that love is richer than money but far less expensive.

'At the end of the Small Faces we were broke and it was ridiculous really when you think back to how big they were,' Jenny says. 'Mind you, Steve wasn't bothered. He just wanted to play and write music. The money or lack of it was totally irrelevant to him. As long as he had enough money to pay the rent, he was happy. I really don't know where the money went. I don't think Andrew ripped them off, he was just as hopeless with money as Steve was.'

Despite the concern over the missing money, the concern over Immediate's short term future, Marriott retained Andrew Oldham as band manager and signed Humble Pie to his label. Why? Why return to a label whose future is uncertain and who you have just argued badly with? The Small Faces contract had expired in June of 1968 so the company had no hold over him contract wise.

Maybe the answer lies with Marriott's impatience to start afresh, build a new career, get things moving. He certainly didn't want to spend time hawking his wares round town although they had approached a couple of other companies, Island being one.

The owner, Chris Blackwell told Marriott, sorry, he wanted to devote all his time to Traffic. Marriott accepted Blackwell's honesty.

In contrast, Oldham pledged him everlasting love. Maybe it was then that Marriott figured better the devil you know than the one you are yet to meet. Plus, Immediate were the only company in town who would allow him to get his own way.

As far as they were concerned, if Steve Marriott wanted to walk away from the spotlight and stand in the dark shadows, then he could do so with all their blessings.

They knew his talent, loved his character, respected his views. He had always brought them success. Why tamper with the formula? What more could a musician want from his employers?

In April of 1969, Humble Pie were unveiled to the press. In a press statement, journalists were informed that the band had been rehearsing in secret for months, first at Jerry Shirley's house in Waltham Abbey and later at the Magdalene Laver village hall in Essex.

'I've never been so excited about anything as I am about the group,' Marriott told *Melody Maker*. 'We're going to be a heavy music group.'

The press instantly dubbed them a 'Supergroup.' Supergroups were the latest fashionable development within rock circles, as epitomised by Blind Faith formed one month later and featuring Eric Clapton, Stevie Winwood, Rick Grech and Ginger Baker. It's why the band decided to include the word 'humble' in their name. It was an attempt to stop pigeonholing, to evade expectation.

'Humble Pie was one of Steve's suggestions,' drummer Jerry Shirley recalls. 'One of mine was Evil Cardboard which was the end of a joint. Anyway Evil Cardboard did not get the vote. We all thought Humble Pie was just perfect. It was a reaction against the whole supergroup thing. The idea of being called a supergroup without even playing a note was quite disturbing.'

It was the press who dished out such tags and it was the press who remained blissfully unaware that Brian Jones from the Rolling Stones had nearly joined the band.

During the early part of 1969, Jones had called Marriott, asked him if he could come up and rehearse with the band. His career with the Stones was finished and Humble Pie were deep into their six month rehearsal period, a period of time that was only interrupted by Marriott having to finish off remaining Small Faces obligations. As a songwriter, Jones was no great shake but as a musician he still had huge respect from his peers.

Marriott readily agreed to Jones's offer but a few days later, the daddy Rolling Stone drowned in his swimming pool at Cotchford Farm, the residence that once belonged to author AA Milne, the creator of *Winnie The Pooh*.

Supergroups may have sparked huge press attention but it proved far harder translating that interest into heavy sales. Humble Pie was no exception. Although the line up was well known, Marriott had already anticipated the press and moved quickly to play down people's anticipations. He knew that the British public hate foregone conclusions.

'The thing that does give me the horrors,' he told *NME*'s, Nick Logan, 'is getting out of the screaming bracket and getting landed in a supergroup bracket. We don't want people to think we are ego freaks who left their groups to form a supergroup. We didn't think we were capable of what audiences expected from us. That's all.'

He also revealed that it was Pete Townshend who had first alerted him to Frampton's talents.

'My first reaction was, "Come off it, man," Marriott told Logan, the man who would edit the *NME* in the '70s and create *The Face* and *Smash Hits* in the '80s.

'When I heard him play I couldn't understand why he was in such a group. People only have to hear him play to know where he's at. I don't want to be rude to Pete or The Herd but he was in a Mickey Mouse band before.'

For his part, Pete Frampton believes that Marriott's every action at this point in his life was solely designed to reduce the pressure that had made his last months with The Small Faces so very unhappy.

'Steve, by his own confession, was going through a period of dreadful self doubt,' he states. 'It was a state of mind most famously brought on by the commercial failure of the Small Faces last single, 'The Universal,' but also by the business and financial disasters which had precipitated that band's demise and were still churning behind the scenes as Humble Pie got started. Steve had even given up songwriting temporarily and in the beginning he pushed me to the front. He just wanted to stand behind me and get really stoned and just play along.'

Marriott needn't have worried so. The band would not find true success in Marriott's homeland. Instead, they would find it in the country that created the music he adored so much.

Success in America meant that Steve Marriott would spend the best part of his next five years in that country and in that wild and dark time, discover a new kind of fame, one which would include the usual ingredients – groupies and drugs and party adventures and hangers-on – but one that was now based on respect for his talents.

Marriott would throw himself headlong into this lifestyle and lose himself in the dark haze of stardom. Many things would happen over the next seven years. He would become a superstar, a drug fiend and lose the love of his life. He would marry for a second time, again be denied his rightful earnings and end by returning to Britain not in triumph but in desperate need of healing.

‡ ‡ ‡

With the demise of pop as a powerfully inventive force, a trend signalled (as ever) by The Beatles and Paul McCartney's doomed attempt to take The Beatles back to their rock'n'roll roots, a much heavier rock sound now took its place. Gone was the emphasis on invention, on new sounds, new ideas. Gone too was the idea of the pop single as the arbiter of success and talent.

The album was now firmly centrestage, propelled there by musicians anxious to replace creativity with musicianship. The musicians didn't know what else to do. Unable to sustain the magic of pop, they now opted to cover up their shortcomings with crashing drums, howling guitars. 'Jamming' with your 'axe' took prominence over imagination or inspiration.

At the same time, the blues assumed a central musical importance, elevated there by guitar virtuosos such as Jimmy Page and Jeff Beck. The guitar became the sacred instrument and the man who could play it, the high priest of rock – a trend epitomised by some infamous London graffiti proclaiming 'Clapton Is God.'

The start of this new style can be heard on the Jeff Beck Band albums from '68 and '69, *Truth* and *Beck Ola*. To see where it led to, look to Led Zeppelin (featuring fervent Marriott admirer Robert Plant on vocals) who managed to put together all the pieces the others couldn't and cleaned up everywhere they played.

When Steve Marriott heard one of their early songs, 'Whole Lotta Love' with its famous 'Woman, you need loving' refrain, he was driving a car in America. Far from being angered at Plant's blatant lift of his vocal phrasing, Marriott started laughing, recalling his days in the Small Faces, thinking about little Percy Plant, the kid who used to follow us around everywhere. Go on, my son, he shouted at the radio, go on, my son.

If in the '60s, these artists had been too stunned, too seduced by the life to fully keep their eyes on the moolah pouring into various pockets, in the '70s that attitude would change. Many had grown weary of facing uncertain financial futures, weary of being ripped off and working in an industry where managers and record company personnel lived better than they did. Enough, they decided. It was time, time to make some serious bread.

'The radical was in decline,' writes Ian Rakoff about the start of the '70s, in his book *Inside The Prisoner*. 'Something unpleasantly different was creeping in. Materialism and hard ambition were back in the ether.'

‡ ‡ ‡

To sustain their image as serious musicians, Humble Pie decided that the stage was as good a place as any to make clear their intent. Their early concerts therefore can be read as live musical jams which the public were invited to.

They debuted at Ronnie Scott's in August, 1969, a music biz show, Dave Gilmour of The Floyd in the audience. They played a five-song set.

Afterwards, they went out and bought acoustic guitars, harps, bongos and headed off to tour Belgium, Holland and West Germany. The support act was the as-yet-unheralded Deep Purple, the first date at the Bilsen Festival, Belgium.

'The Bilsen festival,' Marriott recalled to Hellier, 'was washed out. All our equipment went out of tune, the pianos, the generators failed, it was a complete mess. Then we did The Paradiso in Amsterdam and I remember Andrew being carried out over the shoulder of his chaffeur, Eddie. That sort of sums up the road thing. It was just one big party.'

Frampton would start the show alone, one man and his guitar. Greg Ridley would join him, then Jerry Shirley but on electric piano, not the drums. He would move there when Marriott walked onstage and the band would finish the acoustic set, turn electric and start belting out versions of Dr. John's 'Walk On Gilded Splinters,' and Ray Charles's 'Hallelujah, I Love Her So'. There was time for new Marriott material such as 'The Sad Bag Of Shakey Jake,' before ending on 'Natural Born Bugie,' their debut single which would reach top ten status in September of that year.

'I don't like these new sounds of yours,' Bill Marriott told his son, quite early on in the band's career. Steve shrugged his shoulders.

'It's what the kids want to hear, dad,' he explained. 'It's what they're into.'

Marriott was going with the times, not attempting to shape them anymore.

The album *As Safe As Yesterday Is* was released in August, 1969. It reached sixteen in the charts. The album bore little resemblance to either Marriott's or Frampton's previous work. Melody was the first casualty, replaced by loud, heavy rock guitar workouts. The magical twists and turns that made the Small Faces output so exciting were absent. So were the inventive arrangements. This was the straight ahead rock that Marriott believed the kids wanted to hear.

The former Small Faces frontman contributed six songs to the LP, one a co-write with Frampton. The former Herd man delivered two solo efforts. The rest of the songs were made up from a cover version of Steppenwolf's 'Desperation,' and a new song, 'Growing Closer,' from Ian McLagan, the Small Faces organist.

McLagan had actually rehearsed with Humble Pie very early on with a mind partly set on joining their ranks rather than his former colleagues in their new venture The Faces. He finally opted for his old band but not before telling Marriott that maybe the band had lost a member 'but they had gained a friend.'

'Isn't that great,' Marriott exclaimed to *Record Mirror*. 'It really helped me.'

It was probably just drunken talk. In truth, Marriott and The Faces wouldn't speak to each other for years. It didn't help either that Marriott's role had been taken by one Rod Stewart whose relationship with Jenny Rylance had inevitably soured Marriott's view of the man.

The recording of the first Pie album took place at the Olympic Studio (the band always used Studio Two) in South West London. Jerry Shirley, young, eager, recalls meeting idols such as The Stones and Jimi Hendrix in Studio One. He's still buzzing on the memory today.

'Yeah!' he exclaims, 'a wonderful learning experience.'

‡ ‡ ‡

A tour of the UK started in September, 1969. First date, Coventry. *Top Pops* and *Music Now* were there at the scene.

Their reporter, Tony Norman, said that the highlight of the Humble Pie set was their segue from 'The Sad Bag Of Shakey Jake' to 'Walk On Gilded Splinters.'

'This had everything – Harmonies, controlled guitar phrases and guts. Beautiful.'

Norman later concluded that the Pie could become 'one of the most versatile bands around.' After the show, he spoke with Frampton. The guitarist told him, 'Working with Steve has really helped me. Whereas I wasn't sure of my guitar playing, he was the first person that came up to me and said, "I really like your guitar playing." That really gave me a big nice feeling. He's a lovely lad.'

Penny Valentine from *Disc and Music Echo* was also present, said the same school reportish thing. Good, but could be better.

There were a host of support acts on tour with the band. Samson, Griffin, Love Sculpture and, prior to Pie's arrival, David Bowie on acoustic guitar. Another nice surprise, said Valentine. Then she turned to Steve, asked him his view.

'That was the best opening night I ever had,' he told her. Then he went off for a drink.

Yet to Marriott's sensitive mind there was a problem. The band had not rid themselves of their supergroup tag. Every time they were mentioned in the UK music papers they were referred to in this manner.

America was the answer. They were hardly going to be called a supergroup by a country that had granted them just one hit single between the four of them ('Itchycoo Park').

A six week tour supporting Santana was arranged. It started in late September and when it finished the band found themselves in Los Angeles where from the 3rd to the 6th of December, they staged their own shows at the famed Whiskey A Go Go club. (In 2001, Castle Music issued a live recording of one of these shows.)

The concert begins with a nine-minute version of The Yardbird's 'For Your Love,' followed by an eleven minute version of Johnny Kidd's 'Shakin' All Over.' There are two 'quickies' – 'Hallelujah I Love Her So' and 'The Sad Bag Of Shakey Jake,' before the band take a deep breath and head into Dr. John's 'I Walk On Gilded Splinters' ('probably the most innovative record we'd heard in years,' Jerry Shirley says), which lasts nearly twenty two minutes.

As they were playing this lengthy set all over the States, their second album in a year emerged. It was called *Town and Country*. According to Frampton, it had been 'hastily assembled' from various early recording sessions, and was mainly acoustic in its nature.

Given Immediate's precarious finances, the company obviously believed that their best chance for survival lay in releasing anything with Marriott's name on it. Bizarrely, no single was released from the album although a recent re-issue by Sanctuary of the two albums unearthed a slew of new songs that could have served that purpose.

Most of them were ordinary but a version of the Ray Charles song, 'Drown In My Own Tears,' may well be one of the best things the band ever recorded. Certainly, it stands as a prime example of the genre known as blue-eyed soul, the art of white boys singing black.

In this song alone, Marriott places himself as the number one practitioner of the art. Utilising a tasteful line up of brass and electric piano, the song's pace is stately, the arrangement beautiful.

But it is Marriott's vocal performance that dominates and it is nothing short of masterful. His phrasing is immaculate, his control exemplary, his ability to stay right on top of the song unquestionable.

It is one of the best things Humble Pie ever did and it lay dormant at Abbey Road tape studios for over thirty years. You can see why. At this juncture, Humble Pie had two musical thrusts – heavy rock and meaningful acoustic. Where would such a soulful gem such as this fit in?

It wouldn't have worked on either of the two Immediate albums, that's for sure and this problem, where to place Steve's R&B leanings most productively, would be one that would occur again and again throughout the band's career.

Eventually, the subject would help bring the band down.

‡ ‡ ‡

'Yesterday is gone but not my memories.'

Steve Marriott sang those words in late 1968 and months later they were made available on Immediate's first Small Faces compilation, *The Autumn Stone*. The album was a strange beast, comprising, as previously stated, hits, live recordings, demos, cover versions and the '1862' songs.

Apart from the interest in hearing the demos and live material, the album serves to highlight two distinct musical styles open to Marriott at the time, two roads the band could have taken to had they stayed together.

The clues are in the title track and the band's excellent version of the Tim Hardin song 'Red Balloon.' Both songs feature prominent acoustic guitars, full of dark mood and rhythm that are coloured up by tasteful touches from the electric piano or in the case of the exquisite *Autumn Stone*, a flute. There are no dashes of humour, musical or otherwise. Instead, we hear a songwriter who has truly matured. *The Autumn Stone*, in particular features a touching melody that brilliantly highlights the lyrics.

The version of Tim Hardin's 'Red Balloon' (there is also a live romp through Hardin's 'If I Were A Carpenter') has a similar feel, beautifully enlivened by some delicate lead guitar playing. It's superb acoustic soul but a direction that Marriott opts not to follow.

His future is signalled by the presence of new songs. 'Call It Something Nice' and 'Wide Eyed Girl On The Wall' are heavy rockers, driven by ringing guitars, crashing drums, Marriott's tempestous vocals.

This was the musical baton he chose to pick up.

The Autumn Stone contains nine of the Small Faces's top forty hits, three live recordings from Newcastle City Hall, two of which are covers, four new songs, some in demo form, some B-sides and some recorded covers.

The live material is marked by the band's heavy musical bluster epitomised by Marriott's vocal which is forced to take on the waves of screams hurled at him from the front rows. Worth considering as well is the demo of the instrumental 'Collibosher' which veers slightly towards Northern Soul territory. Again, another intriguing musical marker ignored.

The collection appeared in November, 1969. Chart-wise, the album badly stiffed. Calder and Oldham had miscalculated. No one cared about the Small Faces any more and Immediate plunged further into trouble.

'There was a time at Immediate when we didn't have any songs at all,' Marriott told Hellier. 'All we had was a couple of new songs that Andrew didn't want because he didn't like them. Later on, he put them out on *The Autumn Stone*. He didn't like the song 'The Autumn Stone' but he had the cheek to call that Immediate thing *The Autumn Stone*. We thought, 'You bastard.'

‡ ‡ ‡

Three albums out in a year and then the company that released them goes bust, taking your manager with you. Whilst the fallout was being dealt with Marriott retreated to the countryside and Jenny.

The other members of Humble Pie took on session work. Frampton worked with the soul singer Doris Troy, who had just signed to Apple, The Beatles' label. At the session, Frampton recorded with Steve Stills, Ringo Starr and George Harrison.

(Stills would later feature on a Humble Pie recording.)

Not long after, Harrison invited Frampton and Jerry Shirley to play on his debut solo LP, *All Things Must Pass*, with Phil Spector producing, Eric Clapton on guitar, Billy Preston on organ, a whole host of name musicians wandering in and out.

Greg Ridley and Jerry Shirley also helped out ex-Pink Floyd man Syd Barrett on his second solo album whilst Marriott carried on writing, breaking off to play with his four dogs, twelve cats and assortment of ducks and geese.

It was an idyllic time for Jenny and he, the lull before the storm that would break them into two.

Bobbie Korner, wife of Alexis, was a close friend to Jenny and she and her husband often went to visit The Marriotts at weekends.

'We spent a lot of time at the cottage,' she says. 'I would be with Jenny and Alexis and the boys would go off to the back room to play music,' she recalled, 'I was very fond of Jenny indeed. She was very happy because at that point they were living the life they dreamt of – the animals, the country – and Jenny had a very big influence that way. She wanted to keep Steve anchored. A lot of Jenny is seeing that people are grounded, that they have a solid base, and at that time she was successful.'

'Most of the day Alexis and Steve and whoever else was there would be playing. Alexis thought Steve a great guitar player. I would spend time with Jenny and there would always be this terrific smell of roast meat that Jenny was cooking. Then the sizzling joints would come out of the oven – and they would be thrown to the dogs! Jenny was a vegetarian. I swear that people were tempted to go into the garden and fight it out with the dogs!'

Damian her son also accompanied his parents to these get-togethers. It's where he learnt to love Marriott.

'He was a lovely geezer. He was generous, he was kind, he was thoughtful and that's why Steve and Jenny had such an idyllic time. At the time he didn't have kids but he always had time to talk to children. My brother Nico was deadly scared of dogs and Stevie took time away from other things to take Nico to the dogs and show him that they were not going to do anything. Little things like that stick out for a kid. It's the little glimpses that tell you more when you're a child about someone's personality. He was a lovely person to know.'

One trait his mother Bobbie noticed was how Marriott kept the television on whether he had company or not.

'He would have the sound down and just as you managed to work out what was going on by lip reading he would get up and turn the channel over.

So then you'd have to start all over again.'

Still denied permission to build a studio in the smaller second cottage where Ronnie Lane and his wife, Sue once lived, Greg Ridley and his partner Mandy had moved in for the time being. Marriott meanwhile kept on at the council. Everytime they turned his request down he started telling journalists who visited him that his phone was tapped.

‡ ‡ ‡

Oldham hadn't gone so skewiff that he couldn't help out his former clients. He phoned Jerry Moss at A&M Records in America and raved to him about Humble Pie. He did a good job. Pretty soon, Larry Yaskiel, the head of A&M in England, began making overtures.

Sensing a deal, the managerless band quickly contacted ex-Animals bassist Chas Chandler who had brought the unknown Jimi Hendrix to London and built the platform for his groundbreaking music and subsequent success.

On Pie's behalf, Chandler went straight to Atlantic Records and started a bidding war for the band's talents which A&M finally won, paying the band $400,000 to secure their services. Shirley now alleges that they only saw half that sum.

'It was yearly advances adding up to $400,000.' he states. '$133,333 per year for three years that we divided between the four of us. We saw the first year and the second year and those were the last royalties I ever saw.'

Chandler having negotiated the deal, lost out on the vacant manager's position. That honour would go to one Dee Anthony, a man referred to by some as, 'America's Don Arden,' a man who would help them to years of American success, years of sold out concerts, appreciative crowds, years of high selling albums.

To do so Anthony knew one thing; his first job would be to get Steve Marriott back in the spotlight.

Born Italiano, possessor of the kind of voice usually heard in gangster flicks, Dee Anthony grew up tough on the streets of New York. He served in the Second World War and afterwards earned his corn impersonating Al Jolson. He soon quit the stage, landing a job as singer Tony Bennett's numero uno roadie. The knowledge this work brought him would stand him in good stead when he began working with British musicians keen to break the States. It was Anthony who taught them to apply showbiz technique to their rough rock act.

Joe Cocker, Traffic and King Crimson were just three UK artists who benefitted from his guidance.

In his book, *Mansion On The Hill*, author Fred Goodman describes, Anthony as 'short, barrel-chested and thickly built... Anthony looked more like a professional wrestler than a professional manager.'

Anthony was a hard headed, bright, energetic manager who had been introduced to Humble Pie through the Spooky Tooth roadie, Danny Farnham. Once in charge, he quickly set about making huge changes.

Journalist Keith Altham remembers: 'When I first met Dee Anthony I was very suspicious of him and warned Steve Marriott against him, he's sharp to say the least. Now I'm a big Dee Anthony fan. Other managers are either accountants, lawyers or roadies but Dee is a manager. There's no doubt he made Humble Pie what they were in America, he broke them wide open when everybody had given up on them. He's the most competent manager I've come across. He fought, clawed and scratched his way up.

'He always had such a lot of energy and was also an amazing intellect. He certainly knows how to motivate an artist, he's never boring although he does go on at length sometimes. I've never seen Dee Anthony show any doubts about any of his artistes in their presence and that's what basically makes him such a great man.'

Marriott certainly agreed with this assessment. He told Hellier, 'Dee Anthony managed Humble Pie and did a great job. As far as managers go, Don Arden and Dee Anthony were the best managers I've ever come across. Dee Anthony goes back to Tony Bennett, Frank Sinatra. Old school management. Dee did a classic on Humble Pie. He was at every show, 100 percent of his time, whistle around his neck, blowing when he thought we were slacking off a bit. He was like a fight trainer and that's what a good manager should be. He'd give you a pep talk before you went on, like a sport. It's a happy family that way.'

The use of the word family is apposite. Dee Anthony has often been linked with the American Mafia.

'Intimations that Anthony was mobbed up were rife,' journalist Fred Goodman claimed, 'an impression encouraged by Anthony's friendship with Joe Pagano, a reputed soldier in New York's Genovese crime family...'

Given the amount of money that the music industry generates, it can be of little surprise that the Mafia should be drawing funds from this particular well. As far back as the 1920s, many musicians, including Louis Armstrong were patronised by mobsters such as Al Capone. In the late '30s and early '40s, big Mob men such as Frank Costello and Sam Giancana moved in on the lucrative jukebox business, netting themselves a valuable income totalling millions of dollars. Later they began to cross-promote singers of their own choosing by supplying only records selected by themselves for the machines.

'The gang could literally turn no-talents into national sensations,' Gus Russo wrote in his mafia study *The Outfit*. Inevitably, the Outfit (the name of the Chicago mob) moved into the record companies. The hoods' relationship with Jules Stein at MCA in particular caused a whirlwind of suspicion to swirl around that company's every success. To this day it is safe to assume that the Mob still wets its beak in the music industry. The much-troubled singer Michael Jackson recently cemented a seventy million dollar deal in a Los Angeles hotel room which prevented a humiliating slide into the dark and very deep waters of bankruptcy. One of his saviours was a businessman, freely acknowledged to possess 'dubious' contacts.

Marriott, whether he knew it or not, was in with the big boys.

New label, new manager. Now there had to be a new album, one which would reflect the changes. Up to this point, Andy Johns had produced the band. Now they opted for his brother, former Small Faces producer Glyn Johns. His acceptance spoke volumes about Marriott's talent. After all, Johns was hardly the biggest fan of Marriott's personality but he was more than willing to work with the man, no problem whatsoever. At their first meeting, Johns argued that the band contained a world class singer in Marriott, that they were foolish not to place his talent centrestage. Furthermore, the previous albums had been too confusing for their audience. One was mainly heavy rock, the other mainly acoustic. The diversity was off-putting to people. Why not do what everyone was doing and mix the two up, give yourself a real sound and identity?

The idea appealed and the band retreated into the studio, emerging a month later with a work simply entitled *Humble Pie*. It contained lengthy numbers featuring the band jamming, as well as simpler acoustic songs. The album was far more of a band effort, Steve writing two songs 'Theme From Skint' and 'See You Later Liquidator,' – and helping out with group compositions.

In their July 18th issue, *Melody Maker* declared that 'the third and by far the best Humble Pie album will be out at the end of the month.'

On its release the album didn't sell massively but no-one was duly fussed. The year was 1970, a time when record companies were content for bands to record, one, two, three albums before questions pertaining to their band's commercial potential started surfacing.

Thin Lizzy for example stayed at their record company for five years before cracking success with their *Jailbreak* LP.

Nowadays, if your first single flops, tough, go straight to the dole queue. For Humble Pie and many other rock acts a long-term approach was taken. Record an album, play live, build up an audience. Repeat until success comes a-knocking on your door.

That was Dee Anthony's strategy. He was convinced that Pie could crack the States but it would take years of touring, years of staying on the road, years of playing every dive that would take them until finally the Gods smile upon you and the sky opens bringing them all their dreams, realised in gold and silver and applause.

Yet no-one calculated the other cost, the biggest price you have to pay to pass through the golden gates. Jenny Marriott was Steve's sacrifice and in retrospect maybe the biggest and costliest he ever made.

‡ ‡ ‡

'I'm going to get a short back and sides tonight,' scowled Steve Marriott beneath his years of long hair… 'It's about time. Me barnet is too long. You can't tell if people are stoned anymore. The whole point of long hair was to be different and individual. It doesn't look that way anymore.'

It's November 1970.

Hair is still a battlefield upon which the young and the old fight. The month's big singles run the gamut from soul to heavy rock and beyond: 'Band Of Gold' by Freda Payne; 'War' by Edwin Starr; 'Ball Of Confusion' by The Temptations; 'Black Night' by Deep Purple; 'Paranoid' by Black Sabbath and 'Woodstock' by Matthews Southern Comfort.

The year's biggest albums are Simon and Garfunkel's *Bridge Over Troubled Water* and *Led Zeppelin II*. Both albums outsell The Beatles' last two efforts, *Abbey Road* and *Let It Be*, two to one: a sign of changing times.

Marriott is back from another American tour, talking to Chris Welch at *Melody Maker*, the confidence and fire inside starting to re-emerge. Although a Humble Pie single, 'Big Black Dog,' has stiffed, America's positive reaction to the band cancels out all disappointments.

'We've dropped the acoustic numbers and play our ass off,' says Marriott, notably using American slang. 'The whole act is an up – all the way. It's such a gas to play there. We get a respect we don't have here. American audiences make us think we are good.'

Then, a meaningful comment on how he copes with touring is let slip. 'When I'm on the road, I completely detach myself from everything that is at home. I just become a dummy and work for each night's gig, improving the numbers, getting it right. It's being completely schizoid.'

That Marriott was able to adopt another persona to deal with life on the road was not at all surprising given his background in acting. Yet this schizophrenic trait would also surface in Marriott's later personal life. That was when he would become a character he called Melvin – Melvin the bald headed wrestler.

‡ ‡ ‡

Humble Pie operated at a breakneck pace, constantly touring and recording, rarely resting. Yet the work was starting to pay off. In summer of that year, they returned from America to play a free gig in London's Hyde Park supporting Grand Funk Railroad. Thanks to their extensive work in the States, Humble Pie were now a seasoned live act, capable of giving all of their contemporaries a run for their money. That was certainly the case on this particular day. Marriott's voice, according to *Melody Maker*'s Chris Welch was 'amazingly powerful,' 'so emotional and vibrant.' Peter Frampton's guitar was 'mature and confident,' able to combine 'melodic with a funky feel,' and Jerry Shirley and Greg Ridley provided 'a frequently explosive backing.'

The result was that 'the crowd roared.'

'Hyde Park,' says John Hellier, 'was the gig that established Humble Pie in this country. Everyone thought that, even the band. By the time Grand Funk Railroad came on, the park was half empty.'

Another member of the crowd, Glen Matlock, who would later play two Small Faces tunes ('Whatcha Gonna Do About It' and 'Understanding') with his band The Sex Pistols, was also present, also massively impressed. He recalled the power of the band, their dynamics and above all the 'tasteful' green flowered suit that Frampton took to the stage with.

‡ ‡ ‡

Two Pie albums were released that year, one of which, *Performance – Rockin' The Fillmore*, would give the band the biggest seller of their career.

Their USA boss, Jerry Moss, once told them it would take three albums for them to hit home. When he said it, Marriott got mightily miffed with the man. With the release of *Rockin' The Fillmore* he saw the truth.

Prior to this double live album came *Rock On*, released in early '71. It broke no new ground as far as the Pie style went but it did contain 'Song For Jenny' which would prove to be significant.

Not only was it Marriott's acknowledgement that work was starting to push into his marriage – 'I wonder how you think of me when I am so far away,' he sings – but with its use of PP Arnold, Doris Troy and Claudia Lennear on backing vocals, introduced a soul element which he would now seek to increasingly incorporate over the next few months.

His drive to do so would not only cause friction within the band but more importantly would signal his new found confidence and desire to assume leadership of the band, lead them where he said they should go.

He couldn't help himself. Steve Marriott was not born to stand in the shadows. His time there was over now. Now he was ready to grab the spotlight.

Dee Anthony loved Steve's new attitude even if it meant creating the band's first crisis. Pete Frampton and Steve Marriott had up until his point got on well. Both had come to music at a very young age, had experienced the pop star life, found it to their disliking and sought respect elsewhere.

Frampton found Marriott a source of comfort, a source of fascination. The non-stop chatter, the devil-may-care attitude and the relentless energy that he had brought to the Small Faces had been somewhat subdued when Humble Pie began. During its inception, Marriott often displayed a quieter, more reflective mood which suited Frampton's more laid-back demeanour.

Yet with Marriott's confidence returning, buoyed by a sympathetic record company and a strong manager, his overwhelming need to control strongly upset the balance of the relationship.

'He was no longer prepared to share the limelight with anybody,' Frampton recalled. 'It was now His band rather than Our band. Also the musical direction had changed to the point of being a lot heavier. We had released a couple of albums on A&M and both had their moments but it was the next album, the live set, *Performance – Rockin' The Fillmore*, that really established the band. I left just before its release but I had no regrets.'

The break up occurred when Frampton refused a Pie rehearsal because he wanted to attend a Who concert at the Albert Hall. It was a decision that absolutely infuriated Marriott. All his life, despite everything going on in or around him, work was an absolute priority for Steve Marriott. He told the guitarist to leave. Frampton gladly walked away.

'Steve was very hurt when Peter left the band although he would never admit it,' Jerry Shirley reveals. 'Steve was solely responsible for getting Peter accepted as a serious musician with the media. Before Steve's public admiration for Peter he was simply thought of as just another pretty boy pop star. Peter left just as we cracked America.'

The album that would bring the band all that they yearned for was a work that manager, Dee Anthony had planned all along.

Aware that his protégés were far more effective in a live situation than on record, he reasoned that their best bet would be to issue a double live album showcasing the band's undoubted onstage power.

Whatever one's thoughts on the heavy rock Marriott was now engaging his talents in, *Performance – Rockin' The Fillmore*, certainly achieved that aim. The album showcased a band who had now nailed down every element of the genre. Their riffs were loud and relentless, the rhythm section suitably crushing, the power of Marriott's vocals a vital part of the recipe.

The band had spent countless nights on the road perfecting this sound, this style and although they may not have been the world's most creative group they knew how to move any young, rock-orientated audience put in front of them.

Sex Pistols bassist Glen Matlock calls the album 'one of the best live albums ever made.' He is not alone. So do many others.

The Fillmore in San Francisco was deliberate. Over the last two years, Humble Pie had built up a good reputation at the venue and thoroughly enjoyed playing there.

Greg Ridley told author Dan Muise for his book, *Gallagher, Marriott, Derringer and Trower*, 'There was shagging going on, drugs going on... it was just outrageous. Loved it!'

The band used the producer, Eddie Kramer to record their set over two nights at the club, using facilities from New York's Electric Ladyland studios. Both nights, Humble Pie took to the stage just knowing their time had come.

'It was all very magical,' Shirley told Muise. 'Everything was going right. All the plans that we were making and everything that Dee had said he was going to achieve was being achieved. We were A&M's golden boys at the time. We were absolutely on a roll. Far and away the most sparkly time of the band's existence.'

The record was mixed back in England by the band. Dee Anthony then flew over to hear their efforts. Played the album in its entirety, the boisterous, irrepressible manager turned to his protégés and declared, 'Great, except for one thing. It's a live album and you've forgotten to include the audience in the mix.'

A silence falls. Stoned grins turn and greet him. Shit, man, the musicians reply, forgot about that. Loud laughter. Back to the mixing board.

In September, 1971, *Performance – Rockin' The Fillmore*, appeared, with the audience now clearly audible. Every song played on it was a cover version except for 'Stone Cold Fever.'

'That was something that went through their career, I think,' says Mick Fish, successful book publisher now, Humble Pie fan back then. 'They just didn't produce enough of their own material. They always went back to covers and with a varying degree of success. 'Hallelujah I Love Her So' was great but 'Walk On Splinters' was dragged out and killed. You could go out of the room, make a cup of tea or whatever and come back fifteen minutes later and it was still on.'

Marriott fan and writer Paul Gorman felt the same way. Talent wasted.

'They were big for a while,' he recalls. 'Marriott was obviously a bit of a character and gave good interviews at a time when there were a lot of bores around. Unfortunately the music didn't match up to his spiel. I bought *Rockin' The Fillmore* blind on the basis of his charm and history but it was pretty dull. The only song which swung was 'Hallelujah I Love Her So' which I played incessantly for a while before buying Small Faces and Ray Charles records and switching to those.'

Within a month of its release, the album had sold hundreds of thousands in America, testament to the hard work the band had put in.

Humble Pie were made and Steve Marriott had achieved his every aim since dumping the Small Faces and setting out on this particular road. He had success but above all he had respect and on his own terms.

Now he could smile at himself in the mirror.

Success. How sweet it is to be loved by you.

‡ ‡ ‡

Alexis Korner came on the phone, asked Steve down to a recording session he was organising for BB King. The idea was to cut an album in London with the great bluesman surrounded by the best British guitarists.

Korner was saying that Marriott was a part of that group and Steve heard him. After he put the phone down, a warm feeling engulfed him. Out there, somebody respected him. Didn't judge him by his look, his voice, his attitude, just his talent. It felt great, the way it should be.

Marriott's playing can be heard on the 1971 *BB King Live In London Sessions*. This was a real highlight in Steve's career. He idolised BB King and a photograph of Steve, Alexis and BB King hung in Steve's various houses right until he died.

‡ ‡ ‡

The success of the Pie live album did not bring great joy to Dee Anthony. In fact, he actually became resentful and frustrated. His dark mood had been engendered by the contract negotiated by Chas Chandler. Anthony received no royalties from the multi-million selling *Performance* album and that rankled the gregarious manager. With a big selling album behind him, he decided to renegotiate with A & M Records.

At the conclusion of these talks, Anthony called a band meeting where he revealed he had set up a corporation in which the band effectively became his employees. It was a ploy, he explained, to keep the taxman from the doors. But, he added, for the scheme to work, he, Dee Anthony would have to become the sole proprietor of the corporation.

'As soon as we signed those pieces of paper, we effectively signed, in perpetuity, our entire rights away,' Jerry Shirley would tell author Dan Muise many years later. 'That was it, end of story. Everything we did as Humble Pie was no longer a four-shared business partner in the group. We were just the employees of a corporation and it was our job to supply our musical services to that corporation.'

Hindsight always makes clear that which is murky. By his own admission, Shirley stated that the band were too busy watching the 'cocaine and brandy' to even bother themselves with tiny crucial details.

'By the time the practice came into place,' Shirley revealed to Muise, 'We were on such a roll and so friggin' high that we could have been told the moon was green and we would have said, "Fine. Where's the blow?"'

The oldest story in the music business, it never stops running.

‡ ‡ ‡

Humble Pie needed a new guitarist to replace Frampton. And quickly. There were massive auditoriums to fill, bags of dollars to make. Their forthcoming US tour was worth a quarter of a million dollars alone. Their first choices were Rick Derringer, who having left The McCoys was now engaged in a solo career, and Joe Walsh from the Cleveland-based power trio The James Gang. But both men turned the job down.

Humble Pie began the search again. Clem Clempson was the guitarist with Colosseum, a progressive outfit that mixed rock with blues and jazz. It was laudable stuff but hardly a huge money-spinner.

Some of the Colosseum musicians were now feeling the financial pinch, looking for a way out. Clempson was one of them. He had bumped into Humble Pie once before at an airport and got on well with them. Now, on hearing of Frampton's departure, he decided to call Marriott, find out what was happening.

'When I phoned Steve's house,' the guitarist recalls, 'he was a bit wary as he didn't know much about me and Colosseum was not exactly Steve's cup of tea. But he went out and bought *Colosseum Live*, listened to my blues solo and rang back to ask if I could come up to Beehive Cottage immediately. We sat and jammed together on 'Natural Born Woman,' for fifteen minutes and he asked me to join the band.

'Next day I turned up for a full rehearsal with Jerry and Greg to find most of London's music press waiting for pictures of the new line up and I still hadn't had a chance to speak to the Colosseum guys!' Marriott said don't worry, consider yourself one of the family.

‡ ‡ ‡

In January, 1972, Humble Pie were on homeland, touring British soil and for the first time, enjoying it. The crowds were not massive but they were appreciative of the Pie's ninety minute set of hard rock, often calling them back for three or more encores.

'There's nothing quite as nice as being cheered and being called back for more in your own country,' Marriott told *NME's* Roy Carr backstage in a Bristol venue.

'We've done what we wanted to do in America. Now we want to come home.'

Smells like PR speak. The band adored playing America. Bigger crowds, bigger adulation, bigger everything. In Britain, it was middle-sized venues, middle-sized hotels, middle-sized everything.

In the States, they could play rock star games, and hire private jets to zip them across that vast continent, limos to pick them up, a bundle of dollars waiting for them at the hotel to spend every night on that which is best termed 'the source of all great sorrow' – money was everywhere.

For their recent prestigious Madison Square Garden show, they had their families flown over, all expenses paid. Steve's Mum filled with that pride which only a parent can know, said of the Pie audience: 'They listened and applauded and a lot was mixed. There were a lot of black people and I noticed that they weren't at all enamoured at certain things. The band used to play a number a long time and go into their bits and riffs.'

Steve's wife Jenny also came over but she didn't like the trip at all. Steve on tour was a completely different person to the one she knew from Beehive Cottage, the Steve of long walks and of gentle persuasion.

She went home as soon as she could, a little worried, a little uncertain now about the man she had pledged to spend the rest of her life with.

‡ ‡ ‡

Marriott carried on, regardless. On a flight to Detroit he lit a ciggy in the non-smoking section. The stewardess who remonstrated with him was told to fuck off. The police were called but couldn't touch him when he landed. Arrest him and the large crowd waiting to see the band would have turned the town upside down.

In Florida, he had to be hidden from the police and smuggled out of the auditorium after swearing profusely onstage.

The waiting lawmen cottoned on, raced to the airport and chased the band's private plane down the runway. Steve sat watching them, his body convulsed with laughter. This was it, this was what it was all about, the highest form of fun, enrage the bastards and then disappear before they can take action.

His humour sometimes strayed into surreal fields. Off tour, he had taken to riding his horse, Bim, down to the local pub, tying the animal up outside the boozer and then entering the premises like a John Wayne character and loudly ordering a drink. He had reason to celebrate.

The council had now granted him permission to build a studio in the second building. Marriott was so buoyed by the news he started the renovation himself, building a staircase which still stands to this day. Within six months, the studio was complete. Here Steve could write and record to his heart's content.

In the same period he bought his parents a house in Sawbridgeworth, Hertfordshire, a few miles from Beehive Cottage.

'He took out a mortgage on the property for them,' recalls Laurie O'Leary who would work with Marriott in the mid-'70s. 'You'll hear stories about his relationship with his parents but the gospel truth is that he loved them.'

Kay his mum was working part time in pubs and on many occasions Steve would ask her to quit. He would give her any money she needed.

'I said to him, "Don't feel guilty Steve, it's the best thing that happened to me," Kay recalled. "I've got a really good job and I love it. I felt like a woman again but he did feel guilty about it".'

Kay Marriott still lives in the house her son bought her.

And she still works.

‡ ‡ ‡

Soon, too soon, it was time, time to make yet another album. They called it, *Smokin'*, rock slang that denoted greatness.

Again, the most significant songs were those which featured Steve's soul influence. On Greg Ridley's 'You're So Good For Me' he had fashioned another striking vocal which strongly brought out the blues in his voice. Behind him, Doris Troy and Madeline Bell created a great vocal backdrop.

'Thirty Days In The Hole' was a far more dramatic R&B tinged affair, a signifier to where Marriott wanted to take the band musically.

The album also featured songwriter and guitarist Stephen Stills. He had been working in the studio next door and agreed to play on the opening song, 'Hot And

Nasty.' No stranger to the white powder, Stills and the band took three lengthy days to cut the tune properly.

The album helped sustain Pie's hard rock reputation in Britain.

'I remember seeing *Smokin'* splashed all over the record shop window displays in Hendon and Golders Green and Finchley,' writer Paul Gorman recalls, 'and kids at school walking around with it under their arms, talking about them being really "heavy". That was what they were known for, being really heavy.'

'You know I often used to wonder,' Mick Fish says 'about how people close to them took some of the songs. I mean by this time all they were writing about really was life on the road and all that entails. One song from this period opens up with the line, "You've got your hot pants around your neck," I wonder how he explained that particular nugget to his wife?'

‡ ‡ ‡

Sometimes, usually the day before he was due to pack his bags and head off on yet another tour, another round of playing the rock star, of working the stage, of working the audience, of draining himself of all energy, Steve would turn to Jenny and beg her to say that if he went, she would leave him.

'Things had soured so much,' she recalls, 'that he used to say things like, "Please tell me that you'll leave me if I go on tour again because if you say that I'll have justification not to go. If I have to go and be that other person again, I'll just go mad," Jenny says.

'That was said in a moment of truth but the next day he'd change his mind and he'd be up and off. In order to cope with the pressure he had to become this other person and that's really when our relationship started to go wrong'.

‡ ‡ ‡

In July of 1972, Humble Pie played a festival in Pennsylvania, America with Marriott's old sparring partners, The Faces. Marriott had maintained the upper hand over his ex-bandmates.

'Took two of you to replace me,' was the line he would always taunt them with, referring to their recruitment of Rod Stewart and Ronnie Wood. It was the truth and he never tired of reminding them. Never.

Not that The Faces were short on self-esteem. Since leaving Marriott, the band had initially struggled to impose themselves upon the public consciousness. It wasn't until their singer Rod Stewart hit big with his solo single 'Maggie May' (numero uno on both sides of the Atlantic) and the Faces' third album *A Nod's As Good As A Wink* followed, did the skies open for them. Artistically, Lane had made tremendous steps since walking away from Marriott. Songs such as 'Richmond,' 'Love Lived Here,' and the classic 'Debris,' showcased a songwriter of unique character, one able to reflect working class life while retaining an almost pastoral feel. His sense of melody, style and reflective lyrics put Lane in a class of his own. Yet if Marriott had any hopes of a joyful reunion with his old buddy they were about to be heavily crushed. The band, apart from Kenney Jones, refused to acknowledge his presence.

'I mean Ronnie Lane ignored him,' Clem Clempson told the *NME*. 'Steve went up and asked him how he was doing and Ronnie looked just straight through him.'

Maybe the fact that singer Rod Stewart had started to play the big star was getting to Lane. That day, Stewart had demanded his own private helicopter to travel to the gig. Or maybe Lane just couldn't forgive Marriott for taking his half of Beehive Cottage back in 1969. It would be another three years before Lane could even stand to be in the same room as Marriott. And when he did Marriott flattened him with a punch. Fame, eh?

‡ ‡ ‡

Despite the success, he was starting to get bored, bored silly with the music he was making. It made money but when did he ever give a fuck about that? All his life it had been far more important to keep things interesting. No point doing it otherwise. He was restless, needed new stimulation.

Again, he felt that familiar urge inside of him, the instinct to change, make life interesting. The truth was that for some time he had been thinking about changing the band's sound and direction. The only problem was working out how to successfully do so.

His mind wandered back to a record he treasured and played often. It was the first live Ike and Tina Turner album, recorded in Fort Worth, Texas. One of the things he loved about the work was the Ikette's backing vocals. They were so powerful, so musical. He took down the sleeve, looked for names. His eyes rested on that of Venetta Fields. Where was she now?

Actually, Venetta would prove relatively easy to find. She now sang in her own group, The Blackberries, alongside Billie Barnum and Carleen Williams. Despite Pie's heavy rock image, Venetta readily agreed to meet with the skinny white boys. White acts were nothing new to her and her fellow Blackberries. Stephen Stills, Graham Nash, Delaney and Bonnie, Joe Cocker, Burt Bacharach, Andy Williams, they had all sought out their services. Indeed, they had just got home after working with those drug addled Rolling Stones in France on their latest album, *Exile On Main Street*, had sung on the songs 'Tumbling Dice' and 'I Just Want To See His Face.'

Face facts – if they could work with that lot then they could work with anyone.

After making contact, Marriott started getting enthused, excited, even began talking up the idea of even adding another musician to the line up. The man he had in mind was Sydney George, a sax player who had played with Marriott's beloved Booker T and the MG's before joining the Memphis Horns. Nothing came of Marriott's overtures to him but The Blackberries proved amenable.

Once their contracts had been sorted, the girls would join the band as full time members, equal partners. Given the uneasy racial climate both in the UK and America, this was an audacious move by Marriott and within rock culture, totally unexpected. Rock and soul music operated in parallel lines at the time; there was little cross fertilisation. The rest of the band instantly had their doubts.

'That didn't go over well at all at the beginning,' Jerry Shirley told Dan Muise. 'To his undying credit Steve was way ahead of his time because now nearly everybody has at some time or other used a three-piece, black girl chorus. Still, it was resisted by the record company and management until he was in a position where they could no longer say no to him. Whatever he said went at that point.'

‡ ‡ ‡

Due to significant changes within the black culture of the time, it could be persuasively argued that soul music in the early '70s was displaying much more potency and imagination than rock music.

Two significant developments have to be taken into account.

In the late Sixties, an increasing political awareness amongst both musicians and their audience had created a demand for a music that would stretch further and say much more than the three minute single could. The assassinations of Martin Luther King and Malcolm X, the riots in America that ensued, the rise of black power, the Vietnam War, these were issues of major importance in many people's minds and the music they listened to was duty bound to reflect that. As in rock music, the album was about to take centrestage.

At the same time there arose a determination amongst major musical talents such as Marvin Gaye, Stevie Wonder and Curtis Mayfield, to be treated and respected as seriously as their white counterparts. As far as they were concerned they were high level artists whose work transcended all barriers. The result was a series of albums such as *What's Going On* (Marvin), *Talking Book* (Stevie) and *Back In The World* (Curtis), to name but three examples that were huge successes both commercially and artistically.

Such work helped put soul music on a roll. In Memphis, the Stax label found a second wind and was now charging ahead with acts such as William Bell and The Staple Singers.

(Marriott adored the latter act, especially Mavis Staples' voice. He once rang Stax and offered to produce her. The voice at the other end of the phone had no idea who he was and cut short the conversation. That didn't stop him in the latter part of the Pie career covering and recording The Staples song 'Oh La Di Da.')

Donny Hathaway and Bobby Womack were still in fine musical fettle, Aretha was still the Queen Of Soul whilst the newly created Blaxploitation genre of film had given birth to a number of fabulous soundtracks, not least Isaac Hayes' score for the film, *Shaft*.

To top it all, the Godfather Of Just About Everything, Mr. James Brown was right in the middle of his funkiest ever period. Say it loud. But the most pertinent musical development for Steve Marriott was the musical direction of The Isley Brothers. Since leaving Motown Records in 1968 and starting up their own label, the band had moved into another fertile period of creativity.

Their 1971 album, *Giving It Back*, featured them covering a batch of contemporary rock numbers such as Bob Dylan's 'Lay Lady Lay,' Stephen Still's

'Love The One You're With,' Jimi Hendrix's 'Machine Gun,' and Neil Young's 'Ohio.'

This album, along with the work of maverick musicians such as Sly Stone and George Clinton, helped create the climate which gave Marriott the chance to return the compliment with Humble Pie.

Soon, he would be standing in front of a microphone onstage and singing the line, 'My skin is white but my soul is black.'

‡ ‡ ‡

On issues such as civil rights Marriott's natural inclination was to always side with the underdogs, the oppressed. Bringing in The Blackberries served the dual purpose of shaking things up musically and making public his stance.

The idea that within the groovy world of music, no place for discrimination existed was shattered when the band undertook their umpteenth USA tour with the girls in tow.

'In 1972,' Jerry Shirley recalled to the author Dan Muise, 'in Beaumont, Texas with a bunch of long-haired white boys, it did not go down well at all. It was very powerful. The audience would stand there staring at us. "Well, what are those niggers doing on your stage?" It was really weird 'cuz I thought all of that stuff was long gone. But it still exists today let alone thirty years ago.'

No other rock band tried as hard to bridge the gap between black and white as Humble Pie did. Many rock acts used black singers on their albums and many insisted on using black artists for support slots.

But none invited any black artist to join their ranks, to get equal pay, equal status. But Steve Marriott did. Because it was right and because it was proper.

‡ ‡ ‡

In March 1973, Steve Marriott stood sound-checking on the stage of the London Palladium. Outside the board said 'Sold Out' whilst inside Marriott was unable to stop his mind flashing back to his dad, his old Manor Park home, that night in 1963 when he told his dad that the group he was watching on TV were rubbish and how his father had turned on him, snapped back that when he had sold out The Palladium as The Beatles had just done, he would be entitled to say such things but until then, keep quiet and Marriott, the cocky fifteen year old, replied, 'One day I will sell out the Palladium,' and meant every word because somehow inside he knew it to be true.

John Hellier was at this March 1973, show. He recalled Marriott coming onstage wearing a dinner suit, a jokey nod to the numerous Variety shows staged at this venue over the years. The band opened up with 'Up Our Sleeve' and by the end of their set the crowd were on their feet, 'and Steve was strutting around the stage full of Cockney confidence…letting everyone know who was boss.'

Encores included the band played for about an hour and a half, left the audience demanding more. 'One of the most memorable nights of my life,' says Hellier.

‡ ‡ ‡

Back to America they go. Work, work and work.

'With the addition of their American female vocalists, The Blackberries, Humble Pie now produce a thundering rock Niagara which sounds as though Phil Spector has got into the act.'

That's the *NME* reporting on Humble Pie's May 1973 performance at the Los Angeles Forum. Afterwards, the reporter Douglas Jones went backstage and met Marriott for an informal chat. He started off asking why the band performed so many cover versions. The Stones' 'Honky Tonk Woman,' and The Staple Singers' 'Oh La Di Da,' being prime examples.

'I hate to force my music,' Marriott said about the surfeit of cover versions he was playing, 'and it's relaxing to feel that you do not have to write. There are other people writing songs that you feel say something for you.

'I don't think you should be too intense about making music. If you lose the joy you should stop. There's nothing intense about it – it's funny!'

'Just a load of bleedin' notes, innit?' suggests someone frivolously.

'That's just what it isn't,' Marriott replies. 'A lot of my songs are so personal that it really hurts me to write them or even sing them out loud. Sometimes I think it's very important to reveal a truth and then at other times I think it's silly to expect anyone to identify or feel strongly with something deeply personal. They can't be expected to feel the same.'

Another person in the room ventures to disagree and hits Marriott's bad spot.

'When did you ever write a fucking song?' he snaps. His reaction was indicative of the way Marriott toughened up on the road. A close friend once described him as 'kind and sensitive at home, but on the road he turns into a little nutter to protect himself from being trod on...'

Unfortunately for Jenny, it was the little nutter rather than the kind sensitive soul that was coming home to her.

'Over three years they did nineteen US tours,' she states, 'and to cut a very long and painful story short, Steve was totally whacked at the end of it. For a lot of the time he was quite unapproachable and not the person that I had met and fallen in love with a few years earlier. In order to cope with the pressure he had to become this other person and that's really when our relationship started to go wrong.'

With his home studio up and running, Marriott now had a choice when he came home. He could relax with his wife, rekindle their love or he could carry on in tour mode, locking himself away in his studio with his music, his band, his drugs. He chose the latter.

'He was married to his music and I didn't mind that especially in the early years when he would play me new songs on an acoustic guitar,' Jenny says, 'but what didn't make me happy was when he was in the home studio out of his brain trying to come up with the next album because he was being pressurised into it. He would just disappear into the studio for three or four days at a time.

'He never slept and there would be all sorts of strange people in there with him. It was a crazy business and even the nicest people get mixed up. All sorts of chemicals were presented to him and he became addicted to them in the end. It was drugs that destroyed our relationship. Before the home studio was built Beehive Cottage was our sanctuary. Afterwards it just became his workplace.'

Marriott's drug of choice at the time was cocaine – then enormously popular in both the music and film industries. LSD and amphetamines and cannabis had driven the mover and shakers in the '60s but in the '70s the stars blew their wads on cocaine.

According to writer Harry Shapiro, author of *Waiting For The Man,* the best study yet of the link between music and drugs, the popularity of cocaine in the twenties and thirties could be traced to its easy availability from legitimate pharmacies. This practice was stopped when the police began leaning heavily on the pharmaceutical companies.

'Coke pretty much disappeared off the recreational drug scene at the end of the '30s,' Shapiro states. 'In the late '60s you get the musicians starting to pick up on it. That scene in the film, *Easy Rider* with Phil Spector selling the drug? Well that's the beginning of coke having its second go.'

The drug contains truly seductive powers. Lovely to take, not too bad a comedown the next day, let's do it again.

'I remember talking to somebody who was in Cocaine Anonymous,' Shapiro says. 'He was a regular heroin user for twenty years and he could function reasonably well. He worked in the music industry, did his job and all the rest of it. As soon as he got into coke he said that everything fell apart within six months.'

Rendered from the earth and soiled chemically, Marriott was just one of many to be taken in by its allure, just one of many unable to resist its sweet voice.

'Steve's downfall was cocaine,' Jerry Shirley categorically states. 'It was when he started doing it in a big way that his world started collapsing round him. He became verbally violent and he'd get physically violent as well – if he thought he could get away with it. He knew he couldn't get away with it with the guys in the band.

'I could handle myself and back then Greg was a tough cookie but, yeah, if he thought he could get away with it he would. I've seen him dropped on his arse a few times.'

Yet it was during this period, marked by its chemical cravings and exhaustion and unpredictable behaviour, that Steve Marriott would produce his best work of the '70s, namely his production of The Blackberries album, *Wrap Yourself In My Color*.

The Blackberries adored Steve. They thought him generous, open-hearted, blessed with an embracing spirit. When he suggested they make an album together, they readily agreed. Recorded at his Beehive Studio with Humble Pie backing them, the results of their endeavours were never released apart from a single, a funky slowed-down take on The Isley Brother's record, 'Twist and Shout,' written by Bert Burns and released by A&M.

Like that song the rest of the album was infused with the sound of the black American church, Marriott providing an earthy instrumental sound, the girls singing and swooping in time honoured fashion. Eight songs were recorded, two released. It deserved a better fate, still does, but it did serve to signal the start of Marriott's mission to turn Humble Pie away from heavy rock and turn them into a blistering rock-soul outfit.

‡ ‡ ‡

In 1973, the Humble Pie double album, *Eat It*, appeared in the shops. It did so in the midst of a great comeback for the single format. Despite Pink Floyd's groundbreaking and massive-selling *Dark Side Of The Moon* album, 1973 was not the time of the album, the time of the serious. Instead young Britons were mesmerised by the emergence of Glitter Rock – a genre dominated by classic disposable singles.

T. Rex, Gary Glitter and to a lesser extent, Slade, had hit home and grabbed the airspace by creating simplistic sing-along records for a sophisticated screaming teen audience. Following close behind these acts but sans the make up mystery – were Mud and Sweet and the RAK label artists, Hot Chocolate and Suzi Quatro (subject of a million male fantasies with her bass guitar and leather trousers) and from America were The Osmonds and David Cassidy, all of them competing for the same teenage hearts, the same shilling from the same purses. Most significantly, 1973 was also the year that Marriott's previous support act, David Bowie broke through, big time. He started the year with the huge selling single 'Jean Genie,' and ended it with 'Sorrow.'

Humble Pie had no business in this musical territory. They were a rock act. Their audience didn't buy singles, didn't buy musicians in glitter and dresses ripping off old blues riffs. (Interesting to note how the main protagonists of this style – Bowie, Bolan and Roxy Music's Bryan Ferry – had all been devout Mods.) No, the Pie fan was young and male, serious about his music, serious about rock culture, seemingly careless about his carefully put together look of a greatcoat, jeans, cheesecloth t-shirt and long hair. Therefore *Eat It* had been deliberately designed to show off the band's range and versatility. On one side, typical Pie rock numbers, on the other side slow acoustic songs. On one side, soul-influenced material featuring The Blackberries, on the other, a batch of live songs no doubt to remind everyone of the band's biggest selling album.

The album features some of Marriott's best singing within the Humble Pie framework, specifically on three songs. Ike and Tina Turner's 'Black Coffee,' Otis Redding's 'That's How Strong My Love Is,' and, most memorably of all, 'Is It For Love?' where he part-parodies The Faces' sound and just for good measure, gives Rod Stewart a master class in singing.

Close your eyes and it could be Rod singing amongst the mandolins and the liquid guitar sound, but singing with far more range and depth. The message to Marriott's rival was clear – you're good but you ain't me.

The other stand out track is the short acoustic song, 'Say No More,' slightly reminiscent in its raw feel of the ambience created by his last Small Faces single, 'The Universal,' and written for his wife Jenny who was slowly fading away from him.

'You held my soul in your hands / It sifted through your fingers like fine silver sand / Well, I don't need a swimming pool / I don't need to hang records on the wall

/ I just want you babe and that's all/ Say no more.'

He had written 'Afterglow (Of Your Love)' to win her and now he again reached for the guitar to save the relationship. Yet Marriott was not the only guilty party here, say some.

'He caught her with one of his friends,' Kay the mother coolly claims. 'She said, "Well, I'm 30, I want to eff around," and that's when he said, "Well, that's it, you don't do that while I'm around."'

You can imagine. Mayhem, absolute mayhem.

'He used to be out in his grounds screaming, "I want my wife back",' Kay, the sister recalls. 'Oh, it was awful.'

The couple attempted to right things. A two week holiday in Nassau was arranged. It only served to bring home sharply the problems that beset them.

'There was this beautiful property in Nassau that the band thought they owned,' Jenny recalls, 'but it turned out that it was never in their name to start with. When Steve and I were going through one of our rough patches we went over there to try and salvage our relationship. The holiday turned into a total disaster after just one day.

'Steve was doing a lot of coke and turned into a real monster. I stuck it out for two weeks but I was so glad to get home.'

Even on holiday, Steve kept the white powder close. Just one more time, then I'll quit, I promise.

'It just seems to turn people into monsters and they are impossible to live with,' Harry Shapiro states. 'They're aggressive, violent, etc but what you have to be careful of is that cocaine does not make you that way, it exacerbates whatever is in there.'

And what was inside Marriott was a bald-headed wrestler called Melvin.

‡ ‡ ‡

The space allotted music on TV in the '70s was minimal. If you were an albums-oriented band, *The Old Grey Whistle Test* was the only show in town.

Humble Pie first appeared on the show in March 1973. They returned seven months later and then on New Year's Eve contributed to the show's special which was then cancelled due to an energy crisis in Britain.

As *The Old Grey Whistle Test* was Pie's only chance of TV exposure, any chance to appear on TV had to be grabbed with both hands. Which is why on a BBC 2 arts programme named *Full House*, hosted by a Joe Melia, Marriott and Clem Clempson turned up with acoustic instruments to deliver 'Say No More.'

Ironically, given the nature of the song's creation, when the cameras turn to Marriott, straight away you can see he is bombed out of his head. His eyes are tellingly screwed up. He looks skinny and wasted and forgets the song's opening line.

But then he performs a trick he had perfected during his life as a musician and a hedonist – within a second he sobers up and delivers a mightily affecting performance, rough but mesmerising.

He dedicates the tune to, 'the girl who cut my hair this morning.' Only that same girl, Jenny Rylance, no longer wanted to hear that record anymore. She was tired of hearing it, the same promise day after day after day.

'It broke my heart to leave Steve, Beehive Cottage and the animals,' she states, 'but it had to be done. I was ultimately the stronger.'

Damian De Korner: 'I don't think he wanted the divorce to go through. He wanted his freedom to be with whoever he wanted but he also wanted to go back to Jenny and be with her when he wanted to be. And he wanted his coke and he wanted his road life and he wanted his studio life and inevitably he lost it all.'

It took Marriott years to get over Jenny.

'Steve used to call me a lot afterwards even when I was married to James, my second husband,' Jenny says. 'James would answer the phone and Steve would say, "Is my old lady there"?'

A pause.

'It all stopped when I told him I had had a baby. I never heard from him again.'

‡ ‡ ‡

One casualty from the divorce, Steve's friendship with Alexis Korner.

Damian De Korner: 'Stevie asked us to take sides and we thought his treatment of Jenny was appalling and so when asked to take sides we did – we told him to grow up.'

Someone telling him to what? To grow up? Marriott didn't like that, didn't like it at all. He stopped seeing Korner, dropped him from his phone book. They would meet again when Steve appeared on German TV in 1975 with Korner on the Bremen-based *Musikladen* series. They played four numbers together, including the gospel a capella 'Diamonds In The Rough.' That meeting apart, the two men remained estranged right up until Korner's death in 1984.

'He couldn't apologise to dad,' Damian says, 'he just couldn't do it, but he did send flowers. There was a friendship there and while it couldn't be rekindled it was respected and it was honoured.'

Chapter Eighteen

The Buttermilk Boys

Watch out children, there's a bad moon on the rise.

The *Eat It* album had been recorded at Steve's Beehive Cottage studios which he had named Clear Sounds. Its nickname was The Racket Club, a reference to a phrase much used by cocaine users. When requiring a hit, users ask whoever is holding the drug, to 'rack 'em out.'

As Jerry Shirley would later comment, 'that was when complete control was lost.'

At the same time as recording *Eat It*, Dee Anthony's new contract kicked in, effectively diverting money away from the band. Marriott moved quickly to protect himself. He told the band that the studio belonged to him and no one else.

'His rationale,' Shirley told Muise, 'was, "Well, after all, I'm doing all the writing so by the time all the publishing money comes in, I'll have that much more owed to me anyway. So I'll just have the studio." And we all said, "Oh, uh, ok." I guess there's a certain amount of sense to that argument although it was never mathematically worked out. He just ended up with the studio in his house. What we didn't do was we did not have it acoustically scoped, we never had it tested acoustically. So what sounded great in the studio, once you got out and tried to cut it, sounded like shit.'

During the marathon recording sessions for *Eat It*, a divide between Steve and the rest of the band became apparent, the first time a fault-line had occurred within the band's structure.

Steve's manic work rate was at the heart of the problem. He would spend the day recording and producing with the band. When they called it a day and left for home, Steve would just carry on into early morning.

The results of his efforts would then be played to the band when they appeared at the studio the next day.

'Some of the stuff that Steve had done in those circumstances was ok,' Clem Clempson told Muise, 'and sometimes we didn't like some of the things he had done. But it became difficult because we had gotten to that position where we had to take a stand about certain things. And up to that point we had always been united.'

Both Shirley and Clempson state that with Steve's marriage rapidly detoriating, they had taken the decision to let him assume full control of the album in a bid to keep his mind off his personal life.

A more likely scenario is that Marriott's force of personality, part fuelled by his extensive drug use made the band powerless to stop him assuming complete control. As ever, they hadn't handed him the reins, he had just grabbed them.

His work in the studio covered all aspects including playing other band member's instruments in their absence, adding new riffs or melodies or, worse, actually playing over their own work.

'I mean,' Clempson continued, 'there's no reason why he couldn't have done that occasionally but because it was done after everyone had left it created some bad feelings. His intentions were never malevolent in anyway but he was just full of energy and wanted to keep on working.'

Other problems now surfaced, mainly caused by the band's profligate ways. A tour of Japan and America that year, would lose the band a massive hundred thousand pounds – at least a million in today's money. It was Dee Anthony who was to blame. Having seen the huge box office success of singer Joe Cocker's tour film *Mad Dogs and Englishman* Anthony wanted to repeat the tactic with his band.

To that end, he hired a Boeing 707 plane which took forty passengers – musicians, roadies, liggers – to Japan. The film crew meanwhile travelled separately. Footage was duly shot but such was the inexperience of those involved, nothing was salvagable. No film reached the screens, no money was ever earnt back. It was typical of the organisation's blasé use of money and the huge amount of money available within rock circles. On tour in America, the band thought nothing of hiring two planes to traverse the vast continent. The band and their entourage travelled in one plane, the other plane transported everyone's luggage.

As the money poured out of their accounts, behind the scenes, battle lines were being drawn up. Not everyone connected with the band were happy with some of Steve's decisions. The management and record company disliked the addition of The Blackberries for financial reasons (they were on the wage bill and were potentially alienating narrow minded fans) whilst the band members harboured serious musical doubts about the soul revue direction that Marriott was so obviously trying to push Humble Pie into. The fans were also making known their discontent. On its release, sales of *Eat It* in no way matched that of previous albums.

Mick Fish: 'He wanted to bring in a brass section and a sax player, things like that and I think the rest of the band thought, we're a rock band. We don't want to be this. That said, they were exceptionally good. They used to do about twenty five minutes as a band then the Blackberries would come on and they would do 'Black Coffee', material like that and it was great. In retrospect some of it would seem a bit embarrassing now because what was starting to creep into it was that black language – the "Oh Lords", the "baby babies", that kind of black vernacular that the soul revue singers would use and *Thunderbox,* the next album, had a lot of that on it, that sort of Wilson Pickett way of going about things.'

Marriott remained true to his vision, stubborn in his ways. The presence of The Blackberries had rekindled Marriott's love of R&B and in doing so kept him interested.

'I've got a lot more confidence now and these women don't half make you want to sing,' he enthused to the *NME*.

His onstage demeanour now took on that of the earnest soul singer, Marriott began delivering statements in between songs that were couched in hip black speak. It didn't go down well with a lot of audiences.

'His attempted "street rap" only two numbers into the set showed a lot of nerve,' the *NME*'s New York correspondent wrote after one show, 'and I thought how they'd laugh him off the stage at a place like the Apollo... he reminds me of Sammy Davis Jnr doing an imitation of a black man singing the blues. Somebody send that boy a scholarship to church school so he can get it all out of his system and get back to what he does best.'

Jerry Shirley would later reveal that at this point, Steve spent far more time hanging out with the girl singers than the band, that his language now began reflecting his choice of company. Unfortunately, Shirley concedes, Marriott sometimes used inappropriate words. He is directly referring to Marriott's use of the word 'nigger.' Used by the white man to insult and humiliate, the American negro had cleverly cauterised its vile effect by taking back the word and applying it to themselves. Yet Marriott, much to The Blackberries horror, remained oblivious to this clever use of linguistics and started using it to refer to himself on stage.

'They told him off a number of times for talking like that onstage,' Shirley revealed to Muise.

The issue soon worked itself into the press. Under the most reprehensible headline the *NME* has ever used ('Don't Call Me 'Nigger' No More,') Marriott robustly defended himself.

'Frankly, I couldn't give a shit,' he told the writer James Johnson, 'I've never thought about anything else other than enjoying myself. I've never analysed it or anything. I've never thought should I do this or should I do that.'

Bringing up the subject of the band's version of the Ike Turner song, 'Black Coffee,' Johnson honed in on Marriott's use of the lyric, 'My skin is white my soul is black.' Marriott delivered a scathing reply.

'I've heard these comments,' he stated, 'people on the radio saying, "Who does he think he is?" But you know, Tina Turner sang, "My skin is Brown and my soul is black," – even funnier if you think about it. What do you expect me to do? Change the lyrics completely? I just sang it 'cos I loved the song and it was an interpretation of somebody else's lyrics. People should have known that I've been into black music for years anyway.'

His mind flashed back to 1968, Chiswick Park, the making of the *Itchycoo Park* video, the LSD daze.

'The only time I changed was when I OD'd on certain drugs and started wearing straw hats and kimonos. Other than that I've dug it for years.'

Marriott remained suspicious of the press, kept them at arms length if he could. Their criticisms annoyed him and he often rubbished the adverse comments. Yet he also respected the interview format, used it sometimes to make perceptive comments about himself.

'You see for a long time,' he told James Johnson of the *NME* in 1973, 'I went through a spell where I had to prove myself. After doing things like 'Lazy Sunday,' …' Marriott winces at the memory which makes him stumble over his words. 'You have to… You have to find it all again.

'I personally got to the point a few years back where I couldn't even sing a twelve bar blues which is vocally where I first started. In a way I've come full circle. Like I'm almost back now to things I was doing with The Moments only hopefully better.'

Was he embarrassed now by songs such as 'Lazy Sunday,' Johnson asks? Marriott confirms his discomfort, tells the writer that the humour he lavished on many of the Small Faces's most famous songs was down to insecurity as a songwriter.

'Those sort of songs,' he said, 'eased the strain of thinking I've got to write something or sing something real good. Then it got to the point where I couldn't sing right, anyway… To me all those things like 'Lazy Sunday,' 'Itchycoo Park' and *Ogden's Nut Gone Flake* were all right in the terms of a good pop record but they were a substitute for anything with any kind of feeling.'

‡ ‡ ‡

Kay the mother felt helpless, powerless. She knew the price that was being exacted from her son, the one made up of touring, of travelling and partying and writing and recording and staying in blank hotel after hotel and sitting on buses and watching the white lines disappear under you, singing the same old song to the band, to the audience and to the next morning's pretty face and the world outside of the band has no meaning and the people you travel with bore you silly and the record company are false and the manager's a shark and when you get home you'll discover that your ability to make music has gone because you're so tired to the soul that you can hardly stand and Kay the mum knows this and all she can do is sit at home and wait and hope, wait and hope, the envy of the street, in truth the most worried woman in the world.

If only he would let his family be with him. Maybe then he would think twice before indulging himself. She sighed because she knew her son, knew there were two chances – slim and none.

‡ ‡ ‡

Naturally, Steve wanted to record the next Humble Pie album at Beehive Cottage. Convinced that *Eat It* had stalled due to its muddy sound and inability to leap out of the radio and grab the listener, the band disagreed and insisted on returning to Olympic Studios.

Steve told them bluntly, fine. I'll just get a load of new musicians in and carry on at Beehive without you. The band looked at each other and gave in. One proviso, though – the studio sound had to be cleaned up, had to be raised to another level.

‡ ‡ ‡

Soul music – it always brings out the best in people.

Thunderbox remains Humble Pie's finest album. Why? Because out of all their albums, the R&B influence is most pronounced here.

Despite the growing tension between the band and Marriott, all concerned maintain they had a good time making the album. Jerry Shirley refers to its creation as a 'lot of fun,' going on to relate how he and Clem would lock into a groove and play without thinking, as if the magic was coming through them without any struggle on their part.

Twelve songs were recorded, many of them covers. Ann Peebles's 'I Can't Stand The Rain' (once referred to by John Lennon as the perfect single), Arthur Alexander's 'Anna,' The Staple Singer's 'Oh La De Da.'

Of their own songs, Marriott's 'Groovin' With Jesus,' is the stand out track, full of stabbing organs and clipped guitars, Marriott on fine form vocally.

Incidentally, the word thunderbox is a seventeenth century slang word for the toilet. Guess who unearthed that little gem and insisted they call the album it?

Of all the band members, drummer Jerry Shirley's relationship with Steve yields the most insights. When he met him, Steve was his idol.

The relationship was imbalanced, the young drummer looking up, Steve playing the youngster coolly.

'I idolised him so much that he'd developed this aura with me,' Shirley clearly states. 'Often in an instance like that you end up being very disappointed when you get to know the person. With Steve, particularly early on, there was a good person in there who was always striving to please people who treated him normally.'

Yet as the years flashed by, gaining perceptible speed with each New Year, so Shirley got to see Marriott from all angles. Some good, some bad. And if bad, Shirley says, it was probable that the white powder had been near to hand.

'The first Steve that I knew was generally speaking a decent guy but he was never the same person once his marriage to Jenny started going wrong. He developed a self-destruct button that wasn't there before. He became a bitter man as his drugs intake increased. There were signs of it happening earlier but back then he managed to curb it. Steve's marriage to Jenny was his only piece of normality and when that went down the pan so did he. Bigger and stronger men than him would have overcome it but he wasn't equipped to deal with it. The marriage was probably the first failure in his life and that led up to lots of other failures.'

In fact, Shirley's take – perceptive, sharp – is that Steve now started actively courting failure, left success at the altar unable to cope with its many demands.

‡ ‡ ‡

'Every time success started to come at him he would do everything he could to mess it up,' the drummer states. 'I think his attitude was, "I better mess this up before it messes me up." I saw him blow a million dollar record deal intentionally because he knew if he didn't do it they would end up screwing him.'

Success was Marriott's rawest nerve point, he knew its tricky ways intimately, had lived with them now for ten years. He knew what only the famous do – success is a dream and a nightmare all rolled into one terrifying whole. Success seduces, then it kills. No wonder he yearned for a life of just getting on stage, playing music.

Fuck money, fuck audiences, fuck the business. Just let me play because when I do that's when I am most alive, that's when I am at my most truthful as a human being and that's how I serve my purpose.

'If only he had remained the person that Jenny originally fell in love with it could have lasted forever,' Shirley says. 'He was a star on stage and couldn't turn it off when he came home. Musically, he'd deteriorated as well. All of a sudden he'd settle for second best and he developed a 'that'll do' attitude. Mind you, Steve's half-hearted efforts were better than most people's best efforts.'

It was a wretched time. Jenny had finally gone and most felt that the damage caused by her departure would be deep and long lasting.

Kay, his sister: 'I think from then on he wasn't as good to women as he was before Jenny. I think Jenny made him very bitter. In Steve's mind he had given her everything and he was so hurt. They walked all over him. You wouldn't think so but the women honestly did.'

The nature of his song-writing now suffered, his prolific nature notably slowing down. Fuck it. He'd rather get wasted than work. It is why the album *Thunderbox*, good as it is, is laden down with cover versions. He couldn't be bothered to call upon himself anymore to produce the songs and there was no one else around to successfully pick up the slack. Day by day, Marriott was starting to lose interest and the nature of his life reflected that state of mind...

'He really let himself and his house go to pieces,' Shirley reveals. 'The back door would be left open and cats, dogs, ducks and chickens would come in and shit all over the place. He never cleaned and the place was disgusting. All the local tradesmen had blacklisted the address. When Jenny was there the cleanliness was pristine. By early 1974 it became a crash pad for every drug addicted bastard in the business.'

Soon Shirley started avoiding the place he helped build, his workplace.

'When I walked in,' he recalls, 'some stranger would say, "Who the fuck are you?" I'd say, "I'm the cunt who helped pay for this place."'

Marriott would just look over at him and smile.

‡ ‡ ‡

In 1974, Humble Pie played the Charlton Football Ground with The Who headlining. It was a homecoming of sorts for Marriott. Humble Pie were still viewed as an American success but today, he would have a British crowd, old musician friends such as Townshend and Moon watching in the wings.

Writer Paul Gorman was there.

'His look around 1974 was great: grown-out skinhead with long sideburns and jean jacket and denim parallels with big turn-ups and boots. I'd only seen scallies up north wear that style before. That's what he wore when they played Charlton and it ran contrary to what everyone else was wearing (apart from Lou Reed, who looked magnificent that day). Also, Marriott's attitude was very anti the post-hippie spirit of the times. He sprang onstage in that clobber saying something like: "Awright? How's it faakin' going then?!" and started playing these power chords, which was a bit of a wake-up, because it was a nice, warm day and everyone was a bit drowsy.

That day they played unremarkable boogie blues stuff but I was pleased they did 'Hallelujah, I Love Her So.'

'I don't recall them going down a storm but it was a funny old bill: Widowmaker, Maggie Bell, Lindisfarne, people like that, so he and Lou Reed stuck out like sore thumbs.'

Manon Piercey was also present, her friendship with Steve now rekindled, back up and running.

'Humble Pie were just awesome,' she enthuses, 'The Who just couldn't follow them. Another gig I particularly remember was at The Colisseum. We were right at the top and with the noise and the movement it felt as though the place was going to fall down. The support band was Heavy Metal Kids with Gary Holton on lead vocals. All the way through their set the fans were chanting for "Stevie, Stevie, Stevie." Holton stormed off stage and said, "You can have your precious Steve." Steve was great that night, as he was most nights but he was so thin, he looked ill.'

Thunderbox did not perform well in the charts.

Not rocky enough nor soulful enough to crossover either way. Dark clouds started to surround the band. The energy levels dropped. Everything felt like a slog. Everyone had an opinion why the album had flopped but no one listened. The band were talking into mirrors.

And another gruelling tour of America was about to begin.

‡ ‡ ‡

'I first met Steve on February 25th, 1975. A friend of mine, Peter, met him at a Humble Pie concert and invited him back to his place for drinks. I was living in an apartment in downtown Atlanta with Peter's girlfriend Katie and somehow they and about nine others ended up in our flat. Steve had been up for about three days without sleep. One minute he was sitting up on a couch playing guitar next he'd passed out. Everyone just went home and left him there. Katie and I didn't know what do with him. We knew who he was but didn't know who to call or what hotel he was staying in. We managed to carry him into a bedroom. At that time I was a flight attendant and I had to go to work. When I got back some 12 hours later he was still asleep. When he did eventually wake up he thanked me and invited me to go to Pittsburgh to see his show. I wasn't really one for rock'n'roll but flatmate Katie told me to go. I went with the band and just three weeks later I quit my job and ran off to England with him. I've got a working class Christian family and it was devastating for them. In fact my mother had a massive heart attack three days later after I left with Steve.

'Steve hired me a Lear jet to go and visit my father in hospital. My mother said she would never speak to me again. By the time I got to England I'd lost my job, my family and was in a strange country. I think at the time Steve just intended having fun with me for a couple of weeks and then sending me home again. Because I'd lost my family we were stuck with each other. It made us closer.'

Meet Pam Stephens, Mrs Marriott the Second, described by Jerry Shirley as the proverbial 'fish out of water.' Pam was totally different to Jenny, not averse to The Life, the having of a good time.

'She was my favourite,' Kay the sister states. 'I loved her. She was so funny. We really, really got on. We were mates. We used to go out clubbing and all that when he was away.'

Within a few months Pam fell pregnant and Marriott was hit hard by the news. He and Jenny had tried for years for a child and their failure to produce one naturally made him think of himself as infertile. Now he knew he wasn't.

'And then he was a bit suspicious,' Kay the sister recalls.

It wasn't just his first wife's behaviour that aroused his suspicions. Marriott now started questioning those around him about money, how much, how little. The management and record company became his prime targets. Jerry Shirley took the other point of view, defended his employers, stood up to Marriott, told him that neither Dee Anthony nor the record company had secretly stashed away millions. Marriott refused to believe him. The bastards had it somewhere. Shirley heard the depth of Marriott's bitterness, exacerbated no doubt by prolonged cocaine use, and knew for sure the band were finished.

'Steve's only way of dealing with a problem,' Shirley told author Dan Muise, 'was either completely confrontational or just blow it off. You know. Fuck you, fuck you, fuck you. That was it. All or nothing. Sitting down and having a quiet, intelligent, lengthy compromising, seeing both sides of the fence type of solving a problem talk was just not in Steve's scheme of things.'

In response to the lack of answers, Marriott threw himself into work, embarking upon three separate albums at the same time; a Pie album, an album with Greg and his own solo album.

For the Humble Pie album, A&M insisted that the band now bring in a producer. The band fought them on this issue but finally compromised bringing in none other than their old label boss and manager, Andrew Loog Oldham.

Oldham had now moved to New York. He was glad to work with Marriott again but remembers the sessions ruefully, particularly one Friday night when Marriott and the band suddenly launched into a full on version of Chris Montez's 'Let's Dance.'

As the music roared through the speakers, Oldham could hardly contain himself. Throughout the whole sessions nothing of real value had been put down on tape and it seemed like nothing ever would. This was a band approaching the finishing line. But this, this was magnificent music they were making. Fuck, he thought, we've got a monster hit on our hands here. Unbelievable.

Abruptly, Marriott stopped the music.

'Got you that time, didn't I, Oldham?' he shouted through the mike, evil grin on his face. 'You think I'd do that fucking song?'

Recalling the incident in his book, *2Stoned*, Oldham went straight to the root of Marriott. 'He already knew he could not handle fame again. It was enough to grin and bear the pain; it was enough just to live.'

Steve Marriott could do nothing except sing and play music. Yet success only made him unhappy. Catch 22.

'I know I'd hate to be a coalman,' Marriott told the *NME*, 'but I don't know what I'd do other than be a musician. I'm not skilled at any other trade. Even if it is a matter of playing to fifty people, what the hell, you're still an entertainer. I don't think I could ever end that.'

He was trapped with no easy way out or down.

The sessions with Loog Oldham never worked out.

The final Humble Pie album, *Street Rats*, was eventually cobbled together from old tapes and demos. Whatever lay close to hand, bung it on there. No one gave a fuck.

Yet there was one song of worth amongst this haphazard selection, a real gem, a reminder of both Marriott's great musical imagination and his vocal skills. It is his slowed down bluesy version of The Beatles' 'We Can Work It Out.'

Marriott does a superb job, renders the song unrecognisable from the original, takes it to another level. Entering the track on a falsetto note and creating a slow funky backdrop for the rest of his vocal, Marriott strips the song and places it in another context. It makes for an impressive piece of music. Unfortunately, such high quality is conspicuously lacking throughout the rest of the album.

There is no cohesion on *Street Rats*, no direction, no way home. The band were at war. When it came to the album sleeve, they even refused to pose together. The photographer for the sleeve was forced to visit each member separately at their homes to shoot them. He then cropped the four solo pics into a band composition, made it look like a group photo.

Their last effort to stay alive was a feeble attempt to find new management. A young Bill Curbishley, the man who would one day manage The Who, was approached by Shirley and Clempson and he agreed to see Dee Anthony on the band's behalf, see if he could negotiate the band away from him.

A week later, Curbishley invited the band to his office to report back on his meeting with Anthony.

'We got a business meeting, 'ave we?' Marriott snarled when told of the arrangement. He loved taunting the rest of the band with the word business. Business, business, business.

Marriott turned up for the meet but he was wrecked and in no condition whatsoever to talk, let alone listen. Still, at least he made it to the office. Greg Ridley didn't even bother to show up.

The meeting began. Bill looked at Steve's condition and grimaced to the others. Jerry and Clem looked at each other, and that was it. Say no more, it was all over.

Humble Pie were finished. Marriott got himself back to the Racket Club as fast as he could.

‡ ‡ ‡

In 1975, the Rolling Stones announced – to no one's real surprise – that the ex-Faces guitarist Ron Wood would replace the recently departed, Mick Taylor. Ron Wood. Well, he would wouldn't he?

It could have been Steve Marriott. Following a call from his friend, Keith Richards, Marriott went to audition for the band. Before he did so, the Rolling Stones guitarist called up Marriott with some friendly advice: whatever you do, don't upstage Mick. Go onstage, stand at the back and play guitar. Don't sing. Don't move.

Pam Marriott: 'Steve told me, "I was good and stood at the back for a while but then Keith would hit this lick and I just couldn't keep my mouth shut." Keith wanted him in but there was no way that once Steve opened his mouth Mick would have him in the band. He knew Steve would never stay in the background. They were the one band in the world that Steve would have loved to have been in. He just wanted to work with Keith.'

But he never would, never did.

‡ ‡ ‡

A Humble Pie farewell tour of America – final chance to cash in, boys. It began in March 1975. Karen, a keen fan, waited for them at Los Angeles airport. Marriott spotted her, came over and thanked her straight away for her birthday card from two months ago. Karen was staggered. 'I was so totally zonked out I couldn't believe my ears,' she wrote.

They drive to the band's hotel. Marriott and Pam check in but as with most of the tour party, they leave their room doors open for people to wander in and out.

'Steve was so funny,' Karen recalls, 'and talk about obnoxious. He'd make this loud noise with his hands and mouth –a duck call? – then he'd yell at the top of his lungs, "RUBBISH!" Then would calmly say, "Other than that I'm perfectly alright." After a while of that and other nonsense – like Steve pouring beer on the car below, spitting etc, Steve said he was gonna close the door 'cuz it was getting cold and why don't we go down to the coffee shop and he offered us some money if we needed it.'

During her brief stay with the band, Karen notes that Marriott would often start conversations with himself. 'Hello.' 'How are ya?' 'Good mate,' etc. and that with Pam accompanying him, she and Steve had little time to themselves. When they do chat at the Sacramento gig, Steve tells Karen he has been 'on the junk' but had now kicked it.

Pam Marriott: 'He just told people whatever they wanted to hear.'

Their tour of the USA, as a five piece band with keyboardist Tim Hinckley, finished in Philadelphia. Before the last number 'I Don't Need No Doctor', Steve announced to the large audience: "Before we disappear into the depths of Rock has-beens, we would just like to say we've always had a very special spot for Philadelphia and I think you know it. Such nice people! Nice people!

With the tour completed, Steve and Pam headed back to England, back to Beehive Cottage, back in fact to harsh reality.

His Humble Pie days were over.

PART FOUR

SAYLARVEE?

Humble Pie 1969   *(Patrick Scanlon)*

Steve 1971   *(Unknown)*

Steve 1973   *(SKR Photos)*

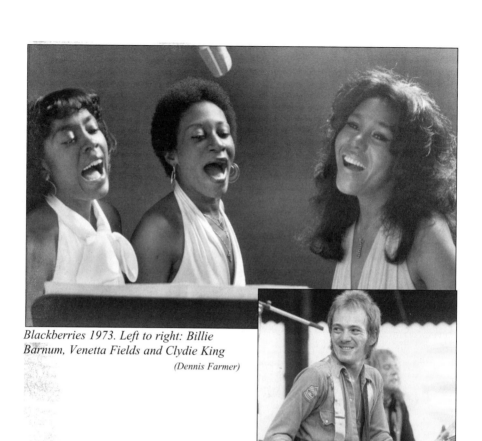

*Blackberries 1973. Left to right: Billie
Barnum, Venetta Fields and Clydie King*
                              (Dennis Farmer)

Steve 1974
(Unknown)

Humble Pie 1974
(Roger Stowell)

Steve Marriott's All Stars 1975   (Dennis Farmer)

Steve and PP Arnold 1977

(London Features Ltd)

Small Faces Mk 2 1977

(London Features Ltd)

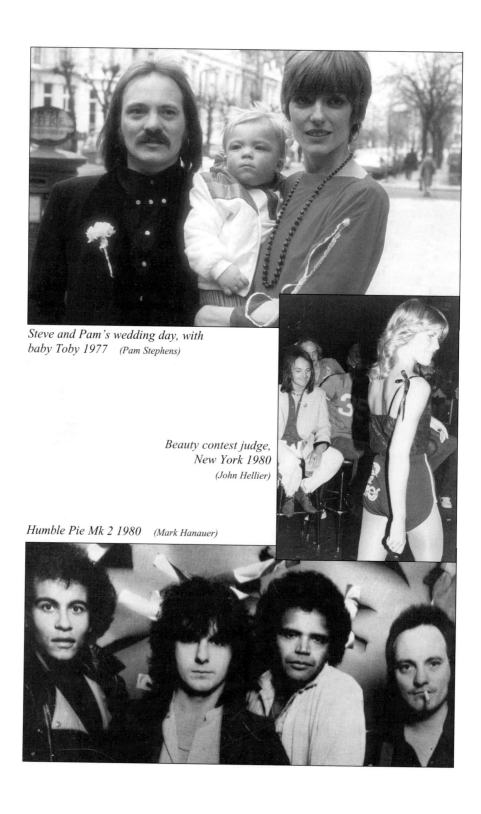

*Steve and Pam's wedding day, with
baby Toby 1977*   (Pam Stephens)

*Beauty contest judge,
New York 1980*
(John Hellier)

Humble Pie Mk 2 1980   (Mark Hanauer)

Hand written poster for Steve and Ronnie's Bridge House gig in 1981. They would go out themselves, in the middle of the night, fly posting around the East End.

Majik Mijits.
Steve and
Ronnie on
stage together
1981
    (Gordon Irwin)

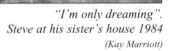

"I'm only dreaming".
Steve at his sister's house 1984
    (Kay Marriott)

Steve 1984   *(Uli Kniep)*

Christmas dinner with Mum and Dad 1984   (Kay Marriott)

Steve 1985   (John Hellier)

Steve with partner,
Manon Piercey, and daughter
Mollie Mae 1985 (Manon Piercey)

Steve on his narrow boat with wife,
Toni and Dad, Bill 1989 *(Toni Marriott)*

The last ever line up.
Packet Of Three 1991
(Toni Marriott)

Steve and Peter
Frampton
together on
stage at the
Half Moon in
Putney shortly
before Steve
died
(John Hellier)

(London Features Ltd)

Chapter Nineteen

Singing The Blues

Once again, there was no money. The minute Humble Pie folded so Marriott's regular wages ceased. Once again, after selling truckloads of records, after playing to the thousands upon thousands, Steve Marriott was skint, alarmingly so.

'We were so broke,' Pam his wife says, 'that we were stealing food. Me and Steve would creep to the next farm at midnight and steal corn and potatoes. Steve thought it was a great laugh but you have no idea how it felt.'

Typical of the indefatigable Marriott to laugh in the face of adversity. Life threw many things at him but he refused to be beaten, refused to be knocked off his perch although it was clear he needed to make a move now, needed to form another group. He was down to borrowing cash from friends such as musician Joe Brown just to keep going.

'Financially,' Brown says, 'we did help them a lot. We had to. They were friends who had fallen on hard times. Steve always promised to pay us back but of course he didn't.'

The men had met through a roadie, hit it off straight away which wasn't at all surprising. Brown and Marriott shared similar backgrounds, similar tastes.

Brown had come to prominence in the late '50s during the skiffle era, gone onto play rock'n'roll guitar with luminaries such as Johnny Cash, Gene Vincent and Eddie Cochran. In 1960, he formed Joe Brown and the Bruvvers and hit the charts, most notably with 'Picture Of You.'

Brown didn't just stick to pop. A genial East Ender whose distinctive haircut was a forerunner to the look made famous by Rod Stewart, Brown kept his name alive by moving into film and theatre work.

'I liked him,' Brown says of Marriott, 'and most of the time he was good company. Only most of the time, though. When he was on certain substances he became quite unbearable. When he was sober or even when he was pissed he was a very funny man. On many occasions we'd sit up all night at either his place or mine, just exchanging jokes. We had the same sense of humour.

'We'd often pull out a couple of acoustic guitars and spend hours playing old country tunes. Steve loved country music, particularly Hank Williams and Willie Nelson. Steve's not known as a country music fan but he really dug the Nashville scene. I also remember that he'd love to play old Everly Brothers songs. He was a smashing musician that could play almost any instrument put in front of him. He also had that great voice.'

He also needed work, needed a band and moved quickly to secure one. He named them The Steve Marriott All Stars. The line up consisted of Ian Wallace on drums, Mickey Finn on rhythm guitar and ex-Pie man, Greg Ridley on bass. Marriott launched them in August 1975 via the UK's best selling music weekly, the *NME*. At this notable interview, conducted by writer Steve Clarke at Marriott's cottage, photographer Joe Stevens, who had visited the house previously, asked about a horse he recalled grazing in Marriott's field.

Marriott laughed and then casually admitted that he and his wife were so broke, they had been forced to kill and eat the animal.

The story did its job, put Marriott straight onto the front cover. 'The Horse That Steve Marriott Ate' was the headline accompanied by a photo of Marriott looking slim and sporting a moustache, sideburns and a Modish haircut.

The interview itself had been conducted with his band the All Stars present although all the questions were directed to Steve.

Asked about his parlous financial state, Marriott initially claims he has spent all his money on Clear Sounds, the home studio. Clarke doesn't buy this. Pressing him further, Marriott then admits that his manager, Dee Anthony, had invested a lot of his money in property on the island of Nassau.

'We earned a hell of a lot of money but we spent a hell of a lot of money,' Marriott revealed. 'The land is a bad thing. There's about ten acres with six houses and a lot of beach.'

Ridley can't resist a dig. 'Our manager likes it there too,' he quips. Marriott chuckles at Ridley's dry remark but within seconds is silencing the bassist.

'The situation between me and Dee is fine,' Marriott says assuringly. 'He's not ripped me off.'

Ridley ignores orders, butts in again. 'You couldn't say it even if he had,' he sneers. 'You can't say things like that to a paper.'

Ian Wallace adds, 'Yeah, who's gonna get their legs sawn off?'

Marriott moves quickly to provide cover . 'Dee hasn't ripped me off,' he says. 'He's spent whatever money in the best way he thought. He made us so we have got a lot to thank him for. He's still about the heaviest manager to get for America. As a manager he's the best.'

End of conversation.

Marriott's defence of his manager is not at all surprising if there is any truth in the story that Pam now tells.

'By the time we got back to England, Humble Pie were finished,' she told Hellier. 'And Dee Anthony cut Steve off completely, absolutely completely. We had no money at all. Steve was convinced that Dee had used Humble Pie money to promote Peter Frampton's live album [*Frampton Comes Alive*] an album that became the biggest selling live album of all time and made Peter a superstar in the States... It got frightening. We got calls from the Mafia threatening death to us and Steve's family if we spoke out against Dee Anthony. Steve was going through great anguish, you have no idea. He wouldn't even answer the phone in the end.'

Knowing of Dee Anthony's loose link with, amongst others, the Genovese family, Marriott's other significant comment halfway through the *NME* interview now makes a hell of a lot of sense. He tells Clarke, 'There's a lot I'd love to say but not right now. Maybe in six months time I can say a lot more than I can say now.'

He never would or could, of course, but a certain tone for the third part of Steve Marriott's musical career and life had just been set, a tone of wild turbulence that would be marked by money problems, women problems, music problems. His response to these situations was to take it on the chin, smile and move on. Yet every incident took its toll, every incident lightly whipped his soul, however much he protested otherwise.

‡ ‡ ‡

Laurie O'Leary entered Marriott's life for the second time.

Along with Joe Brown, O'Leary would prove to be a loyal and staunch ally to Marriott. O'Leary had been raised in the East End and clawed his way upwards. As a teenager he had gone into club management, ended up running the famed Speakeasy club in the Sixties and Seventies. Thanks to his work there, he became acquainted with numerous celebrities including the notorious Kray twins. (In the '80s, O'Leary would take Marriott to meet Reggie Kray in his Broadmoor prison. It was an East End request, one that couldn't be turned down. Marriott went, signed a photo, got out of there as quick as he could.)

O'Leary was a Marriott fan, had become one after the Small Faces show he promoted at the Top Rank in Southampton back in 1966. When ex-mod Mickey Finn turned up at his office and told him Marriott now required management, O'Leary didn't hesitate.

The pair of them drove straight out to Beehive Cottage.

'We met Steve out in the garden,' he recalls. 'He said, "Hello mate [sniff]," I remember a distinct sniff up the nostril. "Alright mate [sniff]," he said. It was obvious even to me who had never done drugs that he was on the coke. "You gonna be my new manager, [sniff]?" he asked. I said, "Well, let's talk. How many managers do you want? You've got Dee Anthony." Steve said, "He's left me potless, ain't got a pot to piss in".'

'I told Steve that I had always respected Dee Anthony, Steve snapped back, "Nah, he's just fucking Mafia, always threatening this and that." I said, "Forget Dee for a moment. What do you want out of a manager?"'

'He said, "I wanna graft, I wanna work. I've got a new band."'

'I said, "Well what do you want to achieve? You can't do record deals 'cos your already tied to A&M." I went through all the rigmarole and ended up by saying, "Look I'll manage you on a handshake. As soon as you mess me around I'm off and if I don't suit you, you're off. That way we won't owe each other anything." Steve's reply to that was, "Smashing mate. Let's go down the boozer".'

Which they did, Steve, Laurie, Pam and Mickey Finn.

After the pub, where according to O'Leary not a lot of alcohol was consumed, they returned to Beehive Cottage.

'It's getting dark by now,' O'Leary recalls, 'and I find he's got no electricity. He said, "Nah, they cut it off mate. Dee's stopped my money, no electricity, Pam's up the duff and all I've got is candles." As I went in there I couldn't believe the state of the place. I went into the kitchen. There were ducks and chickens running about, tipping over waste paper baskets looking for scraps of food. Steve would just shout at them, "Get out of the fucking way!" I'm thinking he's had all these hit records, he must have an income somewhere.'

O'Leary began looking into the legal nuts and bolts that held together Marriott's career. One of the first moves he made was to call his friend, Derek Green who looked after the UK end of A&M Records. In that conversation, Green revealed that he had already received a directive from Dee Anthony not to deal with O'Leary. Furthermore, the overall A&M boss, Jerry Moss, had already advanced Anthony money for a Marriott solo album none of which Steve had seen.

'Derek said, "We want the album out and if I have to work with you we'll do it discreetly, off the record." He told me he would deal with me if Steve gave it the OK. I had to deliver Steve to the studio which I did and A&M advanced Steve twelve thousand dollars to help with the band.'

O'Leary now set up two meetings. One with a Dave Clarke, who, through his liaison with Dee Anthony, was still handling Steve's affairs, and one with Marriott himself later on that day at Beehive Cottage.

'I went over to Dave's house, somewhere in Essex to collect Steve's paperwork for Clear Sounds Productions,' O'Leary recalled. 'I got to Dave's house and it was sparkling clean and very plush. It was a grand house and very well looked after.

'I could see he was a different proposition. I liked and enjoyed meeting Dave but wasn't quite sure where he was going to fit in. I told him I was now representing Steve and that the man had nothing. He just said, "Well that's 'cos it's all gone up his nose." I said I wasn't interested in that and told Dave that I was going to manage Steve in England to the best of my ability.

'Steve was a tough cookie, you had to be tough yourself to handle Steve and Dave must have done a decent job in getting Steve to gigs and liaising with Dee Anthony. Anyway we now had the advance and it was off to Beehive Cottage to hear some new songs.'

Over the past year or so Marriott had written and recorded at least twenty songs for a planned solo album. The LP had two working titles: 'Scrubbers,' or 'Lend Us A Quid.'

'Steve took me across the yard, up some stairs and into his studio. I couldn't believe it. He'd only recently told me that he had no electricity in the house and even I know you've got to have electricity to run a studio. I said "Steve, How come you've got electricity in the studio but not in the house?" He said, "A mate of mine is an electrician and he's come off the pylon."

'In other words one of his buddies had cut into the pylon. I said, "Steve, you'll get nicked." he said, "No we don't do it until after eleven at night. That's why we don't have it in the house. They don't come out after eleven." Later on, in the grass just outside the kitchen I picked up a piece of paper. It was a court order. I'd noticed the heading Court Order Urgent and picked it up. I said Steve's what all this about? This is a court order and you've got five days left to answer it.

'That was the beginning of my management of Steve.'

Keyboardist Tim Hinckley had served the order, claiming co-authorship of songs he had recorded with Marriott. O'Leary instantly killed the claim. 'I just told him, "Musicians don't do that to each other and anyway you get high, Steve gets high, whose to remember who wrote what?"'

Case dismissed.

‡ ‡ ‡

As far as the solo LP was concerned, the obvious action was to give A&M the tapes that Marriott had been working on for the past year. According to Pam, Marriott was 'so proud,' of the music he had created during these sessions. Despite the financial hardships, the threatening phone calls from phone-boxes or social clubs on Mulberry Street, in New York's Little Italy district, Marriott had continued writing and recording. Nothing, not even the mobsters such as John Gotti, could take that away from him.

'It was wonderful music, we all loved it,' Pam recalls. Yet A&M passed on the tapes, opting instead to send Marriott to America to record.

Marriott baulked at the idea of setting foot in Dee Anthony territory.

'He wanted me to go with him,' O'Leary says, 'I just said, "Go on your own. Dee isn't a problem." See, I had spoken to Anthony already and he was totally unperturbed. He was getting into much bigger things.'

Which was true. Peter Frampton, Anthony's new client, was about to release his multi-million selling album, *Frampton Comes Alive*, an album which, as stated above, would somehow top the charts for months on end. The mob had moved on from rigging jukeboxes to rigging all important radio play, with breathtaking results.

Once in America, Steve started making enquiries about the money he should have received for the album he was about to make. He hadn't seen a cent of it. Who had? He got his answer soon enough.

'While we were doing that *Marriott* album we actually went to a Godfather meeting,' Pam Marriott says. 'It was at that meeting that Steve was told he'd receive no money at all from his past and nothing was going to be done about Dee Anthony. From that meeting we knew we were never gonna get anything back. That was really horrible, people just have no idea what he went through.

'Not only could he not work and get any of his back dues, he couldn't say anything either. We were dealing with the big boys! I was pregnant and they would threaten to hurt me. It was a terrible terrible time.'

Pam states that the meet took place at the Ravenite Social club on Mulberry Street, the main artery of New York's Little Italy district. Present was the Dapper Don himself, John Gotti, plus Frank Locascio and Paul Castellano all from the Gambino family. Steve and Pam walked away knowing they now had to forget monies that were rightfully theirs. It must have been a tense, devastating time. You're broke, you're owed money but any chance you have of claiming it back could result in real physical damage.

A miracle then that the resulting album had some moments of note. On the American side head for, 'You Don't Know Me,' a big band soul strut. Check also a funky workout of the Freddy Scott song, 'Are You Lonely For Me Baby?' and a sweeping ballad, 'Early Evening Light,' written by Steve and made distinctive by its unusual sound and arrangement.

On the British side, Pam contributes the lyrics to 'Midnight Rollin'' which deal with her strict religious upbringing and the band also resurrect 'Wham Bam Thank You Ma'am,' which falls quite short of the original Small Faces version. The reason for its inability to match up to the original may, as Marriott inadvertently pointed out in an interview from the time, be the absence of producer Glyn Johns at the controls. Both men may have rubbed each other up the wrong way but both men brought out the best in each other.

'I think,' Marriott admitted to writer, Jim Girard in 1975, 'that the Small Faces did make good records but that had a lot to do with our engineer, Glyn Johns.'

The *Marriott* album came and went, nothing more, nothing less.

'That *Marriott* A&M album,' Pam spits, 'how he hated it.'

Well, what more can you expect from a piece of music made by a man working against a backdrop of Bada Bing Boys making veiled threats and very real whispered hellos?

How glad must Marriott have been to get back to the relative safety of Beehive Cottage where there was not a silk suit or a cup of espresso to be had for miles around?

‡ ‡ ‡

By 1975, former Immediate boss, Andrew Loog Oldham had quit Britannia but his partner, Tony Calder, remained in London and now worked at NEMS, the company once owned by Beatle manager, Brian Epstein. Calder persuaded his boss Patrick Meehan to buy up the Immediate Small Faces back catalogue. Calder sanctioned the re-release of 'Itchycoo Park,' as a single, sending it out to do battle once more with the other chart hopefuls.

'It's one of my all time favourite records. I still think it's a hit today,' says Calder. He had backed a winner. 'Itchycoo Park' became a chart hit, Christmas '75.

In the press, the word 'Reunion,' started to gather currency every time the Small Faces were mentioned. That's how exciting music was in early 1976.

‡ ‡ ‡

Promoter John Curd got in touch, offered to promote five All Stars gigs, two of which he placed at the Roundhouse in Chalk Farm, London and one for the Fairfield Hall, Croydon. Curd correctly figured that with Marriott back in the public eye thanks to 'Itchycoo,' ticket sales shouldn't be a problem.

'The Roundhouse went very well,' O'Leary remembers, 'next up the Fairfield Hall.'

At eleven on the morning of the Fairfield gig, Marriott called O'Leary. He wanted him to pull the show. Marriott had been up for days now, was far too wasted to get on a stage that night. He wanted to sleep, not play. Fuck the gig.

O'Leary called Curd. The promoter was succinct in his response. He told O'Leary that to pull the show would prove ruinous for all concerned. O'Leary called Marriott back, said sorry, but you gotta play. Marriott replied that he was too ill. O'Leary ignored him, insisted that his good name was at stake here and no way was Marriott going to ruin it. Anyway, he said, consoling his wasted client, if you keel over onstage from a heart attack, think of all the publicity.

'I was being hard with him in a nice way,' O'Leary says. 'We did the gig. Halfway through, John Curd the promoter came up to me and whispered to me that the venue's manager had just said Steve's been swearing too much onstage and could I stop him?'

O'Leary made his way to the side of the stage, waited for the band to finish a song and then went onstage. He whispered to Marriott to calm down on the swear words. Marriott nodded and as O'Leary exited, turned, grabbed the mike and addressed the audience.

'I wanna tell you something,' he announced. 'That geezer that's just gone off is my manager and he's a diamond, a real Eastender and the best manager I've ever had and I'm so proud of him. Well, not him but the manager of this gaff here, the guy that owns the place, well he's told my manager to do the dirty work and go and tell him to stop swearing but I don't think I really swear much, but the manager, no not my manager, don't blame him 'cos it wasn't his fault, he's come out and told me to cut down on the swearing. So you know what I'm gonna say and this isn't for my manager 'cos I love him, this is for the manager of this poxy building. You know what I'm gonna say to him and I want you all to repeat with me – BOLLOCKS!'

In unison, the audience joyfully shouted out the word. Marriott, pressed on.

'BOLLOCKS. One more time for me. BOLLOCKS.'

Laurie O'Leary: 'I just stood there and thought, 'He's a star, ain't he?'

‡ ‡ ‡

Since quitting The Faces in 1973, Marriott's brother in Mod, Ronnie Lane had embarked upon a very singular musical journey. Disgusted at Rod Stewart's offensive rock star behaviour Lane had put together Slim Chance, and in 1974 Lane had taken this motley band of fiddle and banjo players on the road, setting up gigs in a circus tent wherever they felt like playing.

Lane's skill as a songwriter was now beyond doubt. Notwithstanding his sterling work with The Faces, Lane's solo shots such as 'The Poacher' and 'How Come' had given him two top 40 hits, established his name once more. Yet any money he had accrued from these and past records had been quickly swallowed up by the huge expense of sustaining what was in effect a travelling circus.

With 'Itchycoo Park,' back in the charts it was becoming increasingly apparent that Lane's best financial bet lay with his former rather than his current band members. Calder had already set up 'Lazy Sunday,' as the follow up to 'Itchycoo Park,' thus increasing the chances of the Small Faces returning in some form or another.

In January, 1976, Lane was back on the road with a much slimmer line up and an itinerary of rather more established venues to play. One of them was Colchester University. The day before the gig, Laurie O'Leary received a phone call at his London office:

'[It was] Mark Fenning of E&G Management who asked if I could get Steve Marriott to a gig in Colchester to jam with Ronnie Lane's Slim Chance. At the time, Ronnie wasn't suffering from MS [Multiple Sclerosis] or at least nobody knew about it back then plus I loved his band, Slim Chance. I wasn't over keen on Ronnie Lane as such but that didn't matter, I enjoyed the music.

'I put the idea to Steve and told him it would be good promotion. Their relationship had soured tremendously over the previous five or six years but it seemed like a good idea to me. It would have been wonderful if Ronnie had rung Steve and said, ' "Come on you, prat, let's do a gig." Steve would have loved that.'

(Always direct in his dealings, Marriott never got to grips with music biz protocol. Why do people call his manager, when they want something, he would angrily demand. Why not talk directly to me? That one always puzzled him.)

Steve agreed to the proposition. Ronnie and he onstage together could only help push sales of 'Itchycoo.' Plus, there were other reasons to re-connect with his old flame. *Top Of The Pops*, the country's biggest TV show, wanted to film the original Small Faces performing both 'Itchycoo Park,' and 'Lazy Sunday.'

Over Christmas, the respective managers exchanged phone calls. By January, all four members had agreed to take part in a loose reunion. In mid-January, 1976, Marriott, Pam and Laurie travelled to Colchester University where Marriott was finally reunited with his old friend and partner, Ronald 'Leafy' Lane. It was some moment although O'Leary did detect 'a little animosity,' between the former song-writing duo, a little verbal sparring that revealed the distance and hurt that still lay between them.

'Then Ronnie Lane went onstage,' O'Leary recalls, 'and did a whole set, had a break and then got back onstage for the second half. I hadn't been told when Steve was going on but I'm expecting it to be the second half. Steve was quite happy, quite chirpy. He's all keyed up and looking at the stage but Ronnie's avoiding all eye contact.'

Lane keeps playing, keeps announcing song after song as Steve waits impatiently in the wings. Finally, Marriott snaps. 'The little bastard,' Marriott growls, 'come on let's go.'

Which is when Lane suddenly announces, 'Well, now we have got a little surprise for you, an old mate is gonna come up and jam with us.' Despite everything, Lane hadn't forgotten how best to play his former best friend.

Laurie O'Leary: 'Steve gets up and pandemonium breaks out. They did three numbers and it was magic. I'm glad Ronnie kept his word and called him up. I pick up on vibes and I felt for Steve. I thought he was getting the elbow.'

According to *Sounds* reporter Jonh Ingham, they actually played five songs – closing the show with 'All Or Nothing,' and then encoring with, 'Whatcha Gonna Do About It,' The Stones' 'Honky Tonk Women,' the Slim Chance song, 'Going Down,' before recalling their music hall roots with a rendition of the Thirties song, 'Side By Side,' the lyrics of which would remain pertinent to both men throughout their lives. 'We ain't got a barrel of money/ Maybe we're ragged and funny/ But we'll travel along / Singing our song / Side by side…'

'By the end Steve has completely taken over,' Ingham wrote, 'adopting full frontal mike strangler position while Ronnie is content to pump bass patterns with a small smile. It's strange to watch him adopt a background role but that's probably how it was in the Small Faces… Rather than being any indicator of a permanent Small Faces re-union, it was a confirmation of both musician's strengths.'

The *NME*'s Steve Clarke had a different take: 'One is left with the impression that Ronnie Lane's Slim Chance are a very happy band indeed but its odds on for a Small Faces reunion of some description.'

‡ ‡ ‡

From Jonh Ingham's review of the Colchester show:

'Really it doesn't say much for the state of rock when The Great Burning Question concerns a possible reunion of a not overly legendary group that broke up seven years ago.'

The man certainly had a point. By 1976, rock was top heavy with ageing bands – Led Zeppelin, The Stones – whose muse had deserted them years ago, whose relationship with their audience had grown stale as their ponderous albums. Worse, the takeover in music by musicians of a cerebral bent had ushered an era marked by pomposity and pretension.

'You want to intellectualise music,' the singer, Patti Smith once growled, 'go and read tea leaves in a cup.' Pop was originally a working class phenomenon and that was when it was at its best. Now the stadiums were filled with 'performances' from acts such Genesis and Emerson, Lake and Palmer and Yes and Barclay James Harvest, their music running round and round in ever decreasing circles. A musical cycle was coming to an end, a new one about to begin, in the shape of punk.

Through punk, rock was delivered back to the young, the rebellious, the angry, the discontented. The bands eschewed musicianship for energy, three-minute blitzes of furious guitars, hurried vocals. One of the movement's leading combos, The Sex Pistols, even included two Small Faces songs in their very early repertoire – 'Understanding' and 'Whatcha Gonna Do About It?'

Although their singer John Lydon would change the opening lyric of the latter to, 'I want you to know that I *hate* you, baby,' and would mockingly refer to the band as 'the Small Faeces,' it was the bass player Glen Matlock who never wavered in his admiration for Marriott.

As the Pistols, along with The Clash, The Buzzcocks, the this and the that, made garish headlines and rejuvenated the industry, not even Matlock could have guessed that those two songs, along with a few other Small Faces tunes were about to be played live by three of the men who made them in the first place.

The Small Faces were about to find themselves once again in the spotlight.

Life.

‡ ‡ ‡

Two days after the Colchester gig, *NME*'s Steve Clarke travelled to Hammersmith, London to attend the filming arranged by *Top Of The Pops*. With 'Itchycoo Park' falling down the chart that week a decision had already been made to switch the resulting footage to the adult-oriented rock show, *The Old Grey Whistle Test*.

Marriott appeared wearing the top he wore at the Slim Chance gig whilst Mac wears a jumper and Levis and a 'pensive' Kenney Jones sits quietly, looking like 'a well groomed hairdresser.' Lane is in the pub across the road, downing a few brandies before filming starts.

When Lane does appear the band run through 'Itchycoo' twice. 'Lazy Sunday,' demands a bit more time. On the latter, Marriott suggests they mimic the band Status Quo by head banging. At the end of the filming, Marriott wants to break open a bottle of brandy but Lane's having none of it. His wife and kids have arrived – time for home.

A few days later, Clarke travels to Beehive Cottage for another one-on-one with Marriott. The writer asks about the possibility of the Small Faces playing gigs; Marriott plays it cagily.

'I think there is a definite possibility of something. But what annoys me is that someone puts it in the paper that we're going to do gigs in the summer – which could be wrong and makes everybody look like an asshole. All we can say is that it would be lovely to play together but we haven't played together as yet. If there was anything positive I'd give it to you.'

Despite Marriott's wariness, the truth was simple. Both he and Ronnie were biding their time, keeping their options open. Marriott had the All Stars and the *Marriott* album, Ronnie had Slim Chance. Both men would naturally prefer their own efforts to work out than fall back on their old band to find success. Plus, there were other complications which centred around the issue of management.

'I was called to this meeting at E&G management in the Kings Road, Chelsea,' O'Leary recalls, 'It seemed that Ronnie Lane wanted them to manage the band. He was saying things like, "I've got an active band, why should I want to change? As long as my management are involved, I'll do whatever you want."

'I told Steve and he said to me, "No, fuck that, what about you?" I said, "No, I'll continue to manage you but I don't want to manage the Small Faces".'

Those managerial wrangles would continue for months although it was agreed in principle that once everyone's commitments were fulfilled they would go ahead with an album and a set of gigs in the summer.

The Small Faces were back. Nice?

‡ ‡ ‡

On 20th February, 1976, Pam Marriott gave birth to her first child, a son, Toby. Kay his sister recalls the celebrations.

'I drove up to the hospital to visit Pam and Toby and as I was staying the night with Steve, after we went back to Beehive, he said, "Come on celebrate, let's have a drink." So we went to his local pub and everyone was making a fuss, he was so chuffed, so chuffed. I left him for just two minutes to go to the loo, they had outside toilets, all of a sudden I'm in the loo and I could hear all this shouting and yelling.

'I come out and Steve is staggering out of the pub and he's got a black eye. Someone had come in and went, "Are you Steve Marriott?" and he went, "Yeah," and the guy punched him in the face. He said, "That's for my wife fancying you. She's fancied you for years."

'I looked at him – I did want to laugh – and I said, "Are you alright?" and he went, "I'm standing aren't I? You don't get me down." So we went back and finished our drinks. I think it was the first punch he ever had, he always got away with murder.'

Marriott did not make a great dad. To raise children successfully requires a full acceptance of responsibility; the attraction of the music life is that precisely the opposite is on offer.

Pam Marriott: 'Steve just didn't like kids, full stop. He was just waiting for Toby to grow up so they could drink together and possibly make music together.'

Kay, his sister, read Steve's discomfort in another way. She believed the warm but always distant relationship between Steve and his father had forever shaped Marriott's attitude towards male children.

'My dad would never ever lay a finger on me,' Kay states, 'and he didn't to his dying day. My mum seemed to chastise me. She'd give me the slap, she'd punish me and I'd get cuddles off my dad which Steve was always a bit jealous about. But in that day and age it was the old school, you don't sit and cuddle a boy. My dad didn't know how to. And Steve was exactly the same with Toby. I think if Toby had been a girl... Steve often said to me, "I want a little girl so I can spoil her like dad has spoilt you".'

Joe Brown and his wife Vicky were selected as godparents and as a sign of his respect and love, Marriott honoured his friend by giving his new son the middle name "Joe".

'His first name Toby was taken from a Toby Jug,' Brown says, 'so he was named after a beer glass. We were quite chuffed to be asked to be his godparents especially when Steve gave him my name. Steve only ever referred to him as "Toe Rag," and it's a wonder that the boy didn't grow up deaf. I remember Steve just propping him up against an amplifier and just plugging in. No damage was intended but Steve didn't stop and think. He wasn't cruel but he was never cut out to be a father.'

Apparently, Pam also wasn't too schooled in child-raising.

'My wife Vicky,' Brown states, 'would teach Pam all the virtues of motherhood, including basic things like nappy changing. Of course, Vicky would have to pop out and buy the nappies first. They just weren't equipped, never had a clue.'

‡ ‡ ‡

Instead of waiting for a deal, the Small Faces decided to press on and record an album at Joe Brown's studio in Chigwell, Essex, sell it afterwards to the highest bidder. The sessions did not go well, not well at all. Lane was still in dispute with his band members over management duties. He still wanted his firm, E&G management to look after the band plus he wanted to keep the Slim Chance project alive. The other members of the band were insulted.

On top of that, Lane was not the man they knew. He had begun acting strangely, acting as if he was drunk every minute of the day.

Marriott told Hellier, 'Ronnie kept falling over in the studio and I couldn't work it out and got angry with him. He was trying to sing and he'd sway and he'd fall.'

Marriott's growing anger at what he perceived to be Lane's drunken behaviour erupted very early on in the recording schedule. Ian McLagan documents the argument in his riveting memoir, *All The Rage*. Having worked through the night with Steve, fuelled by 'vast amounts of Charlie,' the band retired to the local pub for lunch.

'We'd been having a jolly time in the pub garden,' Mac writes, 'the sun was out and Steve and Joe [Brown] were telling jokes, one after the other when all of a sudden Ronnie got pissed off and started talking about going home. He'd never been much of a drinker, not that it had ever stopped him from drinking to excess, but that afternoon he got nastily drunk. The dark mood passed, but when we were back in the studio and began singing background vocals Ronnie threw down his headset, saying it was, "All a load of old bollocks," and made for the door. It had all turned to rat so quickly, we were floored. We tried talking to him, but he wouldn't listen and sulked, and said he'd had enough and wanted to go…'

When it came to work, Marriott always threw himself into the job at hand. He might play hard but he toiled as well. As a consequence, he hated wasters or wasting time.

'If you're onto something,' Marriott once explained to Hellier, 'you're with a sound and you want to finish it, then go for it. Don't say, "Well I think I'll go to bed, have a listen tomorrow." I hate that attitude. I'm hyperactive, and I can't deal with that "Let's go to bed attitude".'

In the ensuing argument, which would end with Steve and Mac chasing Lane out of the studio, the bass player angrily informed Marriott he hadn't written anything worthwhile since leaving the Small Faces in 1969. That was when Marriott went for him and went for him good. He was fiercely proud of his work with Humble Pie. No way would he stand there and allow it to be denigrated.

'I didn't witness the famous Steve and Ronnie fight,' says Joe Brown, 'but I do believe Steve chinned him after Ronnie had been less than complimentary about Steve's songwriting.'

Out of respect, Mac does not document Marriott attacking Lane. Either way,

Lane was now out of the band. It would be five years before Marriott would discover the real truth about his friend's behaviour, five long years before Lane would finally lay bare the truth and bring burning, heavy tears to Steve Marriott's face by explaining that his staggering demeanour and slurred words were not the result of drunkenness but the early symptoms of his multiple sclerosis illness. Furthermore, he knew he had the illness, he just didn't want his old brothers in mod or indeed the world to know.

At which point both men started crying hard, harder than we could ever know or imagine.

‡ ‡ ‡

One of the better side effects to emerge from this reunion was the revival of Steve Marriott's relationship with Ian McLagan. Wary of meeting him again after such a long time, the keyboard player had travelled over to Beehive Cottage in early 1977. Yet within an hour of his arrival, he and Marriott were busy writing new songs, new material as though the past had never happened.

Now with Lane's abrupt departure, the band faced a big problem. Half of their creative talent had just walked out of the door. Marriott though seemed completely unfazed by this turn of events. He suggested they bring in a bass player, named Rick Wills. Marriott had met Wills a few times. He had even cheekily given the bass player a big thank you on the sleeve of the Humble Pie album, *Smokin'*. Wills hadn't played a note on the album but he had rolled numerous spliffs when he visited the studio. For which, many thanks.

Wills's last job had been a tour of America with Roxy Music but on his return, work had dried up. To make ends meet he had taken a job on a building site, waiting for that one phone call to rescue him. When it arrived it did so just as night was turning into day.

'I was living in a small house in Wembley at the time,' he recalls, 'and Steve rang me about four or five in the morning. He was as bright as a bee, as if it was the middle of the day. It probably was for him.'

Marriott asked Wills to get up and come to the studio. Wills explained that he had a day job, no way could he come over. Marriott responded in typical fashion.

'Oh fuck off man,' he said, 'come down the studio. I'm here with Mac and Kenney. I've just had a fight with Ronnie and he's fucked off.' Wills could hardly take it all in. Here he was at four in the morning being asked to join the Small Faces, a band he was 'very much in awe of.'

Life.

'When I did go to the studio, which was the next day,' the bassist continues, 'I found it very daunting. I couldn't believe this was happening to me. I knew where Joe Brown's studio was as I'd been there before. I was the first to arrive and stood around chatting to Joe and his wife Vicky whilst waiting for the others. Steve arrived followed by Kenney and Mac. We just plugged in and started playing some Booker T. stuff. Kenney was really nice right from the beginning and Mac was very funny. Because I was taller than the other guys, Mac suggested they cut a hole in the stage and lower me down a foot. I remember Steve getting me an enormous Gretsch bass so that it counteracted my size.'

According to Wills, Marriott wanted to erase Lane's bass completely from the tapes, except for the song, 'Lonely No More,' the tune they were working on when Lane walked. It is the only song from this period to feature all four original band members.

Steve's style of writing had changed and he was writing a lot of stuff with Mac,' Wills recalls. 'Mac's style was very R&B and Steve was leaning towards country. He was even playing a telecaster at the time. The songs on the album were very basic. Went into the studio, recorded and left, didn't mess about with them at all. Joe and his talented wife Vicky were also involved. The first album, [which would be called *Playmates*], was really fun to make but really I wished it could have been more like the Small Faces of old, you know carry on from where they left off.'

Instead the album represented the musical leanings of Steve Marriott and Ian McLagan, both entering their thirties. The music was bluesy, R&B with tinges of New Orleans and nods towards the Faces sound and style which had brought them so much success these past five years.

In an age when young bands were taking over, preaching revolution and energy and attitude, the *Playmates* album was in the wrong place at the wrong time. There was no way it was going to shake up the world. Plus there were other problems.

Under the band's instructions, promoter Mel Bush had flown to New York and negotiated a six hundred thousand dollar deal with Warner Brothers for two albums. Yet of the first advance on this deal, much of it went to extricate Marriott from his previous record and management deals.

'I got so much more than the others,' bassist Wills recalls, 'because they had all spent theirs before they had got it. In fact, Steve's total was minus or something. He got nothing and I got a cheque for £14,000 which was a lot of money back then.'

Still that didn't deter Pam and Steve. On March 23rd, 1977, they were married at Chelsea Registry office. Afterwards, they and several guests including all the Small Faces retired to a restaurant down the road for a party. Everybody had a good time; everybody let their hair down.

The next thing you know, the composer Andrew Lloyd Webber was knocking on the door.

‡ ‡ ‡

Laurie O'Leary, he tells a good story.

'I got a call one day from Andrew Lloyd Webber asking to talk to Steve about his new London production of *Evita* [a musical based on the life of Eva Peron]. When I told Steve he just said, "Why the fuck didn't he ring me then?" I once again explained that it was ethical to go through the manager first. Lloyd Webber was totally in awe of Steve and invited us both to Eaton Place to meet and run the idea past Steve. We had to be there for 11.00 am so I picked Steve up at Beehive Cottage at nine. I gave myself plenty of time as I knew it was difficult to motivate Steve at that time of the day. He was up and washed when I got there which was surprising.

'Even more surprising was when he went to the laundry basket and pulled out a silk shirt from somewhere near the bottom. Talk about crushed silk! It was totally unwearable to my mind, screwed up beyond belief. He just put it on and was ready to meet Lloyd Webber. We got to the studio in Eaton Place and went to this incredibly posh hall with a baby grand [piano] and all the works. We were asked if we would like a drink. I opted for a lemon tea, Steve a large brandy that was delivered to him in a large decanter.

'Andrew Lloyd Webber really was in awe of Marriott and wanted him to record two songs as Che Guevara for the album. There was no talk at this stage of Steve appearing on stage but I'm sure that would have been proposed. We had to sit through the whole score with Steve knocking back the brandy. At the end of the score, which seemed to go on forever, Steve just stood up, looked at me and said, "What the fuck was that all about? Don't think so, mate. I'm not a puppet."'

Hard to think of Lloyd Webber as a Marriott man. Certainly wasn't from the same side of the road as Steve, nor does his music in any way touch upon the roots that Marriott's did. Yet here he was, in O'Leary's words, in awe to a man who wore silk shirts as crumpled as a tramp's soul. Proof then that the unique Marriott voice, the ensuring talent was strong enough, sure enough, to reach some very far places.

‡ ‡ ‡

The reconvened Small Faces went on tour – did so after playing a try-out show in Harlesden, North West London, for friends and family only.

'I remember,' Rick Wills recalls, 'Dave Gilmour of Pink Floyd telling me that it was fun and just the type of thing that fans would want to hear. There were about three or four hundred people there and everyone was of the opinion that we should take it on the road.'

The set list they settled on put the big hits – 'Lazy Sunday,' 'Itchycoo Park,' 'All Or Nothing' – next to songs from the *Playmates* album with covers such as Bob Seger's 'Fire Down Below,' thrown in for the encores. Then they took to the road. Halfway through the schedule, Steve Marriott had a mighty close brush with death.

It was in Edinburgh that he suffered his near fatal heart attack. Rick Wills and Ian McLagan both remember that terrible night but do so differently. Wills claims that after a show, the band returned to the hotel and stayed up drinking with comedian Billy Connolly. In his book, Mac confirms that statement but says that afterwards he and Marriott returned to his room where they cut out lines of coke.

After sniffing a line, Marriott suddenly fell unconscious in his chair. Mac tries to wake him, fails to and then desperately administers the kiss of life to Marriott. The singer comes to and angrily demands to know why his friend is trying to kiss him. Then he slumps back into unconsciousness again. Mac phones Dave Robinson, a band roadie, who quickly arrives accompanied by another roadie called Dennis Hills.

Dave places Marriott on the floor, Dennis calls for an ambulance and Mac keeps thumping Marriott, trying to keep him awake.

The medics soon arrive but unfortunately are followed by a number of policeman who proceed to search all the entourage's rooms, unearthing little except for some cannabis.

'We learned as a consequence of the unfortunate evening in Edinburgh,' Mac concludes, 'that Steve had experienced several of these heart tremors or palpitations before. I don't know what was wrong with his heart but I do know he was the most highly-strung person I've ever met. As anyone whose done drugs with him could tell you, he was a heart attack waiting to happen.'

In Rick Wills' recollection, a slightly different story emerges, he claims that after finishing their drinks with Connolly, Marriott had smashed the hotel fire alarm, causing the whole hotel to be evacuated. The police were called and searched every tour member's room. Steve hid in Mac's room which is when he collapsed.

'Yeah the man did have an heart attack,' Wills confirms with a short laugh. 'All this mayhem was going on, police cars everywhere, fire engines… just another night with Steve basically.'

A warning shot had been fired right across Marriott's bow but he paid it little attention. Another year of drugging and drinking would take place before his weary body would finally force him into hospital.

'With Steve you were living on the edge all of the time,' Wills plainly states. 'I must say it was pretty scary at times. I loved working with him but you never knew if you were going to be thrown in jail or get the crap beaten out of you. It terrified me really. There was this craziness that surrounded the band and you just had to go along with Steve. He was the glue that held it all together.'

‡ ‡ ‡

In 1977, The Small Faces appeared on the *David Essex Show* and played a beefed up version of 'Whatcha Gonna Do About it.'

David Essex, real name David Cook, had actually grown up on the same street as Marriott and prior to the show invited Steve to sing a duet with him. Unknown to Essex, however Marriott had his own private beef with the man.

Growing up, his mum Kay Marriott always spoke well of Essex, that 'lovely polite boy from down the road.'

Steve resented her admiration. In arguments with her, he would often shout, 'I'm your son, I'm not David Essex. You'd have loved him for a son wouldn't ya? If he farted he'd do a silent one, wouldn't he!'

At the TV studio, Marriott, looking nearly unrecognisable from the boy wonder in the '60s, immediately turned down his host's offer to duet on a song together. 'He's taking the piss, isn't he?' was Marriott's response.

‡ ‡ ‡

The last album to be recorded at Steve Marriott's Clear Sounds studio was the fifth Small Faces album, *78 In The Shade*. There had been some great music made in this space but this album did not include any of it.

'Instantly forgettable,' says Mac.

'Had some nice moments but could have been so much better,' adds Rick Wills.

The producer was Shel Talmy, the man who had sonically guided the early Kinks. Unfortunately, he and Steve did not get on well, not at all. Very soon into the recording, Marriott was up to his wicked tricks.

'Shel is almost blind,' Wills explains, 'and in front of the studio was a large car parking area. We'd wait for Shel to settle in the control room and then we'd go outside and move the cars around. Shel had this sixth sense and remembered where everything was which is how he would manoeuvre his way around. With us moving the cars about he'd come out and walk into everything. Wicked really but we laughed.'

The album did have one highspot, though. In interviews conducted in 1976, Marriott talked about recording a Joe Brown composition called 'Soldier,' which took place in Los Angeles, complete with an orchestra directed by one David Foster.

The recording has never come to light. The first sighting of this emotive song is on the *78* album although an acoustic demo which would later surface, feels far closer to Brown's original intentions.

'This was a song,' Brown says, 'that I wrote about my father. We cut several versions, one of which featured Steve on vocals with an orchestral backing which I believe was done in America somewhere. It's all a bit vague now and the track is long lost which is such a shame as it was considered good enough to be talked about as a possible single.'

Either way, 'Soldier' is the album's standout song but still far too adult, far too deep to find favour with a young music audience that had been weaned on the energy of punk and New Wave.

The Small Faces' timing had been disastrous. Maybe a couple of years previous the band would have found themselves cast in a far more favourable light but punk had made them an anachronism and Marriott knew this better than most. In a vain attempt to appear 'modern,' he turned his onstage demeanour into one of aggression, the singer even mimicking the punks and spitting onstage to demonstrate his tough street credentials

'He went through this spitting phase,' Wills confirms. 'He would just gob up into the air and think it was funny if it landed on Kenney's drum kit. Kenney used to get furious with him. He also became so scruffy that I couldn't believe it was the same person as the sharp Mod that I had admired from afar in the '60s. He had very few clothes and those that he did have didn't fit him.'

By trying to align himself with the punk and new wavers Marriott had only succeeded in making himself look somewhat ridiculous. The spitting soon ceased.

'For the second tour,' Wills recalls, 'we went out as a six-piece band with Jimmy McCulloch and PP Arnold added to the line up. PP was always around anyway and had sung on *Playmates*. She was brilliant, her voice was terrific and she was in great shape. Jimmy and Steve had been pals for years and Jimmy would often visit Steve at Beehive Cottage and get completely out of their minds together. Jimmy was quite unhappy with his situation in Paul McCartney's Wings.

'He was finding Paul very restrictive in as much that Paul wanted things done his way and that was the way it had to be. Jimmy was a very talented guy but he had that Scottish mentality and when he had a few drinks inside him he would tell you to fuck off – whoever you were. That didn't go down too well in the McCartney camp.

'Without consulting the rest of us, Steve asked Jimmy to join the band. I remember McCartney ringing Steve at Beehive Cottage and saying, "You're welcome to him." With him in the band it filled the sound out. Jimmy and Steve shared the solos with the other supplying the rhythm. But Jimmy being in the band was a bad influence on Steve. Kenney and I used to drink but Mac and Steve were social in another way. Mac could sort of control it but Steve and Jimmy couldn't and they sort of let themselves go, Steve more so.

'There were some great gigs on that second tour, though. I remember one evening in Manchester when Steve hadn't been to bed for a few days and he just didn't have any voice left at all. He told the audience. "You know the songs, well sing them." And they did! They sang every word to every song. Absolutely incredible.'

‡ ‡ ‡

If there was a growing sense that time was running out for the reformed Small Faces, the fact that the reunion had not generated the anticipated riches to those involved brought about the band's inevitable demise. As all his money had gone towards extricating him from various management and record company deals, available cash was still a major problem for Marriott.

By 1977, he had to face up to facts. He had no band and no money. He and Pam decided to sell Beehive Cottage, his home since 1968, and move to London. They told friends and family that they needed to be closer to the cut and thrust of the music business but in reality, Marriott was in Pam's words, 'a very broke country squire,' with a family to support. The studio went first, then the house and it's hard to believe that for all his front. Stevie Marriott did not feel a jot of sadness at being uprooted from the space he had occupied for nearly ten years.

So many of his memories lay there, dormant and seeped into the lush green grass, the wooden stairs, the hard concrete floors.

Laurie O'Leary handled the sale.

'We sold Beehive Cottage for £165,000 to the local baker, Mr Shepherd,' he says, 'The place was in disrepair and the upkeep was now out of Steve's reach.'

Time to move on. Which they did, first to a rented flat in Queensway, London, then the Royal Garden Hotel in Kensington.

'We went for a meal there on his "straight" night,' O'Leary recalls. 'There was his mum, his dad, me, my wife, my sister in law and her uncle. We had full waiter service, the whole works, must have cost a fortune. The next night he had a coke night with all his music cronies and that must have cost even more.'

With money from the sale of Beehive, the Marriotts bought a semi-detached house at 11 Woodlands in Golders Green, London's heavily populated Jewish area.

'We lived right in the middle of the Jewish community and the neighbours didn't like Steve's humour,' Pam recalls. 'He would fry bacon every morning with the windows open.'

Just couldn't stop himself, could he?

‡ ‡ ‡

Despite his heart scare in Edinburgh, Marriott's penchant for losing himself in the mist of drugs and drink did not abate. On numerous occasions, Steve would disappear, bingeing for days on end. Then the phone at his house would ring and Pam would be there to answer.

'One day after a two day binge in Golders Green,' she recalls, 'we found him asleep on a neighbour's couch. He didn't even know these people. I was always getting the 'please come round and get your husband call.' I got him out of quite a few fixes and so did Laurie. A week later we'd just laugh about it but at the time he'd just say, 'Well I don't know, mate, I just don't know.'

In August, 1978, with the remaining Small Faces members now occupied elsewhere (Mac with the Stones, Kenney with The Who) Marriott borrowed members of Joe Brown's band to play a one-off pub gig at The Bridgehouse in Canning Town. He called this loose aggregation of musicians, Blind Drunk. The bass player was Jim Leverton, the drummer Dave Hynes, Joe Brown played guitar.

'The idea,' Brown recalls, 'well Steve's idea actually, was that we'd all start the gig with a bottle, not a glass, but a bottle of brandy each and slowly get pissed as the evening wore on. We filled the place, over 400 people, and played good old rock'n'roll.'

It was a taster of the kind of life that Marriott would come to experience in the mid-to-late '80s.

‡ ‡ ‡

If Marriott's instinct was to lose himself in substances when things got tough, then the next shock he received should have been enough to send him on a year long binge. In late 1978, the Inland Revenue informed him that he owed them £100,000 in back taxes from his days with Humble Pie. Marriott was stunned. He had naturally assumed that Dee Anthony's company had made all the necessary payments. As he had told his dad many years before, his job was to play music. The business side he paid others to look after. It was an admirable artistic strategy but it left him wide open, exposed to the sharks.

Now he had five days to find an impossible amount of money.

He turned to Laurie O'Leary for help. His personal manager's advice was blunt, to the point. Leave England or go to jail, simple as that.

Marriott had no choice. The very next day, he and his family packed their bags, flew to California.

Laurie O'Leary, ever the friend, agreed to sell their house in Golders Green in their absence. When he arrived at the empty house to begin valuation, what he encountered was pretty symbolic of Marriott's life at this point.

'The front door was open,' O'Leary recalled, 'and all the electric fires were turned fully on. It was empty apart from a rented television that had to go back. Unbeknown to Steve, some of his friends, knowing it was empty, had been partying in there.'

The Marriotts decamped to Santa Cruz, to the house of Pam's friend Chris Farthing. The first thing Steve did was to set about forming a band. Impressed by their playing at the Blind Drunk gig, Marriott flew Dave Hynes and Jim Leverton over to live with them.

He also recruited the ex-Mountain guitarist Leslie West who moved into the house as well. The guitarist was well respected but his opinion of himself matched his weight.

'Leslie was always problematic,' Leverton recalls. 'He thought he was worth a lot more than he really was.'

Marriott christened the band, The Firm and the unit moved to a larger house in Boulder Creek.

'It was crazy,' Pam recalls, 'we all lived together and we were all broke. Instead of having to feed a wife and a child now he had to feed them all.'

For Toby Marriott, life at Santa Cruz forms some of his earliest memories. He recalls, 'a real funky house with a nice big garden,' remembers sneaking into Leslie West's room to steal biscuits from his massive cookie jar. He recalls his dad deliberately hiding food from the guitarist. It was a joke West never quite got over.

After rehearsing for some weeks, Jim Leverton's work visa ran out and he was advised to fly to Canada and apply from there. On his arrival back in the States he was refused entry and in his own words, 'The Firm just died a death.'

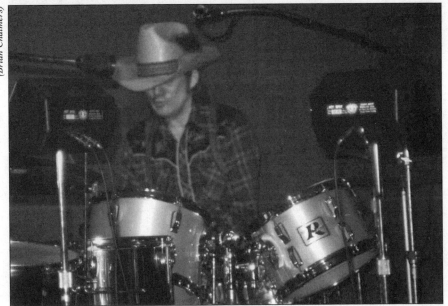

Chapter Twenty

Lend Us A Quid

With the demise of The Firm, Steve Marriott found himself in familiar territory so financially stricken, he was forced to collect empty glass bottles and redeem them for small change.

'He was living in California,' Jerry Shirley, who had now moved to New York, told author Dan Muise, 'collecting the deposits from Seven Up Bottles to get his cigarettes. Pretty awful.'

The story is confirmed by a musician, name of Gary Putnam, who played in a Detroit band, Deluxe. The band had met Marriott at a gig in a local Santa Cruz bar and Marriott, ever the enthusiast, had invited them to the studio to rehearse and record some of his new songs.

'The resulting demo tape,' Putnam recalls, 'included what I believe were the first recordings of 'Infatuation,' 'Big Train Stop In Memphis,' and Steve's rendition of 'All Shook Up.' It also included a reggae number Steve called 'Wass Name,' [he never could figure out what to call it] and 'Midnight Rolling.' Upon hearing the tape, Punch Andrews, Bob Seger's manager, set up a showcase gig at the Center stage in Detroit for Steve Marriott's Deluxe band. In the meantime we did another showcase in Santa Cruz.

'Again, don't know for a fact, but I'd guess this was one of the worst, if not the worst, financial time for Steve. I remember him telling me one night he had to round up some empty bottles that morning to get money for something to put on the table for breakfast.'

Yet if the last two years had taught Marriott anything it was that if you carry a successful past on your shoulders, someone in the present will always want to make money off it.

'It's great to have a reputation to fall back on,' Marriott told Hellier in 1984, 'otherwise I'd have no living at all.'

Thus, when Marriott learnt that drummer Jerry Shirley was living in New York, he called the drummer and put forward the idea of a Humble Pie reunion. At the time, Shirley was in a band called Magnet, managed by Leber Krebs, Aerosmith's management. The band were on the brink of dissolving. Both manager and drummer knew it which is why, on hearing of Marriott's wish to reform Humble Pie, Shirley's manager paid for a plane ticket to bring him to New York.

On his arrival, the manager brought the two musicians together and told them they had the weekend to conjure up a hit single. If they could do so, a studio was booked for Monday morning.

Retreating to Shirley's New York abode, the two men came up with a tune called 'Fool For A Pretty Face,' which they duly recorded using a local bass player by the name of Anthony Jones. On hearing the song, Krebs was convinced enough to start seeking a deal. Within a month, Humble Pie Mark 2 were signed to Atco, an offshoot record company of Atlantic Records. In England their records were released through Jet Records, a company owned by one Don Arden. Marriott had to laugh.

In 1976, a court had ruled that Don Arden owed The Small Faces £12,000 in unpaid royalties. Arden agreed to pay the bill in monthly instalments, made one payment and then disappeared. The band never heard from him again. Until now. The old bastard, Marriott thought to himself, he's still milking me dry.

Marriott's next move was to contact Clem Clempson. Clempson said thanks for the call but he was too busy putting a band together with guitarist Bobby Tench.

Marriott said, no problem, why didn't both musicians fly over to New York? No reason why they could not all play together. Clempson and Tench agreed but after only a couple of days of rehearsing, Clempson upped and left, unable to handle Steve's hyper personality. Tench stayed on, joined the band. Marriott and Shirley then offered the vacant bass player's spot to Anthony Jones.

Now all they had to do was come up with a hit album.

At the same time, Marriott made a great final gesture to the Deluxe band he had been working with prior to these events by going into the studio and working around the clock with them to produce a demo tape of good quality.

'He gave us a week's worth of studio time,' Putnam states. 'He owed us nothing but chose to give us some of the studio time he needed to launch his next project. It was pretty generous.'

‡ ‡ ‡

Melvin is bald, he is a wrestler, an unpredictable man, prone to terrible rages, which often lead to violence. Melvin never appeared when Steve was sober, only when he had been on the sauce. Noticeable too that Melvin also appeared when a relationship was no longer interesting Marriott and he was looking for a way out. Melvin may well have been the perfect device.

Pam first met Melvin some two years into their relationship.

'The more broke he got, the more he drank,' she says of her husband, 'and that's when the famous Melvin came out. He became this character Melvin the bald headed wrestler. He was totally schizophrenic. The next day he'd have no recollection whatsoever of what he did the night before as Melvin,'

Pam pauses, then adds, 'Melvin was a total nightmare.'

Did Steve Marriott suffer from schizophrenia? Or was he the device Marriott used to end his relationships? Melvin certainly put Marriott's women through a terrible time, maybe in the hope that they would get so exasperated with him they would leave of their own accord and thus save Steve the heartbreak. Melvin, always appearing after bottles of brandy had been sunk, after the nose had been sufficiently powdered.

In raging arguments, Pam would shout out 'Steve!' and he would roar back, 'I'm not Steve, I'm Melvin, Melvin the bald headed wrestler.'

Then he would go for her. In the morning he would survey the damage he had wreaked upon his wife, be unable to believe his actions, unable to remember fighting or indeed Melvin himself. He would spend the day distraught, in absolute turmoil.

'At one time,' Pam recalls, 'he had considered going on the same medication that Keith Moon was on. When Keith died [1978] he changed his mind. He'd heard it was an overdose of that medication that killed him.'

Melvin only seems to have appeared before the women in his life, never in front of family, or managers, or friends, or musicians. It was just the women who got to know Melvin and wish they never had. .

‡ ‡ ‡

Meanwhile, the young Toby Marriott found himself being shunted back and forth between his father's abode in America and his grandparent's house in Sawbridgeworth.

'Grandad [Bill Marriott] was very quiet,' Toby recalls of his time there, 'and didn't have the same parental qualities as Nan. Dad's relationship with his dad was domineering. He'd shout at him a lot especially when he had been drinking. I only ever heard him shout at his mum once. He knew with her he'd met his match. He owed them a lot really, I mean they raised me.

'My dad just didn't understand kids. He was always waiting for me to be eighteen so we could get pissed together. Mind you I managed that when I was six or seven. I visited him in Atlanta when he was recovering from a broken leg. He was pissed the whole time but in a good way. We were in a bathtub together and dad kept playing this old rock'n'roll record, 'Tutti Frutti,' by Little Richard over and over again. He was plying me with beer and I got drunk. I was only seven. Most people just thought he was a rude little bugger but he was a very smart man, very book read. He used to love reading about King Arthur and all that, he turned me onto Excalibur and all that stuff.'

Toby looks up, you can see his dad in his eyes.

'Sounds like I'm making excuses for him,' he says softly, 'but he never really got the chance to be a real father.'

‡ ‡ ‡

With Humble Pie functioning once more, the Marriotts spent Christmas of 1979 in England at Steve's parents house and then moved to New York. They settled first in Mahopac then moved to an apartment on 11th Street in Greenwich Village.

A Humble Pie single 'Fool For A Pretty Face' had been released by Atco and was gaining airplay, hovering around the top forty. The follow up album, *On To Victory*, released on March 21st, 1980 also gained respectable sales even if, according to Pam, the band's promoter played it safe, booking the band into a series of what she calls, 'little rat hole places.'

Steve kept to his usual pace, working hard, playing hard, spending days and nights fuelled only by alcohol and coke. He slept little, ate even less.

One night, the inevitable. Collapsing to the floor, holding his stomach in agony, Steve Marriott was rushed into hospital with a suspected burst ulcer.

The warning shots he had ignored these past few years had just turned into a severe hammer blow. He was forced to take note of his body, made to realise he couldn't sustain his lifestyle.

Yet Marriott was always too wild to maintain a careful approach. He believed in living for the day, never the morrow. He had done so all his life. It was too late to change.

He understood just how fragile life is so take it while it's there. Within a month of hospitalisation, Marriott had resumed his old habits, not to the extent of previous use but enough to eventually chase Pam his second wife away.

On To Victory's initial sales suggested some longevity for the album but this encouraging surge quickly died out. Unsurprisingly really; it was not a great album. Marriott had co-written seven new songs and the band tackled three covers, a rocked up version of 'Baby Don't You Do It' (the record he had played to death whilst smashing up his room in Australia with Keith Moon), 'Over You,' and a terribly misjudged version of Otis Redding's 'My Lover's Prayer.'

The rest of the songs sounded dated, clichéd, unable to find their niche. Marriott merely sounds as if he is going through the motions. Which he was according to Pam.

'Steve didn't want to reform Humble Pie in the first place,' she states, 'it was just a vehicle to pay the rent.'

Which pretty much sums up the album.

‡ ‡ ‡

America, September, 1980, Humble Pie plays support to the heavy metal man, Ted Nugent. One reviewer opines that the band – 'led by sewer mouth, Steve Marriott,' – easily 'lacked the fresh energy of its early '70s version.'

Later Marriott told *Scene*'s Brian Chalmers, 'Every time the critics write me off I bounce right back. They hate me because I keep coming back on their arses.'

It was untrue but fighting talk always helps to paper over the truth.

‡ ‡ ‡

In December, 1980, John Lennon stepped out of his limo and was met by Mark Chapman's gun. It was a shocking death, brutal in the way it needlessly, senselessly, robbed a family of a father, the world of an outstanding artist.

Out of all the Beatles, it was Lennon the outspoken that most appealed to Marriott. He loved the biting one-liners Lennon delivered to the press, the radical edge he had displayed in his later years, his couldn't give a fuck stance.

His death was enough to goad Marriott into writing a new song, 'Teenage Anxiety.' The song starts with an intriguing piano melody which engages the listener straight away and throws up interesting musical possibilities. Unfortunately, Marriott doesn't follow them through.

He throws them away, opting to burden his song with an arrangement full of crashing instruments which in no way enhance the song's potential.

'Teenage Anxiety,' was placed second song on Pie's second album for Atco. Name, *Go For The Throat*.

The cover depicted an unattractive couple about to sink their teeth into each other's throats and that was about as imaginative as it got. Amongst the heavy-laden guitar workouts the band even presented a version of Marriott's classic Small Faces song 'Tin Soldier.'

Needless to say, their effort got nowhere near the original's angry brilliance. Maybe hearing the finished version was when Marriott's inner voice told him it was time to quit.

'The final nail in the coffin came when Atco managing director Michael Drowne came to see us in our dressing room at a gig somewhere,' Jerry Shirley reminisces. 'Steve promptly told him to 'Fuck off out of it'. Drowne was insulted and rightly so. Next day back in his office he pulled the plug on us.'

Certainly the Gods felt the band should finish. Having now planned a *Live At The Marquee* London album as a follow up (no doubt hoping to ignite *Rockin' The Fillmore* style sales), on the day of the show Marriott crushed his fingers in a hotel door and the scheme and the band simply fizzled out.

His next project would again be one that was forged from his past.

‡ ‡ ‡

In 1981, Pam and Steve found themselves in England on a long holiday. Marriott was keen to see Ronnie Lane whose MS illness had forced him into a wheelchair. After an emotional meeting, Marriott suggested they gig together, just like the old days.

Pulling together his old mates Jim Leverton on bass and Dave Hynes on drums, he put Zoot Money on keyboards and Mel Collins on saxophone. He again called the band Blind Drunk and as before booked the Bridge House pub in Canning Town, an area of London's East End. The night before Marriott went round the area advertising the night by sticking up his own hand written flyers. They read, 'HURRY, HURRY, HURRY TO THE BD CLINIC, PERFORMING WITHOUT A NET.'

And so it was that twelve years after the final Small Faces show in the Channel Islands and five years after his guest slot with Slim Chance in Colchester, Steve Marriott and Ronnie Lane again stood side by side on a stage.

'It was great fun,' bassist Leverton recalls. 'I remember we changed all the song titles that night. 'Five Long Years' became 'Five Long Beers.' 'Don't Fight It,' became 'Don't Spill It' and so on. We were rightly called Blind Drunk that evening as we all had our own bottle – not glass – of brandy on stage with us.'

Joe Brown couldn't make the show but his sixteen-year-old daughter, Sam Brown did, and in doing so made her stage debut.

The gig was recorded on Ronnie Lane's mobile studio. Soon the two musicians began talking about making an album together. They even had a name for the project The Majik Mijits. Marriott put the idea to Laurie O'Leary and, as the men started composing together for the first time in years, O'Leary agreed to finance the project.

Given the success of their live show, it was decided to record the material live at the Corbett Drama Theatre in Loughton, using Lane's mobile studio to record the performances. The crowd noise you hear on the album is from the students watching at the bar.

'The way the album was intended,' Leverton recalls, 'was that you'd get a Ronnie song followed by a Steve song followed by a Ronnie song and so on throughout. It was great fun. The whole of the fortnight was really pretty much of a drinking situation and I also remember daily pilgrimages to the local pie and mash shop in Loughton.

'Ronnie loved the stewed eels and Steve just had to have his daily intake of pie and mash. Then of course there would be mercy dashes into Notting Hill to get certain substances.'

After the album was completed, a party was held at The Grapes pub in Islington.

'It was quite a flash restaurant,' Leverton recalls, 'and they had a grand piano there. Marriott got on the piano and with Ronnie sat on a stall beside them they knocked out a few songs, that was nice.'

The search for a deal began but it soon became apparent that every record company (even the Rolling Stones' operation) thought the same thing. Lane's illness was a major stumbling block. It prevented the men touring and such an album required live work to successfully promote it. Even Marriott saw that.

'Steve and Ronnie went to America to see Clive Davis of Arista Records,' Leverton recalled. 'They played him the tape. Clive Davis was tapping his foot and tapping his very expensive pen on his very expensive desk. He said, "Yeah, that's great, man." Steve said, "So you like the tape, Clive?" Steve then stopped the tape, ejected it and said, "Well you can't fucking have it!" The story that Steve told me was that it would have meant touring and Ronnie just wasn't up to it. No tour, no album. That's why the Mijits never came out at that particular point.'

The album would eventually surface in 2000, courtesy of New Millennium

Records and in many ways would have fared better had it remained behind closed doors. Between its making and release, a myth had grown up around the work, many fans seeing it as a 'legendary lost album.' Listening to it today, the album has its moments but they are few and far between.

The album starts well, 'Lonely No More' is a catchy tune even if it does walk a well worn musical path, thus making it a minor song in the Marriott canon.

You have to wait for Ronnie's lovely 'Bomber's Moon' (a Second World War pilots' term for a full moon) before the album catches. The tune begins with a play on Booker T and the MGs' great riff for 'Time Is Tight,' before exploding into a trademark Lane song, full of great poetic images ('There are stars on my ear,' he sings, 'And the moon is on the water,') warm acoustic guitars, tuneful verses, memorable in its chorus. His 'Son Of Stanley Lane,' is also up to scratch as is Marriott's pub-cum-music-hall-style tune, 'That's The Way It Is.'

Apart from that, there is little to set the pulse racing, little to spin you round. There are highlights and moments as mentioned but nothing to match the brilliance of these two men when they were young and in Mod.

‡ ‡ ‡

After the Majik Mijits stalled, Marriott returned to New York in his usual chirpy manner, ready as ever to see what was next. But next was nothing new, nothing he had not experienced before. Next was another lengthy bout on the road as a solo act, another round of small time clubs, with the occasional interview after soundcheck, a few drinks before the show, a small audience, a melange of heavy and screaming guitars, and then the night opening up in front of him, beckoning him forward, and, he, Steve Marriott filling himself up, plunging into the darkness, seeing where he would end up come morning light. Then back on the coach and repeat ad infinitum.

Around him the world was again surely but slowly changing. In England Margaret Thatcher was into the third year of her Premiership and only those with bullish souls would prosper. The nation's soul remained sorely wounded. British pop music lost its anger, its bite, also its ideals. Once driven by ideals of community and fairness, equality, the times had changed. 'When they stopped sharing the drugs,' George Clinton once said, 'that's when it came to a halt.'

Now punk was dead and the New Wavers had run out of melody. Intense young men in raincoats stepped forward to howl into microphones, backed by ominous, eerie sounds.

To counteract them, pop threw up a new generation of young unashamed capitalists whose desire for fame and money mirrored that of the Prime Minister. Wham rhymed with Duran rhymed with spam.

The *NME* floundered, the new glossies – *The Face* and *Smash Hits*, shot ahead.

In America, in Marriott's New York, DJ Kool Herc and then Grandmaster Flash were holding block parties in the Bronx, inventing rap, inventing hip hop, creating a music that was true street, true poetry.

Just as punk in the UK had attacked the rock dinosaurs, so the rappers attacked New York's Studio 54 culture, the rich hedonism, the party they were not allowed to attend. Soul music had capitulated to the growing black middle class and thrown off its rawness, its toughness. Now when you turned on the radio James Brown was not telling you to say it loud, you're black and your proud. Teddy Pendergrass was whispering turn off the lights and light a candle.

The worst musical decade ever was gathering pace and there were very few able to stop its terrible progress.

Where did that leave Marriott's musical career? Who knows? He certainly didn't give a fuck about it. All he ever wanted was to get onstage and play. As long as he could do that, be the stage large or small, then he was happy. And that's precisely what he did for the next year and a half. Played the clubs, made the best of what he had.

Throughout it all he remained unbroken. Whatever life threw at him – the music no one would release, broken friendships, the Mafia, the Inland Revenue, hard times, rich times, out of control times – whatever he got, he just took it on the chin and sailed right on through.

Remember him in the field with Pam stealing food? She's mortified, he's cracking up with laughter. Life. He knew and saw life for what it was and was strong enough to not let it scare him. He laughed at its joke, operated by his own set of rules.

Sometimes you're up, sometimes you're down. But who gives a fuck for the world keeps turning, round and around and around and around and there ain't nothing you can do about it except smile.

‡ ‡ ‡

In New York, Steve and Pam now began drifting apart, wanting different things from life. Steve still wanted to party, Pam less so. She wanted out of New York, out of the madcap lifestyle and back to Atlanta to be on her own, to be normal. Marriott was content where he was.

To help her get away, fulfil her wish, Marriott made the kind of gesture that would endear him to so many. He went to see his old buddy, Keith Richards and borrowed five grand which he then gave to Pam to help her relocate.

Then, at the last minute, he decided he couldn't do without her and booked himself a ticket as well.

'I wasn't particularly happy with that,' Pam admits, 'but he promised me things would be different and he would get his act together. This wasn't to be and when we got to Atlanta, he got worse. He started hanging out with all these crazy Southern people and off he went again.'

Pam got her old job as a flight attendant back and tried to lead a normal life. The drugs, the drink, the partying had taken their toll, wearied her soul. She left Steve, lived at home.

Even so, she could not rid herself of her love for Steve Marriott, could not stop the worry, especially when the element of fire came back to haunt him, to warn him of the actions it would take one day, one terrible day, to remove him from this earth.

'He had two accidents with fire whilst with me,' she reveals. 'On one occasion we were talking in bed and we both had a glass of wine. Steve had put a lighted candle in the empty wine bottle. We were chatting away and he reached over me and grabbed the bottle. The candle fell out onto his head and set his hair on fire! His whole head of hair was on fire and I had to pat it out. The other time was on one of the many occasions that we had split up. He called me on the telephone and said, "I can't get the oven to heat up." I said, "Well, what are you doing?" He replied, "It's a gas oven." I told him to turn the pilot light and strike a match. All of a sudden I heard this great whoosh, he had had the gas fire on all the time we were talking on the phone. When he lit the match it just exploded. I was frantic on the telephone, screaming "Are you alright?"

'It burnt his hair, his eyebrows and singed his face. Many people thought he was going bald in his later years because of the high hairline but he wasn't. The receding hairline was down to this accident. We both laughed about the accident afterwards but he was pretty messed up for a few weeks.

She can't help but make the connection, join up the dots.

'The whole fire thing kept re-occurring throughout his life,' Pam points out. 'That's one of the reasons he started rolling his own cigarettes. He was forever sitting them down at the edge of a table, he never used an ash tray. There were constant burn marks on everything we had.'

Then the analysis of the man she still misses to this day

'Steve wasn't a person who should be left alone. He hated to be alone and it wasn't safe to leave him on his own. I had to baby sit him more than I baby sat my own son.'

‡ ‡ ‡

The next year and a half of Marriott's life was spent on the road, playing and travelling, with what was essentially Humble Pie Mark Three. Bass player Jim Leverton accompanied him every step of the way.

'Normally wherever Steve played in America with whatever line up it would be called Humble Pie,' he explains. 'I went over and worked the road for about eighteen months non-stop on a tour bus. There was me, Steve, Goldy McJohn (ex-Steppenwolf) on keyboards and a brilliant black drummer called Fallon Williams. We were doing some Small Faces and Humble Pie songs in the set and we were going to call ourselves The Daggers. I remember getting to the venue of our very first gig and there were all these posters outside claiming, 'Tonight…HUMBLE PIE.' Steve just couldn't get away from it.

'The name Humble Pie filled houses so you could see why they did it but Steve was never happy with that situation and for a while we compromised and were called Steve Marriott and the Pie.

'After a while we had a falling out with Goldy McJohn over his drug abuse which was affecting his playing onstage. He was sacked and we became a trio. We were the Three Trojans [Trojan being an American term for condom].'

After a short while, Jim himself left the band and returned to England.

Steve's personal manager was an experienced record promotion man named

Michael 'Mo' Martin. Having left Pam, Marriott moved into the Atlanta house of Mo and his partner, Debbie.

The band's tour manager was Bill Hibbler. He recalls Capricorn Records, a big label in the '70s with acts such as the Allman Brothers, approaching Marriott with a view to a deal. The owner of the label was Phil Walden who had been working with Otis Redding at the time of his tragic death in 1967. He had seen the name Humble Pie back in circulation and thought it could make him bucks.

'Mo had been speaking with Phil Walden about a deal for Steve,' Hibbler recalls, 'Walden was very responsive but then suddenly stopped taking Mo's calls. Initially, there was a deal on the table and Capricorn even requested that Steve cancel several tour dates to come in and make a record. We didn't know it at the time but Capricorn was in trouble. They finally called and requested that the band come down to Macon, Georgia, to record demos before they tended an offer. That was pretty insulting given Marriott's track record but he and Mo went along because they were in a pretty desperate financial state.'

'Fallon, Steve, Mo and myself went down to Macon for a week', Hibbler continues, 'and they recorded three or four songs. We later discovered that Capricorn had blown their distribution deal and wanted to use Steve's demos to secure a new deal. The guys from Capricorn were in way over their heads and the whole label collapsed within weeks.'

Following this disappointment, which would only serve to strengthen Marriott's hatred of the business, the band resumed touring. When not playing, Marriott, and everyone else connected with him would party most nights at his manager's Atlanta abode. It was a large house, a leftover from Mo's successful time as a record company man.

'We were broke,' Hibbler states, 'but we were staying in this huge house with a hundred gold records on the walls. We were living on peanut butter sandwiches yet there was a party almost every night. It all seemed a bit funny. People assumed because of the house, which was rented, that everyone had plenty of money. One person would call wanting to stop by and Steve would say, "Ok mate but do you mind picking up a couple of bottles of Stoli (vodka) and some orange juice on the way." Another person would ring. "Great, love to see you. Be here at seven and if it's not too much trouble, could you grab a gallon of Jack Daniels and a couple of litres of coke and some ice?"

'Of course, one or two would have a little coke and a little grass. Most of these party-goers just wanted to impress their dates and didn't think anything of picking up some groceries on the way. So yes there were drugs around but the drug use wasn't out of control. The liquor consumption was much larger than the drug use.'

On Monday nights, the entourage would visit a club named Hedgens. The house band were The Satellites and local musicians would drop in for jam sessions which would stretch into the early hours. It was here that Marriott would meet and recruit musicians such as Keith Christopher, a bassist who was invited to join Humble Pie Mark Three, and Tommy Christopher who played guitar.

When Tommy missed two shows in Florida through car trouble, he was dismissed although that didn't stop Marriott making advances to the young girl who had flown down specifically to see the missing guitarist. Her name was Bunny and they ended up living together for a brief spell.

Afterwards, thanks to the income from his live work, Steve was able to rent a house in Georgia which Mo and Deborah also moved into. Before Christopher's dismissal, the band recorded three songs at the Pyramid Eye Recording Studios in Chattanooga. Hibbler's favourite from these sessions was Marriott's rendition of Brenda Lee's 'Sweet Nothings.'

To replace Christopher, Marriott brought in a guitarist named Phil Dix and after many internal arguments over his appointment, the band headed out on tour.

'Steve was looking really well during this time frame,' Hibbler reports. 'He'd dropped a few pounds, got a nice tan and cut his hair. He looked much younger than he had in 1982. By the time of the tour, the band appeared lean and mean. They didn't look like a bunch of old farts on the nostalgia circuit. They were very good and the crowds loved it. We played small clubs, large clubs, theaters, arenas and huge outdoor shows.'

In Oklahoma, the band supported Foghat, a mildly successful American rock outfit. At the soundcheck, Foghat deliberately took ages to get their sound, giving Humble Pie only a few minutes to rehearse.

Marriott retaliated in typical fashion. First, he employed the same tactics as Foghat by repeatedly stopping the band in full flow. Then at show time he walked out onstage wearing a bathrobe and slippers.

'Steve gave one of the best performances I've ever seen,' Hibbler states. 'It was perfect. Foghat couldn't come close to it yet Steve appeared to be so unconcerned about playing with Foghat that he hadn't even bothered to get dressed for the occasion. Foghat proceeded to give a very lacklustre and uncomfortable performance.'

At the end of the tour, Steve returned to Atlanta. Within a week of being back, Marriott sacked Phil Dix and brought in Rick Richards from the recently deceased band The Satellites on guitar.

'The chemistry was amazing,' Hibbler reports of this pairing. 'It was everything I knew it could be but more so. Rick was the perfect foil for Steve. I wish we had taped it. Everyone, including Steve was blown away.'

Unfortunately, Rick Richards was cut from the same mould as Marriott. That night he and Keith Christopher went celebrating, missed the next day's rehearsals. Marriott, true to form, immediately fired the pair of them. Despite his indulgences, work always came first.

They carried on regardless. Marriott, Fallon Williams and a keyboard man named Dave Hewitt went to producer Eddie Offord's studio and recorded as a trio (Offord was best known for his work with Yes). Marriott suggested dropping the Humble Pie name in favour of a new moniker, 'the Packet Of Three'. This appeared to be the action of a man keen to start something fresh and new but in fact Marriott was about to do a runner. His erratic personal life demanded it.

Not long after recording, Marriott secretly cancelled some forthcoming shows, booked a ticket to London and then phoned Hibbler. He told the tour manager that his father was ill and that he had to return to England. Straight away Hibbler knew that Marriott had no intention of returning.

'I think he desperately wanted to get out of the responsibility of supporting Mo and Deb who was pregnant and probably hated living with them,' Hibbler states. 'But he also probably felt guilty since they had helped him out. Whether his dad was actually ill, I have no idea but the implication was that his father was dying…'

‡ ‡ ‡

Pam had now found a new man, moved in with him. Meanwhile, Marriott had been seeing a Canadian girl, Terri Elias. She had come to a gig of his in Atlanta and soon they were an item, a serious item. That's what he told his mum, Kay.

'Mum,' he barked down the phone once, 'talk to the new Mrs Marriott.'

In the quiet of her Sawbridgeworth house, Mum raises her eyebrows, tries to talk nicely to this strange girl on the line. Upstairs, Steve's father sleeps soundly.

Yet Pam never left Marriott's mind. For him, she was unfinished business. It seemed that she felt that way too.

Regularly, he called her, suggested a reconciliation. At first, she resisted but not for long. Her love for him was her Achilles' heel. Finally, against her better judgement but fooled by the hope of a lifetime love, Pam agreed to restart the relationship.

'Steve kept on and on about going back to England for a holiday with a view to moving back over there. I gave into him and we were on the plane when he hit me with another bombshell. Terri was pregnant with his child.'

A daughter, Tonya Elias was born on 16th February 1984.

For Pam, this was the final act. Women will endure all kinds of aberrant behaviour caused by their men's use of drink and drugs. But bring another woman's baby into the equation and they will fly away faster than Concorde.

Pam stayed at Joe and Vicky Brown's for a week, then hot footed it back to Atlanta. There she received a phone call from Steve; he would stay in England. Their partnership was finished. But Pam still cared, would do so all her life. She told him she would go to his house, rescue his guitars and send them back to him.

'When I got to the house where he had been living, the place was empty,' she recalls. 'Everything was gone including Steve's guitars. I made a few hysterical calls and was told that Steve owed a lot of money to a cocaine dealer and they had cleared him out as payment. I think Steve knew this was going to happen and that was why he had been so anxious to get back to England, the little bastard.

'Steve being Steve, he told everyone in England that I was a bitch and I had stolen all his money. In truth I was back in Atlanta, sleeping in my car for a couple of weeks until I got back on my feet. I never received one penny from Steve, ever! No child support, no alimony, nothing so it's very hurtful when I hear these implications that I took our money. We never had any money!'

The hurtful memories, the brazen anger, yet still her love rises to the surface. The girl can't help it.

'We had our good times,' Pam states, 'but he was a man robbed. All those years of hard work for nothing. We just kept going thinking the next band was gonna be the one to make it. But of course it never happened.'

‡ ‡ ‡

He moved in with his sister, Kay, in her council house in Sawbridgeworth in Hertfordshire, near his mum and dad. She was married now to John who ran his own glass business. Kay worked part time in a local pub, The Good Intent on Station Road. Marriott meanwhile was absolutely skint. He had returned from America with nothing to show for his time there except two plastic carrier bags and a mindful of memories. He needed to get earning.

By sheer co-incidence, just after Marriott's return, the drummer Dave Hynes walked into Kay's place of work. Kay told him Steve was back in town. Phone calls were made, including one to bass player Jim Leverton.

Within weeks, Steve Marriott had a new band. And he knew what to call them. The Packet Of Three were ready to do business.

They rehearsed in a warehouse belonging to Kay's husband, John. At the same time, Kay set about finding them gigs. Her first place of call was the Memorial Hall in Sawbridgeworth, a building owned by the local church. Kay arranged to see the vicar. At the meeting he asked to hear a sample of the kind of music that would be played.

Kay went home and recorded a tape of Small Faces and Humble Pie songs. She then invited the collared man round to listen. Which is how Steve Marriott auditioned for the Church of England without even being there.

Suitably impressed, the vicar who had never heard of Steve Marriott or any of his bands, signed the necessary forms. When the gig was announced, the tickets sold straight away. On the night, Kay had to turn people away. Naturally, the band played a somewhat different set of songs to the ones the Vicar had been led to expect, Marriott ignoring his past songs for a far more bluesy workout.

Afterwards, the Vicar asked to see Kay.

'Oh my God,' she remembered thinking, 'here it comes. But you know what? He shook my hand and he went superb, absolutely superb.'

He booked them for two further shows.

In the week leading up to this gig, Steve's old friend Manon Piercey was sitting at home when her phone burst into life. She picked up the receiver.

A voice shouted, 'Ello mate, you alright? Do you wanna talk to my sister?' Manon doesn't recognise the loud voice but says, uncertainly 'alright then.'

Kay Marriott comes on the line laughing, tells her it was Steve.

'He then came back on the phone,' Manon recalls, 'and said, "I've got a gig on Friday at the Sawbridgeworth Memorial Hall, do you wanna come?"'

She went on her own and found herself backstage after the show. Steve talked the most, told her all about splitting up with Pam, how he was back living at his sister's now.

'He'd come back to England,' Manon recalls, 'with just three T-shirts and a couple of pairs of jeans. He didn't even have a guitar. Joe Brown had lent him a guitar for the gig.'

The pair returned to Steve's sister's house nearby where Toby his son was staying. It was there that their relationship took on a new depth and meaning.

'They were at it all night,' Toby Marriott recalled in language reminiscent of his dad's ribald nature. 'They were in Kay's spare bedroom and I'm sure the neighbours half a mile away could hear them they were so noisy.'

Shortly after this noisy coupling, the Packet Of Three began recording in a small studio on Tottenham Court Road. Manon went to visit, popped out for a drink with Steve and Jim Leverton.

'We were walking past a music shop near the junction with Oxford Street [Denmark Street] and Steve saw this Gibson 335 guitar in the window. He said, "I'd love to play that." So we wandered in and he played it. There were loads of people about but nobody took any notice of him until he started playing. Then they were all around him.

'He put it down and told the shop assistant, "I can't afford it, mate." The guy dropped the price. Steve said, "Still can't afford it." But I saw in his face he so wanted it. I said, "He can't afford it but I can. Put it in the case and I'll take it." When we got outside he just screamed at the top of his voice.'

‡ ‡ ‡

The drummer boy, Dave Hynes, couldn't take the pace, wasn't physically strong enough for the rigours of touring. Steve let him go and phoned America – brought back Fallon Williams into his fold. Then he called Laurie O'Leary, asked him to find the band a booking agent.

They got themselves one, a Mick Eve who had once played with Georgie Fame and the Blue Flames. He now occupied an office above Ronnie Scott's in Frith Street, today an extremely desirable location.

'I started by booking them on the Greater London pub circuit at such places as the Half Moon in Putney, the Royal Standard in Walthamstow, the Torrington in Finchley,' Eve recalls. 'Everywhere Steve played it was a full house and in a very short while they were playing four or five gigs a week around the country, averaging 200 gigs a year, pretty hard slog by anybody's standards. In the early years it was always about £500 a gig, cash in hand. Towards the end it was more like a grand a night, still cash in hand.'

There was a compelling reason for Marriott to insist on this financial arrangement. His friends at the Inland Revenue had been made aware of his return. He still owed £100,000 in back taxes.

They had been put on his trail following the Memorial Hall show. They followed him to his next gig which was at a Harlow nightclub called Benny's. As Marriott left the stage, a bailiff appeared and handed Marriott a summons. Marriott argued that he had been out of the country for years, threw away the paper.

Undeterred, the bailiff followed him home. He then parked his car nearby and watched the house, day and night, waiting for the singer to appear. By law, Marriott couldn't be charged on Kay's property and so every day when she left for work, he was forced to stay indoors. One foot outside and he would have been arrested.

'It don't bother me,' he would boast.

Yet often when Kay returned home for lunch her brother would be there, crawling around the rooms on his hands and knees.

'My kitchen looked onto a little courtyard,' Kay says, 'and the lounge had patio doors opposite the road where he was parked. So Steve crawled down the stairs and past the patio door. He was alright when he got in the kitchen to get something to eat. Then he'd crawl and sit in what he called the cupboard because our spare room didn't have a window so he always called it the cupboard. So much for it not bothering him.'

The success of his gigs – the packed houses, the enthusiastic reception, the knowledgeable punters – convinced Marriott that he could now go it alone. No managers, no record companies, total control. He could work when he wanted to and where he wanted to. He told his mum he much preferred it this way. No big money meant no hassles. Bliss.

'It was bloody hard,' Leverton states. 'He'd only work for cash. If he had accepted work for cheques then we could have done legitimate tours and we could have been better looked after. What we were doing was bloody rigorous.'

The touring now extended outside the UK, took in eight weeks in Scandinavia, followed by trips around the rest of Europe. Acting as their own tour managers, the band would roll into town, locate a reasonably priced place to stay, find the venue, set up their equipment, soundcheck, eat, down a few drinks, play the gig, get skiffled, wake up and start it all over again. There were no luxury coaches or hotel rooms, no tour managers to wake them and guide them, just the band and a couple of roadies, working the road and working it hard just to earn a crust.

'It never bothered him,' mother Kay says of her son's precarious finances. 'His dad Bill, he used to worry. He'd say, "How could you let this happen to you? You're right on the floor with nothing." He said, "That's what I like Dad. I enjoy being broke." Bill said, "'Don't be stupid." Steve said, "But I do. I enjoy coming up when I've got it again."'

If Toby was glad that his fighting parents had parted his joy was short-lived. Steve and Manon now moved into the Sawbridgeworth house he shared with his grandmother. The couple stayed a while but then a bad argument between Manon and Kay Marriott erupted.

Steve looked elsewhere, found a two-bedroomed house in a village called Stanstead Abbotts. He insisted that Toby come live with them along with the drummer, Fallon Williams.

'I lived with them at their house in Stanstead Abbotts for about six months,' Toby recalls, 'and it was real hard. Dad wasn't around very much, he'd be away on tour with the Packet Of Three and Manon was very strict... My dad was frightened of her. He wouldn't speak out unless he was drunk.'

For her part, Manon felt for Toby, in his nomadic, insecure existence.

'I felt incredibly sorry for him,' she says, 'and I tried my hardest but it was difficult. I told him one day in anger, "I don't want to be your mother, I want to be your friend."'

'When I told him that he was okay. The poor child was forever being taken from one home to another overnight. We had to change his school, he loved his other school. It was so hard for him.'

Yet Manon undoubtedly exerted a beneficial influence when it came to her lover's social habits. She was a teetotaller, a non-user of drugs, and made very clear her displeasure if Marriott strayed back onto that particular path. He, in turn, duly cleaned up his act and followed her example.

In March of 1984, Steve was unexpectedly invited to appear on Mike Read's TV show, *Pop Quiz*. His fellow guests included singer Paul Jones, Holly Johnson, Tom Robinson, Bob Geldof and PP Arnold.

Talking of PP Arnold; 'they asked me at the show if I remembered her,' Marriott told the *NME* in 1984, '"Remember her?" I said, "I used to bloody shag her."'

Marriott took along his sister Kay to the recording.

'He was taking the mickey out of Bob Geldof,' she remembers. '"Typical Irishman," Steve said, "Look, he's got his paper in the pocket."'

He dressed in a Hawaian style shirt and his hair had noticeably receded. After the show, he and Kay went for a drink.

'Steve said, "Come on let's have a drink". So we walk into this pub and it was only a '60s memorabilia pub and "Sha La La La Lee" was playing. They were all over him. It was autograph after autograph. We had a smashing time.'

‡ ‡ ‡

In August, 1984, Aura Records issued the live album *Steve Marriott – Dingwalls, 6.7.84*. The album looked to the past, couldn't look anywhere else really.

There were two Small Faces songs, 'Whatcha Gonna Do About It,' and 'All Or Nothing,' five Humble Pie-associated songs, 'Fool For A Pretty Face,' 'The Fixer,' 'Five Long Years,' 'Thirty Days In The Hole' 'Don't Need No Doctor,' and 'Big Train Stop At Memphis,' a Marriott original taken from his unreleased 1982 recording session in America.

Also included were covers of 'Bad Moon Rising,' 'Shame Shame Shame,' and 'Walkin' The Dog.' Just to make sure all bases were covered, Marriott also delivers an acapella version of 'The Cockney Rhyme.'

The album sold little compared to his past work but for Marriott that was neither here or there. If someone wanted to put out a live album, great. If it did well, even better. If it didn't, he didn't give a fuck.

In December, he spoke to the *NME*. For the interview, he wore a cap, a silk scarf and shabby overcoat. He had noticeably put on weight now but told the writer that he was happy with his current life, playing gigs, picking up cash, having a laugh.

'Yeah, it's funny,' he said of his current audience. 'You get the fucking tattooed longhaired Humble Pie freaks with Steve tattooed across their chests – bless their hearts. You get all these Mods and bless their hearts. Then you get like punks that have come because their big brother said so – great. It's a right interesting cross section. It seems to work. Like I said, we didn't start it for nothing but a laugh, and all of a sudden it's like interviews and records out. Let me tell you, this is how it started with The Small Faces.'

Questioned about past managers such as Arden and Anthony, Marriott refused to criticise them. Without them he argued he would never have achieved the success he had. He stated that he was finished with drugs and as for modern music, there was 'nothing a good stake through the heart wouldn't cure'. As for plans for the future, he thought he would have another couple of years 'sweating it out in the clubs,' and then move into producing.

'I should pass on any knowledge, if there's any knowledge that I've learned,' he said, 'You shouldn't keep it a secret.'

Some people don't believe Marriott's stance at this time. They believe that once a competitive songwriter, always a competitive songwriter. His 'I'm just having a laugh which is all I wanted to do in the first place,' line simply does not ring true for them. This scepticism is given some credence by the singer's previously discussed encounter with his old school friend from Sandringham, Ken Hawes, at the Mean Fiddler. Having denied his part in the school fire, Marriott had eased up and backstage after the gig was on fine form, but when it came to the subject of Rod Stewart, he no longer seemed laid back.

'I mentioned to Steve something about Rod Stewart and he went ballistic!' Hawes records. 'He said "that fuckin' bastard." He was completely resentful towards Rod Stewart. I remember him saying, "That could've been me". Steve was really quite depressed over what he had missed out on. He was very consumed by this, he really was. It was a sad sight to see, he was really hurting. He looked to me a sad, pathetic figure and I left it at that.'

Another face from the past, Hugh Janes from Marriott's Italia Conti schooldays, recalls a similar encounter. He too went to see The Packet Of Three and got talking to Marriott.

'By then he was a very scruffy individual,' Janes says, 'but he still had the excellent voice and was a greatly improved musician. I spoke with him and he definitely appeared to be very pissed off with the fact that Rod Stewart had stolen something that he had originally started and become a very rich man in doing so. This wasn't really true but Steve was quite obviously very gutted at the success of guys like Rod and David Bowie while he was back playing the pubs. He certainly wasn't the cheeky chappie I'd known in the 1960s. He wasn't happy. But whatever problems he had he was always able to put them to one side whenever he was on stage. I never saw him give a bad performance.'

The stage, that was all he lived for. Whether he was drunk or stoned or wired or frazzled, didn't matter. Soon as he walked on that stage, that was where Stephen Peter Marriott fully came into being. The stage was where he shone and of course, as he knew better than anyone else, the bigger the stage, the higher the high. Hence, the bitterness.

‡ ‡ ‡

Soon Fallon the drummer was causing problems both at home and at work. Manon Piercey: 'He was a brilliant drummer, a lovely singer but he had absolutely nothing between his ears whatsoever. He was about 28-years-old and we'd be getting fourteen year old girls knocking on the door. Steve was like a fatherly figure to him and would say, "You can't do that, you can't bring young girls in here. It's a family home.'"

Of more concern to Marriott was Fallon's ruminations in the music press. They ran along the lines of, 'I'm actually a jazz-fusion drummer, I'm very talented, I'm just treading water, just helping Steve out until something better comes along.'

Which instantly got him the sack. Marriott's choice to replace Fallon was predictable. He phoned Jerry Shirley, asked him back.

'Jerry was tried and tested and Steve knew what he could do,' Jim Leverton explains. 'There was a lot of resentment between those two which went back a long way and did manifest itself in the end. I think Jerry felt he was owed from before and he saw it as an opportunity to catch up with what he thought he was owed. We were working even more then. We toured America, Canada, Scandinavia and all over Europe. We were on the road all the time.'

For his part, Shirley was just happy getting work.

'The idea of playing again with Steve in small clubs and pubs appealed to me,' Shirley states. 'I was out of work at the time and had just moved back to England. It was a fun two years.'

‡ ‡ ‡

To the Manon born – a daughter, Mollie Mae on the 3rd of May 1985.

'We went on holiday to Jaywick Sands with Mollie,' Manon recalls. 'We stayed in the same bungalow where Steve had stayed many times as a child. A great time. He wasn't drinking and we just used to sit on the beach and make sand castles, even if it was raining. I remember this guy walking by who looked at Steve and said, "Good God, Steve Marriott." He looked so different but people still knew him. In the evenings we'd just watch the telly or play games. He was a better father with Mollie than he was with Toby, perhaps because he was older or perhaps it was because she was a girl.'

Marriott had moved into a more stable period, less frenetic. At home with his family, he stayed off the booze, off the powders. He was willing to let Manon rule the roost, lay down the law. He had the ability to stop when necessary.

'He would go on a binge,' Kay his sister remembers, 'and then he'd say, "I'm not drinking anymore". And he'd stop, six weeks, two months. He was very strong willed. If he wanted to, he could.'

Manon: 'After the lease run out on our house in Stansted Abbotts, we moved to Aythorpe Roding in Essex. I didn't like that it was a modern property but Steve disagreed. It had a large kitchen and he loved the kitchen. He was always cooking and would go out for fresh food every day. Cooking was a real passion of his. Another was reading. A favourite book of that time was a Noel Coward biography. Another favourite pastime was simply to go shopping together. He loved helping little old ladies with their shopping. We lived a very normal existence.'

Marriott also set up a little studio where he proceeded to record his new songs, new music that would inevitably lay dormant, rusting away on master tapes as the years rolled by. He put a brave face on did Marriott, kept on writing and recording, but gone were the days when he could write a song, record it, hear it on the radio a few weeks later. Still, he remained musically ambitious, always trying to nail that one song which would turn around his life.

‡ ‡ ‡

Around this time, his mum entered a bad stage in her life. Steve saw it and went to Manon with an idea that took even her by surprise.

'Steve's mum was going through a bad patch and needed a treat,' she recalls, 'so Steve suggested we take her to the ballet. Steve took us both to see Swan Lake at the National Theatre. He spent the night explaining all the moves to us because he had done ballet at the Italia Conti. Other people in the audience were very impressed with his knowledge but not so with his dress sense. He stood out like a sore thumb, he was dressed so scruffily.'

‡ ‡ ‡

On 13 July, 1985, the night of Live Aid, a huge charity concert to raise money for starving African children, the British leg of which took place at Wembley Stadium, the US leg at JFK Stadium in Philadelphia, Steve Marriott played the Half Moon in Putney.

As a procession of his former colleagues and contemporaries – David Bowie, Eric Clapton, Paul McCartney, Ron Wood and Keith Richards, The Who, Elton John, Santana, The Beach Boys *et al* – played for a global audience of billions, Marriott performed for about two hundred and fifty people. The irony would not have been lost on him and it would probably have served to fuel his sense of injustice.

Live Aid was the conclusion of a campaign begun by Bob Geldof's all-star recording group Band Aid, which featured many of the artists that would perform at Live Aid, on the famine relief fund-raising single 'Do They Know It's Christmas Time?'

Thanks to Band Aid's example, in the summer of 1985 the London based Phoenix Modernist Society put together Mod revival bands, such as the Lambrettas and Purple Hearts with an array of '60s stars such as Chris Farlowe, PP Arnold and Eddie Phillips to cut a version of 'All Or Nothing,' for both the Band Aid trust and Ronnie Lane's ARMS trust. The producer, and long time Small Faces buddy, Kenny Lynch managed to persuade Steve Marriott to get involved. Together they produced a version which was released as a single on 7 inch and 12 inch formats under the collective name of The Spectrum.

It came out, then Marriott went back on the road…

After months and months of hard touring, Jerry Shirley started making his displeasure known at Packet of Three's low-level-status. He began insisting that the band go to another level, that they make an album, get a deal and stop poncing around in clubs and crappy cheap hotel rooms. In other words, get taken seriously for God's sake.

At first, Marriott just laughed, not what he wanted. But still Shirley persisted. After all, the band were accepting offers of live work from all over the world. They had spent part of 1986 in America and Canada where Pam, Steve's ex-wife, had set up the dates and in 1987, Mick Eve secured them a tour of Japan.

'I set it up with a very honourable promoter,' he recalled. 'I asked Steve if he had any drug convictions that might stop him getting entry into the country. He just said, "Nah, mate none." The promoter had booked all the venues and made large down payments and all of a sudden we got a knock back on Steve's visa. Apparently, he'd got a £10 fine back in 1970 for smoking a joint in Soho Square. It was nothing really but it was enough to haunt him seventeen years later. It wasn't so much that he had this conviction, it was more to do with Steve not declaring it. Poor promoter over there lost a lot of money. Can't believe it really especially when you think of all the big boys, the Keith Richards of this world, sailing in. So Steve would do regular European tours.

'His stronghold was Germany and Scandinavia. He used to love those. They'd take the van over on the ferry, very back-to-roots stuff, like he was doing pre-Small Faces.'

A return tour of America was offered to the band at this time and they accepted. It would be the last time the Packet Of Three would play together. Halfway through the tour, with Shirley still on about recording an album, Marriott discovered that the small American road crew he was working with were on the take.

Jim Leverton: 'Things like one speaker would be blown in a Marshall cabinet and Steve would ask the roadie to take it to a music shop and get a new speaker put in. They'd come back and say things like, "Actually, three of the speakers have blown," and Steve would be improperly charged for the repair. When I found out about it, I challenged the culprits. Their reply was "Oh he's so out of his head, He'll never know."

'I told Steve and we just fucked off back to England in the middle of the night. We just got on a plane in the middle of an American tour and left Jerry there.'

The band was finished. So too was Marriott's relationship with Manon. Despite his sobriety at home, on tour Marriott could not resist. Now he started bringing his tour habits back home.

'Steve was straight for a long time with me and it was pure bliss,' Manon states. 'But towards the end of our relationship, the drink and the cocaine came back with a vengeance. Because I didn't drink he felt guilty about drinking himself and then he would go on binges. This was a major problem between us. I didn't want Mollie growing up with that. He was very Jekyll and Hyde. I should have seen the split coming but when you love someone you don't look.'

The truth was that Marriott could no longer serve under Manon. He had grown to resent the rules of their relationship. Plus, his eye had now strayed, fixed on another girl, the girlfriend in fact of a roadie who worked for Chas and Dave, the cockney band Marriott had befriended and borrowed equipment from occasionally.

Her name was Toni and she liked to party, have a good time.

Manon shrugs. 'With her Steve could do everything with ease.'

She sounds just like Jenny Rylance, Marriott's first wife. Come to think of it, she also sounds like Pam, his second.

With son, Toby   (Toni Marriott)

Chapter Twenty-One

The DT's

It is the summer of 1968. A group of very young Essex girls, only about seven or eight years old, gather outside Steve Marriott's Beehive Cottage. The girls are keen to get his autograph, all of them except one.

This girl hates Steve Marriott. Despises him. Every weekend her parents have a party that lasts from Saturday night to Sunday night and the record they play over and over again, the one that keeps her awake until the early hours, is 'Lazy Sunday.'

The girl can't stand the song, hates it with a passion. By extension, she loathes the man who created it.

One of her friends now urges, 'Come on, let's just walk to the door 'n' see if he's in.'

'I ain't going in,' she says, her London accent clear in the country air. 'I'll hold the bikes. But you better be out here in five minutes. I've heard about those pop stars and their drugs. If you're not out in five minutes I'm calling the police.'

The girls laugh and then head for the cottage. Judy 'Toni' Poultney stays and peers through the bushes, watching them walk towards the house, hoping that her friends will be okay, that the man she loathes beyond belief doesn't get up to anything funny.

Life. Nineteen years on from that sunny day, Toni will fall in love with that very same man and spend the last four years of his life with him.

Their first meeting came together through Toni's brother, John Poulton. He had organised a couple of Packet Of Three gigs, one in Woking and one in Chelmsford. At the latter gig, he left Toni and his girlfriend downstairs whilst he went to chat with Marriott in the upstairs dressing room. After a while, Toni decided she had had enough of being ignored and marched up the stairs, barged into the dressing room, absolutely fuming.

Her brother introduced her to Marriott – first impressions – she thought, 'What an obnoxious, foul-mouthed, vile and disgusting bloke.'

He thought, 'If that bird wasn't such a miserable-faced bastard she would be very pretty.'

After that, love was inevitable really.

‡ ‡ ‡

In reference to his financial difficulties, Steve had cheekily named his new band, Steve Marriott and the Official Receivers.

Jim Leverton kept his job as bassist, he and Marriott as close now as Steve and Ronnie had been in the '60s. 'Steve had complete and utter admiration for Jim as a musician,' Toni will unequivocally state. 'He often said, "He's one of the finest musicians I have ever worked with."'

They found a Richard Newman, ex-Joe Brown band, to play drums and then Leverton suggested recruiting Mick Weaver, the Hammond organ player from the '60's outfit, Wynder K. Frog to add some different colour to the music.

Marriott prevaricated for a few days on the idea, then agreed.

The Official Receivers were in a lot of fans' minds, Steve's best outfit of the 1980s. The Hammond oriented line-up was a lot nearer The Small Faces' set up than any of the other later outfits. They even got to support Steve's hero Chuck Berry at London's Hammersmith Odeon.

Weaver wasn't the only new face at a Steve Marriott gig. Since their first meeting, Toni was now present at many of them.

'Everyone I was hanging around with was constantly going to his gigs,' Toni says. 'They was all mad about him.'

One night, Marriott told Toni that he had plans to travel to Germany. He had been in touch with his ex, Pam. She had moved there and a reconciliation was on the cards. Toni felt a lump of disappointment appear in her throat but Marriott never made the trip.

Much to Pam's chagrin, he chose to stay in the UK, chose instead to pursue Toni.

'She hates me, Pam,' Toni says laughing, 'another one! They all bloody well hate me.'

Marriott christened Toni 'the little hippy,' ('because I was always stoned,'), made his move (they rented a hotel room one night,) and soon they were living together in his house in Aythorp Roding. Manon had relocated to a council property which she lived in with Mollie Mae. Toni took her place, bringing along her Irish wolfhound and bags of chutzpah.

'From there we looked for a nice place to move into,' she recalls, 'and later moved to Arkesden, North Essex.'

Jim Leverton approved of the relationship and its effect on Steve.

'When he first got together with Toni,' he states, 'he'd be the most together person in the band. First to bed, with all his next day's clothes folded on a chair.'

She was a feisty girl, Toni. Loud, determined, not at all meek. She had a daughter by a previous relationship and before her arrival had worked on her dad's fruit stall in Harlow market. She shared a lot of Steve's characteristics. She loved ribald humour, was fun, took life with a pinch of salt. Soon, she started working with the band, driving the van first before taking on other responsibilities.

When she assumed financial control, she immediately made changes. The band were put onto wages, Steve given a hefty percentage of the takings. As it was his name that was bringing in the crowds, no one had a right to complain.

Steve kept writing away in his little bedroom, sometimes alone, sometimes with Jim Leverton in tow. He still wrote quickly, still occasionally needed a Ronnie Lane-type figure to slow him down, suggest avenues he hadn't thought of exploring.

'He was always writing,' Toni states. 'There were loads of songs he never finished. He kept a book in the music room and every time he got an idea or any words come into his head he'd just bolt in there and write them down.'

Again, the songs piled up but again the songs would stay unreleased for years and years and years.

‡ ‡ ‡

When they made the move to Arkesden, they lived in a 16th century listed house opposite a pub. The property was used for location shots in the television series *Lovejoy*. Marriott turned to Toni and said, 'We'll have to behave ourselves here, doll.'

Wouldn't it be nice to get on wiv me neighbours... Arkesden was small, sleepy and very upmarket. Make a noise here and everyone would be on your case.

A week after moving in, they had a huge row. Toni left the house, stormed over to her friend Jim Skinner's abode. When she finally calmed down, she returned home. As she neared the house she saw what she thought was a huge mound of sand in the front garden. It wasn't sand. It was all her possessions piled up high and on top of the pile, a handwritten note from Steve.

'You can fuck off,' he had written.

Toni went to the front door. Locked. She goes round the back, that door is locked as well. Her Irish wolfhound now bounds up to her. He's been in the garden all this time. She comforts the large animal, looks up, sees the light on in the back bedroom. It's raining but the roof is easy to climb onto. She hoists herself up, starts inching her way towards the window.

When she gets to the window, she looks in. Steve Marriott is lying on the bed wearing a dressing gown, holding a large glass of brandy in one hand, a big spliff in the other. Toni knocks on the window.

'Come on Steve,' she shouts, 'Don't be stupid, this has gone on long enough.'

Marriott gets up, goes to the window and shouts, 'Take your car, take your dog and fuck off.'

Then he pulls the curtains shut.

At which moment, Toni slides all the way down the roof to the ground, landing on her back. When she stands up she is covered in dirt and moss.

Again, she calls up to Steve but the curtains stay closed, the doors locked. She hurls a stream of expletives at him, walks round, gets in the car with her dog, slams the car door shut and drives to Steve's parents' house in nearby Sawbridgeworth. Kay and Bill take her in, comfort her. Bill says he'll ring his son, talk him round.

He gets him on the line but Steve is raging, can't keep his mouth still. The word fuck pours out a hundred times. She can fuck off. I'm not fucking having it. She's a fucker. Fuck. Fuck. Fuck.

Finally, the dad says, 'Come on son, you can't keep saying fuck off all the time.'

There's a second's silence. Then Steve Marriott shouts back, 'Well, you can fuck off as well'

‡ ‡ ‡

He liked Arkesden, liked his life there. At first he was a name, a celebrity to the locals but pretty soon his reckless, behaviour killed off any residue of mystery and glamour that might have attached itself to him.

He became well known in the pub, often popped in to buy bottles of brandy or borrow glasses. One time he walked in wearing just his Converse trainers and a dressing gown. You had to laugh. He certainly did. He was pissed.

And of course, drunk or not, he couldn't resist playing games, winding up those he thought needed it.

A nearby neighbour bought some false sheep for his front garden. Marriott went to the pub, rounded up some local boys and after closing time, crept up the hill in the dead of night and poured bottles of mint sauce all over them.

The landlord of the pub was named Gell. Marriott changed that to 'Jailboy.' Within a week, much to the man's obvious displeasure, everyone was calling him by that name,

One Christmas Eve, two in the morning, Marriott put a ladder against the pub wall, climbed up it and to the tune of 'Noël, Noël,' sang, 'Jailboy, jailboy, jailboy,' through the man's bedroom window.

Incorrigible! He was nearly forty and the man was still incorrigible.

‡ ‡ ‡

The gigs kept coming, enough to pay the rent, keep him happy. He even attended an audition for the reformed group Bad Company – went and played for them, got drunk, insulted Simon Kirke's wife, went home. He didn't get the job and shouldn't have gone for it in the first place. His personality simply did not fit in. He didn't have the desire to win.

Then one day there was an unexpected message. EMI in Germany had been in touch, were talking about a £100,000 deal, invited Steve and Jim Leverton to fly out to Cologne, all expenses paid, to start discussions.

'We met at Stansted airport, the night before the flight,' the bass player recalls. 'We stayed in a Holiday Inn so we'd be there on the spot in the morning. We got up early and were walking to the terminal when Steve just stopped in his tracks and said, "Oh fuck this, I don't wanna go to Germany." He just turned round and walked away.'

Leverton was furious. He was hours away from the biggest break in his life and now his best friend had scuppered the deal. But what could he do? Marriott's fear of the music industry was manifest. Major success hadn't brought him contentment. It had annoyed him, angered him and disgusted him. Happiness for Steve Marriott came from following your heart, going your own way and large record deals would not allow him to do that. So fuck them.

'He figured,' Leverton says, 'that if we signed with them, they'd tell us what songs to record, who to have in the band, what clothes to wear and so on. He may well have been right but you've got to play the game a little bit.'

That didn't stop the bitter envy at his contemporaries rising, although interestingly Marriott never seemed to express his contempt or anger in front of his parents, close family or partners. It was as if he was afraid his bitterness might upset them. Toni insists she never heard him bad-mouth the likes of Rod Stewart. Jim Leverton says the same.

'I don't think he was jealous of them' the bass player says, 'I never heard him tear into anyone's musical ability. I've heard him take the piss out of their appearance, he was always doing that. "Looks like a go go dancer," that was Rod. Kenney was Des O'Jones, because Steve thought Kenney had the same coiffured hairstyle as Des O'Connor.'

Marriott seemed to express his ire only to outsiders, the likes of Ken and Hugh and other people he met at gigs. The only thing that separated him from them was their willingness to play the game. These musicians would bow to anyone if it meant furthering themselves. To Marriott, such behaviour was abhorrent. You don't go cap in hand to any fucker, whoever he may be Music came first, so did talent. That's what mattered, that's what he fervently believed in. Whatever the cost.

'Once the EMI deal was fucked, the band's days were numbered,' Leverton states. 'There was a lot of resentment over that. It was a real pity because during our short lifetime we were received really well wherever we played. I remember at the Half Moon in Putney one night, Toni his girlfriend said, "He's gonna knock it on the head for a bit." I just said, "Great. Best news I've heard all day." To be quite honest I was quite pleased to have a rest from him. He was a very overpowering character, especially at gigs. Away from the stage he was different all together, he was good company, but on the road he'd say things like, "You're fucking boring, you are," and all that.

'Yeah, I was pleased to get a break.'

‡ ‡ ‡

He had seen them a couple of times at his own shows, liked their style. The first time the DT's supported the Official Receivers had been at the Five Bells in Northampton. The band played R&B covers and Marriott enjoyed their set so much that halfway through he leapt onstage and sang an impromptu blues ballad with them. Later that year, he turned up at their gig in Leicester's Princess Charlotte pub and sang a whole set.

Now with The Official Receivers finished, Marriott was in a bit of a quandary. He had to form a band so he could play live, pay the rent. But after the EMI debacle and the years of acting as a leader, he was tired. What he wanted now was to take a backstage role, as he had in the early days of Humble Pie.

The DT's provided the perfect answer. In late '87, Marriott called the band's harmonica player, Simon Hickling, talked about the possibility of joining the outfit. Nothing really happened until May the following year.

In the intervening period, Marriott took time out, relaxed. He was forty-years-old now, had a bit of a paunch, a round full face. No traces of his classic Mod style was discernible in his appearance. Gone were the colourful tops, the creased trousers, the breathtaking shoes. Now he wore tracksuit bottoms with baggy t-shirts whilst onstage, he had taken to wearing denim dungarees and a mullet haircut. He dressed down, dressed very down.

'I remember going to see him in the '80s,' the filmmaker Paolo Sedazzari recalls, 'and he was brilliant. Great voice, great guitarist but what I couldn't get over were the dungarees and the mullet haircut. That was really disappointing.'

One day on the tube into town, a passenger kept looking at Steve out of the side of his eye. After three or four stops had gone by, the man could no longer help himself.

'Excuse me,' he said, 'Didn't you used to be Steve Marriott?'

Funny, but sad also.

At home, Steve listened mainly to old music. Randy Newman, Dr Hook, Willie Nelson, Little Walter, BB King, Howlin' Wolf, Taj Mahal, the blues. He watched a lot of TV. When Channel Four was launched, he would stay up late, watching to the early hours.

Sports wise, he enjoyed boxing most, especially bouts featuring young and up coming fighters. His knowledge of football wasn't great which is why he supported West Ham. He cooked a lot but never did a scrap of housework. Never washed up or cleaned around the house. He far preferred going on holidays, going off to sit in the sun, relax, have fun.

He liked reading, much more so in his later years. Stephen King was a favoured author, so was the science fiction writer, Philip K. Dick. Anything on Noel Coward was eagerly devoured as were biographies of actors, film stars. He even had a book shelf, filled with the likes of The Goons, in his toilet. His vices were few now. He still drank, still smoked spliffs, still snorted occasional lines of cocaine but nothing compared to what he once consumed. Toni talks about a guy called PD coming over, chopping out lines, but to be honest visitors to the Marriott household were a rarity. In his time off, he wanted to stay in, be left alone.

There were even days when he hardly spoke and Toni would try and cajole him out of his silence. 'Come on you old fart,' she would cry, 'liven up.' But he just shrugged his shoulders, meandered on. They had little social life, letting the gigs act as nights out, nights for drinking, smoking, having a giggle. But even that time was marred by the pains he would feel in his kidney and liver region the very next morning.

Home was the place therefore where he went to heal, to repair himself in peace and in quiet.

'He just used to get up,' Toni says, describing a run of the mill day from their life together at this point. 'I'd do the ironing and then he would go upstairs and read. He read a lot. He'd go up in the bedroom and read while I done the downstairs housework and then he'd come downstairs while I done the upstairs. He'd maybe watch a bit of telly, have a little doze, do some more reading and then we'd have dinner and after that he'd just watch telly all night long. We'd go to bed between one or three and four.'

Oh, another fact. Marriott didn't like electric lighting. He much preferred candles.

He had them all over the bedroom.

After five months of this lifestyle, of holidaying, of inaction, Steve was revitalised and ready to return to work. In May 1988, he started rehearsing with The DT's. Apart from Hickling on vocals and harmonica, the band consisted of Steve Walwyn on lead guitar and vocals, Craig Rhind on bass and Chas Chaplin on drums.

By the time they hit the road, the band had a different name – Steve Marriott and the DT's.

They began playing concerts, England and Germany mostly. Marriott could never rein in his more anarchic side in the latter country. At an after show party in a hotel room, Toni recalled Marriott taking a pen to a painting of a German dignitary and turning the man into an Adolf Hitler look-alike.

On another occasion, backstage at a gig, he got into an argument with the promoter, called him 'a cringing Kraut.'

'What does cringing mean?' asked the man.

'It's what Hitler did when he got the gas bill,' Marriott retorted, 'now piss off.'

In Marriott's world, no subject was taboo. Everything was up for grabs. Race was as ripe for mickey taking as anything else was. Toni shared his humour, understood it for what it was. She saw this style of humour as a defence mechanism, protection against the horrors of the world.

'That's why we was just the same,' she says, 'because although I laugh about everything, I don't think it's that funny. It's just a way of dealing with things.'

Other bookings came in, exciting ones. An Icelandic agent saw the band play the Half Moon in Putney and booked them for two nights at a Reykjavik club called Hollywood.

No one in the band had been to Iceland before. They fancied it would be a trip to remember. They met at Heathrow, Marriott smoking endless roll ups, talking non-stop, drowning brandies to cover his nervousness about flying

On their arrival, they were met at the airport by the promoter of the two shows. Marriott's first words to him were, 'Have you got any gear?' Then he nicknamed the man, 'Guff', a phrase that relates to the art of flatulence.

As they loaded up the mini van, Guff asked Marriott if 'Sha La La La Lee,' was in the set list. No way, Marriott replied. 'All Or Nothing,' was the only song they performed from that time, the rest was strict R&B. At the hotel, the promoter went off to make a phone call.

When they arrived at the club they were met by the owner, a man named 'Biggy', who took Marriott aside and demanded he play, 'Sha La La La Lee' that night.

Again, Marriott refused.

The club opened for business. The crowd poured in, started drinking heavily as they tend to do in cold countries where the sun is rarely seen and the day is grey before it has even begun. Five minutes before going onstage, Biggy again approached Marriott, asked him to play 'Sha La La La Lee.'

Marriott ignored him and the band walked out onstage, plugged in, started playing. The alcohol soon began to take its effect on the crowd. Half way through the set, a woman in the front row passed out, face down in the ashtray.

Swaying men, emboldened by drink, started approaching the stage, shouting for 'Sha La La La Lee'.

'Sorry mate,' Steve announced between songs, 'we don't do it.'

For one man in particular, Marriott's explanation simply wasn't good enough. He kept returning to the stage, demanding that Marriott tell him why he wouldn't play the song.

'Cause we don't fucking do it, you nob headed Eskimo,' Marriott shouted back and that was that.

The band went into 'All Or Nothing,' the set's closer. Afterwards, in the van back to the hotel, Biggy curtly told Marriott that as he wasn't going to play the Small Faces material he requested, he was cutting the next night's set down to 45 minutes. Marriott said, good, fine by me.

The next night when they arrived at the club, a long queue of people reached all the way down the street.

Inside the club, a beaming Biggy greeted Marriott.

'Everyone in Reykjavik tells me I am a great man to bring R&B to this club, it is a big big success. Tonight, you must play for 90 minutes.'

'Tough shit,' came Marriott's reply. 'You wanted 45 minutes last night and that's what you're getting.'

Which is precisely what happened. The band played forty five minutes, hotfooted it back to the hotel, drank their mini bars dry, went out on their room balconies, toasted the revellers below, Marriott made a speech to the crowd which had his band in stitches and they all went to bed at six in the morning, shitfaced and happy.

And Iceland never heard 'Sha La La La Lee.'

‡ ‡ ‡

The gigs continued, one after the other. In Liverpool, he was given an escort back to his hotel by a bunch of scooterboys. The act was an old Mod tradition, granted only to special acts such as Prince Buster.

In June 1988, he topped the bill at the Wimbledon Town Hall. Supporting him were three new groups, The Boys, The Clique and Boys Wonder. The Boys' guitarist was one Steve Cradock, later to find fame himself with Ocean Colour Scene.

'It was the first time I was made aware of reefers,' Cradock recalls, 'because

Marriott was chugging on one.'

Two months later, Cradock again played support, got into a longer conversation with the man. He recalls Marriott complaining about his liver and kidneys, telling the young guitarist, 'I ain't got long for this world.'

As he made this solemn announcement, he was downing vast quantities of brandy and marijuana, which he also offered to Cradock. Throughout his life, Marriott remained a generous man both with his possessions and his time. Giles Twigg, the engineer for 'Baker Street' songwriter Gerry Rafferty, was just starting out with his first band, Iago, when he met Steve.

'We were supporting him at the Woolwich Tramshed,' he recalls. 'We arrived there as the rest of his band was doing a soundcheck. He literally told his band to fuck off the stage and give the other guys, meaning us, a chance, which was really nice of him. It was our first major gig and he ensured we had a long time to sort our sound out, which was amazing as most people coming to the gig that night were there to see him. Anyway, while we were playing, he sat out in front and watched us run through our set, giving instructions to the house engineer to get the right sound for us. Later in the evening, just before we were due to go on stage, he walked into our dressing room with a huge carrier bag of dubious substances which he thought we might want to smoke before we went on. The thing was we were really well oiled so we didn't imbibe at the time but that was a really nice thing for him to do for us.'

Top boxing trainer and fan Dean Powell recalls going to see Marriott at the Thomas A Becket boxing pub on London's famed Old Kent Road. 'I went upstairs and Marriott was in a boxing ring pissed and out of his head,' he recalls. 'He kept jumping into the ropes and throwing himself across the ring. He was gone. Yet when he took the stage he didn't put a foot wrong. You would never have known.'

For his agent Mick Eve, the Wimbledon tennis season was always the worst time. Steve's name and reputation had even seeped into that sporting arena, attracting the attention of hipper players such as Pat Cash or Vitas Gerulatis.

'These guys would hook up with him,' Eve says. 'Steve would be at Wimbledon every afternoon for strawberries and cream and whatever. It certainly wasn't for the tennis. Then, instead of turning up at a soundcheck at six, it would be more like nine. It was a nightmare. One Sunday at the Cricketers pub near the Oval cricket ground, he turned up in muddy Wellington boots telling his adoring fans he had been gardening all day. A likely story!'

‡ ‡ ‡

He went to see Manon and Mollie but the visit ended in tears, a raging argument. He came home furious, told Toni he would no longer keep contact with Mollie. 'I'm not gonna dance to somebody's tune just so that I can see a kid,' he shouted. 'Fuck it, I'm doing her a favour walking away.' Then he locked himself in Toni's car with a big bottle of brandy. Steve Marriott couldn't handle kids, wasn't built for them. Didn't have the time, the patience, most of all the necessary sense of responsibility. 'He said to me,' Toni recalls, '"one day, when she's old enough, she can come and find me and then I'll have my own relationship with her.'" That's what he was really waiting for.'

‡ ‡ ‡

His name might not be in the papers anymore but some still remembered. A call came in from an advertising company. They wanted Steve Marriott to sing a song called 'Law Of The Jungle,' for a TV ad promoting Puma trainers. Good money, as well. Marriott duly obliged.

Another unexpected phone call. This time a film composer, name of Steve Parsons, wanted him to sing the title track for a film entitled unpromisingly *Food Of The Gods 2.*'

Easy money. Marriott duly obliged.

At the subsequent recording session, Marriott and Steve Parsons, got on well. Then a small company name of Trax Records, got in touch, wanted Steve to make an album with Parsons producing. They offered him ten grand.

Perfect. For months now, Marriott had set his eyes on acquiring a boat, a long narrow boat that cost ten grand. He went in to the Alexandra Palace studios in North London, laid down his vocals, two takes at the most. Then he went home where he disparagingly referred to the project as 'the narrow boat album.'

He recorded one new tune, the Marriott-Leverton song 'Phone Call Away' (although it was only credited to Marriott), the rest were covers of other folk's songs, including himself. 'All Or Nothing' was played at a slower tempo and there were cracks at Marvin Gaye's 'One More Heartache,' Major Lance's 'The Um Um Um Um Um Song,' Terry Reid's 'Superlungs,' Bob Marley's 'Get Up Stand Up,' Talking Heads' 'Life During Wartime,' (undoubtedly, he would have adored The Staple Singers cover of the same band's song 'Slippery People,') a cover of Johnny Kidd's 'Shakin' All Over' (also placed on the soundtrack for the film *Food Of The Gods 2*), 'Rascal You,' a 1930s song covered by Louis Armstrong, Curtis Mayfield's 'Gyspy Woman,' and a duet with PP Arnold, one of his all time fave singers, on Shirley Ellis's 'The Clapping Song.'

Despite his blasé attitude, all the ingredients were in place to make a striking album. Steve Marriott, the doyen of blue-eyed soul, the man who carried a torch all his life for R&B, singing such a list of fine songs should have produced a musical storm but technology defeated him.

The album should have been recorded live in room with a tight sweaty band. Instead, he is surrounded by synths and synth drums, modern noises to produce a mechanical work of unwonder.

Listen to the opening song, John Fogerty's 'Knocking On Your Door.' Now play Tina Turner's, 'Simply The Best.'

The records might as well be twins.

Yet vocally he is on absolute top form. His phrasing is great, his reach impressive. He knew that as well, told Tone that out of all his records, 'Thirty Seconds to Midnite,' contained some of his best ever singing.

The man was not wrong. Still, at least he got to sit on his boat.

‡ ‡ ‡

Another surprise call. Would Steve be interested in singing a new version of the Ike Turner song, 'Black Coffee,' for a Nescafé coffee advert? Course he would. The session took place at the Sony studios in Whitfield Street. By coincidence, the producer for the day also booked Marriott's old Humble Pie partner, Clem Clempson, unaware of the two men's past.

'Steve arrived late,' Clempson recalls, 'after the backing track had been recorded. He went straight into the studio and once the engineer had sorted the sound he only needed one shot at it. His involvement in the session lasted about fifteen minutes.'

Which meant that Steve Marriott had just earned a grand a minute. After laying down his vocal, he stuck around, shot the breeze with Clempson. Then he headed home.

Clempson was still at the studio, when Marriott called back on the phone, asked if he would consider joining a new band he was planning. Clempson answered in the affirmative although Marriott did make the proviso that he wasn't keen on undertaking lengthy tours.

Clempson said that was fine by him. The men said their goodbyes, promised to keep in touch.

‡ ‡ ‡

On July 14th, 1989, after two years of living together, Steve and Toni were married at Epping registry office. Afterwards, a party at their home, then a honeymoon in Bali. Marriott loved visiting other places, never tired of it. He was a nervous flyer but by this time a seasoned traveller. Bali was a ball.

‡ ‡ ‡

In London first, and then in clubs up and down the land, the young swallowed Ecstasy pills, danced to House music, lost all inhibitions socially and sexually. New music, new drugs, new fashions. Acid house, the most important youth cult since punk had arrived.

Marriott would not have liked or indeed understood the scene but he would have approved. Pills that make you go ummm. Nice!

Meanwhile, he kept to the pubs, the clubs, playing the blues.

One night, after driving through the Blackwall Tunnel, Jim Leverton came across a sign outside the Mitre Club that read 'Tonight – Steve Marriott and The DT's.' He immediately put on the brakes.

'I hadn't seen him for about eighteen months,' he recalled, 'so I just pulled in and watched the gig. They did 'Five Long Years' and it was superb. I said hello, of course, told him I was just passing and no hard feelings and all that. Two weeks later, I got the phone call. 'Gotta put the band back together,' and that was Steve Marriott's Next Band.'

The original line up featured Steve and Jim with Simon Hickling from the DT's on harmonica, Richard Newman from the Official Receivers on drums. Newman didn't last. Marriott had a falling out with the drummer early in the band's life and he was replaced by Kofi Baker, Ginger Baker's son. Like father, like son apparently.

'He was quite amazing,' Leverton says of Kofi's skills, 'and we worked the same circuit as before and toured Europe. But I found the line up confusing with the lead vocals shared by Steve, Simon and myself. Kofi ended up making the same mistake as Fallon Williams had a few years earlier. He was giving interviews and saying things like, "I'm a jazz drummer, just filling in to help Steve out." Not a good thing to say if you want to last. Well, that was the end of him.'

The band recruited the DT's old drummer, Alan 'Sticky' Wickett. Not long after, Simon Hickling quit over money.

'Simon was only on a wage,' Leverton states. 'It was a smaller amount than the other guys in the band and when he asked for the same as them he was ousted. Steve offered him a hundred per cent of fuck all. That was the end of that.'

Noting that they were now a trio, Steve killed the band's title and re-christened them the Packet Of Three.

'From a booking point of view,' his agent Mick Eve states, 'it didn't matter what the current line up was, as long as he had competent musicians onstage with him, that was enough. Steve's audiences were always about eighty per cent male and therefore bar takings were always high. Steve always told me he was happy playing at this level and never wanted anything bigger but it's my belief he could have ended up on the festival circuit, pretty much how Joe Cocker has.'

‡ ‡ ‡

In her time as Prime Minister, Margaret Thatcher created many controversial policies. Her most famous was the 1990 Poll Tax Bill which brought thousands out onto the street, instigating a major riot that would signal the beginning of the end of her reign.

At the same time, the American band the Georgia Satellites, who Marriott had befriended in Atlanta, began a tour of England. Their most notable gig was at the Mayfair club in Newcastle. During one particular song, the band started improvising on a blues riff, before singing "Ain't gonna pay no poll tax no more". The whole audience immediately sang along with it, showering the band with applause for their stance.

A couple of days later Steve hooked up with Satellites manager, Kevin Jennings and Satellites drummer Barrymore Barlow and took them to his local, The Axe and Compass in Arkesden.

Over drinks, the band invited him down to a little 8-track-studio called Carnoustie at Henley-On-Thames to participate in the recording of their new single, 'Poll Tax Blues', written by the band's guitarist Dickey Lee, who would later change his name by deed poll to Keith Richards.

Steve agreed but only if he could sing under the alias of Matt Vinyl. Steve had taken to using aliases of late. They offered him further protection from stardom.

John Hellier recalls attending Steve Marriott gigs where he saw Marriott play under the various monikers 'Hunt Lunt and Cunningham', 'Book Em And Riskett', and 'The Tubby Has Been Trio'.

The Satellites agreed to Steve's request. Two days later, Marriott appeared at the studio along with Jim Leverton and Simon Hickling. They and The Satellites cut the track in an hour. The single was rush released under the name of the Poll Cats.

As they only had time to cut the one number, the same track was used on both sides of the record.

It failed to reach number one.

‡ ‡ ‡

The world of adverts again came knocking. Kleenex toilet paper wanted to use 'Itchycoo Park,' for a TV advert. Marriott's manager, Laurie O'Leary agreed but asked that they allow Steve to record a new version.

That way, his client would get paid, not just the song's publishers. Kleenex agreed and paid for a day at The PRT studios in London's Bryanston Road. Steve arrived on time, spent the day there re-working the famous song.

'It was a great new version,' Mick Eve his agent recalls, 'and everyone was delighted. But due to some technicality Kleenex had to use the original version after all. On the strength of this Steve put 'Itchycoo Park' back in the Packet Of Three's set after saying he'd never do that song again.'

Steve's version has never been released.

After a gig in the Half Moon, Putney, an unexpected guest shows up in the crowded dressing room. The band's ex-drummer Kofi Baker needs a favour. The son of one of his friends is in a coma. The boy is a huge Marriott fan. Would Steve record a message that they could play to him in the hope it might bring him round?

Marriott instantly went shy, backed away. Using his fame to bring people back to life? This was voodoo to him.

'I ain't no good at anything like that,' he brusquely told Kofi. But Kofi knew him a bit by now, so he persisted. No good. Steve stuck to his guns.

Kofi then turned to the other people in the room who took his side, started to encourage Steve to say something.

'Well, what happened,' Toni recalls, 'was that Steve finally said, "Oh, all right, then". And Kofi's turned on the tape recorder and Steve looked into the tape recorder and went, "*WAKE UP YOU CUNT!*" really loud, and then he said, "that'll do, won't it, mate"? And everyone just fuckin' set about laughing. It was really embarrassing, the guy's mum and dad were in the room. But it wasn't that he was hard, he just had an incredibly forward attitude.'

Their son made a full recovery and carries that tape around with him wherever he goes.

‡ ‡ ‡

Having earned enough money, Steve and Toni now cancelled all gigs, headed out for a three-month holiday in Barbados. During their time there, they were joined by Steve's parents, Kay and Bill. True to form, an argument erupted between the four of them, a vicious terrible argument. The parents flew home, Steve angrily swore he would never talk to them again.

When Steve and Toni finally got home, a significant change had taken place. Steve Marriott was starting to tire of the work. He had been playing up to 200 gigs a year and the demands it made, the energy it exacted, was getting to be too much. Schlepping around in a van from town to town, pub to pub, just to pay the rent and nothing else, he simply couldn't face it anymore.

He had just spent three months in the sun and now it was back to the same old thing, the same old venues, the same old road. He wanted comfort now, wanted money because money allowed you to be free.

They played a few more shows. At one, the Borderline in London, Marriott gave a radio interview to John Wilson of the BBC. Wilson was putting together a documentary on Mod and wanted Marriott's input. They met at the club, Marriott in the middle of soundchecking when Wilson arrived. After the band finished, the two men retreat to the dressing room.

'You've got five minutes,' Marriott briskly tells Wilson.

Wilson starts by asking what music had influenced the Small Faces. Stax and Motown came the reply. Was Marriott aware that a lot of bands were now using the same influences as the Small Faces. Marriott said he wasn't but of late had heard a lot of music with a Hammond organ in it.

'Which is great,' he continued, 'because that was a big part of that marvellous sound. I used to go and watch Georgie Fame at The Flamingo when I was about fifteen and that was one of the first English Hammond sounds. It was fantastic. It would send you out of the door. It was fabulous.'

Wilson moves onto street fashion, how a much smarter Mod look was now returning.

'Nothing wrong with that,' Marriott says. 'When you think about what we have been through fashion wise in the last fifteen years, I would never have believed it myself, it's something out of a horror comic.'

Wilson reminds Marriott that he was once an 'ace face,' a style icon. Marriott tells him that he's flattered but was unaware of such praise.

'I'm glad I don't know about it otherwise I might turn my collar up and start wearing shades,' he joked. 'But thank you, whoever it is. I'm glad we had a bit of style that people could look at.'

Were you not conscious of it at the time, though? Wilson asks.

'Sure, yeah,' Marriott says. 'We were Mods, we were kids off the street who dressed that way and suddenly we had enough money to get the same cuts made but in better materials. Very aware of it then but not now. I'm forty-four years old. When I was eighteen it was another world for me, a world I personally wouldn't want to cling onto except for the music which will always be with you, no matter what. But if other kids take that and dress like that, nothing wrong with that, it's a very nice way to present yourselves.'

Marriott expounds further on Mod, says that everything went hand in hand. If you liked that music then you dressed in a certain way to give clues to the world about your stance in life.

Wilson tells Marriott that the musician currently carrying the flame for Mod is Paul Weller. Had Marriott heard of him?

He had. Weller had sent Marriott a couple of letters, some records.

'Very nice,' Marriott stated. 'Nice look, nice music, full applause, very good. [A little laugh.] Again, it's his version of his roots. It's very good, I admire it to the hilt but it's not my particular sort of music. I can admire it but I wouldn't want to play it. Mine's a bit more spikey, his is a bit more smooth.'

Wilson tries some contemporary band names on Marriott. The Charlatans, The Inspiral Carpets, The James Taylor Quartet, do these names mean anything?

'Sure,' Marriott says, 'but unfortunately a lot of it conjures to mind lazy buggers who can't play. Some of it is very good. But some of it is a sham but that's always been the way.'

Are these retro sounding bands relevant, Wilson wonders out loud.

'Of course they are' Marriott quickly states, 'they are today. And God bless them for it. But in today's music you will find that the cream will always rise to the top and the shit will sink.'

Both men laugh, the tape is switched off.

His last ever radio interview is finished.

‡ ‡ ‡

Pete Frampton flew into town, hunted down his old colleague in Arkesden. He had a proposition for him.

'I was at home going through some old tapes,' the ex-Humble Pie man recalled, 'and I realised Steve Marriott was the man I wanted to work with again.'

The offer to reform Humble Pie for the fourth time around could not have come at a better time. Marriott had had enough of being skint, broke, out of pocket. It was too tiring, too soul sapping. He was getting older, wanted security now, and comfort.

As a declaration of his intention to help out, Marriott invited Frampton to his show at the Half Moon in Putney, brought him onstage at the end to play a version of Pie's 'Natural Born Bugie.'

Frampton stayed on in England, writing with Steve at his house, putting together new material. Marriott's studio was small, cramped. They decided it would be better to relocate to Frampton's studio in Los Angeles, carry on writing and recording there.

They left on January 27th, 1991, Marriott determined to make this alliance work but Toni full of doubts about the project.

'When Peter's people got in touch with Steve and asked him if he'd be interested in doing a one-off album and tour reunion with Peter,' Toni recalls, 'they promised they wouldn't call it Humble Pie. They promised that, and he'd get three million quid. And he said, "I want to secure our future and I want you to have what all the others have had", and I said, "I don't want that. I don't want three million fucking quid. I don't want anything like that. I'm happy doing what we're doing and why don't you just stay here and get a deal for what you're doing and just do it as you". I don't know, for some reason he just wanted to go for it and there was no stopping him.'

Prior to his departure, Marriott told Jim Leverton that he was off to work with Frampton. Leverton, his closest ally for years felt badly betrayed again.

'It had been on the boil for awhile,' he recalls, 'and then he told me that Frampton had been in touch with him and he wanted him to go to America to make a record. I thought, "Here we go again." He had me doing all the hard graft with the constant gigging and now he wants to make a record with a guy that all he'd ever done was bad mouth.

'He'd always tell me that Frampton was a big Jessie who couldn't play rock'n'roll if it bit him on the arse. And contrary to what he had previously said, he told me, "I gotta get back in the big time, mate. Then I can start to help people." It was a complete turnaround. I think his wife Toni had a lot of sway. She'd never been to America and she had no idea of what Marriott was going to be like over there. I did tell her before they went, "Watch out, he turns over there, he's a different person." Everything is so accessible, the coke and everything…'

Jim's stark warnings were to prove true. For Toni, the next three months would prove to be hellish beyond belief. The first sign of trouble occurred when Frampton told Steve that he didn't want any women in the studio, including partners.

'And that's when Steve went on the turn,' Toni states. 'See if there was no one to temper him, he'd just go on the piss and he'd get out of control. I'm not saying that I controlled him or anything, but he needed a mate. And I did tell that to Peter. I told him, "You ain't gonna cope with him." Not many people could cope with him, that's what it was. It wasn't a matter of ruling him, it was a matter of whether or not you could cope.'

As Steve started to derail, some record company interest in their project was made known. But preliminary meetings with various executives, only served to push Marriott further off track.

'They told Steve,' Toni states, 'that he had to go to meetings and prove that he wasn't the Steve Marriott of old. The other thing was that he said that he didn't want to front the band, he wanted it to be more Pete's thing and he would just come back and play. But when he got over there everyone was for him, you know what I mean? He was so shot through with all that. I mean, the man nearly died doing all that and he was so scared of getting into all that again.

'He was on his own, and he didn't like doing things on his own. He liked to have a sidekick, you know what I mean? And one that understood him and one that said "Oh, fuck 'em," like he would, and all that. I could see him losing the plot, he was just going off his nut 'cause he was away from everything that he was accustomed to, you know.

'If I was there with him constantly he would have been alright and I'm not saying that he needed me and all that but someone had to deal with him when you see him losing it. You had to know how to deal with him. Otherwise he'd just hit the bottle and that would be it, and then he'd get progressively worse and worse and nastier and nastier until he'd be told, "we ain't taking a risk on it".

Marriott had begun resenting his situation, began resenting himself. He wanted out but, fearful of confrontation, fell back into his old habits. One night, after days of heavy consumption, it happened – Melvin came roaring back to life. It was the first time in their relationship that Toni had been exposed to Melvin, the first time she had witnessed Marriott's schizophrenic behaviour brought on by his heavy alcohol and drug abuse.

'He was a raving lunatic,' Toni calmly says of her husband in this period. 'Pissed out of his head all the time. Yeah. Violent, abusive, everything. It was dreadful. Dreadful it was. At first it weren't so bad but when the pressure started piling on him and I weren't there to alleviate for him, he just went to pieces. You know, he just lost the plot.'

Toni had no idea that Melvin was not a new creation but someone who had lived within Steve Marriott's body for the past 16 years. For her, Melvin was, 'violent, vicious, spiteful, a totally different man to the one that I had married,' and now she was scared out of her mind.

‡ ‡ ‡

The arguing that would rage between them for weeks on end had been sparked by the tragedy that had just scarred Eric Clapton's life forever. In New York, the guitarist's three-year-old baby son, Conor, had walked out unattended onto a balcony, fallen to his death from their high rise flat. The news shook Marriott, badly, made him take a step back, re-assess. Now he looked towards his own children, Toby, Tonya and Mollie, started imagining how he would feel if a child of his should be taken away so suddenly, so brutally.

He knew he had not been a great father but he also knew that time was still on his side. He could make amends, he could reach out to all of them now, try and be the father he had never truly been.

Toni fully understood his motives. After all, she was a mother herself.

Yet Marriott's vow served to set her alarm bells ringing.

If you looked at Steve's marriages or long term relationships, a definite pattern emerged.

When he married Jenny Rylance, he did so at a time when he needed protection from the madness of Small Faces stardom, the hectic lifestyle. With her, he was able to retreat to the country, live quietly. Yet after a couple of years he had grown bored of the quiet life, started feeling the urge for something more exciting. Exit Jenny, enter Pam.

Now follow six, seven years of the high life, of party time. Then the switch occurs, the need to calm down, experience something more sedate.

Exit Pam, enter Manon.

He settles down, curbs his excesses. But this mindset can't last.

Exit Manon, enter Toni.

They had been together four years now. She couldn't help herself. Was it now her turn to be jettisoned? Was her husband bored of her, hankering for the quiet life that she couldn't provide, maybe thinking of using Mollie Mae to return to Manon and a more simple life?

And Melvin. Had Melvin now appeared to scare her away? Was he the sign that she was about to lose the man she loved above everything else, the man she was convinced was her absolute and true destiny?

No wonder she was so frightened. Not only of Melvin but worse, a future with no Steve in it.

‡ ‡ ‡

They wrote and recorded three songs at Frampton's recording studio. They were called, 'The Bigger They Come The Harder They Fall,' 'I Won't Let You Down,' and 'Out Of The Blue.' The songs had potential but the money men were unhappy with Steve and his wayward behaviour. It was the '90s now, different times. The record company men were in control. They held the cheque books, they held the power. To them, Marriott's ways were a throwback to the bad old days when musicians did what they wanted, when they wanted. Not anymore they didn't.

Meetings were held, pressure applied to Toni to clean up her man. It was fruitless. Marriott was getting more and more agitated, more and more reckless. If at first he admired Frampton's playing, the sessions between them had now revealed that Steve was now on a par with him.

Jim Leverton recalls getting phone calls from Toni and Steve, insulting the ex-Herd and Humble Pie guitarist behind his back.

'They'd ring in the middle of the night and just be putting the guy down, telling me what a prat Frampton was.'

‡ ‡ ‡

From the latter part of his stay in Los Angeles come two reports. One is from Peter Stringfellow, the other a fan, Darren Hitchcott.

Club runner Stringfellow was in town to oversee the opening of his new venue. On hearing of the Humble Pie reunion, he got in touch, invited both Marriott and Frampton to lunch. He states now that Marriott seemed to have a grip on himself, that he looked great, had lost weight, wasn't drinking, seemed to be clean and was good company to be in.

'He wasn't pissed, he wasn't drugged,' Stringfellow says. 'He was raving about the songs he had done with Frampton, it was like great man, I was so pleased for him. We arranged to meet back in London.'

Marriott, clean and serene.

Yet Darren remembers Steve differently. In early April, 1991, he and a friend met Steve at The Rainbow bar on Sunset Boulevard. By sheer coincidence, the two friends were actually discussing Marriott's vocals on the *Rockin' The Fillmore* album when Marriott and Toni walked in. They couldn't believe their eyes. They went straight over, introduced themselves.

Marriott enjoyed their company and after a few drinks, told them he had a limo outside, rented courtesy of Frampton. The group left the club, headed up to Stringfellows, drinking copious amounts of whiskey from the limo's bar.

At the club they are unable to contact Peter Stringfellow and gain admission. Instead, they pile back in the car, head for the house on the beach that had been rented for Steve and Toni.

More drinks and then Steve starts playing Charlie and Inez Foxx records to the boys, starts raving about them, just as he had done all his life. Toni meanwhile looks for a cassette player so that the guests can hear Steve's new songs.

'She really seemed like Steve's biggest fan,' Darren says, 'she kept telling us how great Steve's new stuff was and how much we had to listen to it.'

Toni has a problem. The only machine she can find is a small Walkman. Toni pushes the tape into the machine, hits play. Nothing happens. She shakes the machine, hits buttons furiously, tries and tries to get it to play. No joy.

'So we're all standing there in our drunken state looking at this bloody Walkman,' Darren says, 'and then Steve's wife grabs the walkman, holds it really close to her face and says to the Walkman, "WORK YOU CUNT, WORK."

'Steve turns to me and says, "Met the wife have you?"'

They stayed up until 4.30am, playing guitars, singing Humble Pie songs, heading out for more booze, at one point, Steve even ringing Darren's home and singing the first verse of Pie's 'Thirty Days In A Hole,' into his answer machine.

'I still listen to that answer machine cassette tape with Steve singing,' he says, 'and I think that could have been the last time that he ever sang 'Thirty Days In The Hole,' and that the last time he played the song '79th And Sunset,' was with me playing guitar.'

‡ ‡ ‡

After two and a half months, Marriott had decided, enough was enough. Fuck the money, the three million quid. He just wasn't suited to this bullshit. Far better to go back to what he knew best, the pubs, the clubs, where he could do what he wanted, play what he wanted.

'They tried to make him stay,' Toni reveals, 'but I told them he don't want to do it. It's not what you told him it'd be and he don't like it, he's unhappy and he wants to go home and so do I. And that was it, really.

'There wasn't any real nastiness, know what I mean? I thought well, as soon as we get back to England, everything will be alright. Once he started working properly again and playing and all that, yeah, he'd be all right 'cause that's how he got frustrated when he didn't do live gigs. And he loved the pubs and clubs, the gigs.'

Jim Leverton recalls Steve ringing him to invite him back into his future.

'Steve was on the phone saying, "We'll get the band back together, mate. Go back on the circuit." I said, "No." It was the first time I had ever said, no. I said, "Let's make a fucking record then we don't have to do all the dives. Perhaps we can do places like Hammersmith Odeon with two thousand people a night. I'm not looking for places like Earls Court or anything but by playing to two thousand people you don't have to work so hard. You're playing to more people at one time."

'To my amazement he said he was gonna go for it. In the past when I said I wanted to make a record he'd just say, "Well, fuck off and make one then." Now he was up for it. He even suggested using a mobile at his home in Arkesden, North

Essex. We had some great new songs and it would have been smashing to get them down on record.'

That record was never made.

It is also worth pointing out that Darren's answer machine tape could well be the last recording Steve Marriott ever made. Given his passion for music, that mystic force that consumed him, that defined him, that shaped him, and bearing in mind his huge distaste for the business of music, if that fact is true then in many ways, justice on Steve Marriott's life has been beautifully served.

Chapter Twenty-two

All Or Nothing

Stewardess comes over, remonstrates yet again with the arguing couple.

'Sir, madam,' she angrily hisses, 'please, for the last time, can you keep your voices down. You're upsetting all the other passengers.'

It is Friday, the 19th of April, 1991. Steve Marriott and his third wife, Toni, are flying back to England. They are not a happy couple. Since they boarded the plane they have done nothing but argue. Steve is the instigator, the more aggressive. He won't stop challenging Toni. Even when she has conceded the point, he keeps coming back for more. Today, even his clothes are argumentative. Steve is wearing a silver mohair suit, red shirt, red shoes.

Toni is dressed in jeans, a baggy jumper. Her simple look in no way reflects her state of mind. Although her feisty nature can't help retaliating to Marriott's constant taunting of her, in truth she is scared out of her mind. Melvin is sitting next to her. Not her husband, the man she absolutely adores, but vicious spiteful Melvin who won't stop baiting her in his loud threatening voice.

No wonder their fellow passengers have complained to the stewardess.

'He was total hell and I couldn't cope with it,' she says. 'It was such a long and tiresome journey.'

The couple order drink after drink and the bickering never stops.

Waiting for them at Heathrow Airport is Steve's friend, Phil Anthony who had briefly played guitar with Steve in his DT's group. For the last two and a half months, Phil has been looking after their home, Sextons in Arkesden. Unfortunately, in the couple's absence, the house has been burgled, the telly and guitars, including Marriott's favourite Epiphone, removed.

Phil had phoned Marriott in America, told him about the break in. By not being in the house that night, Phil knew that suspicion about the robbery would naturally fall upon his shoulders. But when he first saw the couple come through customs round about midday, he knew straight away that something else was afoot.

'When Steve first arrived at Heathrow,' Anthony recalls, 'he appeared agitated. There was definitely an atmosphere between him and Toni. We had a quick chat. I went away to fetch my car and we arranged to meet in the bar at the airport. After just one drink we loaded up the car and set off for home.'

Tired from the alcohol and jet lag, Toni laid out on the back seat, tried to succumb to sleep. Marriott sat in the front, energetic as ever. He had with him a pack of cigarettes that he had been forced to buy at the airport as no one there served his preferred pouches of tobacco. As the car starts to travel through lush English landscapes, he tells Phil how glad he is to be home, away from LA, the shithole. He points at the flashing scenery, the colours, the shapes and comments on how beautiful it all is. Marvellous.

Then he begins talking about his plans to form a band. He knows who he wants already. Jim Leverton on bass and Kofi Baker on drums. He turns to Phil. You can join as well, he tells him. He already has the band's name. He will call them, 'I Should Coco.'

The men laugh. Toni wakes up but as soon as she speaks Marriott viciously snaps at her.

'Every time she would say something, he would shout her down,' Anthony says.

Their first stop is Phil's house in Old Harlow. There, they drink a cup of tea and then Steve announces he wants to check up on his narrowboat which is docked in nearby Sawbridgeworth. The group leave the house and drive to the river. They check the boat, return to the car. Steve says he is anxious to get home. He wants to survey the damage caused by the burglary, see what has been left him.

They set off, arriving in Arkesden at about five that afternoon. Phil doesn't go into the house.

'I left Steve and Toni at his house,' Phil says. 'They were both knackered, pissed and tired. I presumed that's where they would have stayed for the evening. I was wrong.'

Within a minute of Phil's departure, Steve turns into Melvin again.

'He went beserk,' Toni says, 'and smashed up the telephone and anything else to hand. I was so frightened. I could not handle it.'

Salvation arrives in the form of a mutual friend, Ray Newcomb. Ray is a car dealer from a nearby village called Little Hallingbury. He knows the couple are due back today, has popped round to see if they are home yet. His arrival temporarily stops Melvin in his tracks but Ray can't help being overwhelmed by the awful tension, the dark mood between Steve and Toni.

In an attempt to calm them down, he invites the couple out for a meal, suggests they eat at one of Steve's favourite restaurants, The Straw Hat in Sawbridgeworth.

The couple agree to go and Ray drives to the venue.

On being seated, Marriott orders his favourite meal, roast lamb with mint sauce, and several bottles of wine. The food and drink do not help.

'It was a strained atmosphere,' Newcomb says. 'All evening, Steve was being particularly aggressive towards Toni. I can't remember what the arguments were about but it was really loud. Members of the staff were continually asking them to cool it for the sake of the other customers. By the end of the evening they were both out on their feet.'

Ray, now fearful of leaving the couple alone, insists they accompany him to his temporary home, promoter Bryan Shaw's house in Ongar, Essex.

Bryan will be there, so might some other things.

Steve and Toni think it a good idea.

They get into Ray's car, drive to Ongar, arriving at the house around 12.30. Shaw opens the front door. He welcomes them and having taken their coats, shows them the spare bedroom which is located upstairs. Exhausted now, Steve and Toni decide to say their good nights.

Ray and Phil stay downstairs, drinking. From above, they can hear Marriott's raised angry voice. At about 1.30am, they then hear a door open and footsteps coming down the stairs. It is Marriott. He has decided to go home. Could they call him a cab?

Both men are not at all worried by this turn of events. With the couple now separated, they can sleep off the argument, meet up in the morning, fresh and sober. A cab is called.

'Toni was asleep in the bed; Newcomb remembers. 'She was totally unaware of Steve leaving the house to make the journey home alone.'

The car arrives and quickly. Steve says his goodbyes, goes out and gets in the cab, instructs the driver to take him to his house in Arkesden. On arrival, he pays the driver, steps out of the car, walks to his house, unlocks his front door, steps into the hallway, turns and slams the door shut.

He has about an hour left to live and this is the last time that Stephen Peter Marriott will ever find his way home.

‡ ‡ ‡

At about six-thirty on the morning of the 21st of April, 1991, a passing motorist saw the top half of Steve Marriott's house ablaze. Using the phone box next door to the blazing house he frantically called the fire brigade and then started hammering on the doors of all the nearby houses.

Within minutes, four fire engines arrive. A group of firemen leap out, pull out water hoses and douse the fire from outside. Having made the building safe, they enter the house through the back door. As they do one of them feels his stomach drop. It is obvious to Assistant Divisional Fire Officer, Keith Dunatis that the house belongs to a musician. The memorabilia, the guitars, the pictures of rock stars on the walls, tells him so.

Dunatis knows that the only musician who lived in these parts was someone he greatly admired, whose records he had once bought and loved – Steve Marriott.

'When we arrived, there was smoke pouring out of the building and the flames were really fierce,' Dunatis told the *News Of The World*. 'We had to break in through the back door. When we got in the house we could see tons of pictures of rock stars on the wall. I especially noticed a print of guitarist, Ronnie Wood. All those '60s people, they were his colleagues in the business and my idols.

'It was a tough fight getting upstairs. We searched the bedroom areas and it was very hot – we knew immediately that no one could have survived the fire. We began to feel our way around the walls and discovered him lying on the floor in between the bed and the wall. I would say he had been in bed and tried to escape. As soon as I saw the body clearly I knew who it was.

'I used to be a fan – it's difficult to put my feelings into words. The scene was horrific in that corner of the room. I saw him lying there and thought what a pity it all was. I deal with many fires but this one was like walking down memory lane. We managed to salvage all his guitars and musical equipment. I feel a bit upset – all the firemen do. It was like seeing part of our lives gone forever.'

No one can say for certain what triggered the fire that terrible night, nor how Marriott reacted. The best explanation is that Marriott had fallen asleep with a cigarette in his hand.

He was, after all, absolutely exhausted. He had been on the go for over twenty-four hours in which time he had flown the Atlantic, downed huge amounts of alcohol and, as they would later discover, taken valium and cocaine at some point during the day.

By the time he got home to Arkesden, his mind would have been in no man's land. Thus crashing out onto the bed with a lighted cigarette and then instantly falling asleep, is the most likely scenario. The tragedy is that if he had been able to secure his normal smoking tobacco then the fire which took him would probably never have started. Roll up cigarettes contain no chemicals. If Marriott had fallen asleep with one in his hand it would have just gone out without causing any significant damage

Later enquiries would suggest that after the fire began, Marriott woke up confused after breathing in an unhealthy amount of smoke. The fumes had disorientated him, his bearings gone, and he tried to escape through the door on his right, not his left. He has gone the wrong way, yanked open the storage cupboard door, not the bedroom door. Before he could rectify his mistake, the smoke overwhelmed him.

His body was formally identified using dental records at the Herts and Essex Hospital, Bishops Stortford. Steve Marriott had died from carbon monoxide poisoning due to smoke inhalation. It is pretty certain that by the time the fire got to him he had already passed away. He was forty-four years old.

‡ ‡ ‡

Kay Marriott, the mother, recalling the events of Saturday, April 21st, 1991:

'I'd just washed my hair. I was working in the Good Intent, a pub just down the road. And I was going in. I did a Saturday morning. I expect it was about half past nine when the phone rang. It was Toni, just screaming on the phone, "He's dead, he's dead." When I got it out of her I just went hysterical. And Bill's picked up the phone and he's sobbing and Toni said she was coming over. Somebody was going to bring her over. I think Ray brought her over. And I rang up the pub and I said, "I can't come into work." And they said, "Oh, are you not well.?" I said, "No, my Steve's just died."

Kay Marriott, the sister, remembering the same day:

'It was a Saturday morning and it would have been my birthday on the Monday. And for once Joseph [her new husband] was taking me out to buy me a birthday present. And so I was all excited. I was really looking forward to the day. Getting Lucy dressed, who was what, two-years-old. And he answered the phone. Joseph answered the phone.

'My mum told him. She said, "Please, be gentle with her, it's going to kill her." Which it very nearly did. I had actually thought, "Oh I'll speak to Steve today or see him." Yeah. And well, it was awful. And so of course we just got in the car and went over to mum's and that was it really. It's still a nightmare.'

Jenny Rylance, Steve's first wife: 'Bobbi Korner, Alexis's widow, heard about it on the radio and she called me. I also got a phone call from June Bolan. Because I hadn't seen him for such a long time it took a long while to register. I was deeply saddened by the news. I had always assumed that we would meet up again and work things through.'

Pam Marriott, Steve's second wife. 'I was in the civil reserve for five years and was at Desert Storm. I was actually the first civilian woman to go into Kuwait and I had just got back. There was a party at a friend's house that night. I was at this party and we were watching a boxing match on cable TV when I had an asthma attack. I don't have asthma but I couldn't breathe. It felt like I was choking to death. 'Next morning I got the call and realised I had had the attack at exactly the same time that Steve died. There's no doubt in my mind that he came and touched me.

'Toby had a soccer match that day and I was trying to get to him before he heard the news. He played the game and then I was able to tell him before the news broke on the radio. It's difficult for a fifteen-year-old boy to hear that his father is dead. He was distraught, took it very hard. He'd been planning to visit his father in the summer and he had been rehearsing about three hours a day on his guitar. He really couldn't wait to surprise his dad with how good he was. He was so disappointed that he never got to play guitar with his dad. Then it turned to anger.'

Toni Marriott, Steve's third wife:

'Our mate Ray had gone to work early Saturday morning at his car showroom near our Arkesden home. He saw all the fire engines and police cars in the area and went to investigate. He was horrified to find out that it was Steve that had been burnt to death. Ray phoned Bryan at his Ongar home where I was staying and broke the horrific news to him. They now had the ordeal of telling me.

'Bryan drove me to Ray's garage and they took me in the office. They said they had something to tell me. I sensed that something was horribly wrong. They said, "I don't know how to tell you this but Steve's dead." I thought they meant a mate of ours, a fat geezer with diabetes. I just said, "Oh no, how's Maria his wife?"

'Ray said, "No, Steve Marriott is dead." I couldn't register what he was saying. I said, "What do you mean?" and he replied, "He's dead, honey. He's dead." I just looked at them and said, "You mean my Steve, my husband? You're fucking sick, you are." He just said, "I swear to God he's dead. He died in a housefire." I just lost the plot. I sprang out of my seat and went beserk. I had to be taken to our local doctor to be sedated. I was kicking the shit out of all these motors and punching everything in sight. It took three people to hold me down. Even to this day, I've never been able to get my head around it.'

Tonya Elias, Steve's first daughter:

'He died shortly after my visit to him. I was seven-years-old and had come down with my mother. We had been staying with my sister Mollie and her mother, Manon, having a great time. We went to my aunt's house and awaited his arrival. I remember clear as day exactly what he was wearing and what I was feeling. He walked in wearing green socks with multiple coloured polkadots. He hiked his trousers up quite high, revealing these socks. He also walked [jokingly] with his chest sticking out and had large shades on.

'I remember he got down on his knees and said to me, "Hello love." We then just hugged for what had to be at least five minutes. We went off to a boat house where he taught me to play a song on the keyboard, which I can still play. We hung out there for a while and then went off to a pub. I sat in his lap the whole time.

'The part that always stays in my mind is the goodbye. Everyone else was talking near the car as we were playing and talking on the grass. He held me up in the air while laying on his back telling me how much he loved me and to take care of mom and myself. Little did we know it would be our final goodbye.

'A few months later we got the call about the blaze. I guess you could say I didn't get much sleep that night.'

Jim Leverton, bass player: 'I was home in bed and I got the call from Toni's brother, John Poulton. If at any point from when I started working with Steve, the phone had rung and somebody said, Steve Marriott is dead, I wouldn't have been at all surprised. It was the horrific circumstances that I can't bear to think about. He was as sharp as a razor, his wit was fantastic, One on one he was kind, generous and understanding. But in a crowd, he was a complete arsehole. I don't think that being a star at seventeen years old helped him as a human being.'

Jerry Shirley, drummer: 'He was certainly the most talented person I ever worked with. He was like a brother to me and I was devastated when he died. He always lived on the edge and I was always waiting for a phone call to say that he had died but I never dreamed it would be under those circumstances. He's never got the credit he deserves. He should be in the rock'n'roll hall of fame because he was the greatest white soul singer that England ever produced. I'm certain that if you caught the likes of Rod Stewart and Paul Rodgers in a private moment and asked them who was the main man, they would say, Steve Marriott.'

Chapter Twenty-three

The Big Train Stop

The funeral took place on Tuesday 30th of April 1991. The weather was terrible, the wind howling into people's faces, the rain hurling itself down to the ground from a sky that would stay ominously black all day, as if the Gods themselves had been angered by this senseless loss.

The conditions were so bad that when Kay Marriott arrived at the Great Parndon Crematorium in Harlow, Essex, and stepped out of the car with her daughter Kay and Toni, she thought she saw streaks of lightning flash across the sky. She was wrong. The angry lights were the photographer's flashbulbs firing off in her face.

'My daughter and daughter in law both said, "For God's sake, can't you leave him alone. Let him rest." It was then that I realised it was the flash from all the photographers. I said, "Well, this is his last show. Let him have a good send off."

Mother still knew best.

Steve Marriott's coffin was removed from the black hearse in front of them and the three women followed it into the building. They were watched by hundreds of people. Present were the press, the TV cameras, the locals, even a group of young Mods who tuned up on their scooters to pay their respects. It was the largest turn out the cemetery had ever seen.

Numerous wreaths had been received, one from Rod Stewart and his wife Rachel which read, 'In deepest sympathy,' one from Dave Gilmour of the Pink Floyd, one from Chas and Dave, one from daughter Mollie which read, 'Dear Daddy. Our hearts will always be linked together. I love you, Mollie.' Kenney Jones came, so did PP Arnold, actor Terence Stamp, Jerry Shirley, Greg Ridley. Jenny Rylance was there, so was Manon. Pam and Toby were in America. Nothing was heard from

Ronnie Lane or Ian McLagan.

As the congregation came into the building, Ray Charles's 'Drown In My Own Tears,' came through the speakers. The crowd settled, the hush arrived, the service began. Vicar Duncan McGuffie (and imagine what Steve would have done with that surname) paid tribute. He had spent hours with Bill and Kay and Toni trying to get a grip on the man's character. He said, 'I didn't know Steve Marriott but I have heard a good deal of good things about him. He was known for his humour, wit, inventiveness, kindness and generosity.'

After his speech, he stepped away from the lectern and the song, 'Saylarvee' from the Small Faces' *Playmates* album played.

Not long after it had finished, Steve Marriott's coffin started moving towards the wall. Within a minute, the small doors on the wall shut.

He had gone forever.

Then, it happened. 'All Or Nothing,' began playing through the tiny speakers and as its spiky little guitar riff unfurled itself, bringing back such sweet memories, the crowd as one broke down.

'I thought you'd listen to my reasoning....'

Kenney Jones: 'I can only remember all the fun Steve and I had. But hearing 'All Or Nothing,' during the service broke me up.'

'But now I see you have the other point of view...'

Rick Wills: 'When we walked into the crematorium and saw this tiny white coffin I just couldn't believe that was Steve in there. This guy that had always been so full of life and had given such a lot to the world musically, had gone. I coped well until the end of the service and then they played, 'All Or Nothing.' That song pretty much summed up Steve's life perfectly. The words say it all.'

'Try to make you see, how it's got to be...'

'At that point I lost my composure and just broke down and cried. It brought it all home to me just how stupid all this drugs and drink abuse could be. Steve was given an exceptional talent and it had all gone wrong for him. He was dead way before his time. He should still be out onstage giving it his all.'

'And it's, all or nothing, all or nothing, all or nothing,

For me...'

‡ ‡ ‡

In July, the coroner published his report, recorded a verdict of accidental death. An examination of Steve Marriott's blood revealed quantities of valium, alcohol and cocaine.

Toni explained the valium. 'He always took them when he flew because he was terrified of flying,' she told the local paper, 'He was not into drugs in a big way. He liked to drink more than anything else.'

As for the cocaine, my guess is that right up until his dying day, Steve Marriott was still leading everyone a merry little dance.

A force such as Steve Marriott could never leave this earth quietly. That would be impossible.

The day before the funeral, his panama hat which had hung on the wall in Kay Marriott's house for years inexplicably fell to the ground. The day after the funeral, Kay and Bill are quietly sitting in their lounge, lost in the sadness and helplessness of it all when their unhappy mood is angrily broken by the framed photograph of Steve they keep on the piano, suddenly falling onto the floor and smashing into bits.

The weather outside was filthy. No windows or doors were open. There were no draughts anywhere.

A few days later, he was still hovering close. Kay, Bill and Bill's brother settled down one night to play the card game, Newmarket.

If Steve had been present he would have made up the foursome. He liked such card games. 'Because there were only three of us, we needed to take a complete set out,' Kay Marriott explains. 'Bill took out all the clubs. I said, 'No, leave the clubs in, take out the spades.' But it was too late, we played without the clubs.

'At the end of the evening the cards we had played with were shuffled and put back in the box. The clubs that we didn't use were left in a neat pile next to the box. The next day we came down to find all the spades outside the box and all the clubs put back with the remaining cards. There was only one explanation – it was Steve playing games.'

Stephen Peter Marriott – as in life, so in death.

Aftermath

Still they come to 22, Westmoreland Terrace, the boys and the girls with their cameras and love, to stand outside the black door, to imagine Stevie Marriott and his Small Faces bouncing out of the black front door, full of colour and life and smiles, waving only to them.

Thirty-seven years after he moved out of this house, Steve Marriott still holds a sizeable chunk of the public consciousness. He once told his second wife, Pam, 'When I'm dead, that's when I'll be famous.' He was wrong. Since his passing, he is yet to achieve the level of stardom that Humble Pie afforded him.

Yet instinctively he knew his work would live on, take hold after his passing.

As of writing (October 2003), the last album to be released bearing his name was Castle Music's *The Small Faces – Ultimate Collection*. It sold 64,000 copies, went top thirty. To promote it, Mac and Kenney, the remaining band members spent two hours at HMV on Oxford Street signing autographs. As we all know, 64,000 Small Faces fans can't be wrong.

Some would argue that these impressive facts actually bear witness to the shabby state of contemporary music. They may be right. There are few contemporary bands creating music as potent and as inventive as the Small Faces did. But there is also another different story, one of a group actually gaining more respect as the years pass.

Since the 1990s, the Small Faces reputation as a key band has grown enormously, helped by a mini industry dedicated to examining and celebrating the '60s, the decade they contributed so strongly to.

These include a proliferation of labels re-issuing its music and a rash of music publications such as *Mojo*, *Uncut* and *The Word* running in-depth articles on its history. Book companies have published a slew of books covering the times, TV has weighed in with numerous documentaries. As the spotlight has increased in its intensity, the Small Faces music is now seen in a far deeper critical light, their position in the scheme of things a lot higher than before

In retrospect, this process should not surprise us too much. After all, the group's music and look is timeless and Mod, the source they sprang from, is Britain's most enduring youth cult. Every time it takes on another member it is odds on that the Small Faces will appear somewhere in that person's journey. They always do.

Another reason for their continued presence may be traced back to 1966, the day the The Small Faces played the Atlanta club in Woking, Surrey. As they did so, at nearby Stanley Road lived an eight-year old boy enjoying an idyllic working class childhood.

Like Steve Marriott at that age, Paul Weller was transfixed by music. Music made life magical, wonderful, took him out of the world and deep into his own imagination.

He formed his first band, age 14 in 1972. Four years later he was a top 20 artist. By 1979, his band The Jam were one of the biggest in the land. Musically, Weller aimed high. Through his songs, he sought to enter the national consciousness, capture society's prevailing mood.

Steve Marriott played a notable part in the realisation of his dream. The two had much in common. Working class, brought up in a tight-knit family, energetic, impatient, tremendous lovers of American R&B, perfectionists, blunt, temperamental, clothes obsessed.

The real difference was age. Marriott grew up in the Fifties, became a significant part of the Sixties when Weller was just a boy. By the time Weller had reached his teens, the Sixties was gone, the party finished.

As most contemporary music bored him, he soon found his way back to there, became a Mod. He had loved Small Faces records as a child but in his early twenties they played a much more significant role in his life.

In fact, by the start of the '80s, Weller was so heavily reflecting Steve Marriott's '60s style that even the man himself couldn't help notice.

Asked for his view on the boy wonder, Marriott told the *NME* in 1984, 'Look, I'll be honest with you. I've only seen The Jam once on a video and I thought it reminded me of me in the old days. So for me to say that – sure, I like me. [Laughs] It's not like I can really judge them. They looked exactly like we did and played similarly. At the same time, I admire their taste. [Laughs].'

Musically, Marriott had his most influence on Weller in The Jam's later years – the period that saw The Jam's leader returning the band to their original R&B roots. The Jam not only covered 'Get Yourself Together,' but looked to records such as 'Don't Burst My Bubble' to seek the best way forward.

With the advent of his solo career in the early '90s, Weller again turned to the Small Faces for inspiration. Hear his song 'Out Of The Sinking,' for proof. Look at how singer Carleen Anderson, once of the Young Disciples, became his PP Arnold – she turning up on his records, Weller writing and producing for her.

Ironically, he was playing the Brixton Academy on the day of Marriott's death. It was the end of a solo tour and as Marriott's people grieved his loss, Weller walked out onstage, said 'This one's for Steve,' and opened his show with a version of 'Tin Soldier,' a song he had been playing for weeks.

In the audience that night was one Noel Gallagher.

Noel was a member of the Stone Roses-obsessed generation that had grown up in the '80s despising the pop music of their times. Like Weller previously, Noel turned backwards, found inspiration in the decade of magic. One of the names he found there was Steve Marriott.

When the first ever Small Faces biography, *The Young Mods' Forgotten Story*, was published, the back cover carried tributes from Primal Scream, Oasis, Blur, Ride and Paul Weller.

That fact alone tells us that if Steve had managed to keep himself together, he would not have been able to move for requests to appear on people's albums. Weller, Ocean Colour Scene, Oasis and The Scream would have been the first in line. Many others would have followed.

All would have sought to have located in him his great talent for creating records of such power and grace.

And it wasn't just the musicians the man's talent was affecting. In 1994, Steve Chamberlain and Stuart Wright started *The Darlings Of The Wapping Wharf*, a fanzine dedicated to the Small Faces. They ran it for four issues and then gave up due to financial reasons.

The fanzine was taken over by one of their contributors, John Hellier. He turned it glossy and took its circulation quickly from 100 to a 1,000. It now reaches five thousand people. Every year, 600 fans converge on the Ruskin Arms for the annual Small Faces convention, organised by John and close friend, Dean Powell.

In May 1996 the Small Faces were awarded the prestigious Ivor Novello "Lifetime achievement" award at the Grosvenor Park hotel on London's Park Lane. Steve's award was presented to his mum, Kay, and sits proudly in the living room of the house that Steve bought for her in Sawbridgeworth, Hertfordshire.

No doubt these same people are aware of the two biographies and two TV documentaries that have appeared, helping change the band's fortunes and standing. 1999 saw the release of the US documentary *The Life and Times of Steve Marriott*, produced by Gary Katz along with *Wapping Wharf*'s John Hellier.

On the 20th April 2001, John Hellier, in conjunction with Chris France and Toni Marriott, staged a memorial concert for Mod legend Marriott at the London Astoria. The main man had died ten years ago to the day and the event was sold out six weeks before. It attracted a star-studded cast that included Paul Weller, Noel Gallagher and Humble Pie, as well as the two remaining Small Faces, Kenney Jones and Ian McLagan. The concert was filmed and recorded for CD and DVD.

Meanwhile, the band remain a staple of compilation companies everywhere prompting us to think that maybe Marriott would have finally received at least some of the financial rewards that were taken from him, the money he desired towards the end of his life to secure his future.

Even the cinema was not immune to his appeal. In August 2003, London's National Film Theatre hosted a season of '60s related films under the banner of The Cool World. One night was given over to Steve Marriott and The Small Faces.

The night began with clips from his work as a child actor. Then came the band's appearance on *Dateline Diamonds*, their wonderful performance on the 1966 *Morecambe and Wise Show*, videos of 'Itchycoo Park,' and 'Get Yourself Together,' and 'Lazy Sunday,' their explosive rendition of 'Ogden's' on *Colour Me Pop*, a Len Brown directed documentary, and to end, footage from Bill Marriott's home movies.

In the audience that night sat Steve's mother and sister. Bill, his father had passed away in 1996. After every film clip, the audience applauded, filled that darkened room with huge love and respect. It was such a special sound.

Afterwards, Kay Marriott sat in the Green Room with her daughter Kay and grandson, Stephen. She looked tired, happy but so wistful. All this love and recognition for her son, and he wasn't there to experience it. So sad.

Until mother and son met again, she knew life would never be complete, so best to try and put things aside, get on with things best she can.

Yesterday is gone now but not tomorrow.

Toby Marriott on stage in 2001   (Sarah Robinson)

Afterword

Toby Marriott, Steve's only son: 'Well, for the last five years I've been pretty screwed up with drink and drug problems. During that time I didn't even want to play. But after rehab I'm back and have been playing with a local Mod band, Tender Idols. When I was in England a while back I was expected to live up to dad's image, you know go to the pub and drink twenty pints, the whole sex, drugs and rock'n' roll bit.

'I've got the passion back now. I got to hang out with Keith Richards and Woody last November and that was great. An old manager of mine called them up and they invited me to a gig. Keith's personal manager came and got me and I thought it would be a little handshake and that's it. But they invited me back to their room and I spent a few hours with them.

'They idolised dad. We spoke about dad's audition for The Stones. Anyway, I knew a lot of old pub songs that I'd heard dad sing and the three of us ended up singing those together. They were both great guys and spending time with them spurred me on to keep going. If those guys and people like my dad don't make you do it, no-one will.'

The authors with Kay Marriott, PH on the left, JH on the right

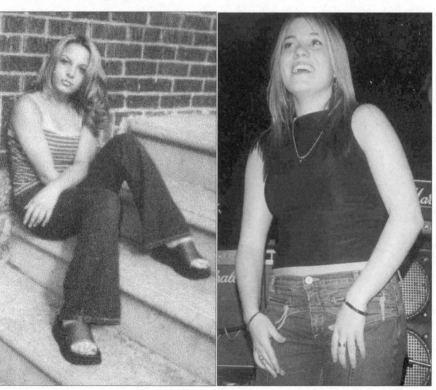

Steve's daughters Tonya (2001, Terri Elias) *and, on the right, Mollie* (2002, John Hellier)

Bibliography

Ackroyd, Peter *London* (Vintage Books 2000)

Bacon, Tony *London Live* (Balafon 1999)

Badman, Keith Rawlings, Terry et al *Quite Naturally* (Complete Music 1997)

Bowman, Rob *Soulsville USA* (Books With Attitude 1997)

Cohn, Nik *Ball The Wall* (Picador 1989)

Cox, Jane *East End Life and Traditions* (Weidenfeld and Nicholson 2000)

Dannen, Fredric *Hit Men* (Helter Skelter, 2003)

Gorman, Paul *The Look* (Sanctuary 2001)

Green, Jonathan *All Dressed Up* (Jonathan Cape 1998)

Guralnick, Peter *Sweet Soul Music* (Penguin 1986)

Hellier, John [Ed] *The Darlings of Wapping Wharf Fanzine 1 – 25*

Hewitt, Paolo *The Young Mods' Forgotten Story* (Acid Jazz 1994)

Jasper, Tony *The Top Twenty Book* (Blandford 1994)

Larkin, Colin [Ed] *Virgin Encyclopedia of the Sixties* (Virgin Books 1997)

Larkin, Colin [Ed] *Virgin Encyclopedia of the Seventies* (Virgin Books 1997)

Lentz, Graham *The Influential Factor* (GEL publishing 2002)

Levin, Bernard *Run It Down The Flagpole* (Atheneum 1971)

Lewis, Peter *The Fifties* (Book Club Associates 1978)

Loog Oldham, Andrew *Stoned* (Secker and Warburg 2000)

McLagan, Ian *All The Rage* (Sidgwick and Jackson 1998)

Marwick, Arthur *The Sixties* (Oxford University Press 1998)

Muise, Dan *Gallagher, Marriott, Derringer and Trower* (Hal Leonard 2002)

O'Neill, Gilda *My East End* (Penguin 2000)

Ritson, Mike and Russell, Stuart *The In Crowd* (Be Cool Books 1999)

Russo, Gus *The Outfit* (Bloomsbury 2001)

Shapiro, Harry *Alexis Korner* (Bloomsbury 1996)

Twelker, Uli and Schmitt, Roland *Happy Boys Happy* (Sanctuary 1993)

'Darlings of Wapping Wharf Laundrette', the ultimate Small Faces and related glossy magazine.

For a free sample copy contact:
John Hellier,
7, Waterdene Mews, Canvey Island, Essex, SS8 9YP
jjhellier@aol.com
www.wappingwharf.com

Paolo Hewitt interviewing Steve Marriott for NME in October 1984   *(Bleddyn Butcher)*

John Hellier with Steve Marriott in 1985   *(Jim Leverton)*

Discography

Early Steve Marriott

Title	Label	Catalogue Number	Format	Release Date	Comments
OLIVER	WORLD RECORD CLUB	Tp151	LP	1960	West end soundtrack. Steve sings lead on three tracks – "Consider yourself", "Be back soon" and "I'd do anything
GIVE HER MY REGARDS/ IMAGINARY LOVE	DECCA	F11619	7" single	1963	Buddy Holly sound alike single, but much better "b" side
MOVE IT	UNKNOWN	Unknown	7" single	Late 1963 Unconfirmed release. Allegedly in Malaysia	Steve Marriott and the Frantics. Band members confirm recording and a release in the Far East, but no copies have surfaced
I CRIED	DECCA	None	7" single	March 1964	Record Mirror report it as the second Steve Marriott single. No demos exist
YOU REALLY GOT ME/ MONEY, MONEY	WORLD ARTISTS	Wa 1032 USA	7" single	Oct 1964	Attempt to hit the US market before the Kinks did
TELL ME/ MAYBE	DECCA	F121	7" single	Feb 1965	Unconfirmed. Test pressings exist
HARD UP HEROES	DECCA	DPA 3009/10	2 x LP	1974	Various Artists. Includes "Give Her My Regards"
POP INSIDE THE SIXTIES	SEE FOR MILES	SEECD 386	CD	Unknown	Various Artists. Includes "Give her my regards"
DADDY COME ON HOME VOLUME 9'	DIG THE FUZZ RECORDS	1559	LP	Unknown	Includes the Moments 'Money, Money'
GREAT SONGS FROM GREAT SHOWS VOLUME 2	WORLD RECORD CLUB	TP 711	LP	Unknown	Includes "Consider Yourself" from Oliver

Early Small Faces

Title	Label	Catalogue Number	Format	Release Date	Comments
WHATCHA GONNA DO ABOUT IT? / WHATS A MATTER, BABY?	DECCA	F12208	7" Single	AUG 1965	
I'VE GOT MINE/ IT'S TOO LATE	DECCA	F12276	7" Single	NOV 1965	
SHA-LA-LA-LA-LEE/ GROW YOUR OWN	DECCA	F12317	7" Single	JAN 1966	
HEY GIRL/ ALMOST GROWN	DECCA	F1239	7" Single	MAY 1966	
ALL OR NOTHING/ UNDERSTANDING	DECCA	F1247	7" Single	AUG 1966	
MY MINDS EYE/ I CAN'T DANCE WITH YOU	DECCA	F12500	7" Single	NOV 1966	
I CAN'T MAKE IT/ JUST PASSING	DECCA	F12565	7" Single	MAR 1967	
PATTERNS/ E TOO D	DECCA	F12619		MAY 1967	
HERE COMES THE NICE/ TALK TO YOU	IMMEDIATE	IM 050	7" Single	JUN 1967	

Title	Label	Catalogue Number	Format	Release Date	Comments
ITCHYCOO PARK/ I'M ONLY DREAMING	IMMEDIATE	IM 052	7" Single	AUG 1967	
TIN SOLDIER/ I FEEL MUCH BETTER	IMMEDIATE	IM 062	7" Single	DEC 1967	
LAZY SUNDAY/ ROLLIN' OVER	IMMEDIATE	IM064	7" Single	APR 1968	
THE UNIVERSAL/ DONKEY RIDES, A PENNY, A GLASS	IMMEDIATE	IM069	7" Single	JUL 1968	
AFTERGLOW (OF YOUR LOVE), WHAM BAM, THANKYOU MAM	IMMEDIATE	IM 077	7" Single	MAR 1969	
MAD JOHN/ THE JOURNEY	IMMEDIATE	ZS7 5012	7" Single	1968	USA AND AUSTRALIA

Small Faces Reissue singles and Eps

Title	Label	Catalogue Number	Release	Format	Comments
WHATCHA GONNA DO ABOUT IT/ WHATS A MATTER BABY/ DONT STOP WHAT / YOURE DOING/ COME ON CHILDREN	DECCA	457091	FRANCE 1966	EP	LATER RE-ISSUED ON EVA
SHA LA-LA-LA-LEE/ GROW YOUR OWN/ IT'S TOO LATE/ I'VE GOT MINE	DECCA	SDGE 81127	FRANCE 1966 SPAIN, PORTUGAL	EP	LATER RE-ISSUED ON EVA
SHA LA LA LA LEE/ WHATCHA GONNA DO ABOUT IT/ ALL OR NOTHING	DECCA	F13727	NEW ZEALAND 1966	EP	
ALL OR NOTHING/ UNDERSTANDING/ HEY GIRL/ ALMOST GROWN	DECCA	457.123M	FRANCE 1966	EP	
HEY GIRL/ ALMOST GROWN/ ITS TOO LATE/ E TOO D	DECCA	SDGE 81162	SPAIN 1966	EP	
SHA LA-LA-LA-LEE/ GROW YOUR OWN/ WHATCHA GONNA DO ABOUT IT/ WHATS A MATTER BABY	DECCA	DX 2396	TURKEY/ GERMANY 1966	EP	
SHA LA-LA-LA-LEE/ WHATCHA GONNA DO ABOUT IT/ I'VE GOT MINE/ HEY GIRL	DECCA	DFEA 7538	AUSTRALIA 1967	EP	
MY MINDS EYE/ I CAN'T DANCE WITH YOU/ SHAKE/ ONE NIGHT STAND	DECCA	457133	FRANCE 1967	EP	LATER RE-ISSUED ON EVA
I CANT MAKE IT/ YOU'D BETTER BELIEVE IT/ JUST PASSING/ YOU NEED LOVING	DECCA	457.146	FRANCE 1967	EP	
HERE COMES THE NICE/ BECOME LIKE YOU/ TALK TO YOU/ GET YOURSELF TOGETHER	COLUMBIA	ESRF 1876	FRANCE 1967	EP	
HERE COMES THE NICE! TALK TO YOU/ ITCHYCOO PARK/ IM ONLY DREAMING	IMMEDIATE	LSE 6034	SPAIN 1967	EP	
ALBUM SAMPLER	IMMEDIATE	AS1	1967	7"	RADIO ALBUM SAMPLER FOR FIRST IMMEDIATE ALBUM

Title	Label	Catalogue Number	Release	Format	Comments
ITCHYCOO PARK/ I'M ONLY DREAMING/ GREEN CIRCLES/ EDDIE'S DREAMING	COLUMBIA	ESRF 1882	FRANCE 1967	EP	LATER RE-ISSUED ON JET RECORDS
GET YOURSELF TOGETHER/ TALK TO YOU/ EDDIE'S DREAMING/ HAVE YOU EVER SEEN ME	TK	TK193	THAILAND 1967	EP	
ITCHYCOO PARK/ GREEN CIRCLES	STATESIDE	K551029	SWEDEN 1967	7" SINGLE	
ITCHYCOO PARK/ GREEN CIRCLES	COLUMBIA	CF117	FRANCE 1967	7" SINGLE	
ITCHYCOO PARK/ I'M ONLY DREAMING/ GREEN CIRCLES/ EDDIE'S DREAMING	ODEON	333.3558	URUGUAY 1967	EP	
ITCHYCOO PARK/ I'M ONLY DREAMING/ HERE COMES THE NICE/ TALK TO YOU	STATESIDE	LSE 6034	SPAIN 1967	EP	
ITCHYCOO PARK/ I'M ONLY DREAMING/ HERE COMES THE NICE/ TALK TO YOU	EMI	NONE	UK 1967	ACETATE	EMIDISC. ACETATES DO EXIST
ITCHYCOO PARK/ I'M ONLY DREAMING/ HERE COMES THE NICE/ TALK TO YOU	STATESIDE	PSE 512	PORTUGAL 1967	EP	
TIN SOLDIER/ HERE COMES THE NICE/ ITCHYCOO PARK/ I'M ONLY DREAMING	EMI/IMMEDIATE	EPOC 40056	ISRAEL 1967	EP	
TIN SOLDIER/ TALK TO YOU/ HERE COMES THE NICE/ ITCHYCOO PARK	IMMEDIATE	IME P1001	AUSTRALIA 1967	EP	
TIN SOLDIER/ TALK TO YOU/ HERE COMES THE NICE/ ITCHYCOO PARK	STATESIDE	CSEP 1001	SINGAPORE 1967	EP	
MAD JOHN/ THE JOURNEY	IMMEDIATE	Z57 5012	US 1968	7" SINGLE	
MAD JOHN/ THE JOURNEY	IMMEDIATE	IM 856	AUSTRALIA 1968	7" SINGLE	
RUNAWAY /SHAKE	PRIDE	PR 1006	1972	7" SINGLE	
FLY IN THE OINTMENT	NONE	NONE	1973	FLEXI DISC	FREE WITH NME MAGAZINE
LAZY SUNDAY/SONG OF A BAKER	DAFFODIL	DFS 1024	CANADA 1973	7" SINGLE	FIRST RELEASE FROM IMMEDIATE IN CANADA
ITCHYCOO PARK/AUTUMN STONE	DAFFODIL	DFS 1036	CANADA 1973	7" SINGLE	FIRST RELEASE FROM IMMEDIATE IN CANADA
ITCHYCOO PARK/ MY WAY OF GIVING	IMMEDIATE	MS 102	1975	7" SINGLE	SOME HAVE "MY MINDS EYE" ON "B" SIDE
LAZY SUNDAY/ AUTUMN STONE	IMMEDIATE	IMS 701	1975	7" SINGLE	
LAZY SUNDAY/ ODGENS	BELLAPHON	B0220	GERMANY 1975	7" SINGLE	
LAZY SUNDAY/ ROLLIN OVER	CHARLY	BF18462	GERMANY 1975	7" SINGLE	
TIN SOLDIER/ AFTERGLOW	BELLAPHON	B0172	1975	7"	
OGDENS/ MY WAY OF GIVING	BELLAPHON	B0173	1975	7" SINGLE	
ITCHYCOO PARK/ MY WAY OF GIVING	IMMEDIATE/ FESTIVAL	K6391	AUSTRALIA 1976	7" SINGLE	
LAZY SUNDAY/ HAVE YOU EVER SEEN ME	IMMEDIATE	IMS 106	1976	7" SINGLE	

Title	Label	Catalogue Number	Release	Format	Comments
LAZY SUNDAY/ ITCHYCOO PARK	IMMEDIATE/ ARIOLA	104 403 100	GERMANY 1977	7" SINGLE	
SHA LA-LA-LA-LEE/ WHATCHA GONNA DO ABOUT IT	ARIOLA		GERMANY 1977	7" SINGLE	ARIOLA DOUBLE HIT SERIES
ITCHYCOO PARK/ TIN SOLDIER	ARIOLA/ IMMEDIATE	103462	GERMANY 1977	7" SINGLE	DOUBLE HIT SERIES
ALL OR NOTHING/ TIN SOLDIER	ARIOLA	103463	GERMANY 1977	7" SINGLE	DOUBLE HIT SERIES
SHA LA-LA-LA-LEE/ WHATCHA GONNA DO ABOUT IT/ ALL OR NOTHING	DECCA	F1372	1977	MAXI SINGLE	IN SUPPORT OF ROCK ROOTS LP RELEASE
HEY GIRL	DECCA	FR 13864	1979	EP	PLUS TRACKS FROM BOWIE, BYRDS AND DOBIE GRAY
LIVE IN EUROPE 1966	QUISH	QUISH 00	1979	EP	BOOTLEG EP OF 1968 NEWCASTLE CITY HALL
ALL OR NOTHING/ COLLIBOSHER	CHARLY	BF 18494	GERMANY 1980	7" SINGLE	
ALL OR NOTHING/ SHA-LA-LA LA-LEE	BELLAPHON	100700	1980	7" SINGLE	OLDIES SERIES
TIN SOLDIER/ TIN SOLDIER LIVE/RENE	VIRGIN	VS 367	GERMANY 1980	EP	
LAZY SUNDAY/ ROLLIN OVER	IMMEDIATE	IMO64	1982	7" SINGLE	
ALL OR NOTHING/ MY MINDS EYE	OLD GOLD	OG 9343	1983	7" SINGLE	
ITCHYCOO PARK/ HERE COMES THE NICE/ AFTERGLOW (OF YOUR LOVE)	LINE	OLS1105	GERMANY 1983	EP	
SHA LA-LA-LA-LEE/ WHATCHA GONNA DO ABOUT IT	OLD GOLD	OG9344	1983	7" SINGLE	
TIN SOLDIER/ LAZY SUNDAY/ UNIVERSAL	LINE	OLS1092	GERMANY 1983	EP	THE ORIGINAL SERIES
LAZY SUNDAY/ TIN SOLDIER	OLD GOLD	OG 9465	1985	7" SINGLE	
ITCHYCOO PARK/ HERE COMES THE NICE	OLD GOLD	OG 9466	1985	7" SINGLE	
ITCHYCOO PARK/ LAZY SUNDAY/ ALL OR NOTHING/ AUTUMN STONE	ARCHIVE4	TOF 103	1986	12" SINGLE	
LAZY SUNDAY/ AFTERGLOW	BR MUSIC	45210	NETHERLANDS 1986	7" SINGLE	
ITCHYCOO PARK/ HERE COMES THE NICE	BR MUSIC	45211	NETHERLANDS 1986	7" SINGLE	
LAZY SUNDAY/ ITCHYCOO PARK	PERFECT	786005	BELGIUM 1986	7" SINGLE	
ITCHYCOO PARK/LAZY SUNDAY/ ALL OR NOTHING/AUTUMN STONE	CASTLE	CD 3-9	1988	3" CD SINGLE	5000 ONLY, SPECIAL EDITION
TIN SOLDIER/ MY MINDS EYE	BR MUSIC	45209	NETHERLANDS/ GERMANY 1988	7" SINGLE	
ITCHYCOO PARK/ LAZY SUNDAY/ TIN SOLDIER	OLD GOLD	OG 6119	1989	3" CD SINGLE	THE ORIGINAL HIT RECORDINGS
ITCHYCOO PARK	COLLECTABLES	UNKNOWN	1991	CD SINGLE	C/W "HANG ON SLOOPY"
ITCHYCOO PARK/ TIN SOLDIER/ LAZY SUNDAY	DISKY	DISK 4504	1994	CD SINGLE	HIT SINGLES COLLECTABLES
ALL OR NOTHING/ SHA/ WHATCHA GONNA DO ABOUT IT/ HEY GIRL	DERAM	SF SAMP1	1996	4 TRACK PROMO CD	SAMPLER FOR "DECCA ANTHOLOGY"

Title	Label	Catalogue Number	Release	Format	Comments
ALL OR NOTHING / SHA LA LA LA LEE	DECCA	BRIT 51	NEW ZEALAND	7" SINGLE	
BECOME LIKE YOU	NONE	NONE	POLAND	PICTURE POSTCARD	PLAYS LIKE A VINYL RECORD
DONKEY RIDES A PENNY A GLASS	STATESIDE	UNKNOWN	INDIA	7" SINGLE	
FEELING LONELY	NONE	NONE	POLAND	PICTURE POSTCARD	PLAYS LIKE A VINYL RECORD
GREEN CIRCLES	NONE	NONE	POLAND	PICTURE POSTCARD	PLAYS LIKE A VINYL RECORD
HERE COMES THE NICE	NONE	NONE	POLAND	PICTURE POSTCARD	PLAYS LIKE A VINYL RECORD
HEY GIRL/ YOU REALLY GOT A HOLD ON ME	DECCA	NONE	NONE	DEMO SINGLE	UNRELEASED- BUT COPIES EXIST
HEY GIRL HITS VOLUME 4	DECCA	DFEA 8663	AUSTRALIA		PLUS TRACKS FROM THE ANIMALS, ALAN PRICE, LOS BRAVOS
HEY GIRL	NONE	NONE	POLAND	PICTURE POSTCARD	PLAYS LIKE A VINYL RECORD
I CANT MAKE IT	NONE	POLAND	PICTURE	PLAYS LIKE A VINYL RECORD POSTCARD	
I FEEL MUCH BETTER	NONE	NONE	POLAND	PICTURE POSTCARD	PLAYS LIKE A VINYL RECORD
ITCHYCOO PARK/ LAZY SUNDAY	IMMEDIATE	Z57 511	USA	7" SINGLE	MEMORY LANE SERIES
ITCHYCOO PARK/ LAZY SUNDAY	ARIOLA	106718	GERMANY	7" SINGLE	
ITCHYCOO PARK	RUSSIAN ALPHABET	RUSSIAN ALPHABET	RUSSIA	33RPM FLEXI	GREEN VINYL
TCHYCOO PARK/ I'M ONLY DREAMING	EPIC	152333	USA	7" SINGLE	SOME ON EPIC MEMORY LANE LABEL
ITCHYCOO PARK/ MY WAY OF GIVING	IMMEDIATE	NEMS 301 0149	BRAZIL	7" SINGLE	
ITCHYCOO PARK/ LAZY SUNDAY/ IM ONLY DREAMING/ I FEEL MUCH BETTER	CAPITOL	EPEM 1028	MEXICO	EP	
ITCHYCOO PARK	RIPETE	R45 127	USA	7" SINGLE	C/W DESMOND DEKKER "ISRAELITES"
LAZY SUNDAY/ ITCHYCOO PARK	IMMEDIATE	Z57511	CANADA	7" SINGLE	
LAZY SUNDAY/ TIN SOLDIER	ELECTROLA	IC006 05219	GERMANY	7" SINGLE	
LAZY SUNDAY/ AFTERGLOW	CHARLY	RISS 8077	PORTUGAL	7" SINGLE	
LAZY SUNDAY/ HERE COMES THE NICE	GIP	GIP 4134	ITALY 7"	SINGLE	
LAZY SUNDAY SOCIAL DEGREE"	IMMEDIATE	NONE	UNKNOWN	ACETATE	C/W BILLY NICHOLLS "LONDON
LENIWA NIEDZIELA	DRIWIEKOWA	M1	POLAND	45RPM FLEXI DISC	RED PLASTIC, POLISH FOR LAZY SUNDAY
MYSTERY	EMI DISC	NONE	NONE	7" DEMO	REALLY "SOMETHING I WANT TO TELL YOU" C/W THE EASYBEATS "FRIDAY ON MY MIND"
OCZKO GLOWIE	CENA	ZK20	POLAND	45RPM FLEXI DISC	MY MINDS EYE C/W DONOVAN
SHA LA-LA-LA-LEE/ MY MINDS EYE	EXPLOSIVE	128.062	FRANCE	7" SINGLE	TUBES DU PASSE SERIES

Title	Label	Catalogue Number	Release	Format	Comments
SHA LA-LA-LA-LEE/ WHATCHA GONNA DO ABOUT IT	ARIOLA	12738AT	GERMANY	7" SINGLE	POP GOLD SERIES
SHA LA-LA-LA-LEE/ GROW YOUR OWN/ WHATCHA GONNA DO ABOUT IT/ WHAT'S A MATTER BABY	DECCA	PEP 1158	PORTUGAL	EP	
SHA LA-LA-LA-LEE/ ALL OR NOTHING	DECCA	810 181	NETHERLANDS	7" SINGLE	GOLDEN OLDIES
SHA LA-LA-LA-LEE/ ALL OR NOTHING	DECCA	810 181.7	GERMANY	7" SINGLE	
SHA LA-LA-LA-LEE/ ITCHYCOO PARK	ELECTROLA	1 C006 95199	GERMANY	7" SINGLE	
SHOW ME THE WAY	NONE	NONE	POLAND	PICTURE POSTCARD	PLAYS LIKE A VINYL RECORD
TALK TO YOU	NONE	NONE	POLAND	PICTURE POSTCARD	PLAYS LIKE A VINYL RECORD
THERE ARE BUT THREE	BEAT	BREP2 SF1	UNKNOWN	EP	TV/RADIO TRACKS
TIN SOLDIER/ SHA LA-LA LA-LEE/ ITCHYCOO PARK/ WHATCHA GONNA DO ABOUT IT	CHARLY	ISI.002	NETHERLANDS	EP	
TIN SOLDIER/ ITCHYCOO PARK	BELLAPHON	100 7006	GERMANY	7" SINGLE	OLDIES SERIES
TIN SOLDIER/ ITCHYCOO PARK	EMI	EPOC 4003	ISRAEL	7" SINGLE	
TOP GEAR SESSIONS 68	BOOTLEG		BOOTLEG	EP	BOOTLEG RELEASE
THE UNIVERSAL	NONE	NONE	POLAND	PICTURE POSTCARD	PLAYS LIKE A VINYL RECORD
THE UNIVERSAL	IMMEDIATE	IM069/IM067	ITALY JUKE BOX RELEASE	7" SINGLE	C/W PP ARNOLD "ANGEL OF THE MORNING"
WHATCHA GONNA DO ABOUT IT/ ALL OR NOTHING/ SHA LA LA-LA-LEE/ ITCHYCOO PARK	TONPRESS	N50	POLAND	EP	OLDIES BUT GOLDIES SERIES

Small Faces LPS

Title	Label	Catalogue Number	Release	Format	Comments
SMALL FACES	DECCA	LK 4790	MAY 1966	LP	
FROM THE BEGINNING	DECCA	LK 4879	JUNE 1967	LP	
SMALL FACES	IMMEDIATE	IMLP 008	JUNE 1967	LP	
ODGENS NUT GONE FLAKE	IMMEDIATE	IMLP 012	JUNE 1968	LP	
THE AUTUMN STONE	IMMEDIATE	IMAL 01/02	MARCH 1969	LP	

Small Faces Compilation LPS

Title	Label	Catalogue Number	Release	Format	Comments
GULLIVERS TRAVELS	INSTANT	INLP003	1968	LP	MIKE D'ABO MUSICAL WITH MANY SMALL FACES RELATED ITEMS ON THE ALBUM
THERE ARE BUT FOUR	IMMEDIATE	Z12 52002	USA 1968	LP	US RELEASE OF FIRST IMMEDIATE ALBUM
Title	Label	Catalogue	Release	Format	Comments

		Number			
TONITE LETS ALL MAKE LOVE IN LONDON	INSTANT	INLP	1968	LP	SOUNDTRACK ALBUM, INCLUDING AN ALTERNATE VERSION OF "HERE COMES THE NICE". RE-RELEASED ON SEE FOR MILES IN 1990 IN USA IN 1991
IN MEMORIAM	IMMEDIATE	C048 90201	GERMANY 1969	LP	UNIQUE RELEASE FOR GERMANY AND ALSO IN SINGAPORE. RE-RELEASED IN 1975
IN MEMORIAM	IMMEDIATE	2C05491871	FRANCE 1969	LP	COMPLETELY DIFFERENT TRACK LISTING TO GERMAN RELEASE
SMALL FACES	EMI/COLUMBIA	SOEX 10122	AUSTRALIA 1969	LP	AUSTRALIAN RELEASE OF IN MEMORIAM – THE SAME TRACKS
ARCHETYPES	MGM/CAPITOL	SW95723	USA 1970	LP	US RECORD CLUB DECCA COMPILATION. LATER RELEASED IN UK ON MGM
FIRST STEPS	WARNER BROS	7599263762	1970	LP	ACTUALLY A FACES ALBUM, EVEN THOUGH TITLED SMALL FACES
WHAM BAM	IMMEDIATE	IC04850719	GERMANY 1970	LP	ALSO RELEASED IN SOUTH AFRICA, AND IN AUSTRALIA ON AXIS. LATER RE-ISSUED ON EMI DISC
(SMALL FACES AND) AMEN CORNER STORY OF POP	ARIOLA	25155ET	GERMANY 1972	LP	SPLIT LP ONE SIDE SMALL FACES
BIGGEST SMALL FACES	IMMEDIATE	IMSP050	NEW ZEALAND 1972	LP	ISSUED IN AN AUTUMN STONE STYLE SLEEVE. ONE SIDE OF THE ALBUM IS LIVE. RARE
EARLY FACES	PRIDE	PRD001	USA 1972	LP	DECCA COMPILATION 10 TRACKS
SMALL FACES	A/Z RECORDS	AZ STEC 112	FRANCE 1972	LP	LANDMARK RARE RECORD. THIS LP IS FULL OF DECCA ERA OUT-TAKES
(SMALL FACES AND) AMEN CORNER	NEW WORLD	NW 6001	1973	SPLIT LP	ONE SIDE SMALL FACES
FAMOUS POP GROUPS OF THE '60s VOL 1 – SMALL FACES & AMEN CORNER	MFP / EMI	1C146 50250	GERMANY 1973	2 X LP	THE SMALL FACES ALBUM IS THE SAME TRACK LISTING AS "IN MEMORIAM"
HISTORY OF BRITISH POP VOLUME 2	IMMEDIATE	SC 052 05	NETHERLANDS 1973	LP	FAMED AS THE FIRST ALBUM TO CONTAIN THE RARE "B" SIDE VERSION OF WHAM BAM THANKYOU MAM
SMALL FACES (FIRST HIT ALBUM)	NEW WORLD	NW 6000	1973	LP	INCLUDES ALTERNATE VERSIONS. STRONG SIMILARITIES WITH "SORRY SHE'S MINE" ON PLATINUM AND "SMALL FACES" ON A/Z RECORDS. RE-ISSUED IN 1980
EARLY HITS AS ROD STEWART AND THE FACES	TRIP TOP		USA 1973	LP	INCLUDES SMALL FACES OUTTAKES
HISTORY OF	PRIDE	PRD0014	USA 1974	LP	8 TRACK AND 10 TRACK VERSIONS BOTH EXIST
IMMEDIATE STORY VOLUME 2 THE SMALL FACES	SIRE	SIRE 3709/2	USA 1975	2 X LP	GATEFOLD. NICE PACKAGING. 28 TRACKS.
"THE VINTAGE YEARS" ROD STEWART AND THE FACES	SPRINGBOARD	SP4030	USA 1975	LP	PEOPLE SAY THIS IS WHERE THINGS GOT COMPLEX. REALLY THIS IS A SMALL FACES ALBUM, PUTTING A BUNCH OF ALTERNATES AND INSTRUMENTALS ON TO THE MARKET FOR THE FIRST TIME UNDER WEIRD TITLES

Title	Label	Catalogue Number	Release	Format	Comments
SMALL FACES	CHARLY	CR 3024	1975	LP	
MAGIC MOMENTS	NEMS/ IMMEDIATE	IML 1008	AUSTRALIA 1976	LP	ALSO RELEASED IN SOUTH AFRICA
ROOTS ROCK VOL 5 THE SMALL FACES	DECCA	ROOTS 5	1977	LP	RE-ISSUED ON SEE FOR MILES CD
GREATEST HITS	IMMEDIATE	IML2008	UK/ NETHERLANDS 1978	LP	MAINLY A SINGLES COLLECTION
LIVE UK 1969	CHARLY	CR 300025	1978	LP	
PROFILE SMALL FACES	DECCA/TELDEC	624 002	GERMANY 1979	LP	DECCA COMPILATION
BIG HITS	VIRGIN/ IMMEDIATE	V2166	1980	LP	RELEASED AS A GATEFOLD ALBUM, LATER IN A SINGLE SLEEVE, AND ALSO RE-ISSUED ON LONDON RECORDS
FOR YOUR DELIGHT THE DARLINGS OF WAPPING WHARF LAUNDRETTE	VIRGIN/ IMMEDIATE	V2178	1980	LP	UNUSUAL COMPILATION – FAMOUS FOR THE FIRST EVER APPEARANCE OF DONT BURST MY BUBBLE
HISTORIA DE LA MUSICA ROCK	DECCA	47005	SPAIN 1981	LP	SAME TRACK LISTING AS DECCA'S "GREATEST HITS" RELEASE IN NETHERLANDS
LEGENDS OF ROCK	DECCA	628 556 DP	GERMANY 1981	2 X LP	DECCA COMPILATION
SHA LA LA LA LEE	DECCA	TAB 16	1981	LP	DIFFERENT CATALOGUE NUMBERS IN NEW ZEALAND AND AUSTRALIA
BY APPOINTMENT	ACCORD	SN7157	USA 1982	LP	DECCA COMPILATION,WITH MANY RARITIES
HISTORY OF BRITISH ROCK VOLUME 2	ORBIS	HRL011	1982	LP	5 SMALL FACES TRACKS, PLUS THEM AND JOHN MAYALLS BLUESBREAKERS
IN MEMORIAM	IMMEDIATE/ OUTLINE	LINE OLLP 5270 AS	GERMANY 1982	LP	DIFFERENT TRACKS TO THE ORIGINAL IN MEMORIAM RELEASE
ROD STEWART RIDING HIGH	JOKER	SM 3985	ITALY 1982	LP	INCLUDES 3 SMALL FACES RARE OUTTAKES
SHA LA LA LA LEE	PHILIPS	6495 104	ITALY 1982	LP	LINER NOTES IN ITALIAN
ITCHYCOO PARK 6 ORIGINAL HITS	LASERLIGHT	12208	GERMANY 1983	CD	NICE PACKAGING FOR A BUDGET CD
SORRY SHES MINE	PLATINUM	PLP 29/LP 2045	1983	LP	ALSO ISSUED ON GERMAN ASTAN LABEL
BACK TO THE '60s	ASTAN	9007/3	GERMANY 1984	3 X LP	ONE LP SMALL FACES. OTHERS ARE TROGGS AND EQUALS
COMPLEAT COLLECTION	COMPLEAT/ BIG MUSIC	672 004-1	USA 1984	2 X LP	COMPLEAT IS FROM NASHVILLE, TENNESSEE. THE GATEFOLD COVER SPORTS A LARGE PICTURE OF HUMBLE PIE! THE SLEEVE ADVERTISES RARE TRACKS – WHICH ARE EXACTLY THE AME AS THE GERMAN RARITIES RELEASE ON LINE 1984
GOLDEN HITS	ASTAN	20049	USA/ GERMANY 1984	LP	SAME ALBUM AS NEW WORLD'S "SMALL FACES" & PLATINUM'S "SORRY SHE'S MINE"
RARITIES 14 TRACKS HAVE FUN	OUTLINE	LMLP 5283 AS	GERMANY 1984	LP	LIMITED ISSUE ON WHITE VINYL. SIMILARITIES WITH THE TRACKS ON THE COMPLEAT RELEASE.
COLLECTION	CASTLE	CC SLP 108	1985	2 X LP	COMPILATION USES A COMBINATION OF MONO AND STEREO TRACKS. LATER RELEASED ON CD AND REISSUED ON VINYL IN 2001

Title	Label	Catalogue Number	Release	Format	Comments
IMMEDIATE SINGLES TWENTY BY TEN	COMPLEAT	672007	USA 1985	2 X LP	SIDE 3 ALL SMALL FACES RELATED
SMALL FACES	RITZ	RMLP 4507	GERMANY 1985	LP	CAREER COMPILATION
OLDIES BUT GOLDIES	DECCA	823 408	1986	LP	DECCA COMPILATION
QUITE NATURALLY	CASTLE SHOWCASE	SHLP 145	1986	LP	RELEASED ONE YEAR LATER ON CD
BEST OF BRITISH ROCK	PAIR	21153	USA 1987	2 X LP	THERE ARE 15 TRACK AND 13 TRACK ISSUES IN EXISTENCE
IMMEDIATE YEARS	ACCORD	13928	1987	CD	
COLLECTION	POSSUM	SPLP1075	AUSTRALIA 1988	LP	SAME COVER AS CASTLE COLLECTION.
NIGHTRIDING	KNIGHT	KNLP 10007	1988	LP	COMPLETE WITH A VARIETY OF SPELLING MISTAKES. 12 TRACK PRESSINGS AND 13 TRACK PRESSINGS BOTH EXIST.
20 GREATEST HITS	BIG TIME	261 552	KOREA 1988	LP	
COLLECTION	LINE	IMCD 960657	1989	CD	
EARLY DAYS OF ROCK VOL1	LIV LEG	LLRCD021	1989	CD	VARIOUS ARTISTS CD, INCLUDING 3 SMALL FACES LIVE TRACKS
GREATEST HITS	CASTLE	CLACD146	1989	LP/CD	RE- RELEASE OF IML2008. VARIOUS OTHER VERSIONS OF THIS EXIST, EG ON JUGOTON (YUGOSLAVIA) AND POWDERWORKS (AUSTRALIA)
BEST HITS 18	TEICHIKU / IMMEDIATE	TECX18796	JAPAN 1990	CD	18 TRACK IMMEDIATE COMPILATION
COMPLETE COLLECTION	CASTLE	CCS CD 302		CD	RE- RELEASED IN 1993 WITH DIFFERENT PACKAGING
GREATEST HITS	RANGE	ONN 65	SWITZERLAND 1990	CD	BUDGET RELEASE, BUT PACKED WITH OUTTAKES AND ALTERNATIVE VERSIONS
LAZY SUNDAY	SUCCESS	SUC 2198	1990	CD	BUDGET CD, BUT WITH MANY RARITIES, LATER RELEASED ON PICKWICK
LAZY SUNDAY	ARIOLA EXPRESS	ARICD 973	1990	CD	2 COMPLETELY DIFFERENT FRONT COVERS EXIST
SINGLES A's AND B's	SEE FOR MILES	SEE 293	1990	LP	ALSO RELEASED ON CD WITH 8 EXTRA TRACKS
ULTIMATE COLLECTION	CASTLE TV	CTV LP 004	1990	2 X LP	LATER RE-ISSUED AS "THE COMPLETE COLLECTION"
GREEN CIRCLES	SEQUEL	NEXCD 163	UK 1991	CD	
LAZY SUNDAY SMALL FACES BEST	ZOUNDS	CD 27200194	GERMANY 1991	CD	
QUITE NATURALLY RARE	DOJO	CD60	1991	CD	RE- ISSUE OF "QUITE NATURALLY". RELEASED AGAIN IN 1992 BY SOUND SOLUTIONS IN GERMANY
ALL OR NOTHING	SONY	AK 5247	USA 1992	CD	23 TRACK IMMEDIATE COMPILATION
CASTLE MASTER COLLECTION	CASTLE	37403076	1992	CD	IMMEDIATE COMPILATION
READY STEADY GO WITH SMALL FACES	EVA	EVA 700	FRANCE 1992	LP	THE 4 FRENCH EPS. LATER RELEASED AS A CD AND AS A 4 CD BOXSET
VERY BEST OF CHARLY	CHARLY	CPCD 8260.2	1992	2 X CD BOX	40 TRACKS, SINGLES PLUS ODGEN'S AND AUTUMN STONE TRACKS

Title	Label	Catalogue Number	Release	Format	Comments
25 GREATEST HITS	REPERTOIRE	REP 4255 W6	GERMANY 1992	CD	CLAIMS TO BE THE FIRST RELEASE OF THE STUDIO VERSION OF "EVERY LITTLE BIT HURTS".
ALL THE HITS AND MORE	ELECTROLA	7243	1993	CD	NETHERLANDS COMPILATION
GREATEST HITS CLASSIC ROCK	CHARLY	IMB500	GERMANY 1993	CD	CAREER COMPILATION, MAINLY SINGLES
ROD STEWART BABY COME HOME	SOUND CARRIER	1021 2027-2	SWITZERLAND 1993	CD	INCLUDES RARE SMALL FACES
VERY BEST OF	ARCADE	99 02 140	1993	CD	18 TRACKS DIGITALLY REMASTERED
16 ORIGINAL HITS	DELTA	12208	GERMANY 1993	CD	
BEST OF	EMI	8141842	AUSTRALIA 1994	CD	18 TRACK COMPILATION, MAINLY SINGLES "A" SIDES
GET YOURSELF TOGETHER	JIMCO	JICK 89379	JAPAN 1994	CD	SINGLES AND LIVE TRACKS
GREATEST HITS	ARC TOP	940 500	1994	CD	
HERE COMES THE NICE 16 ORIGINAL HITS	LASERLIGHT	12221	GERMANY 1994	CD	CAREER COMPILATION
ACID FACE PSYCHEDELIC COLLECTION	JIMCO	JICK 89457	JAPAN 1995	CD	16 TRACK COMPILATION
BEST OF 16 ORIGINAL RECORDINGS	CHARLY/ SUMMIT	SUMCD 4001	1995 FRANCE	CD	MANY BUDGET VARIATIONS OF THIS CD EXIST
DEFINITIVE ANTHOLOGY	REPERTOIRE	REP 4429	1995	2 X CD BOXED	55 TRACKS, CD 2 IS FULL OF RARITIES. INCLUDES 48 PAGE BOOKLET
IMMEDIATE YEARS	CHARLY	CD IMM BOX1	1995	4 X CD BOXSET	EXCELLENT PACKAGING AND COMPREHENSIVE ANTHOLOGY
ITCHYCOO PARK	ABRACADABRA	AB 3034	1995	CD	
ITCHYCOO PARK	MASTERTONE MULTIMEDIA	10065	1995	CD	
LAZY SUNDAY	SOUNDWINGS	101 1001 2	SPAIN 1995	CD	THE CD EXISTS IN SEVERAL FORMS. THIS COVER IS OF A RAILWAY STATION. A VERSION ON SOUNDCARRIER HAS A SUMMERY PHOTOGRAPH. A LIMITED EDITION VERSION HAS A PSYCHEDELIC FLOWER POWER COVER
MOD FACE	CHARLY	JICK 89546	JAPAN 1995	CD	
SMALL FACES	ITS MUSIC	22579	1995	CD	
THERE ARE BUT THREE	THIRD EYE	NONE	1995	CD	TV AND RADIO APPEARANCES
COMPLETE SINGLES WORKS	RARITIES ON RECORDS	WWW 007	1996	CD	14 "A" SIDES THEN 14 "B" SIDES. EXCELLENT. A CD WITH SAME TITLE, TRACKS AND COVER AND WAS RELEASED ON "WESTWOOD ONE RADIO NETWORKS"
DECCA ANTHOLOGY	DECCA/ DERAM	844 583.2	1996	CD	DEFINITIVE DECCA ANTHOLOGY WITH GREAT REMASTERED SOUND
FACES FAMILY ALBUM	CONNOISSEUR COLLECTION	VSOP CD231	1996	CD	BUILT AROUND PETE FRAME'S ROCK FAMILY TREE. CONTAINS MANY SMALL FACES & RELATED TRACKS
GET YOUR GARAGE	SOUL IMMEDIATE	TECW 20058	JAPAN 1996	CD	VERY GOOD 27 TRACK IMMEDIATE COMPILATION
GOLD	GOLD	111	NETHERLANDS 1996	CD	SHORT 8 TRACK SINGLES CD
GREATEST HITS	REPERTOIRE	REP4597WL	1996	CD	28 TRACKS MAINLY "A" SIDES AND "B" SIDES

Title	Label	Catalogue Number	Release	Format	Comments
GREATEST HITS	SONY	RAJ4013	AUSTRALIA 1996	CD	RE- RELEASED IN 1997 ON WARNER MUSIC AUSTRALIA
LAZY SUNDAY	ITS MUSIC		1996	CD	
LONDON INVASION	TRING	JHD062	1996	CD	INCLUDING 3 SMALL FACES TRACKS
BEST OF	TEICHIKU / IMMEDIATE	TECW 20475	JAPAN 1997	CD	IMMEDIATE COMPILATION
BEST OF	IMMEDIATE CASTLE	RENCD 124	1997	CD	VARIOUS ARTISTS CD, BUT CONTAINS MANY SF & RELATED TRACKS
THE MASTERS	CHARLY/ EAGLE RECORDS	EOM CD023	1997	2 X CD	36 TRACK IMMEDIATE COMPILATION
GREATEST HITS	CRIMS	CRIMCD	CANADA 1997	CD	RARE COMPILATION
COOL BRITTANIA	SUMMIT	SCDD BX 3659	1998	3 X CD BOXSET	1 CD SMALL FACES BEST OF – OTHERS BY THE YARBIRDS AND THE ZOMBIES
DOUBLE DECKER TRIPLE TRACKER	SNAPPER	RECALL 177	1998	2 X CD	VARIOUS ARTISTS CD, INCLUDING 3 SMALL FACES AND 3 HUMBLE PIE TRACKS
ROD STEWART MINDS EYE	BCI MUSIC	BCCD 463	1998	CD	INCLUDES SIGNIFICANTLY DIFFERENT SMALL FACES VERSION OF RED BALLOON
SMALL FACES (MASTER SERIES)	DECCA/ POLYGRAM	844 836 2	GERMANY 1998	CD	DECCA COMPILATION
THREE CLASSIC ALBUMS	CASTLE	ESM BX 302	1998	3 X CD BOXSET	SMALL FACES, ODGEN'S AND AUTUMN STONE
BBC SESSIONS	BBC	SFRS CD081	1999	CD	COMPILATION OF BBC TV & RADIO APPEARANCES. AVAILABLE ALSO ON LIMITED EDITION 180g VINYL
BIG HITS	DRESSED TO KILL	METRO282	1999	CD	COMPILATION OF IMMEDIATE ALBUM TRACKS
CLASSIC SMALL FACES UNIVERSAL MASTERS	DERAM	844 9422	1999	CD	DECCA COMPILATION
DARLINGS OF WAPPING WHARF LAUNDERETTE	IMMEDIATE	NEECD311	1999	2 X CD	DEFINITIVE IMMEDIATE ANTHOLOGY. FIRST 5,000 HAD ORIGINAL WHAM BAM INSTEAD OF ME, YOU AND US TOO
DEFINITIVE COLLECTION	CHARLY / SNAPPER	SMCD 183	1999	2 X CD	RECALL BUDGET RELEASE
ITCHYCOO PARK THE BEST OF THE SMALL FACES	CASTLE/ PIE	PIESD 019	1999	CD	SPARSE PACKAGING, 15 TRACKS
ME, YOU AND US TOO	REPERTOIRE	REP 4818 WG	1999	CD	COMPILATION CENTERED AROUND THE FIRST OFFICIAL RELEASE OF THE MYTHICAL ALTERNATIVE VERSION OF WHAM BAM THANK YOU MAM
PURE GOLD	NEON	NE 34521	1999	CD	ALSO RELEASED ON DISKY IN THE NETHERLANDS
SINGLES COLLECTIONS	ESSENTIAL / CASTLE	ESB CD725	1999	6CD BOXSET	6 IMMEDIATE SINGLES IN ORIGINAL PICTURE SLEEVES. LOVELY PACKAGING
SUPER BEST OF	IMMEDIATE	TECW 20846	JAPAN 1999	CD	IMMEDIATE COMPILATION
BEST OF	DERAM	845 569.2	GERMANY 2000	CD	DECCA TRACKS PLUS 5 IMMEDIATE SINGLES
BEST OF	IMMEDIATE JVC	UNKNOWN	JAPAN 2000	CD	IMMEDIATE COMPILATION
BEST OF THE '60s	DISKY	S1990782	2000	CD	18 TRACK IMMEDIATE COMPILATION

Title	Label	Catalogue Number	Release	Format	Comments
GREAT SMALL FACES	REDX	UNKNOWN	AUSTRALIA 2000	3CD BOXSET	NICELY PACKAGED BOX SET
IMMEDIATE BLITZ OF HITS	CHARLY	CDBOOK 101LC 08477	2000	2 X CD BOOKSET	4 SMALL FACES TRACKS AND 2 HUMBLE PIE TRACKS
NICE	NMC	PILOT 66	2000	2 X CD	MATCHING CD-ROM WITH VIDEO
RARITIES	UNKNOWN	VICP 61141	JAPAN 2000	CD 25	RARE TRACKS FROM IMMEDIATE
ULTIMATE COLLECTION	CHARLY	CD VAL 115.2	2000	2 X CD	40 REMASTERED TRACKS
LAZY SUNDAY	CASTLE/ SANCTUARY	SEL CD 522	2001	CD	20 TRACK IMMEDIATE COMPILATION
ABSOLUTELY THE BEST	VARESE SARABANDE	30206112429	USA 2001	CD	INCLUDES RARE MIXES AND ALTERNATIVES
ALL OR NOTHING	SONY		2001	CD	20 TRACK CAREER COMPILATION
BEST OF	DECCA	8829732	2001	CD	DECCA COMPILATION
SMALL FACES FOREVER	GOLD	F 6093	2001	CD	MAINLY SINGLES COLLECTION
IMMEDIATE HITS MOD RARITIES	GET BACK	GET 612	ITALY 2002	2 X LP GATEFOLD	REMASTERED IMMEDIATE RARITIES
ODDS AND MODS	IMMEDIATE	302 061 2272	2002	CD	PER THE TITLE, A NUMBER OF CURIOS ON THIS CD
ULTIMATE COLLECTION	SANCTUARY	CD SAN 004	2003	2 X CD	TRIUMPHANT RETURN TO THE UK TOP TEN IN 2003 WITH THIS DECCA AND IMMEDIATE COMBINED COLLECTION
ALL OR NOTHING	BOOTLEG	J60	BOOTLEG	CD	TV, RADIO AND OUTTAKES
ALL OR NOTHING THE SMALL FACES STORY	DROFTEL	LET 33		CD	BBC RADIO TRANSMISSION.PHIL DANIELS NARRATION
BBC CLASSIC ALBUMS ODGENS NUT GONE FLAKE	BOOTLEG	NONE	BOOTLEG	CD	60 MINUTE RICHARD SKINNER RADIO PROGRAMME
BEST OF +3	LONSDALE	TFCK 87516	JAPAN	CD	INCLUDES 3 TRACKS BY QUIET MELON
BEST OF	BELLAPHON	CR3025	GERMANY	2 X LP	24 TRACK CAREER COMPILATION
BEST OF	WORLD RECORD CLUB	WRC 5/5043	AUSTRALIA	LP	VERY SOUGHT AFTER RARE AUSTRALIAN RELEASE
BEST OF ALL OR NOTHING	IMMEDIATE	CSL 6031	USA	CD	IMMEDIATE COMPILATION
BEST OF THE NICE,SMALL FACES HUMBLE PIE,ERIC CLAPTON MAYALL	IMMEDIATE	IC 148 92 661	GERMANY	2 X LP	INCLUDES 6 SMALL FACES TRACKS
DEEP JOY	INTERACTIVE	DEZ02	BOOTLEG	CD	MAINLY TV APPEARANCES.STRONG COMPILATION OF UNRELEASED TRACKS + I've Got Mine With Dubbed Screaming from Film Dateline Diamonds
DIE GROSSES ER FOLGE EINER SUPERGRUPPE	BIEM/ STEMRA		GERMANY	LP	THE BIG HITS OF A SUPERGROUP
EARLY FACES	UNKNOWN	MALPS 378	NEW ZEALAND	LP	
GREATEST HITS	DECCA	H 09	NETHERLANDS	LP	DECCA COMPILATION
GREATEST HITS	DECCA	LP005	SPAIN	LP	DECCA COMPILATION
GREATEST HITS	GOPACO RECORDS	CAT 111	USA	LP	
GREATEST HITS	FESTIVAL/ IMMEDIATE	L36377	NEW ZEALAND	LP	
HISTORY OF BRITISH POP	VEE JAY		USA	LP	VERY RARE ALBUM,CONTAINING AN ALTERNATIVE VERSION OF "GET YOURSELF TOGETHER"
MMEDIATE YEARS	IMMEDIATE	IMLP008		CD	RE- ISSUE OF 1ST IMMEDIATE ALBUM PLUS ADDITIONAL RARITIES

Title	Label	Catalogue Number	Release	Format	Comments
IMMEDIATE YEARS	IMMEDIATE	TECW 20058	JAPAN	CD	27 TRACK COMPILATION
ITCHYCOO PARK AND OTHER CLASSIC TRACKS	WOODFORD MUSIC	WMMC 4525	NETHERLANDS	CASSETTE	MAINLY SINGLES COMPILATION
ITS A MOD MOD WORLD	J60	NONE	BOOTLEG	LP	TV AND RADIO APPEARANCES. NICE COVER
LA GRANDE STORIA DEL ROCK	ARMANDO CURCIO	GSR 75	ITALY	CD	SOLD AT NEWS STANDS IN ITALY TO PROMOTE AN ENCYCLOPAEDIA. SPLIT CD WITH AMEN CORNER
LEGENDARY	BELLAPHONE	DR 3044	GERMANY	2 X LP	VERY CLOSE TO IMMEDIATE FIRST ALBUM PLUS OGDEN'S
MAGIC COLLECTION	ARCRE	UNKNOWN	NETHERLANDS	CD	
MODS A GO GO	BOOTLEG	MODS 002	BOOTLEG	CD	10 TRACKS BY THE WHO,10 TRACKS BY THE SMALL FACES. RARE VERSIONS
ROD STEWART BRIGHT LIGHTS BIG CITIES	PULSAR	PULS 011		CD	INCLUDES 6 SMALL FACES RARE OUTTAKES
ROD STEWART STEAMPACKET	SPRINGBOARD	SPB 4065	AUSTRALIA	LP	VARIOUS SMALL FACES ODDITIES ON THIS ALBUM
SHAKE, SHUDDER, SHIVER	GOLD STANDARD	ZA52	BOOTLEG	CD	BILLED AS SMALL FACES, BUT IS THE FACES LIVE ON THE BBC
SMALL FACES	MFP SUPER	IM 048 90472	GERMANY	LP	REALLY THE OGDEN'S ALBUM
SMALL FACES	WORLD RECORD CLUB	IVRC S483	AUSTRALIA	LP	QUITE RARE AND EXPENSIVE
SMALL FACES	RAJON	RJBOX43	AUSTRALIA	2 X CD	CD1 IS SINGLES AND "B" SIDES, CD2 IS OGDENS PLUS EXTRA TRACKS
SMALL FACES	CR/ JASRAC	F003	JAPAN	CD	SUPERSTARS BEST COMPILATION
SMALL FACES	TEICHIKU / IMMEDIATE	TECX 2073	JAPAN	CD	
SPOTLIGHT ON	CHARLY	450.04	NETHERLANDS	LP	MAINLY SINGLES COLLECTION
STOCKHOLM	BOOTLEG	NONE	BOOTLEG	CD	6 LIVE SMALL FACES TRACKS25/11/66
THATS EVIL LIVE	BOOTLEG	NONE	BOOTLEG	TAPE	FACES LIVE IN BOSTON 1970,BILLED AS SMALL FACES
TOP OF THE POPS	BBC TRANSCRIPTION	BBC 122081	"182 WEEK 21"	LP	3 SMALL FACES TOP GEAR TRACKS PLUS HOLLIES, FLEETWOOD MAC ETC
WIEN	BOOTLEG	NONE	BOOTLEG	CD	6 TRACKS LIVE 12/1/69 IN VIENNA
16 GOUDEN SUCCESSEN	CHARLY	541.672	NETHERLAND	LP	MAINLY SINGLES COLLECTION

Humble Pie Singles

Title	Label	Catalogue Number	Format	Release Date	Comments
NATURAL BORN BUGIE/ WRIST JOB	IMMEDIATE	IM 082	7" Single	1969	
NATURAL BORN WOMAN/ I'LL GO ALONE	IMMEDIATE	IMOC001	7" Single	USA 1969	PROMO ALSO EXISTS WITH MONO/STEREO VERSIONS OF NATURAL BORN WOMAN
NATURAL BORN WOMAN	IMMEDIATE	IMOC001	7" Single	USA PROMO 1969	ONE SIDE MONO, ONE SIDE STEREO
SAD BAG OF SHAKEY/ COLD LADY	IMMEDIATE	C006 90917	7" Single	GERMANY, NETHERLANDS 1969	
HEARTBEAT/ DOWN HOME AGAIN	DAFFODIL	DFS 1023	7" Single	CANADA 1969	
HEARTBEAT/ SHAKEY JAKE	IMMEDIATE/ TOSHIBA	IMI 518	7" Single	JAPAN 1969	
BIG BLACK DOG/ ONLY A ROACH	A&M	14711 AT	7" Single	1970	GERMANY

Title	Label	Catalogue Number	Format	Release Date	Comments
BIG BLACK DOG/ STRANGE DAYS	A&M	AMS807	7" Single	1970	INCLUDING GERMANY
BIG BLACK DOG	A&M		7" Single	USA PROMO 1970	ONE SIDE MONO, ONE SIDE STEREO
BIG GEORGE/ STONE COLD FEVER/ 79TH AND SUNSET/ THE LIGHT	A&M	2206006	EP	HONG KONG 1971	
ONE EYED TROUSER SNAKE RHUMBA/ I'M READY	A&M	AM147	7" Single	JAPAN 1970	
SHINE ON/ MISTER RING	A&M	10031	7" Single	GERMANY 1971	
SHINE ON/ MISTER RING	A&M	N3528	7" Single	PORTUGAL, SPAIN 1971	
SHINE ON	A&M		7" Single	ITALY JUKE BOX 1971	C/W ARTIST "BILL & BUSTER"
I DON'T NEED NO DOCTOR/ SONG FOR JENNY	A&M	AMS 862	7" Single	GERMANY NETHERLANDS 1971	
I DON'T NEED NO DOCTOR/ JENNY/ FOUR DAY/ SOUR GRAIN	A&M	AME67	EP	MEXICO 1971	
I DON'T NEED NO DOCTOR/ BIG GEORGE	A&M	AM102	7" Single	JAPAN 1971	
I DON'T NEED NO DOCTOR	A&M	AM1282	7" Single	USA PROMO 1971	ONE SIDE MONO, ONE SIDE STEREO
HOT N NASTY/ YOU'RE SO GOOD TO ME	A&M	AMS7003	7" Single	1972	
HOT N NASTY	A&M	AM1349	7" Single	USA PROMO 1972	ONE SIDE MONO, ONE SIDE STEREO
HOT N NASTY/ SWEET PEACE AND TIME	A&M	AM1349	7" Single	CANADA 1972	MONO
'SMOKIN' – "HOT N NASTY", "30 DAYS IN THE HOLE", "C'MON EVERYBODY"	A&M	MC 969	EP	THAILAND 1972	
THIRTY DAYS IN THE HOLE/ SWEET PEACE AND TIME	A&M	AM 1366	7" Single	USA	1972
THIRTY DAYS IN THE HOLE/ C'MON EVERYBODY	A&M	Unknown	7" Single	PROMO JAPAN 1972	
THIRTY DAYS IN THE HOLE/ ROADRUNNER/ C'MON EVERYBODY	A&M	AM 047	EP	THAILAND 1972	
THIRTY DAYS IN THE HOLE	A&M	AM1366	7" Single	US PROMO 1972	ONE SIDE MONO, ONE SIDE STEREO
BLACK COFFEE/ SAY NO MORE	A&M	1406	7" Single	1973	
GET DOWN TO IT	A&M	AMS 7070	7" Single	USA PROMO 1973	ONE SIDE MONO, ONE SIDE STEREO. ALSO IN THE UK
BLACK COFFEE/ HONKY TONK WOMAN/ SAY NO MORE/ GET DOWN TO IT	A&M	2206015	EP	1973	
GET DOWN TO IT/ HONKY TONK WOMEN	A&M	AMS 7070	7" Single	GERMANY, UK 1973	
GET DOWN TO IT/ GOOD BOOZE & BAD WOMEN	A&M	PR 019	7" Single	FRANCE 1973	
SHUT UP AND DON'T INTERRUPT ME/ BLACK COFFEE	A&M	Unknown	7" Single	GERMANY 1973	'DOUBLE "A" SIDE
OH LA DE DA/ THE OUTCROWD	A&M	AMS 7090	7" Single	1973	
NINETY NINE POUNDS/ RALLY WITH ALI	A&M	13373AT	7" Single	GERMANY, SPAIN, JAPAN 1974	
NINETY NINE POUNDS	A&M	1530	7" Single	USA PROMO 1974	ONE SIDE MONO, ONE SIDE STEREO

Title	Label	Catalogue Number	Format	Release Date	Comments
ROCK N ROLL MUSIC/ SCORED OUT	A&M	13949 AT	7" Single	GERMANYPROMO 1975	ALSO RELEASED IN THE UK
ROCK N ROLL MUSIC/ ROAD HOG	A&M	1711	7" Single	1975	USA
ROCK N ROLL MUSIC	A&M	1711S	7" Single	USA PROMO 1975	ONE SIDE MONO, ONE SIDE STEREO
BUTTERMILK BOY/ ONLY YOU CAN SEE	BELLAPHON	B0170	7" Single	1975	
NATURAL BORN BUGIE/ SHAKEY JAKE	BELLAPHON	BF18512	7" Single	GERMANY 1975	
NATURAL BORN BUGIE/ HEARTBEAT	ARIOLA	103459	7" Single	GERMANY NETHERLANDS 1977	
FOOL FOR A PRETTY FACE/ YOU SOPPY PRAT	JET	JET180	7" Single	1980	
NATURAL BORN BUGIE/ WRIST JOB	IMMEDIATE	IM082	7" Single	GERMANY 1982	PICTURE SLEEVE OF CLEMPSON ERA BAND
NATURAL BORN BOOGIE (SIC)	OLD GOLD	OG6136	3" CD Single	AUSTRIA 1989	C/W ATOMIC ROOSTER
HOT N NASTY	A&M	AM 025	EP	THAILAND	C/W TAKE IT EASY (EAGLES)/ POWDER BLUE MERCEDES (QUEEN), CONQUISTADOR (PROCUL HARLUM)
I'LL GO ALONE/ ALABAMA '69'	BELLAPHON	B0171	7" Single	GERMANY	
LOST AND FOUND	IMMEDIATE	M 082	EP	ISRAEL	"BANG", "DOWN HOME AGAIN", "GROWING CLOSER", "HEARTBEAT"
NATURAL BORN BUGIE/ STICK SHIFT/ DESPERATION	IMMEDIATE	12006	EP	ISRAEL	

Humble Pie Albums

Title	Label	Catalogue Number	Release	Format	Comments
AS SAFE AS YESTERDAY IS	IMMEDIATE	MSP 025LP	1969	LP	
TOWN AND COUNTRY	IMMEDIATE	IMSP027	1969	LP	
HUMBLE PIE	A&M	AMLS 986	1970	LP	
ROCK ON	A&M	AMLS 2013	1971	LP	
ROCKING THE FILMORE	A&M	AMLH 63506	1971	2 X LP	
SMOKIN	A&M	AMLS 64342	1972	LP	
EAT IT	A&M	AMLS 6004	1973	2 X LP	
THUNDERBOX	A&M	SP 3611	1974	LP	
STREET RATS	A&M	AMLS 68282	1975	LP	VERY DIFFERENT MIXES ON UK AND US RELEASE
ON TO VICTORY	JET	JET LP 231	1980	LP	
GO FOR THE THROAT	ATCO	SD 38 131	1981	LP	
GEMINI	BOOTLEG	TKBWM 1810	1974	LP	ONE SIDE PETER FRAMPTON, ONE SIDE HUMBLE PIE
POP CHRONIK	A&M	88771	GERMANY 1975	2XLP	21 TRACKS
HUMBLE PIE	CHARLY	CR 3032	1975	LP	IMMEDIATE COMPILATION
CRUST OF	DISC	C.048.50.72	GERMANY/ NETHERLANDS 1975	LP	IMMEDIATE COMPILATION
BACK HOME AGAIN	IMMEDIATE	IML 1005	1976	LP	LATER RELEASED ON PYE
GREATEST HITS	IMMEDIATE/ PYE	IML 2005	1977	LP	IMMEDIATE COMPILATION

Title	Label	Catalogue Number	Release	Format	Comments
BEST OF	A&M	SP 9048	CANADA 1980	LP	A&M BEST OF (8 TRACKS)
BBC ROCK HOUR	LONDON WAVELENGTH	226	1981	LP	ON TO VICTORY ERA. EXCELLENT ALBUM
INNERVIEW	INNER VIEW	SERIES 16 SHOW 13	1981	CD	JIM LADD INTERVIEW WITH MARRIOTT/SHIRLEY
KING BISCUIT FLOWER HOUR HUMBLE PIE/ LOVER BOY	DIR		1981	RADIO PLAY TAPE	CIRCA RELEASE OF "GO FOR THE THROAT". RECORDED AT PRIVATES NEW YORK
KING BISCUITFLOWER HOUR HUMBLE PIE/ GARY US BONDS	DIR	NONE	1981	RADIO PLAY TAPE	TRACKS FROM PRIVATES NEW YORK
RECAPTURED	ATCO		1982	LP	ON TO VICTORY" AND "GO FOR THE THROAT" COMPILATION
BEST OF	A&M	CD 3208	1982, 1987	LP	A&M BEST OF (9 TRACKS). RELEASED ON CD IN 1987
GREATEST HITS	JUGODISK	LPS 1072	YUGOSLAVIA 1984	LP	
COLLECTION	CASTLE	CC SLP104	1985	2 X LP	LATER ON CD WITH FIVE EXTRA TRACKS
SLICE OF	COMPLEAT	672009	1985	2 X LP	
BEST OF BRITISH ROCK	PAIR	SPCD 2.1152	US 1987	CD	IMMEDIATE COMPILATION
CLASSICS	A&M	AAM0002512	US 1987	CD	A&M BEST OF
IMMEDIATE YEARS	ACCORD	139240	1987	CD	IMMEDIATE COMPILATION
BEST OF	BIG TIME	3215012	WEST GERMANY 1988	LP	RE-RELEASED ON CD. MADE IN KOREA
KING BISCUIT FLOWER HOUR HUMBLE PIE/FRAMPTONS CAMEL	DIR	NONE	1988	RADIO PLAY CD	PHILAPELPHIA 1975 LIVE TRACKS
LIVE USA	IMTRAT	IMT 900 029	1989	CD	PIE LIVE, SHARED WITH FRAMPTON LIVE
GREATEST HITS	SOUNDWINGS	101 1024.2	CZECH, SWITZERLAND 1990	CD	IMMEDIATE COMPILATION
GREATEST HITS	WOODFORD	WMCD 5527	NETHERLANDS 1990	CD	
KING BISCUIT FLOWER HOUR HUMBLE PIE/ LITTLE CAESAR	DIR	NONE	1990	RADIO PLAY CD	SAN FRANCISCO WINTERLAND 73 SELECTION
SGRS (SUPER GOLDEN RADIO SHOWS)	SGRS	SGRS 19	1991	CD	SAN FRANCISCO WINTERLAND 1973 SHOW
SMOKIN BOSTON 72	RC RECORDS	6832-2(1)RC	1991	CD	THERE MAY HAVE BEEN AN ORIGINAL LP RELEASE IN 1976
SAD BAG OF SHAKY JAKE	PULSAR	PULS 026	1992	CD	TOWN & COUNTRY TRACKS
BEST OF	CHARLY	503 UK	1993	CD	IMMEDIATE COMPILATION (10 TRACKS)
EARLY YEARS	DOJO	EARL04	1994	CD	ALSO RELEASED ON GRIFFIN MUSIC
HOT N NASTY ANTHOLOGY	A&M	AAM 540164	1994	2 X CD	31 TRACKS AND NICE PACKAGE
PIECE OF THE PIE	A&M	3154.0179.	CANADA, NETHERLANDS 1994	CD	"SONGS FROM THE ERA OF BLACK VINYL"
IMMEDIATE YEARS	CHARLY	CD IMM BOX3	1995	CD BOXSET	24 TRACKS IN QUALITY PACKAGING
ALTERNATIVE COOKING	OUTLAW	OTR1100014	1996	CD	IMMEDIATE COMPILATION
KING BISCUIT FLOWER HOUR	BMG	7071 88015-2	1996	CD	SAN FRANCISCO WINTERLAND 1973 CONCERT. LATER RELEASED ON KING BISCUIT FLOWER HOUR RECORDS AND ON SONY IN JAPAN.
BEST OF	TECW	20480	JAPAN 1997	CD	IMMEDIATE COMPILATION

Title	Label	Catalogue Number	Release	Format	Comments
IN THE STUDIO	BULLET/ ALBUM NETWORK	SHOW NUMBER 446	1997 RADIO PLAY RELEASE	CD	RADIO PROGRAMME AROUND THE ROCKING THE FILLMORE ALBUM
NATURAL BORN BUGIE	BAND OF JOY	BOJCD 010	1998	CD	BBC SESSIONS
NATURAL BORN BUGIE THE IMMEDIATE YEARS	RECALL	212	1999	CD	
NATURAL BORN BUGIE	NEON	NE 34524	1999	CD	
RUNNING WITH THE PACK	NMC	PILOT 48	1999	CD	LARGELY TRACKS EARMARKED FOR THE MARRIOTT/ RIDLEY "JOINT EFFORT" LP
BEST OF	INTERSCOPE		2000	CD	"20TH CENTURY MASTERS. THE MILLENIUM COLLECTION"
EXTENDED VERSIONS	EXCELSIOR	75517-457682	2000	CD	KING BISCUIT 1973 LIVE SHOW
NATURAL BORN BUGIE IMMEDIATE ANTHOLOGY	IMMEDIATE/ SANCTUARY	CMDDD 54	2000	2 X CD	EXCELLENT RELEASE, WITH MANY THE RARE TRACKS, AND INCLUDING THE DEBUT APPEARANCE OF "DROWN IN MY OWN TEARS"
UNRELEASED MASTERS	BOOTLEG	NONE	2000	2 X CD	IMMEDIATE OUTTAKES
LIVE AT WHISKY A GO GO	SANCTUARY	CMRCD 368	2001	CD	1969 US TOUR
NATURAL BORN BUGIE	CASTLE/SANCTUARY	PIESD 282	2002	CD	IMMEDIATE COMPILATION
UP YOUR SLEEVES	DISKY	SI 794132	HOLLAND 2002	CD	KING BISCUIT 1973 SAN FRANCISCO TRACKS
GREATEST HITS LIVE	KING BISCUIT FLOWER HOUR		2003	CD	RE-RELEASE OF 1973 SAN FRANCISCO CONCERT
NATURAL BORN BUGIE	BLACK BOX	BB271	NETHERLANDS 2003	2 X CD BOXSET	RE-RELEASE OF CHARLY IMMEDIATE YEARS BOXSET
WINNING COMBINATIONS	UNIVERSAL	A&M B0001 13902	2003	CD	C/W NAZARETH
BBC ARCHIVES	BOOTLEG	NONE	BOOTLEG	TAPE	69, 70, 71 BBC COMPILATION
BBC (1)	BOOTLEG	NONE	BOOTLEG	TAPE	AUGUST 69 SESSIONS. "NATURAL BORN BUGIE", "SHAKEY JAKE", "HEARTBEAT" AND "DESPERATION"
BBC (2)	BOOTLEG	NONE	BOOTLEG	TAPE	LATER RELEASED AS LIVE AT WHISKY A GO GO"
BBC (3)	BOOTLEG	NONE	BOOTLEG	TAPE	TOP GEAR, RECORDED AT AEOLIAN HALL, EAST LONDON, AND INCLUDING "I WALK ON GILDED SPLINTERS", "ONE EYED TROUSER SNAKE RHUMBA", "BIG BLACK DOG" AND "FOUR DAY CREEP"
BBC (4)	BOOTLEG	NONE	BOOTLEG	TAPE	RECORDED IN SEPTEMBER 1970 AT THE PARIS CINEMA, LOWER REGENT ST LONDON. 9 TRACKS BROADCAST ON JOHN PEEL'S "SOUNDS OF THE SEVENTIES"
BBC (5)	BBC TRANSCRIPTION SERVICE	UNKNOWN			RUMOURED TO HAVE BEEN RELEASED UNDER THE TITLE "THE LIGHT" TAPE MARCH 71, STUDIO T1, KENSINGTON HOUSE, SHEPHERDS BUSH. "FOUR DAY CREEP", "I'M READY", "I DON'T NEED NO DOCTOR", "ROLLING STONE", "THE LIGHT"

Title	Label	Catalogue Number	Release	Format	Comments
BBC (6)	BOOTLEG	NONE	BOOTLEG	TAPE	FEB 72, MAIDA VALE STUDIO "SOUNDS OF THE SEVENTIES" WITH PETE DRUMMOND. "ROADRUNNER", "C'MON EVERYBODY", "SWEET PEACE AND TIME"
BBC (7)	BOOTLEG	NONE	BOOTLEG	TAPE	MARCH 73, "BLACK COFFEE"
BBC (8)	BOOTLEG	NONE	BOOTLEG	TAPE	23 OCTOBER 1973 "I DONT NEED NO DOCTOR"
BBC (9)	BBC TRANSCRIPTION SERVICE	127968-S	NONE	VINYL RECORD	"PICK OF THE POPS – FOR YOUR DJ"
BEST OF	PS RECORDS	NTLP 246	SINGAPORE	LP	UNUSUAL IMMEDIATE AND A&M COMBINATION
BEST OF	JICK	89381	UNKNOWN	CD	IMMEDIATE COMPILATION
BEST OF BRITISH ROCK LIVE	STCLAIR	CST52152	CANADA	CD	VARIOUS ARTISTS. INCLUDES "30 DAYS IN THE HOLE" AND "HOT N NASTY"
FAMOUS POP GROUPS	MFP/ EMI		GERMANY	SPLIT LP	COUPLED WITH THE NICE. 1 SIDE EACH
FOOL FOR A PRETTY FACE	TENDOLLAR	TDR033	JAPAN	CD	LIVE, TV APPEARANCES AND RARITIES
GREATEST HITS	MUSIC MIRROR	1001 2008.2	GERMANY, SWITZERLAND	CD	IMMEDIATE COMPILATION
LAST SLICE	GOLD STANDARD	NONE	BOOTLEG	CD	TV, RADIO, 1991 FRAMPTON / MARRIOTT RE-UNION
LEGENDARY	BELLAPHON	CR 3403	GERMANY	2 X LP	IMMEDIATE COMPILATION
LOST & FOUND	A&M	SP 3513	USA	2 X LP	1ST TWO IMMEDIATE ALBUMS IN A DOUBLE SET WITH GOOD SLEEVE NOTES
NATURAL BORN BUGIE	IMMEDIATE	CSL 6034	USA	CD	IMMEDIATE COMPILATION
ON STAGE	MIDAS TOUCH	72611	1970'S	CD	1970 JOHN PEEL RADIO SHOW
QUEENS & NUNS	FIVEDOLLAR	014	BOOTLEG	CD	RARE TRACKS & "B" SIDES
ROUTE 66	DYNAMITE STUDIOS	DS 94	BOOTLEG	2 X CD	LIVE 1975 AND 1981
RUMBLE HUMBLE	TRYSTAR	TR0013	JAPAN	CD	LIVE IN TOKYO MAY 73
SHINE ON	A&M		GERMANY	LP	
STONE COLD FEVER	BOOTLEG	NONE	BOOTLEG	CD	LIVE 1969 – 1973

Post Humble Pie Singles

Title	Label	Catalogue Number	Release	Format	Comments
STAR IN MY LIFE/ MIDNIGHT ROLLING	A&M	AMS 723	1976	7"	
STAR IN MY LIFE/ EAST SIDE STRUTTING	A&M	17063	AT NETHERLANDS 1976	7"	
STAR IN MY LIFE	A&M	1825 S	USA 1976	PROMO 7"	ONE SIDE MONO, ONE SIDE STEREO
LOOKIN FOR A LOVE/ KAYOED BY LOVE	ATLANTIC	ATL K10983	1977	7"	ONE SIDED ACETATES ALSO EXIST
SMALL FACES MK II STAND BY ME/ HUNGRY AND LOOKING	ATLANTIC	K11 043	1977	7"	
SMALL FACES MK II FILTHY RICH/ OVER TO SOON	ATLANTIC	K11173	1978	7"	
SMALL FACES MK II WHATCHA GONNA DO ABOUT IT/	AURA	AUS 145	UK 1985	7"	

ALL SHOOK UP

Title	Label	Catalogue Number	Release	Format	Comments
ALL OR NOTHING/ CLAPPING SONG	POSSUM	POS 5112	AUSTRALIA 1989	7"	
THE UM UM SONG/ I NEVER LOVED A WOMAN	TRAX MUSIC	7TX8	1989	7"	
POLL TAX BLUES	CELTIC MUSIC	BOL AXT	1990	7"	THE POLLCATS
A SMALL FACE	BUBBLEHEAD	BH004	1996	CD EP	"I NEVER LOVED A WOMAN"/ "STAY WITH ME BABY"/ "OH WELL"
LOOKIN FOR LOVE/ PLAYMATES	ATLANTIC	NONE	NONE	DEMO TAPE	

Post Humble Pie Albums

Title	Label	Catalogue Number	Release	Format	Comments
MARRIOTT	A&M	AMLH 64572	1976	LP	
PLAYMATES	ATLANTIC	K50375	1977	LP	SMALL FACES MK2 FIRST STUDIO ALBUM
78 IN THE SHADE	ATLANTIC	50468	1978	LP	SMALL FACES MK2 SECOND STUDIO ALBUM
PACKET OF THREE	AURA	AUL 792	1984	LP	7 TRACKS. TWO EXTRA TRACKS ON THE CASSETTE RELEASE.
PACKET OF THREE	BELLAPHON	28807139	1986	LP	7 TRACKS. LATER RELEASED ON CD IN 1990
30 SECONDS TO MIDNITE	TRAX MUSIC MODEM	BMG MODCD 1037	1989	LP & CD	
ROCK OVER LONDON	WESTWOOD ONE RADIO NETWORKS	RL 89.41	1989	2 X LP	INCLUDES STEVE MARRIOTT TRACKS & INTERVIEW
DINGWALLS	MAU MAU	CD 609	1991	CD	COMPLETE 78 MINUTE VERSION OF PACKET OF THREE ALBUM
SCRUBBERS	ELASTIC CAT	CDEC1	1991	CD	
PACKET OF THREE	ALFA	ALC8617	1992 JAPAN	CD	13 TRACKS
PACKET OF THREE LIVE	GUITAR RECORDINGS	9714 993 01 2	1993	CD	8 LIVE TRACKS FROM DINGWALLS 84
ALL STARS	OUTLAW	OTR 1100012	1996	CD	SOLO, MAJIC MIJITS AND SMALL FACES COMPILATION
ALTERNATIVE HISTORY	OUTLAW	OTR 1100017	1996	CD	COMPILATION OF SOLO STEVE MARRIOTT
ANTHOLOGY	OUTLAW	OTR 1100021	1996	2 X CD	34 TRACK COMPILATION
INTERPRETATIONS	OUTLAW	OTR 110002	1996	CD	COMPILATION – MAINLY "30 SECONDS" TO MIDNITE TRACKS
LIVE AT THE GEORGE ROBEY	ZEUS	501 8766	1996	CD	PACKET OF THREE LIVE 1985
MARRIOTT, & THE ALLSTARS/ HUMBLE PIE/ PACKET OF THREE	OUTLAW	OTR 1100016	1996	CD	MISCELLANY OF TRACKS
PURE ENERGY BEST OF SMALL FACES LIVE	OUTLAW	OTR 1100015	1996	CD	
RARITIES	OUTLAW	OTR 1100023	1996	CD	COVER VERSIONS. MAINLY FROM "30 SECONDS TO MIDNITE"
SCRUBBERS	REPERETOIRE	REP 4603 WP	1996	CD	ALSO RELEASED ON BARSA, SPAIN 1996, SEE BELOW
ALL OR NOTHING LIVE	RECEIVER	RRCD 251	1997	CD	LIVE FROM ONE OF STEVE'S LAST SHOWS
ANTHOLOGY SAMPLER	ORANGE	OR 003	1997	CASSETTE	6 RARE TRACKS

Title	Label	Catalogue Number	Release	Format	Comments
SCRUBBERS	ARCHIVE	ACH 80001	USA 1997	CD	ALSO RE-RELEASED IN THE USA AS "HUMBLE PIE" ON EAGLE IN 1999
AFTERGLOW	NEWSOUND	NWST017	1999	CD	LIVE AT THE GEORGE ROBEY 85
CLEAR THROUGH THE NIGHT	NMC	PILOT 22	1999	CD	MID 1970s FROM CLEARSOUNDS STUDIOS
OFFICIAL RECEIVERS	NMC	PILOT 23	1999	2 X CD	FIRST RELEASES WITH BONUS CD EP
SCRUBBERS	BARSA	CD0029	SPAIN 1999	CD	COMPLETELY DIFFERENT COVER, AND STUDIO CHATTER. ONE ADDITIONAL TRACK CALLED "MUTTERING INTERVAL"
SCRUBBERS	EAGLE	50 34504	US 1999	CD	BILLED AS HUMBLE PIE
LIVE IN GERMANY 1985	CASTLE	ESMCD 898	2000	CD	STEVE MARRIOTT'S NEXT BAND. THE CD TITLE IS WRONG – IT'S ACTUALLY EARLY 1990
MAJIK MIJITS	NMC	PILOT 58	2000	2 X CD	
SING THE BLUES LIVE	EDEL	EDI 182202	USA 2000	CD	
SING THE BLUES LIVE	SANCTUARY	CMRCD23	2001	CD	RE-RELEASE, WITH MANY CORRECTIONS
VOICE OF HUMBLE PIE	BIG EYE BIG	4038	2001	CD	LIVE AT DINGWALLS 1984
SIGNED, SEALED	ALCHEMY	STRTR 165	2003	CD	NICE COMPILATION OF LATTER DAY MARRIOTT
BBC	TRIDENT	NONE	NONE	5" TAPE	"STAND BY ME" FOR JOHN PEMBERTON
BBC SESSION (SMALL FACES MK2)	BOOTLEG	NONE	BOOTLEG	TAPE	"ALL OR NOTHING", "HIGH AND HAPPY", "WHATCHA GONNA DO ABOUT IT"
BEDROOM TAPES	BOOTLEG	NONE	BOOTLEG	TAPE	WONDERFUL 1980S HOME RECORDINGS
CHALK AND CHEESE	BOOTLEG	NONE	BOOTLEG	CD	THE COMPLETE 1991 FRAMPTON/ MARRIOTT SESSIONS
CLEAR THROUGH THE NIGHT (ORIGINAL VERSION)	BOOTLEG	NONE	BOOTLEG	CD	SIGNIFICANTLY DIFFERENT TRACK LISTING FROM THE RELEASED ALBUM
LAUREL AND HARDY TAPES	BOOTLEG	NONE	BOOTLEG	TAPE	THE FIRM, WITH LESLIE WEST
LIVE AT FUNKAUSSTELLUNG	BOOTLEG	NONE	BOOTLEG	TAPE	1975, WITH ALEXIS KORNER BAND ON GERMAN TV
MAGIC MORSE CODE	BOOTLEG	NONE	BOOTLEG	CD	1987 STUDIO ALBUM. EXCELLENT
MIJIT REHEARSALS	BOOTLEG	NONE	BOOTLEG	TAPE	REHEASALS AND DEMO VERSIONS
PYRAMID EYE	BOOTLEG	NONE	BOOTLEG	CD	1982 STUDIO ALBUM. EXCELLENT
STEVE'S SOUNDS OF THE '60s	SILVER SURFER	GMcI 01	BOOTLEG	TAPE	STEVE MARRIOTT HOSTING A RADIO PROGRAMME
30 SECONDS TO MIDNITE ROUGH MIX	BOOTLEG	NONE	BOOTLEG	CD	ALTERNATIVE VERSIONS

Guest Appearances

Throughout his career, Steve Marriott made many guest appearances on other people's records, helping both vocally and instrumentally. His reputation for producing records was also significant, and at one stage he was close to becoming the house producer for Led Zeppelin's record label Swansong.

Please find below a summary of these sessions

Apostolic Intervention
The single 'Have You Ever Seen Me' / 'Madam Garcia' was long rumoured to actually BE a Small Faces record. In actual fact, it was Jerry Shirley's group (complete with the unfortunate name), but Steve WAS very much in evidence in the studio control room. Some outtakes which have come to light quite recently now prove this conclusively

Arnold, PP
Significant help was given to fellow Immediate stablemate PP Arnold, particularly on her single 'Everything's Gonna Be Alright' and by writing, producing and performing 'If You Think You're Groovy' with Pat and Ronnie Lane and the other Small Faces

Art
This may well have been the first meeting between Steve Marriott and Greg Ridley. Steve helped on the production of 'Supernatural Fairy Tales' for the group that would soon become Spooky Tooth. In particular, he is responsible for the phasing effect on the title track.

Atlantis 2000
It's unusual to hear disco licks from Steve Marriott. But some great vocals in any case on the track 'Here and Now'

Black Coffee
In 1989, Steve and Clem Clempson guested on a TV Commercial for Nescafe Coffee's new product - Blend 37.
By all accounts, in typical fashion, Steve laid down a great vocal in one or two takes - and the commercial itself was strong enough to win some of that year's end of year awards.

Blackberries
Steve recorded an entire Blackberries album at Clearsounds Studios, with a backing which sounds obviously Humble Pie.
The album was never released, but the most prominent tracks 'Twist and Shout' c/w 'Don't Change on Me' were released as a single in 1973.

Blue Goose
Our man Steve Marriott appears, along with Alexis Korner, on this 1979 album, released on Anchor Records - although I would say they are extremely difficult to detect

Brown, Joe
Steve collaborated with Joe Brown a number of times. He can be heard on Joe's self-penned version of 'Soldier', which Steve himself later recorded with the LA Philharmonic Orchestra, definitely a potential Number One single, as it was tipped to be, by all accounts, had it been released. A version later appeared on the Small Faces album *78 in the Shade*. Steve also helped on Joe's mid 70's 'Let it Rock'.

Brown, Vicki
The backing band on Vicki Brown's 1977 album is like a Steve Marriott's 'who's who', including Steve, Joe Brown, Dave Hynes, Rick Wills, Jim Leverton, Mel Collins, Zoot Money and Madeline Bell. Steve was spending a lot of personal time with Joe and Vicki Brown at the time, and his influence is felt throughout the entire album

Capaldi, Jim
Typical Marriott vocals appear on Capaldi's 1984 album *One Man Mission* on the track 'Young Savages'.
Steve, of course, had known Jim from Traffic days back in the 60's.

Cochise
Steve helped out old friends BJ Cole and Rick Wills on their 1971 *Swallow Tales* album, with some roaring vocals on the single 'Why I Sing the Blues'. Steve later attended Rick's wedding not long after this, and Rick of course went on to work with Peter Frampton, Roxy Music, Small Faces, Foreigner and Bad Company.

Donovan
Excellent guitar work from Steve on the track 'There is a Boy for Every Girl' from the very good 1973 album *Essence to Essence*. Steve actually met and

reconciled with Peter Frampton during these sessions - leading to Peter wearing the Steve Marriott t-shirt on the cover of his eponymous 1974 album.

Easybeats
Fabulous vocals on the single 'Good Times' in 1968, from the LP *Vigil*. It caused Paul McCartney, when he heard it on the radio, to stop his car and telephone the radio station to ask for details and request a replay! Check it out!

Farlowe, Chris
Steve contributed guitar and vocals on Chris Farlowe's single 'My Way of Giving', which was produced by Mick Jagger and of course written by Marriott/Lane.

Lindenberg, Udo
This German superstar seems an unlikely collaboration for Steve, who joined him on Gene Galaxo, Part 1.

Grunt Futtock
Now here is a very rare single from 1972 'Rock n Roll Christian' c/w 'Free Sole'. Producer Andrew Oldham confirms that Roy Wood sings lead vocals, backed by Frampton, Marriott, Andy Bown and others.

Hallyday, Johnny
Hallyday famously hired Peter Frampton and the Small Faces to record on his 1969 album. Amongst their contributions are 'Amen', Reclamation' and 'Regarde Pour Moi', which are variations of Small Faces and Humble Pie tracks. However, they can be heard playing throughout the album. Often forgotten is Hallyday's rare single and EP from the same sessions - but which doesn't appear on the album - 'Que Je T'aime'

Herd, The
Steve took the controls and produced 'Sunshine Cottage' as the group made a last gasp effort to retain Peter Frampton

Hermann Ze German
Former Scorpions drummer Herman Rarebell made a 1986 album, including vocals from Steve on the track 'Having a Good Time'

Illusion
Strong vocals contributed by Steve on the 1985 eponymous album on the track 'Weighs a Ton'

King, BB
'Alexis Boogie' was written by Alexis Korner, and is included on *BB King in London*, with Steve prominent on harp and assisted by other Humble Pie bandmates.

King, Freddy
Reliable sources report Steve Marriott's involvement in the making of the classic jazz blues track 'Tore Down'

Korner, Alexis
Marriott was hired as a guitar player for both UK and European tours in 1975. He produced an absolute classic with his acappella duet with Alexis Korner on 'Diamonds in the Rough', immortalised on German TV footage. Steve also appears on several tracks on the *Get Off My Cloud* album, including the title track, 'Strange and Deranged' and 'Tree Top Fever'.

Law of the Jungle
A TV Commercial for Puma Trainers, written and sung by Steve!

Lee, Alan
Singer/songwriter and guitarist Alan Lee was a good friend of Steve Marriott and recorded an entire album at Clearsounds Studios in 1973, with Humble Pie back-up. Tim Hinckley, BJ Cole and Dave Hynes were said to have been involved also, which points to slightly later sessions. 'Rainy Changes' emerged as a single on Decca, but the album wasn't released. More recently a version has emerged with Steve himself handling the vocals.

McCullough, Henry
Contributions from Steve on Hank Williams' 'Mind Your Own Business' - Hank himself an early idol to a young Steve Marriott. This appeared on the album of the same name by ex-Grease band Henry McCullough

Meek, Joe
A controversy. There are a couple of demos produced by Joe Meek in the early 60's, 'City Lights' and 'Love Gone Home', which are believed to be sung by a young Steve Marriott throughout the Joe Meek fraternity. However, there are mixed feelings among Marriott fans about their authenticity.

Miller, Frankie
Another controversy, as it happens, over whether the backing to an excellent collection of 80's tracks was provided by Packet of Three.

Input from band members, friends and family suggest that P3 were indeed heavily involved.

Mott the Hoople
Steve can be heard vocally, rocking on 'Midnight Lady' from 1971

Nicholls, Billy
Steve made a major contribution to Billy Nicholl's landmark 1968 album *Would You Believe*. In some versions of the title track Steve is very high in the mix. Other notable contributions are 'It Brings Me Down', and his guitar pyrotechnics on 'Girl from New York City'

Oldham, Andrew Loog Orchestra
Steve claims to have played on many ALO records in pre-Small Faces days, mainly on harmonica, and under a variety of different monikers.

This continued right through the Small Faces Immediate period.

Pink Floyd
Well, not Steve, but his dog Seamus made a big contribution to the *Meddle* album by howling the blues, just like Steve taught him to, on the track 'Seamus'. The Pink Floyd guys were dogsitting Seamus while Steve was away on tour.

Poll Cats
Memorable single from Steve and the Georgia Satellites in 1990, 'Poll Tax Blues', protesting against Margaret Thatcher's most infamous tax. Steve handles lead vocals in his inimitable style

Quik, The
Unconfirmed rumours do persist of Small Faces involvement on 'Bert's Apple Crumble', a 1967 'B' side from this obscure Welsh band.

Redding Noel
1976, at Basing Studios in London, Steve gets engineering credits on some of Noel Redding's *Missing Album*.

Rivers, Tony & The Castaways
Tony Rivers and The Castaways secured Steve's help in 1966 on 'Can't Make It Without You' when he walked into the studio and offered to sing.

Rolling Stones
Backing vocals and guitar on 'In Another Land' from the 1967 album *Their Satanic Majesties Request*.

Shannon, Del
Steve plays keyboards on the *Home and Away* album for one of his earliest influences, in sessions recorded by Andrew Oldham.

Listening to these sessions reveals a typical period 'Immediate' sound.

Skip Bifferty
Their 1968 single 'Man in Black' was arranged by Steve and produced by Ronnie Lane

Smiley, Brett
Brett Smiley was a protege of Andrew Oldham, otherwise a collaboration with Steve Marriott may have been unlikely! Brett was called 'the most beautiful boy in the world' by *Disc* Magazine, and he did share the distinction with Steve of starring in *Oliver* - in his case on Broadway. Anyway, in Nashville, Steve contributed lead guitar to the track 'Va Va Vroom' while Oldham was recording the 1974 album *Breathlessly Brett*

Snape
Alexis Korner, Peter Thorup and King Crimson were all supporting Humble Pie on tour in the US in 1972, when the support acts kind of imploded and became Snape - generating the album *Accidently Born in New Orleans*, with Steve most prominent on organ and vocals on the track 'Country Shoes'. He contributes backing vocals throughout - and can be heard on 'Don't Change on Me' which he recorded the next year with the Blackberries.

Spectrum
Vocals from Steve as part of the Spectrum 'All or Nothing' charity single in 1985

Thunders, Johnny
Take Phil Lynott, a couple of Sex Pistols, ex New York Doll Johnny Thunders, and Steve Marriott, and you get the explosive mix which is 'Daddy Rolling Stone' from the 1978 album *So Alone*. Steve sings a verse, and adds piano and harp.

Tornell, Monica
The Swede's *Big Mama* album is graced by a collaboration with Steve on 'I Just Wanna Make Love With You'

Traffic

Mr Marriott appears on the *Mr Fantasy* album, and can clearly be heard on the track 'Berkshire Poppies', which was recorded during some relaxing times in...Berkshire

Twice as Much

Strong rumours of Small Faces involvement on the Twice as Much duo's Immediate cover 'Green Circles'

Steve on stage 1990

Index

Other Titles available from Helter Skelter Publishing

Coming soon

Everybody Dance
Chic and the Politics of Disco
By Daryl Easlea
Everybody Dance puts the rise and fall of Bernard Edwards and Nile Rodgers, the emblematic disco duo behind era-defining records 'Le Freak', 'Good Times' and 'Lost In Music', at the heart of a changing landscape, taking in socio-political and cultural events such as the Civil Rights struggle, the Black Panthers and the US oil crisis. There are drugs, bankruptcy, up-tight artists, fights, and Muppets but, most importantly an in-depth appraisal of a group whose legacy remains hugely underrated.
ISBN1-900924-56-0 256pp   £14.00

Available now

The Sharper Word: A Mod Reader
Ed Paolo Hewitt
Hewitt's hugely readable collection documents the clothes, the music, the clubs, the drugs and the faces behind one of the most misunderstood and enduring cultural movements and includes hard to find pieces by Tom Wolfe, bestselling novelist Tony Parsons, poet laureate Andrew Motion, disgraced Tory grandee Jonathan Aitken, Nik Cohn, Colin MacInnes, Mary Quant, and Irish Jack.
  "An unparalleled view of the world-conquering British youth cult." *The Guardian*
  "An excellent account of the sharpest-dressed subculture." *Loaded*, Book of the Month
ISBN 1-900924-34-X 192pp £9.99

Smashing Pumpkins
by Amy Hanson
Initially contemporaries of Nirvana, Billy Corgan's Smashing Pumpkins outgrew and outlived the grunge scene and with hugely acclaimed commercial triumphs like *Siamese Dream* and *Mellon Collie and The Infinite Sadness*. Though drugs and other problems led to the band's final demise, Corgan's recent return with Zwan is a reminder of how awesome the Pumpkins were in their prime. Seattle-based Hanson has followed the band for years and this is the first in-depth biography of their rise and fall.
Paperback   ISBN 1900924684   256pp   156mm X 234mm, 8pp b/w photos
UK £12.99   US $18.95

Love: Behind The Scenes
By Michael Stuart-Ware
LOVE were one of the legendary bands of the late '60s US West Coast scene. Their masterpiece *Forever Changes* still regularly appears in critics' polls of top albums, while a new-line up of the band has recently toured to mass acclaim. Michael Stuart-Ware was LOVE's drummer during their heyday and shares his inside perspective on the band's recording and performing career and tells how drugs and egos thwarted the potential of one of the great groups of the burgeoning psychedelic era.
ISBN 1-900924-59-5   256pp   £14.00

Be Glad: An Incredible String Band Compendium
Edited by Adrian Whittaker
The ISB pioneered 'world music' on '60s albums like *The Hangman's Beautiful Daughter* – Paul McCartney's favourite album of 1967! – experimented with theatre, film and lifestyle and inspired Led Zeppelin. 'Be Glad' features interviews with all the ISB key players, as well as a wealth of background information, reminiscence, critical evaluations and arcane trivia, this is a book that will delight any reader with more than a passing interest in the ISB.
ISBN 1-900924-64-1   288pp   £14.99

Waiting for the Man: The Story of Drugs and Popular Music
Harry Shapiro
From Marijuana and Jazz, through acid-rock and speed-fuelled punk, to crack-driven rap and Ecstasy and the Dance Generation, this is the definitive history of drugs and pop. It also features in-depth portraits of music's most famous drug addicts: from Charlie Parker to Sid Vicious and from Jim Morrison to Kurt Cobain. Chosen by the BBC as one of the Top Twenty Music Books of All Time. "Wise and witty." *The Guardian*
ISBN 1-900924-58-7   320pp   £12.99

The Clash: Return of the Last Gang in Town
Marcus Gray
Exhaustively researched definitive biography of the last great rock band that traces their progress from pubs and punk clubs to US stadiums and the Top Ten. This edition is further updated to cover the band's induction into the Rock 'n' Roll Hall of Fame and the tragic death of iconic frontman Joe Strummer.
   "A must-have for Clash fans [and] a valuable document for anyone interested in the punk era." *Billboard*
   "It's important you read this book." *Record Collector*
ISBN 1-900924-62-5   448pp   £14.99

The Fall: A User's Guide
Dave Thompson
Amelodic, cacophonic and magnificent, The Fall remain the most enduring and prolific of the late-'70s punk and post-punk iconoclasts. *A User's Guide* chronicles the historical and musical background to more than 70 different LPs (plus reissues) and as many singles. The band's history is also documented year-by-year, filling in the gaps between the record releases.
ISBN 1-900924-57-9   256pp   £12.99

Pink Floyd: A Saucerful of Secrets
by Nicholas Schaffner £14.99
Long overdue reissue of the authoritative and detailed account of one of the most important and popular bands in rock history. From the psychedelic explorations of the Syd Barrett-era to 70s superstardom with *Dark Side of the Moon*, and on to triumph of *The Wall*, before internecine strife tore the group apart. Schaffner's definitive history also covers the improbable return of Pink Floyd without Roger Waters, and the hugely successful *Momentary Lapse of Reason* album and tour.

The Big Wheel
by Bruce Thomas £10.99
Thomas was bassist with Elvis Costello at the height of his success. Though names are never named, *The Big Wheel* paints a vivid and hilarious picture of life touring with Costello and co, sharing your life 24-7 with a moody egotistical singer, a crazed drummer and a host of hangers-on. Costello sacked Thomas on its initial publication.
   "A top notch anecdotalist who can time a twist to make you laugh out loud." *Q*

Hit Men: Powerbrokers and Fast Money Inside The Music Business
By Fredric Dannen £14.99
Hit Men exposes the seamy and sleazy dealings of America's glitziest record companies: payola, corruption, drugs, Mafia involvement, and excess.
   "So heavily awash with cocaine, corruption and unethical behaviour that it makes the occasional examples of chart-rigging and playlist tampering in Britain during the same period seem charmingly inept." *The Guardian*.

I'm With The Band: Confessions of A Groupie
By Pamela Des Barres £14.99
Frank and engaging memoir of affairs with Keith Moon, Noel Redding and Jim Morrison, travels with Led Zeppelin as Jimmy Page's girlfriend, and friendships with Robert Plant, Gram Parsons, and Frank Zappa.
   "Miss Pamela, the most beautiful and famous of the groupies. Her memoir of her life with rock stars is funny, bittersweet, and tender-hearted." Stephen Davis, author of *Hammer of the Gods*

Psychedelic Furs: Beautiful Chaos
by Dave Thompson £12.99
Psychedelic Furs were the ultimate post-punk band – combining the chaos and vocal rasp of the Sex Pistols with a Bowie-esque glamour. The Furs hit the big time when John Hughes wrote a movie based on their early single "Pretty in Pink". Poised to join U2 and Simple Minds in the premier league, they withdrew behind their shades, remaining a cult act, but one with a hugely devoted following.

Bob Dylan: Like The Night (Revisited)
by CP Lee £9.99
Fully revised and updated B-format edition of the hugely acclaimed document of Dylan's pivotal 1966 show at the Manchester Free Trade Hall where fans called him Judas for turning his back on folk music in favour of rock 'n' roll.

Marillion: Separated Out
by Jon Collins £14.99
From the chart hit days of Fish and "Kayleigh" to the Steve Hogarth incarnation, Marillion have continued to make groundbreaking rock music. Collins tells the full story, drawing on interviews with band members, associates, and the experiences of some of the band's most dedicated fans.
Rainbow Rising
by Roy Davies £14.99
The full story of guitar legend Ritchie Blackmore's post-Purple progress with one of the great 70s rock bands. After quitting Deep Purple at the height of their success, Blackmore combined with Ronnie James Dio to make epic rock albums like *Rising* and *Long Live Rock 'n' Roll* before streamlining the sound and enjoying hit singles like "Since You've Been Gone" and "All Night Long." Rainbow were less celebrated than Deep Purple, but they feature much of Blackmore's finest writing and playing, and were one of the best live acts of the era. They are much missed.

Back to the Beach: A Brian Wilson and the Beach Boys Reader REVISED EDITION
Ed Kingsley Abbott £14.00
Revised and expanded edition of the Beach Boys compendium *Mojo* magazine deemed an "essential purchase." This collection includes all of the best articles, interviews and reviews from the Beach Boys' four decades of music, including definitive pieces by Timothy White, Nick Kent and David Leaf. New material reflects on the tragic death of Carl Wilson and documents the rejuvenated Brian's return to the boards. "Rivetting!" **** Q "An essential purchase." *Mojo*

Harmony in My Head
The Original Buzzcock Steve Diggle's Rock 'n' Roll Odyssey
by Steve Diggle and Terry Rawlings £14.99
First-hand account of the punk wars from guitarist and one half of the songwriting duo that gave the world three chord punk-pop classics like "Ever Fallen In Love" and "Promises". Diggle dishes the dirt on punk contemporaries like The Sex Pistols, The Clash and The Jam, as well as sharing poignant memories of his friendship with Kurt Cobain, on whose last ever tour, The Buzzcocks were support act.

Serge Gainsbourg: A Fistful of Gitanes
by Sylvie Simmons £9.99
Rock press legend Simmons' hugely acclaimed biography of the French genius.
   "I would recommend *A Fistful of Gitanes* [as summer reading] which is a highly entertaining biography of the French singer-songwriter and all-round scallywag" - JG Ballard
   "A wonderful introduction to one of the most overlooked songwriters of the 20th century" (Number 3, top music books of 2001) *The Times*
   "The most intriguing music-biz biography of the year" *The Independent*
   "Wonderful. Serge would have been so happy" – Jane Birkin

Blues: The British Connection
by Bob Brunning £14.99
Former Fleetwood Mac member Bob Brunning's classic account of the impact of Blues in Britain, from its beginnings as the underground music of 50s teenagers like Mick Jagger, Keith Richards

and Eric Clapton, to the explosion in the '60s, right through to the vibrant scene of the present day.

'An invaluable reference book and an engaging personal memoir' – Charles Shaar Murray

On The Road With Bob Dylan
by Larry Sloman £12.99
In 1975, as Bob Dylan emerged from 8 years of seclusion, he dreamed of putting together a travelling music show that would trek across the country like a psychedelic carnival. The dream became a reality, and *On The Road With Bob Dylan* is the ultimate behind-the-scenes look at what happened. When Dylan and the Rolling Thunder Revue took to the streets of America, Larry "Ratso" Sloman was with them every step of the way.

"The *War and Peace* of Rock and Roll." – Bob Dylan

Gram Parsons: God's Own Singer
By Jason Walker £12.99
Brand new biography of the man who pushed The Byrds into country-rock territory on *Sweethearts of The Rodeo*, and quit to form the Flying Burrito Brothers. Gram lived hard, drank hard, took every drug going and somehow invented country rock, paving the way for Crosby, Stills & Nash, The Eagles and Neil Young. Parsons' second solo LP, *Grievous Angel*, is a haunting masterpiece of country soul. By the time it was released, he had been dead for 4 months. He was 26 years old.

"Walker has done an admirable job in taking us as close to the heart and soul of Gram Parsons as any author could." **** *Uncut* book of the month

Ashley Hutchings: The Guvnor and the Rise of Folk Rock – Fairport Convention, Steeleye Span and the Albion Band
by Geoff Wall and Brian Hinton £14.99
As founder of Fairport Convention and Steeleye Span, Ashley Hutchings is the pivotal figure in the history of folk rock. This book draws on hundreds of hours of interviews with Hutchings and other folk-rock artists and paints a vivid picture of the scene that also produced Sandy Denny, Richard Thompson, Nick Drake, John Martyn and Al Stewart.

The Beach Boys' Pet Sounds: The Greatest Album of the Twentieth Century
by Kingsley Abbott £11.95
Pet Sounds is the 1966 album that saw The Beach Boys graduate from lightweight pop like "Surfin' USA", *et al*, into a vehicle for the mature compositional genius of Brian Wilson. The album was hugely influential, not least on The Beatles. This the full story of the album's background, its composition and recording, its contemporary reception and its enduring legacy.

King Crimson: In The Court of King Crimson
by Sid Smith £14.99
King Crimson's 1969 masterpiece *In The Court Of The Crimson King*, was a huge U.S. chart hit. The band followed it with 40 further albums of consistently challenging, distinctive and innovative music. Drawing on hours of new interviews, and encouraged by Crimson supremo Robert Fripp, the author traces the band's turbulent history year by year, track by track.

A Journey Through America with the Rolling Stones
by Robert Greenfield UK Price £9.99
Featuring a new foreword by Ian Rankin
This is the definitive account of their legendary '72 tour.

"Filled with finely-rendered detail ... a fascinating tale of times we shall never see again" *Mojo*

Backlist

The Nice: Hang On To A Dream by Martyn Hanson   1900924439   256pp   £13.99

Al Stewart: Adventures of a Folk Troubadour by Neville Judd
1900924366 320pp   £25.00

Marc Bolan and T Rex: A Chronology by Cliff McLenahan
1900924420   256pp   £13.99

ISIS: A Bob Dylan Anthology Ed Derek Barker
1900924293   256pp   £14.99

Razor Edge: Bob Dylan and The Never-ending Tour by Andrew Muir
1900924137   256pp   £12.99

Calling Out Around the World: A Motown Reader Edited by Kingsley Abbott
1900924145   256pp   £13.99

I've Been Everywhere: A Johnny Cash Chronicle by Peter Lewry
1900924226   256pp   £14.99

Sandy Denny: No More Sad Refrains by Clinton Heylin
1900924358   288pp   £13.99

Animal Tracks: The Story of The Animals by Sean Egan
1900924188   256pp   £12.99

Like a Bullet of Light: The Films of Bob Dylan by CP Lee
1900924064   224pp   £12.99

Rock's Wild Things: The Troggs Files by Alan Clayson and J Ryan
1900924196   224pp   £12.99

Dylan's Daemon Lover by Clinton Heylin
1900924153   192pp   £12.00

Get Back: The Beatles' Let It Be Disaster by Sulpy & Schweighardt
1900924129   320pp   £12.99

XTC: Song Stories by XTC and Neville Farmer
190092403X   352pp   £12.99

Born in the USA: Bruce Springsteen by Jim Cullen
1900924056   320pp   £9.99

Bob Dylan by Anthony Scaduto
1900924234   320pp   £10.99

Firefly Publishing: An Association between Helter Skelter and SAF

The Nirvana Recording Sessions
by Rob Jovanovic £20.00
Drawing on years of research, and interviews with many who worked with the band, the author has documented details of every Nirvana recording, from early rehearsals, to the *In Utero* sessions. A fascinating account of the creative process of one of the great bands.

The Music of George Harrison: While My Guitar Gently Weeps
by Simon Leng £20.00
Often in Lennon and McCartney's shadow, Harrison's music can stand on its own merits. Santana biographer Leng takes a studied, track by track, look at both Harrison's contribution to The Beatles, and the solo work that started with the release in 1970 of his epic masterpiece *All Things Must Pass*. "Here Comes The Sun", "Something" – which Sinatra covered and saw as the perfect love song – "All Things Must Pass" and "While My Guitar Gently Weeps" are just a few of Harrison's classic songs.
  Originally planned as a celebration of Harrison's music, this is now sadly a commemoration.

The Pretty Things: Growing Old Disgracefully
by Alan Lakey £20
First biography of one of rock's most influential and enduring combos. Trashed hotel rooms, infighting, rip-offs, sex, drugs and some of the most remarkable rock 'n' roll, including land mark albums like the first rock opera, *SF Sorrow*, and *Rolling Stone*'s album of the year, 1970's *Parachute*.
"They invented everything, and were credited with nothing." Arthur Brown, "God of Hellfire"

The Sensational Alex Harvey
By John Neil Murno £20
Part rock band, part vaudeville, 100% commitment, the SAHB were one of the greatest live bands of the era. But behind his showman exterior, Harvey was increasingly beset by alcoholism and tragedy. He succumbed to a heart attack on the way home from a gig in 1982, but he is fondly remembered as a unique entertainer by friends, musicians and legions of fans.

U2: The Complete Encyclopedia by Mark Chatterton £16.99
Poison Heart: Surviving The Ramones by Dee Dee Ramone and Veronica Kofman £9.99
Minstrels In The Gallery: A History Of Jethro Tull by David Rees £12.99
DANCEMUSICSEXROMANCE: Prince – The First Decade by Per Nilsen £12.99
To Hell and Back with Catatonia by Brian Wright £12.99
Soul Sacrifice: The Santana Story by Simon Leng UK Price £12.99
Opening The Musical Box: A Genesis Chronicle by Alan Hewitt UK Price £12.99
Blowin' Free: Thirty Years Of Wishbone Ash by Gary Carter and Mark Chatterton UK Price £12.99

www.helterskelterbooks.com

All Helter Skelter, Firefly and SAF titles are available by mail order from
www.helterskelterbooks.com
Or from our office:
Helter Skelter Publishing Limited
South Bank House
Black Prince Road
London SE1 7SJ

Telephone: +44 (0)20 7463 2204 or Fax: +44 (0)20 7463 2295
Mail order office hours: Mon-Fri 10:00am – 1:30pm
By post, enclose a cheque [must be drawn on a British bank], International
Money Order, or credit card number and expiry date.

Postage prices per book worldwide are as follows:

UK & Channel Islands	£1.50
Europe & Eire (air)	£2.95
USA, Canada (air)	£7.50
Australasia, Far East (air)	£9.00

Email: info@helterskelterbooks.com